Sam Smiley
University of Arizona

THEATRE

THE HUMAN ART

1817

HARPER & ROW, PUBLISHERS, *New York*

Cambridge, Philadelphia, San Francisco, Washington,
London, Mexico City, São Paulo, Singapore, Sydney

THEATRE: The Human Art

Copyright © 1987 *by Sam Smiley*

Sponsoring Editor: Phillip Leininger
Project Editor: Jo-Ann Goldfarb
Text Design: Suzanne Dyer Company/Maria Alina Miller
Cover Design: 20/20 Services, Inc.
Cover Illustration/Photo: Jerry Vezzuso
Text Art: Fineline Illustrations, Inc.
Photo Research: Mira Schachne
Production Manager: Jeanie Berke
Compositor: Ruttle, Shaw & Wetherill, Inc.
Printer and Binder: R. R. Donnelley & Sons Company

Cover photograph is a scene from the play *Quarry* presented by LA MAMA E.T.C. at LA MAMA E.T.C., New York, N.Y.

Library of Congress Cataloging-in-Publication Data

Smiley, Sam, 1931–
   Theatre, the human art.

   Bibliography: p.
   Includes index.
1. Theater. 2. Drama. I. Title.
PN2037.S564 1987   792   86–19321
ISBN 0–06–046292–2

87 88 89 90 9 8 7 6 5 4 3 2 1

For Ann

Yul Brynner and
Deborah Kerr in
The King and I

Contents

Part Four   CONNECTIONS

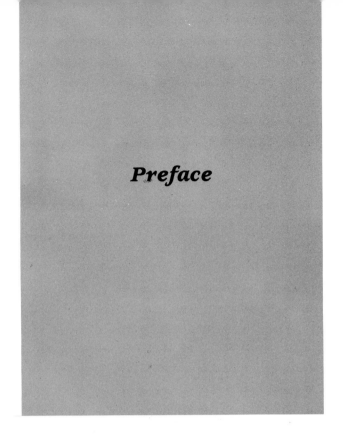

Preface

I wrote this book for college students who are taking a first course in theatre, but I hope anyone might find in it new ideas and fresh inspiration. It offers a comprehensive and humane view of theatre, one that stresses human beings and their wondrous creativity. It is imbued as well with a vision drawn from long experience in the working theatre.

Human creativity is the heart of the book. It reveals the effort, pain, and joy of personal and group creation. The various chapters examine human beings in the theatre—what they do, think, and feel—and what they have accomplished. The book explains how people can and do respond to theatre. It provides insights about the creativity that makes theatre and causes audience response. The book's unique approach to theatre is reflected in its subtitle—"the human art."

The length and flexibility of the book should enable it to serve equally well for theatre appreciation and for introduction to the theatre courses. About half of the text focuses on artists, audiences, and connections. The other half is devoted to history.

Individual instructors can and should tailor the reading of the book to suit their own purposes. For instance, the history chapters may be crucial to some schemes but less so in others. It can thus serve equally well for an academic quarter or a semester. The book's adaptability should make it a particularly useful tool.

The first section stresses artistic and human vision. Its four chapters initiate the book's treatment of theatre from the audience member's point of view; thus the reader is given an immediate psychological and aesthetic orientation. The chief subjects of the first section are the connections of theatre to human nature, the significance of audiences, the types of theatre, and a system of analysis.

Part Two deals with creation, and it penetrates what theatre artists—playwrights, directors, actors, and designers—think about and do while accomplishing their work. Each chapter provides students with an intimate set of insights about the attitudes, ideas, skills, and creativity of the various theatre artists. A reader therefore should gain from this section a fuller understanding of the contributions of each theatre artist.

Part Three, the history unit, comprises nearly half the book and presents a clear, contemporary account of theatre history with a focus on people— who they were, what they thought and felt, and what they accomplished. Each chapter of the history section features a succinct orientation to the ideas and social currents of the time that affected the artists. The book's special emphasis on human experiences gives the historical account a uniquely personal quality.

Part Four makes connections that should appeal to those instructors who wish to discuss such subjects as social and economic concerns, theatre architecture, and cinema. The conclusion emphasizes the relationship of theatre to society. Some of the ideas in the book are classical; some are modernist; but all apply to contemporary theatre and its appreciation.

The discussions in the chapters offer complex ideas right along with simple ones. Why shouldn't a reader's first book on theatre provide the most important ideas, the most intensive materials? This book explains how and why men and women create theatre. It probes theatre's relationships to the contemporary world, and it looks into many of the unsolved mysteries of theatrical creation.

No one could put together a book like this without drawing from the work of others. I've learned from so many people it's impossible to recognize them all. I acknowledge direct sources in the text or bibliography, but I owe special thanks to certain scholars: Stephen Archer, Oscar G. Brockett, Walter Meserve, and especially Hubert C. Heffner.

Many leading theatre artists and teachers read all or parts of this book and offered valuable suggestions, and I wish especially to thank them: Leon Brauner, Lois Carder, Marvin Carlson, Linda Conaway, David Cook, James Fisher, William Grange, Jean Korf, Wesley Peters, Joy Reilly, Thomas Taylor, Richard Weaver, Dorothy Webb, Ron Willis, and Leigh Woods. During the first years of work on this book, E. James Hooks gave me special encouragement and talked with me often about the role and potential of such a work, and I am most grateful to him.

A number of other fine professionals encouraged me during the years the book required: Larry Clark, Roger Cornish, Jerry Crawford, Harold Dixon, Sears Eldredge, Barbara and Tom Evans, Don Finn, Joseph Flauto, Brian Fonseca, Lauren Friesen, Jeff Koep, Felicia Londré, John David Lutz, Harlene Marley, R. Keith Michael, Dale Miller, Clair Myers, Kip Niven, John Steven Paul, Mary Schakel, Arno Selco, David Shelton, John Tammi, Charles Vicinus, Edgar Webb, and David Young.

Numerous fine students, too, have contributed to this book, and many are now theatre artists or scholars of note. I'm most grateful to Sam Abel, Richard Allen, Gary Bayer, Marcia Bennett, Martin Bennison, Norm Bert, Suzanne Blackburn, Duane Campbell, Jim Clark, David Emge, Alice French, Michael Friedman, Ron Glass, Hazel Hall, Claudia Johnson, Paul Kuritz, John David Lutz, David Shelton, George Sorensen, Jane Stout, Steve Timm, Rich Weaver, Louise Williams, Judith Zivanovic, and all my other wonderful students over the years.

I particularly wish to thank Phillip Leininger, senior editor at Harper & Row, whose work was most instrumental in bringing this book to fruition. Nor would the book have had its present finish without the meticulous work of project editor Jo-Ann Goldfarb. I also thank Michael E. Brown, who first asked me to write the book. Others among the wonderful people at Harper who helped so much are photo editor Mira Schachne, editorial assistant Katherine Vuignier, copy editor Robert Brainerd, marketing manager Naomi Collett, and the entire staff.

Without the spirited support of my sons Mark, Steve, and Sean I could never have written the book. My wife Ann Walters Smiley helped me most with research and editorial aid. This book is also hers.

Sam Smiley

P R E F A C E

A Streetcar Named Desire by Tennessee Williams

Part One

VISION

1 The Human Nature of Theatre

Theatre's most significant aspect is *human presence*. For theatre to happen, more than one person must be present. It cannot occur in solitude. As fleeting as life itself, theatre exists as the art form of the present tense. It always involves live human begins.

Theatre is sharing. People come together in a theatre to share perceptions about the joys and sorrows of life. During a drama, actors experience life, and they move on a stage, sharing their living experiences with people in an audience. The sharing is immediate and direct. Both actors and observers face each other with sensitivity and anticipation. The living presence of the two groups in a creative situation makes possible the unique potentials of dramatic art. Theatre is impossible without people there. Theatre persists as the art form of life in action.

Theatre stands as the most human of all the arts because it involves lived experience. The artists certainly live while making drama, and audiences are alive when they partake of it. Even the characters in plays cease to be simple personages on a page and come to life through the personalities of the actors.

The art of theatre can be simple—an acting out of life—or it can be complex—a human creative activity involving imagination, talent, and hard work. It holds endless fascination today as types of theatre constantly multiply. Theatre artists continue now, as in ages past, to respond sensitively to the ceaseless changes in the burgeoning world. Just as theatre requires human presence, so does it demand an immediate view of life. And it always presents a direct response of human beings to life around them.

***Amadeus* by Peter Shaffer**

ESSENTIAL CONCEPTS AND DEFINITIONS

As a word, *theatre* can refer generally to the whole art, to the entire complex of human processes and products that comprise a performed play. *Drama* can mean the same. But theatre people usually distinguish between the two words. Theatre means all the production activities taken together—acting, directing, designing, constructing, operating, and managing. Drama means plays, dramatic literature, and the work of authors who literally dramatize life. "A theatre" refers to a certain building, and "a drama" to a specific play script. To study drama, one acquires knowledge about plays; to study theatre, one learns about production activities.

The proper way to spell theatre is with an "re" at the end, except in newspapers and magazines where it's spelled with an "er." In other words, educated usage requires the French spelling, theatre, and journalistic

Cats

usage requires the German spelling, theater.

The definition of key words permits a more incisive discussion of theatre's foundations. Knowing the definitions of the words that follow can make thinking about theatre more precise.

Art means an acquired skill, a branch of education, an occupation, the creative use of craftsmanship, or a class of objects. The *fine arts* are those highly developed types of human creative endeavor that produce objects of beauty, value, and meaning. Traditionally, there are seven fine arts: architecture, dance, drama, music, painting, poetry, and sculpture. Some people reasonably argue that other arts—for example, cinema— should be included. Many productive human activities can result in fine

4

art, and it occurs whenever craftsmanship becomes creatively innovative. The fine arts are highly sophisticated ways that people of all cultures, periods, and locales can deal creatively with life.

The basic functions of fine art are the same today as yesterday or tomorrow. First, art fulfills the human need for personal expression of feelings. Next, it provides opportunities for societal display, celebration, and communication. Third, art appears when people make utilitarian objects or surroundings beautiful. Last, the creation of art permits human beings to establish some order in the chaos of life. Art infuses life with extraordinary intensity.

Aesthetics is the philosophical study of art. To discuss ideas about art objects, how to make them, or how people respond to them requires aesthetic thinking. This book is one example of a type of aesthetic study, since it presents ideas about the theatre. It is aesthetic because its major objectives are to stimulate in readers a more knowledgeable philosophy about art, theatre, and the potentials of life. Traditional aesthetics focuses on theories of beauty and how people respond to art objects. Contemporary aesthetics pays more attention to human creativity and how people interact in the presence of art.

Action is the word that stands for the most important principle of dramatic art. Action means change, and dramatic action means human change. Theatre depends mainly on human action in everything that happens. Action of all sorts makes good theatre. A physical movement of Hamlet's sword hand when he stabs the King may be as important as his thoughtful soliloquy about suicide. But the best kind of action is the sort of change involved when human beings make significant decisions. Most important, however, action is the total movement of a play. Later chapters explain action more fully, but the easiest way to understand a play's overall action is simply to ask, What is going on?

Structure in a play refers to the relationships that connect actions, characters, or any other elements. Structure includes every connection between particulars, such as between one event and the next, between one character and another, or even between the speeches of a scene. To study a play's structure is to examine the dynamics of how its individual parts relate to each other.

Form is the shape of the completed whole. This word relates to the word *structure* but is not synonymous with it. Take all the pieces of a drama plus all the enclosed relationships together, and overall form appears. The traditional forms of drama are tragedy, comedy, and melodrama. But today most plays mix traditions, and now the identification of a play's general form is often difficult. Nevertheless, to understand the unique form of each play is to comprehend the strategy of its impact.

As today's world grows ever more complex, the study of art and its terminology ought not to complicate things; rather, the process of knowing, like the process of making art, should be the unraveling of complexities. Other concepts, terms, and words, appear significantly in the discussion that follows. But a clear understanding of such important words as art, aesthetics, action, structure, and form provides a foundation for seeing into the nature of theatre itself.

ARTISTS ALIVE

The growth of surging populations, complicated technology, influential media, and other such dehumanizing factors in contemporary life motivate people to commit individualizing acts. Some people try to buy individuality and display it by what they wear, where they live, or how they travel. Others attempt to live in a manner deviant enough from mass norms that they can claim a greater degree of individuality. Everyone wants recognition as a unique human being. As contemporary British novelist John Fowles notes, nowadays artists often create as an individualizing act. Acts of creation express the solitary self.

A creative drama class

Experiencing works of art can increase anyone's zest for life. The world of art, of course, does not consist of artists alone. An artist may express individuality by making a self-revealing, self-asserting object—for instance, a play. Once made, that object stands as a symbol of human individuality. The object may even be worthy enough to survive the test of time. But there is also the spectator. Through contact with the artworks made by others, any person can intensify the value of life. Art provides individualizing experiences both for artists and for spectators.

Three spheres of interest comprise the world of art—the sphere of the artist, of the art object, and of the audience. To know any art, all three spheres need exploration. The sensitive student might well begin by observing artists to see how they work, then examine the nature of individual art objects, and finally notice the response of the spectators who witness works of art. The three spheres are easily confused, and when that happens, serious discussions of art are more difficult.

Creation in art means bringing order into the chaos of life. To create, a human being makes an object of some sort—a painting, a song, or a drama. In the process the creator develops a purposeful conception for the work of art, then selects materials, and in a certain manner assembles or shapes them into an ordered whole. Thus, an artist turns out an artificial object—artificial in the sense of being fashioned by the artist. Natural objects occur in nature, but only humans create fictional ones. Precisely how art imitates nature has long been argued. Simply speaking, many art objects are contrived somehow to resemble a natural model. Others imitate nothing but notions in an artist's head. Most art objects are related to reality yet remain imaginative. But art always gives some sort of order to life.

The basic creative act in a human being consists of an internal experience, partly intuitive and partly cognitive. Benedetto Croce, a twentieth-century Italian philosopher, developed the concept of *intuition* as the action of a human when creating. In fact, with his term *intuition-expression* he meant to emphasize the mental step of noticing something in life and realizing its significance, as when a comic-strip character gets an idea and a light bulb goes on above his head. Whenever a person makes a mental realization, then intuition-expression occurs. Such a mental event is the basis for all internal experience. Whenever a person conceives an idea—any idea, whether realistic or fantastic—that moment is a creative experience. Making a mental image from a physical sensation, a memory, or a subconscious intuition is the basic act of creating. In this sense, creativity means intuition-expression. It happens to everyone. Artists are simply those people who possess the abilities and experiences to externalize their intuition-expressions as works of art. An artist conceives, collects, and unifies a cluster of intuitions and forms them into an artistic object. That's the way every artist creates.

A street mime

From age to age, people have demanded in works of art certain qualities. One of these is especially appropriate to this discussion, the quality of *feeling*. Benedetto Croce was also influential in establishing the necessity for artists to invest their art objects with emotion. As a result, for twentieth-century audiences, feeling is a major criterion for judging art. In order to create art, artists perceive personal feelings, express themselves in works that contain those feelings, and then those works arouse feelings in spectators. Whenever a work of art fails, an observer should first examine the artist's intention—for example, expressing oneself is better than creating for money. Then the observer should study the artwork to see why it contains no emotional potentials and is boring. Sometimes, of course, the possibility exists that the observer is at fault. Perhaps a bad mood, an illness, an irritating companion, or even a lack of sensitivity may prevent a certain spectator from feeling something when looking at a work of art. But in the present-day world, feeling is one of the most useful measures of creative success.

IMAGES AND THE PROCESS OF CREATION

Images have also become significant in contemporary art. An image can occur in an artist, in an artwork, or in a spectator. When an artist experiences intuition-expression, what occurs inside that artist's head can be called an image, an imaginative particular. An image, in this sense, need not be a mental picture. Other types of images besides visual ones can occur. A painter may conceive pictures, but a writer might think of a group of words, a composer a melody, or a dancer a pattern of movement. Figure 1.1 depicts the intuition-expression of one image. An artist conceives an image (represented in Figure 1.1 by the asterisk) and by externalizing puts it into the artwork. There, the image stands independently, existing separately from the artist. Then any spectator who makes the effort may comprehend the artwork and perceive the image within it. When the artistic process succeeds, an artist conceives an image, implants it in an artwork, and thereby communicates it to an

Figure 1.1

The intuition-expression of an image

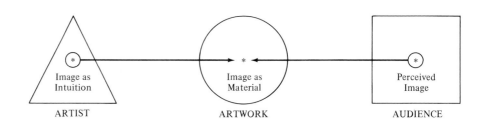

audience. Thus, image making can lead to the sharing of perceptions among human beings.

An image in art amounts to an imaginative particular. The theatre demands from its artists and offers to its audiences images of splendid variety. Images in theatre are the imaginative particulars in playwriting, acting, scenic design, costuming, lighting, sound, and staging. Acting, for example, projects visual and aural images for audiences, but it stimulates mainly internally imaginative and emotional images for an actor. A performed drama can be thought of as a connected series of images, mainly visual and aural. It can also be considered as one major image spanning the entire work.

A person creates on the basis of internal images, and in each piece of art people mostly see imagery. Ultimately, after a person contacts an artwork, one or more images about that work remain in that person's mind. When the artwork is good, its impact remains imagistically implanted for a long time. For example, Arthur Miller, a modern American playwright, wrote *Death of a Salesman* with the basic image of "the inside of a man's head." He wished to show the inner workings of Willy Loman's mind as that character approaches suicide. Likewise, after seeing a good production of the play, a spectator is likely to leave not only feeling sympathy for Willy but also carrying images about the inside of his mind.

An artist at first conceives singular images, but for an art object of large scale, the artist must make the single images multiply. Arthur Miller, for instance, had to envisage many images of Willy Loman and of specific members of Willy's family in order to make a whole play. Beside dreaming up images, an artist must convert those images into concrete materials such as words, paint, or musical notes. Then the artist must unify both the images and the materials into an artistic object or performance. Thus, an artist organizes a work of art.

During a period of creation each artist becomes involved in the *process* of making an art object in order to externalize intuitions and thereby make a *product*. Sometimes people argue about whether process or product is more important. Should society place more value on the human process of creation or upon the product as a material possession? Critics tend to stress the value of art objects, but artists themselves are usually more occupied with the process of creating. Those who consider creative endeavor to be the business of turning out products for con-

Above: An audience responding

Left: *True West* by Sam Shepard with Gary Sinise (left) and John Malkovich (right)

9

sumption usually stress the economic aspects of art. Indeed, the best audiences for art are more involved in the process of experiencing rather than in the fact of consuming art. Artists, of course, still consider art objects important. Stressing the values of creative experiences does not diminish the value of art objects themselves. The contemporary view of art tends to place more value on the human process than on material possessions. Whenever an artist concentrates on the process of creativity, the resultant artwork tends to be better than when the artist focuses on

The Harlem *Macbeth* by William Shakespeare directed by Orson Welles

the business of profiteering. Why? The main reason is that in the process of creating art one creates oneself and in the process of selling art one sells oneself.

Theatre stands as a perfect example of how art is both process and product. In the theatre, human process is more significant, if more temporary, than objects such as properties, scenery, costumes, or play scripts. The live performance of a play is itself a process, one existing in space and time, albeit temporary. It demands a living process for the actors, and once they stop their acting, the process ends.

THEATRE IS CO-CREATIVE

Another traditional argument is about whether theatre people are creative or interpretive. The key question is this: Are actors, directors, designers, and technicians artists or interpreters? Most people agree that playwrights are creative, but are actors interpreters or what? Stage directors are often thought of as mere interpreters and designers as only planners of a bit of scenery. As for technicians, even some theatre people who should know better think of them as lowly mechanics. A creative artist is anyone who contributes to a work of art. Any artisan who assembles or helps to assemble the materials for a work of creative art may correctly be called an artist. The cooperative nature of theatre work demands creativity of all who contribute to the final production. Everyone involved in theatre is an artist.

Theatre is a co-creative art. A work of dramatic art has two strange aspects. First, it is an immediate, live thing, and second, it is the collective creation of a group of people. A playwright puts together the materials of the script. Actors handle the necessary psychological, physical, and vocal experiences to make the script come alive. Designers plan and constructors assemble materials for settings, costumes, properties, lights, and other physical items. A director coordinates all the materials and actions that the others furnish. A performance comes to life because of everyone.

To explain why people become artists and spend their lives creating art objects would require an entire book or perhaps several of them. But some explanation of the rewards of creating is possible. First, an artist normally experiences a special pleasure upon completing a work of art. That experience is called an *aesthetic reaction*. Audience members have aesthetic reactions, too, but not quite of the same sort. Responding physically, emotionally, and intellectually, an artist's reaction has to do with a sense of completion. The work is finally over, the project completed as conceived. An artist simply gets pleasure out of the art object produced. The artist finds involvement and some measure of self-fulfillment in the very activity of creating. The actual labor, more than the objects created, gives more artists a deepened sense of purpose. The lives of artists are more meaningful because they spend their energy making something perceptive, constructive, and beautiful. Artists do not wish to destroy the world; they wish to create it.

Theatre artists of all sorts, like artists in other fields, find life's intensity and meaning in their work. But theatre artists get a bonus. Because they create alone and in concert with others, they get to share life experiences with friends and colleagues as they work. Creating with other people usually stimulates anyone to realize the constructive and social nature of life at its best. How important it is to get outside oneself! Joining others in acts of creativity helps each individual to enjoy a more intense and pleasurable life. In all artistry there is great joy. In the theatre one of the chief ingredients for the stimulation of joy is social creativity. Even the audience gets involved. An artist gets the joy of sending out images, and an audience has the pleasure of receiving them. Both experiences are life-expanding and self-fulfilling. Without art, life is less than it can be. To create and to enjoy what others create are two marvelous delights of being alive.

Art can also affect a community in other ways. It can heighten the awareness of people about noncreative concerns. It can be socially directive by suggesting ideas or patterns of behavior. Some dramas, for instance, are intellectually persuasive. Twentieth-century Irish playwright George Bernard Shaw wrote many fascinating argumentative plays, such as *Arms and the Man*. Other plays offer information as well as entertainment—for example, the history plays of William Shakespeare. Still others prescribe social policy or action—for instance, the Marxist plays of the modern German dramatist Bertolt Brecht. Plays are sometimes written in order to describe social conditions, to protest injustices, or to preach messages. All dramatic art displays social awareness, if not direct social concern. In the process of making theatre, people pursue a type of social action—they join together in a communal effort to create.

Artists create order in the chaos of life. They do so by forming a unified art object and by establishing order through work in their own lives. An artist, like everyone else, is bombarded daily with impressions, pressures, and anxieties. Fortunately, life holds an almost equal number of plea-

Left: *Our Town* by Thornton Wilder

Right: The San Francisco Mime Troupe performs *Spain/36*

sures, joys, and beauties. Out of the welter of personal experiences, the artist selects bits and pieces. From a miscellaneous group of particulars the creator assembles an order whole, one that is beautiful, moving, or somehow memorable.

Every artist is dedicated to constructive work and thereby achieves self-creation. Each labors as an artisan, using previous life energy, employing inner experience, and making some object worthy of attention. Thus, every artist expresses outwardly, in a striking manner, a personal self. But to express the self in a way valuable to others, there needs to be a developed identity to express. Somehow there must be a self in action. In one respect, to create means to identify a self. The human action of creation is self-actualizing. To discipline oneself to learn how to create and then actually to do it requires the development of a vision, a persona, a spirit. By necessity, every artist creates a personal identity in a more self-directed manner than most other people. When a human being creates, the apparent result is an art object, but the most significant result is *self-creation*.

Self-creation alone would justify artistic effort, but something even more important occurs. The greatest sanction, the most important reason for art is *self-transcendence*. That means getting outside oneself, being more than selfish in daily life. Every person who lives up to human potential somehow goes beyond personal interest by loving, creating, and contributing to the well-being of others. Through their creativity, artists reach a level beyond themselves. The greatest sanction for art is self-transcendence by creating for others.

Artistic creation is at best the making of an object for the purpose of sharing. The work of a playwright can serve as an example. Utilizing life details, a writer experiences, selects, structures, and records perceptions; thereby a drama comes into being as a script. But the moment that playwright shares the completed script with someone else, whether actors or readers, then with that work of art the writer goes beyond self-concern. When an artist holds out a work of art—the product of heartfelt labor—the desire is not for an ego boost. The artist is trying to share, trying to get beyond selfishness. To create a work of value to others is more important than self-satisfaction. In this way, artistic creation escapes egocentric concern. Creation of art amounts to sharing what is best in oneself with others. In this special sense, art can produce relationships of love.

This chapter most importantly suggests how art can promote higher ethical values in society. Such matters as self-expression, artistry, awareness, intuition, feeling, image, social action, self-creation, self-transcendence, and love are crucial to all authentic artists. These are also useful for anyone in approaching daily life. Art is far from going out of date. In the world's population more people follow creative pursuits today than ever before, both quantitatively and proportionately. Not one of the seven traditional fine arts, nor any of the newer ones, is in any danger of extinction. In this increasingly depersonalized world, art is more up to date and more essential than most other human endeavors. Indeed, art is no more out of date than human life itself. As long as the human race survives, people will create.

Art in general and theatre in particular are among humankind's most humanizing activities. The theatre offers special individualizing values. It is not separate from daily life. Contact with art, especially when frequent, can make any person more fully human. Any person's act of creativity helps that person perfect an identity, and it contributes to the identity of the human community.

The cast of *Lie of the Mind* by Sam Shepard

2 *Live Audiences*

A thorough study of art requires an examination of all three points of the aesthetic triad—artist, object, and audience. Chapter 1 established some necessary concepts for understanding the first two points of the triad: the artist and the object. This chapter deals with key considerations about the audience.

Apparently drama as an art is essential to humankind. It came into being during the formation of primitive societies, and it has persisted in every age. Today more people attend live theatre than ever before. Right now there are more theatres and more theatre artists than at any other time in the world's history. Although commercial theatre survives only precariously, drama as art endures as a necessity for many people. Why? What are the chief appeals of theatre for audiences? How do spectators respond to performances?

Tickets

AUDIENCE INVOLVEMENT

In theatre the spectators become actively involved in the shaping of the final product. Without spectators, theatre amounts to nothing. Without people present, theatre is impossible. Unless there is a live performance by actors, a play remains a piece of inanimate literature, and unless there is a live audience, a dramatic performance remains an unattended rehearsal. Audiences function in theatre in three principal ways—inciting, contacting, and experiencing.

First, what incites all theatre artists to work is the prospect of an audience coming to see the show. The potential appearance of an audience stands as a goal for the entire theatre community as it plans, prepares, and rehearses a play. For most theatre companies the date of the first performance always looms as one of two climaxes. The final performance, the last opportunity for an audience to attend, is usually the second climax. Of course, no show goes on if no audience shows up. In this sense, audiences incite theatre art.

The best theatre artists know that audience strategy is crucial. They want to stimulate and control the attention, interest, feelings, and thoughts of audiences. In the best productions, every detail comes under careful scrutiny with potential audience reaction as the chief criterion of judgment. Although the artists tune their work to attract and move a particular audience, they need not pander to the tastes of that audience. Indeed, most knowledgeable theatre directors attempt to challenge their audiences. But the better a director knows an audience, the more astutely he can confront and entertain it. Audiences thus stimulate theatre not only through their potential group attendance but also in the very identity of the individuals who usually attend. Thus, social communities incite theatre of a particular sort because of their unique personality. Each audience, meaning the total group that attends a given production, requires a specific strategy from the theatre artists.

The second audience function is the live contact and response between performers and spectators. While a performance is going on, an audience directly affects that work of theatre art. Passive audiences do not exist—

**A Broadway theatre at
curtain time**

16

not for live theatre. People sitting there always affect the performance. In obvious or subtle ways the spectators cause immediate modifications, which they cannot do with film or television. With those media, no direct contact occurs between audience and performer, no live interchange takes place. Through live interaction, audiences participate actively in theatre; they help create it. The degree of participation varies, of course, from one audience to another, or between varying production situations. An American audience of the upper cultural range might respond with

An audience in the auditorium of the Alliance Theatre Company, Atlanta

appropriate laughter and applause during a comedy, but an audience of migrant farm workers might participate more directly in a performance about a labor strike. An audience first gives its presence and then its attention. Each performance, however, must maintain and control that attention. When control operates successfully, an audience responds fully and reinforces the intentions and actions of the performers. The enacted drama, thus stimulated, grows in intensity and improves in quality.

Audiences respond overtly. When an audience is pleased, it laughs, weeps, applauds, or shows its devotion with rapt attention. If an audience loses interest or comes to dislike a play, it can disturb the performers enough to throw them off psychologically and physically. A bored audience lets actors know its reaction by coughing, talking, fidgeting, sleeping, and walking out. Sometimes they react by simply withholding most of their positive responses. An affronted or angry audience answers an offensive performance overtly. Audiences have sometimes stopped shows by throwing vegetables, tearing out seats, or storming the stage. Most audiences, however, neither wholly adore nor thoroughly despise the theatre pieces they see. Usually, a theatre audience furnishes a living and constantly shifting response to a drama—a response by turns happy or sad, excited or bored, and moved but thoughtful. In such ways, positively or negatively, audiences affect performances through the live interchange between themselves and the actors.

People from any particular audience can affect future performances of that play. Word-of-mouth commentary and published criticisms not only can extend or shorten the run of a show but also can establish audience expectations beforehand. Furthermore, for the actors, positive critical suggestions or negative remarks can naturally affect future performances. This sort of feedback, whether delivered publicly or privately, often has a telling effect on the actors in a play, and they always affect those who attend.

The third and perhaps most significant audience function is to experience the dramatic performance. This function of experiencing may seem obvious and self-explanatory, but it is quite complex. It involves two considerations: how the audience contributes through its very act of experiencing, and how that experiencing actually occurs within each spectator's consciousness.

A person entering a theatre joins what can be called an aesthetic community. It is not a crowd, but rather a purposeful group with mutual expectations. After the performance begins, that group becomes, moment by moment, more closely bound together into an aesthetic community because of its commonly shared experiences and responses in that particular time and place. When a person experiences a play in the midst of a like-minded group of "aesthetic friends," then that person's experience is likely to be more vivid and thus more valuable. When such a communal condition comes into being, the actors can sense it, and

Dead End by Sidney Kingsley

they can then better control the effects of their work on that particular audience community. Thus, every person can contribute significantly to a performed drama by simply but sensitively joining with others in a full experiencing of the performance. To hold back emotionally or to retain a doubtful psychological attitude prevents full experience. A negative audience member often signals his attitude to those nearby, and a number of such negative people in one audience can make themselves felt to the actors. The more dynamic the awareness of every spectator present, the higher the work of art may reach for everyone. The communal experience of human beings sharing intense sensations and perceptions is essential to theatre art.

AESTHETIC RESPONSE

An aesthetic experience is a person's life response to a work of art. A genuine encounter with a work of art demands a creative capacity in the viewer. To have a full aesthetic experience, also called an aesthetic reaction, a person must somehow contact a work of art, perceive it, and comprehend it.

Contacting a live drama means more than just being there. Besides physical presence, conscious seeing and hearing are involved. To maintain visual and aural sensitivity requires concentration on the sights and sounds of the performance. When concentration lessens, then attention wanders, and a person hears and sees less well. Real contact between actors and audience requires concentration.

Perceiving a live drama refers to the action a person takes in registering and understanding all the sensory stimuli coming from the stage. A young child, for example, might see and hear a production of Shakespeare's *Macbeth*, but the child cannot grasp many implications of the stimuli striking its eyes and ears. Perception implies not merely the animal senses of eyesight and hearing, but the mature capacity of insight. Insight suggests thought in response to what one sees and hears. Logical thought ought to occur, but logical thought alone is insufficient for total intuitions. A person also needs to feel *into* the work. For instance, to enjoy the humor and irony of *The House of Blue Leaves* by contemporary American playwright John Guare, a person should emotionally enter into the spirit of the fractured urban world of the play. To perceive a performed drama means to follow it emotionally and intellectually.

Comprehending is also an important factor in a person's aesthetic response to a play. To comprehend means to make significance of the physical sensations and intuitive perceptions. One must make significance of them inside one's own head. At the end of a drama, after a person has accumulated and integrated all the projected stimuli and the associated feelings, the human mind then "closes" them and makes a whole of them. Only then can the person somehow comprehend that drama, make sense of it, or attribute meaning to it.

After witnessing a performed drama, a person carries the aesthetic experience of all the physical sensations, emotions, and thoughts in memory. Therefore, any audience member can recall and meditate about the significance of a whole drama. The memory of it remains. An aesthetic experience occurs in a person's body, feelings, and thoughts. What theatre art thus generates is a complete human experience which remains etched in human memory.

Aesthetic experience is genuine, lived experience. It is in no way bogus or phony. Such an experience in response to a work of art like a performed play can be one of the most striking incidents in a person's life. Art may be inconsequential, of course, or downright dull, but it may also make life vivid and memorable. Art assumes value insofar as it make people's lives more responsive physically, more varied emotionally, and more meaningful intellectually. The true value of works of art has little to do with their price as consumer goods; value in art can best be measured as human experience.

Several other concepts about audience responses to art and to drama deserve mention. Each could bear extended discussion, but the brief explanations which follow permit a better understanding of audience response to drama.

The most well-known term is *empathy*. Psychologically, empathy means "feeling into." It refers to the action of a human being who is "feeling for" or "feeling with" someone else. For example, when a person watches a fight on stage, some of the emotional excitement of the fight may rise in the viewer; thus an empathic response occurs. Psychologists suggest that empathy exists as a necessary factor in understanding others. Empathizing is not quite the same as sympathizing. To empathize is to extend oneself psychologically to another person in order to understand and perhaps identify with that person. *Sympathy* refers to a positive set of feelings one person may have toward another; it implies that the other person is somehow worse off than the viewer. Empathy is any emotional response caused by vicarious or interpersonal recognition. It does not suggest any sort of superiority, neither situational nor emotional. Empathy is the human capacity of feeling for someone other than oneself.

Aesthetic distance refers to the number and kind of conventions separating an audience member and the performance. It indicates the number of psychological conditions that make the viewing of art different from life. *Psychic distance* is a more precise term. For example, when one actually experiences an event in life, say, a slap in the face, the psychic distance is extremely short. The experience is immediate and direct. But if during everyday life one sees two friends fighting, and one slaps the other in the face, then the psychic distance is longer. The experience remains, however, still fairly direct because one's life involvement is immediate. In the theatre, psychic distance tends to increase because of many conventions and circumstances. Using the example of a slap in the face, in a theatre one does not know the people who are fighting on stage. Conventionally, one sits comfortably in the dark surrounded by a lot of other people. As a result, when the slap occurs, one can understand it, but the associated feelings are different from those in everyday life. Still, in the theatre, the more one becomes emotionally involved in the experience, the shorter will be the psychic distance. That is why during certain kinds of theatre performances, when an actor looks at or actually touches an audience member, the psychic distance may be so reduced that the person touched receives a psychic shock. Aesthetic distance does not indicate the quantity of emotion an audience may be able to experience, nor does it refer to the physical space between spectator and performer. The term simply points to the conditions in a theatre having to do with impressions and responses of immediacy.

Closure means the mental capacity of human beings to receive a group of stimuli and somehow "close" them, making them an understandable

The Catalonian mime troupe Els Joglars performs *Laetius*

whole. For example, seeing the beginning of a movie with mountain scenery, a stagecoach moving across it, and Indians waiting in the distance, one may "close" the stimuli and say, "It's a western." In a more complicated manner, each person makes sense of the pattern of stimuli that a theatre presentation projects. For instance, when watching a production of *Hamlet*, a viewer may not hear, follow, or understand everything that happens on stage. But that viewer mentally makes a "whole experience" of seeing the production. *Hamlet* becomes meaningful in that person's mind as a totality. Each person makes the closure uniquely, depending on his experience and state of mind. Even watching an incomprehensible drama, such as a piece of abstract theatre, a person somehow "closes" the stimuli of the total experience, makes a whole of it, and in some way comprehends it. Likewise, for some theatre people closure means a sense of completion at the end of a unit or at the close of a whole play.

A significant attitude for an audience member to cultivate is an informed tolerance. Such an attitude means that one goes to the theatre with a single expectation—to accept what the artists present. One should try to understand whatever conditions the artists are working under and to permit them to project whatever experience they choose in any manner they wish. Then, after seeing what the artists are trying to do, one can try to understand and experience the artwork as presented.

Left: The Metropolitan Opera House at Lincoln Center

Right: A rock concert in Central Park

Too many people have aesthetic blind spots, usually because of acquired prejudices. For example, some go to the theatre expecting only to be entertained with songs or with jokes about sex. Some approach theatre hunting only for drama of literary merit, of social protest, or of special originality. Some people are ready only to enjoy Broadway theatre, while others like only Off Broadway theatre, repertory theatre, or dinner theatre. Of course, each person can have favorite types of theatre, but often people are too narrow in expectation and never give a particular production enough of an imaginative chance. Variety of experience is far more possible if one is willing to remain open and tolerant.

Does aesthetic tolerance mean one can never judge? Not at all. But no one can evaluate an experience before having it. Judgment comes afterward; prejudgment means prejudice and self-limitation. One of the marvelous circumstances in the aesthetic world of the twentieth century is the amazing diversity of every sort of art. With a tolerant mental attitude, anyone can more readily understand and accept the new, the original, and the unique in both art and life.

Scale of value refers to all the bits of knowledge and experience plus the ideas and attitudes that help any individual evaluate any work of art. It means a personal set of criteria, a system of judgment. Potentially, each person's scale of value is open at the top and at the bottom. At any time, one may discover a piece of art better or worse than any other he has found before. When a person becomes sophisticated, in the positive sense of the word, then the more that person knows about art the more demanding he becomes. Sophistication tends to permit a well-developed scale of value to operate, but an overly critical attitude can spoil the fun. Everyone's scale of value undergoes continual changes; it should not remain static. What one considers good theatre at age 3 ought to be different by age 23 or 53. Every person can beneficially grow in awareness of ideas and attitudes and thus develop a better scale of value for judging art.

AUDIENCE VARIETY

Today the audience for theatre is not singular in personality. Unlike network television executives or film producers, theatre managers do not have to please an audience of millions. They can appeal to more specific and more particular groups. The mass audience for the camera media is so large and varied that to please it producers must limit the dramatic boundaries of film much more strictly than those of theatre. Films can show more places than the theatre, but theatre can be more intelligent. Film and television have become arts that fulfill commonplace expectations. Music and drama have become arts that fulfill special expectations. The theatre is blessed with small audiences. Each theatre can develop its own unique audience. Still, the potential variety of individual theatre audiences remains great.

Theatres have unique goals regarding audiences. The primary objective of most film producers is to make money, and their secondary objective may be to create good cinema. The primary objective of most theatre producers, even many of those who work in the Broadway arena, is to create good theatre, and their secondary objective is to make enough money to keep going. Unlike so many films, dramatic performances are not merely products to be paid for and consumed but, rather, experiences to be shared and remembered. There are enough different sorts of theatres and plays to suit anyone. In fact, each theatre in existence tries to identify a particular segment of the population within a locale as its particular audience. At best, theatre people want a steady, supportive audience of the most imaginative and educated people in a community.

The impulse to be provincial is healthy in today's theatre. Producers and directors realize that their own particular audiences like both established Broadway plays and unique ones by lesser-known playwrights. In fact, much of the best theatre in the United States now originates outside New York. The Arena Stage in Washington, D.C., the Mark Taper Forum of Los Angeles, and the Long Wharf Theatre of New Haven are examples of innovative theatres that surpass the originality and audacity of most New York organizations. Each American theatre company attracts its own audience, or else it dies.

The variety of different kinds of audiences in America today is astounding. Of course, in Europe many cities have their own theatres with devoted audiences. Also, many other parts of the world are now awakening to the importance of their own theatre, especially countries in

South America, Africa, and the Middle East. But the variety of theatre audiences in the United States appears to be the greatest.

In New York the theatre audience is probably the world's largest and most segmented. London perhaps stands as its leading rival. New York generates audiences for the many commercial productions and for the occasional fine professional works of art. Also, Off Broadway has its special following. The widest audience in the metropolitan area probably goes for the semiunion or nonunion productions of the Off Off Broadway movement. Broadway attracts out-of-towners, of course, for all its successful productions. It also sends out road companies to theatres throughout the country. Thus the audience for the New York professional theatre continues to be a large and lively one.

Audiences of great scope exist, too, for professional theatres outside New York. In the major cities of the country, professional repertory theatres have built excellent followings. The people of their locales persistently support them as long as the productions are good. Other professional theatre troupes draw well, too, especially during summers and holidays. Many dinner theatres throughout the country offer pleasant entertainment. Also, summer stock is once more booming.

Perhaps America's largest and most varied theatre audience is the one for amateur theatre. It is everywhere. In most cities and towns, special audiences support amateur theatre groups and semiprofessional companies—alternative theatre, university theatre, community theatre, outdoor theatre, children's theatre, high school theatre, guerrilla theatre, religious theatre, celebratory theatre, and therapeutic theatre. Each has its own particular following. Some people go to several kinds of theatre. In fact, experienced theatregoers find that a varied theatre diet sharpens their appetite for more and better theatre experiences.

Every audience is unique. The mix inside any theatre auditorium is never the same from one night to another. Still, each theatre organization tends to know the profile of its usual audience. Theatre managers study audiences in terms of education, social background, racial mixture, age, religion, financial status, aesthetic expectation, attention span, and theatregoing experience. But no matter how theatre artists try to predict what their audience may be, each audience is always a surprise. That is one of the strange characteristics of live theatre. From one performance to the next, each audience makes a difference in the work of art. Each particular audience helps theatre as art come into being.

SELF-CREATION

Life and art are, today, deeply interconnected. No doubt they have always been interdependent, but only recently have so many people realized that the realm of art is as real as any other. People used to believe, and perhaps some still do, that art and life were somehow separate, that the realm of art did not connect directly with what they called the real world. But today's artists—painters, writers, musicians, and actors—more consciously understand how life affects art and how art comes to bear on life.

Art is experience. That idea can make all the difference in how one approaches theatregoing. An artist takes the action of creating an art object; for him that process of creation is experiential. Once completed, an art object exists in the real world, just as actually as any other thing. Then, a viewer sees and somehow enjoys that art object. When the viewer makes contact, the art object causes him to have an experience—a real one. At best, the experience is unforgettable. For each artist, creation is experiencing; for each spectator, witnessing art is a significant experience.

Theatre is a particularly life-connected art. A play script as a literary object becomes a work of theatre art only when performed. Indeed, in theatre no art object exists unless actors and viewers are living through an experience together. Art affects life in many ways, but the first significant way is how it can cause experiences—unique, intense, and memorable. To experience creation or to respond to the creation of another is to know art as life.

At least two kinds of reality exist: the inner and the outer. Art objects, paintings, songs, or stage performances exist in both realms. Everyone naturally understands that there are things separate from the self, things out in the world. Everyone is also aware of inner reality. Each person's unique psychological being makes that separate reality possible. A person knows only that which can be registered somehow internally. In that sense, all phenomena are more real inside people than outside them.

The Empire Builders by Boris Vian, University of Missouri

Internal reality exists within the conscious being of each person; all else is external. A person can logically surmise, of course, that a reality exists external to the self, but it is always foreign to the self. A person's inner life is more real than all external objects. Art objects exist outside the spectator, but the experience of them is always internal. Thus, when considering theatre, both internal and external realities are crucial.

Art first exists as an intuition that stimulates feeling, imagination, or thought within the personal reality of an artist. Then the artist goes to work to create something, and he brings an art object into existence externally. But that object is useless and meaningless if unobserved. It certainly exists in the world of things, but it gains an extensive reality when some other human being perceives it and absorbs it as internal reality. At that moment inside that viewer the art object becomes fully real. It comes true.

These thoughts about perception and experience suggest that art exists somewhere other than just in the external realm of reality. Artworks are concrete objects, but *art as experience* is potentially as much a part of any person's inner reality as other circumstances of life. Thus the imaginings of an artist are not to be dismissed as mere fantasy. Within an artist's mind, images are reality. They are the stuff of art objects yet to be created.

Art can also furnish a person's life with *peak experiences*. As each person lives from day to day, events of all sorts occur. But routine oc-

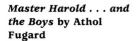

***Master Harold . . . and the Boys* by Athol Fugard**

26

cupies much of human time, and it produces boredom. Much of life is merely to be endured. Art offers a way for human beings to enrich their lives. With art, people can enhance their process of living. Art enriches not primarily through ownership but through experience. To see and to feel the effect of a great painting, to hear a fascinating song, or to partake of live theatre—all such experiences can stimulate peaks of life. In them, life becomes more intense. At such moments, life is not merely a physical circumstance to be endured; life becomes climactic. Other events in life can of course be memorable or touching, but the fine arts are highly developed ways people can, for the sake of pleasure and beauty, partake of peak experiences.

This chapter has featured the special power arising in the confrontation of live actors with live audiences. In *The Actor's Freedom,* Michael Goldman explains that a theatre of live actors functions differently from other kinds of entertainment. A special power arises in the confrontation of live actors with live audiences. That meeting generates a strange energy of concentration, imagination, and consciousness. When enacting a play, actors exercise a unique double power—control over others and the ecstasy of self-surrender to a personality not their own. At its best, theatre is violent and quiet, disturbing and satisfying, ambiguous, and perceptive. But theatre is always thoroughly alive, and that's the foundation of its universal appeal.

Art is self-actualizing. Insofar as art extends from the human experience of an artist and results in the human experience of a viewer, art can touch people's lives. It can affect their very natures. When a person experiences certain moments at a high level of intensity or awareness, such as during a musical concert or a well-performed play, then that individual's inner spirit literally comes into existence more fully. As artists work they create themselves just as much as they create art objects. Whenever spectators give attention to one thing rather than another, they control the actuality of life. With art one develops a self. Art affects life!

CHAPTER 3

Types of Theatre and Drama

This chapter deals with the multiple purposes and amazing variety of theatre as a living art. It explores the various ways plays are organized and the styles of presentation common in drama. It also explains the functions of artistic movements as well as the uses of dramatic art.

FORM, SPECIES, AND GENRE

Every play contains a sequence of scenes, a series of situations and events that taken together comprise an action. A situation refers to a set of relationships between people, or between people and things. An event means a rapid change in relationships. Situation is relative stasis; event is change. An action is a progression of events, a sequential revelation, or simply somebody doing something. In order for something to happen, a person must be in a situation before an event can take place. Thus, when a motive force explodes a static human situation, dramatic action occurs. The structure of a play's action is the spine of its being, and every good play has a pattern of action. An analysis of the structure of a play's action leads to an understanding of its form. Three basic sorts of form are traditionally employed in order to describe particular sorts of dramatic action—tragedy, comedy, and melodrama.

Tragedy is, of course, the most serious form of drama. The basic materials of tragedy are the words and deeds of characters who get themselves into serious situations, matters of life and death. The form of tragedy features a line of action moving from relative happiness through conflict into catastrophe to resolution. The style of tragedy is controlled to express intense human emotion. Tragedy depicts the potential greatness of people as they make errors when facing overwhelming odds. Some of the world's best tragic dramas are *Oedipus the King* by Sophocles, *Hamlet* by William Shakespeare, *The Wild Duck* by Henrik Ibsen, and *Death of a Salesman* by Arthur Miller. These plays indicate the variety of the tragic form.

Comedy is the dramatic form that provokes the most overt responses from an audience. The materials of comedy are the humorous sayings and doings of characters who find themselves in ridiculous situations. Comedy usually deals with how people deviate from societal norms. The form of comedy depends upon a line of action moving from happiness into a predicament to the unraveling and conclusion. The style of comedy exaggerates elements of humor, wit, and irony. Comedy points attention to social excesses, deviations, and mistakes. Some examples of famous comedies are *The Frogs* by Aristophanes, *The Miser* by Molière, *Arms and*

Kabuki theatre

29

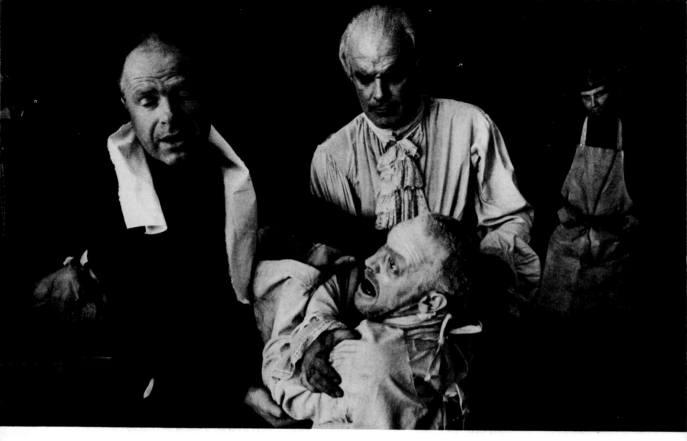

Peter Brook (left) rehearses the cast of *Marat/Sade*

the Man by George Bernard Shaw, and *Brighton Beach Memoirs* by Neil Simon. Through the centuries, different types of comedy have arisen—farce, satire, burlesque, high comedy, low comedy, and comedy of manners. Comedies of all kinds both amuse and communicate perceptions about life's excesses.

Melodrama is the third traditional form. From the time of ancient Greece to the present, many plays have been written neither as tragedies nor as comedies. The word *melodrama* came into popular usage in the nineteenth century to describe the third dramatic type. Melodramas are temporarily serious, but they usually end happily. The materials of melodrama are drawn from the activities of two sets of characters, those essentially good and those essentially evil. The form of melodrama employs a line of action moving from happiness into a predicament containing conflict and then to a double ending with rewards for the good people and punishments for the evil ones. More than do tragedy or comedy, the style of melodrama imitates everyday speech. Melodrama shows man's inventive vitality and the possibilities of justice in the world. Some good examples of melodrama are *Andromache* by Euripides, *Liliom* by Ferenc Molnar, *Look Back in Anger* by John Osborne, and *Deathtrap* by Ira Levin.

A growing number of contemporary dramas do not fit into one of the three traditional categories. For example, *Our Town* by Thornton Wilder,

Waiting for Godot by Samuel Beckett, and *Rhinoceros* by Eugène Ionesco are all plays that defy conventional classification. Theorists therefore continually develop fresh terms to describe such new types of drama. Three useful terms that offer a different approach to dramatic form are *mimetic, didactic,* and *imagistic.*

In *mimetic drama,* action is the unifying factor. The pattern of human change apparent in a series of events is the key to the structure of a mimetic play. Such plays usually have good stories. *Cat on a Hot Tin*

**John Barrymore in
*Hamlet***

Roof by Tennessee Williams is an example of a mimetic drama. Most of Harold Pinter's plays are mimetic, as are those of Edward Albee, Lanford Wilson, and Marsha Norman. Mimetic dramas present characters in action simply for the sake of a fascinating story.

In *didactic drama,* ideas unify the play. Every detail in an idea-centered play is there for the sake of certain thoughts. A complex of ideas lies at the heart of didactic plays. They have stories, characters, and dialogue like mimetic plays, but in didactic plays all such elements somehow help project the central complex of ideas. Of the many different types of didactic plays, some are more obviously persuasive than others. Among the best writers of modern didactic plays are Max Frisch, Clifford Odets, and George Bernard Shaw. *The Good Woman of Setzuan* by Bertolt Brecht demonstrates the high level of artistry possible in plays with a significant message.

In *imagistic drama,* a cluster of images, all somehow interdependent, form the heart of the play. An image is any imaginative detail in a play that stimulates a sensory response. Images can be pictures, words, melodies, movements, or other sensations. An image cluster represents a pattern of free association in a playwright's mind. An entire current in modern drama is imagistic, and it spans the decades from George Büchner's *Wozzek* and Alfred Jarry's *Ubu Roi,* to the surrealist dramas of the 1920s, to the post-World War II absurdist plays of Samuel Beckett and

Eugène Ionesco. Sam Shepard, with plays such as *Curse of the Starving Class* and *Buried Child,* is a noteworthy American imagist of the 1970s and 1980s. Imagistic plays focus more on unusual situations than on lines of action, and they do not present ideas very clearly. What's more, they don't usually have stories to follow. Dramas of the imagistic species are put together to provide vivid sensory and emotional experiences.

Another way to distinguish between dramas is to examine the generic variety of their production in the theatre. Some common generic types are straight plays, musicals, documentaries, and improvisations. Straight plays are those plays with normal dialogue and action presented in professional or amateur theatres for entertainment. Musicals have songs and dancing as major elements. Documentary dramas feature nondramatic materials adapted to the stage for didactic purposes. Improvisations sometimes happen spontaneously in front of an audience; sometimes, however, they are the results of careful rehearsal. The dramatic genres are unlimited in their variety.

STYLES OF DRAMA

Style in drama refers to how the speeches and action of characters are rendered in a play script. The type of selection and exaggeration employed in a play are keys to its style. *Style in theatre* refers to how the director, actors, and designers render the action, the characters, and the

V I S I O N

Above: *The Cashier* **by Glen Merzer, Indiana University**

Right: Jean-Louis Barrault in *The Nights of Paris*

settings concretely on a stage. An easy way to identify dramatic or theatrical styles is to notice how close to or how distant from everyday life the details are. The term *stylized* usually suggests a large degree of exaggeration. Theatre artists have some obligation with each play to harmonize their production style with its dramatic style in order to communicate the spirit of the play to their audiences. Identifying dramatic and theatrical styles means being aware of how the playwright, director, actors, and designers have handled the details of action, speech, and place.

The words *representational* and *presentational* are also useful in discussing different types of drama. Authors of representational plays attempt to present life on stage in an illusory fashion. The details are selected and arranged so that a viewer has the illusion of watching everyday life. Writers of presentational plays make less of an attempt to establish an illusion of ordinary life. A presentational drama is more frankly a play, one that expects viewers to enjoy a more ritualized version of life. The realistic plays of Henrik Ibsen, such as *The Wild Duck*, are examples of representational drama, whereas the classical plays of Sophocles, such as *Oedipus the King*, are apt examples of presentational plays. The two terms are, however, relative and best used comparatively. *Death of a Salesman* by Arthur Miller, for instance, falls someplace between the two extremes. Presentational and representational, then, are relative terms that are sometimes useful in describing plays.

One set of stylistic terms persists in discussions of theatre art. They are often called "the isms." Because these terms have been used so often and so generally, they need repeated definition. Of the large number of such terms, only a few are defined here—classicism, neoclassicism, romanticism, naturalism, realism, symbolism, expressionism, and surrealism. For the most part they are simply convenient labels, and one must be careful in critical discussions not to count on them too heavily. Later chapters, especially the historical ones, expand these definitions and furnish others.

Classicism originally referred to the best of Greek art, with its features of order, simplicity, and beauty. Eventually, Roman art came to be included in the term. Today, classicism still suggests the styles of those two periods—the Greek and the Roman. Classicism also has come to mean the application to art of the best of traditional, time-proven principles. The dramas of Sophocles provide examples of classicism. Classical drama suggests the dramas first presented in ancient Greece or during the Roman Empire.

Neoclassicism was a style developed in France during the eighteenth century by such writers as Corneille and Racine. Those who established the style made it far more restrictive than classicism. In drama, the doctrine of neoclassicism required strict observance of the unities of time, place, and action. Even more important, it required decorum in the display and evocation of emotion. Throughout the twentieth century, critics have employed the term *neoclassical* more generally, and now it suggests merely a contemporary concern for classical values in art.

Like the other great styles, *romanticism* grew out of a system of philosophic ideas. The romantics believed in the importance of the individual,

The ancient Greek theatre at Epidauros

The Adding Machine by Elmer Rice

and they thought that human beings are perfectable. Each person, they said, can with effort be better. Romanticism in drama focused on the valorous deeds of heroes, and it brought sentiment to the stage. Its heyday occurred in the late eighteenth and early nineteenth centuries, and it gave birth to melodrama and sentimental tragedy. The plays of Victor Hugo and Alexandre Dumas *fils* are examples of French romanticism. *Cyrano de Bergerac* by Edmond Rostand well illustrates the neoromanticism of the late nineteenth and early twentieth centuries. Romanticism still persists in some of the attitudes and practices of most artists of the twentieth century. Far from being a sweetly sentimental viewpoint, today's tendencies toward romanticism stress the threats of mass society to the sanctity of the individual.

Naturalism surfaced in the artistic world during the last half of the nineteenth century. It represents the application of the scientific method to art. The naturalists, led by Emile Zola, who wrote *Thérèse Raquin*, observed and recorded the details of life around them. They employed the concepts of environment and heredity to analyze the behavior of characters. Also, not wishing to make life sound more grand than it really is, they attempted to create artistic works without permitting intellectual predilections to interfere with the depiction of life as it is. Furthermore, they opened new realms of subject matter, dealing with such problems as poverty, crime, and pathology. Naturalism persists today in the apparent desire of many writers to record truthfully what they see and hear.

Realism is a style closely associated with naturalism. The early realists usually experimented with naturalism and found that they wanted more artistic freedom than the strict rules of such theorists as Zola permitted. But they still wished to maintain truthfulness and reproduce real life on stage. Henrik Ibsen (*Ghosts*) and August Strindberg (*The Dance of Death*) were for long spans of their careers devoted to the realistic style, but in plays like *Uncle Vanya*, Anton Chekhov probably most nearly achieved perfection with dramatic realism. Following its development in the late nineteenth century, realism rapidly became the most popular dramatic style, and it persists today.

Derek Jacobi in *Cyrano de Bergerac* by Edmond Rostand

Symbolism was developed as an almost immediate reaction to the movement of realism. Arising first in the late nineteenth century, symbolism found its way to the stage in the particularly memorable plays of the French writer Maurice Maeterlinck—for example, *The Intruder*—and the Irish poet W. B. Yeats—for example, *On Baile's Strand*. Although their objectives were not simple, one of their aims was to set symbolic images before audiences so that spectators could experience the same feelings as when the artist first witnessed the striking event. Especially in its idealistic and humane conception, symbolism kept alive some of the best features of the romantic tradition. Today's playwrights find some of the symbolist methods still useful. Although symbols must be understood to have much effect, the symbolists wished less for their audiences to hunt for symbols in their works than for them to let the symbols work dynamically on their imaginations. Josef Svoboda, a contemporary Czech theatre artist, often uses symbolism in scenic designs. Many outstanding contemporary film makers—such as Ingmar Bergman and Federico Fellini—utilize visual symbolism in much the same way Maeterlinck hoped it would work. Ultimately, the symbolists wish to communicate what life is like, not by showing its realistic detail but by setting forth the symbols best representing its spirit.

Expressionism reached its artistic peak in the 1920s in Germany and the United States. Georg Kaiser (*From Morn to Midnight*) and Ernst Toller (*Man and the Masses*) of Germany plus Eugene O'Neill (*The Hairy Ape*) and Elmer Rice (*The Adding Machine*) of the United States wrote outstanding expressionistic plays. One of the key attitudes of most expressionists was to present the world as they saw it *inside* their own minds. Thus, most expressionistic plays present a purposely distorted version of people and events. The plays are episodic and illustrate the imaginations of their authors; many of them contain sharp criticism of undesirable conditions in society. The expressionists often utilize a mixture of other styles, as well, to achieve desired effects, and most of their plays have strong story lines. Expressionism persists in its influence into the final quarter of this century, especially in some of its specific techniques of episodic progression of story and psychological distortion of characters.

Surrealism is a French version of expressionism, and its best practitioners rose to prominence in the 1920s. Even though relatively few artists were devoted to surrealism, its influence strongly persists into the latter part of this century. André Breton, the chief theorist of surrealism, wished

The Death of Von Richthofen as Witnessed from Earth by Des McAnuff

Judith Malina and Julian Beck, founders of the Living Theatre

to treat the process of human thought as a chief artistic objective, and he thus established the principle of "automatism," or the free flow of ideas in the act of creation. The surrealists claimed that the subconscious mind ought to control the artistic process. They mixed familiar images with surprising ones, and they often made surprising combinations of elements for the sake of shocking effects. At its best, surrealism utilizes the subjective side of the imagination to create fresh artistic images. Guillaume Apollinaire wrote the first surrealistic play, *The Breasts of Tiresias*, and it remains the most representative.

Each of the major styles discussed in this chapter persists in some measure in today's theatre. All the styles have aided some artists to write down their visions as plays, and they have helped others to stage those dramas appropriately. Of course, other less influential styles have blossomed, and new ones are in vogue today. Style in an art object is a result of the way a particular artist has worked, and style comes from that artist's imaginative selections and exaggerations.

MOVEMENTS, SCHOOLS, AND FUNCTIONS

There are still other ways to understand the great variety in the world of the theatre. To study it from another angle is to review the movements, schools, and functions of theatre in the human community.

Through the history of art many tendencies in the handling of material, structure, and style have arisen and then passed. When a number of artists follow similar tendencies at about the same time, their creative production is called a *movement*; and when a group of artists communicate with one another in order to concentrate on certain aesthetic goals, the group is called a *school*. The rise of movements and schools in art has been frequent in the nineteenth and twentieth centuries, but in the theatre schools are less frequent than movements.

One of the major movements in recent theatre is theatre of the absurd. French philosopher and playwright Albert Camus first brought the word *absurd* into vogue among intellectuals. He referred to man's inner sense of finitude when facing a hopeless world. Later, critic Martin Esslin applied the term to drama in describing the works of such playwrights as

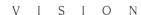

Biloxi Blues **by Neil Simon**

Samuel Beckett and Eugène Ionesco. Since the early 1950s, many playwrights have written in a similar vein. Most movements in modern drama are smaller than the absurdist movement. Two examples are the "angry young men" of England, including John Osborne and N. F. Simpson, and the improvisationalists of the United States, such as Megan Terry and Jean-Claude van Itallie. Some plays, then, can be associated with a movement, but most cannot.

Often in the history of theatre, artists have banded together to form a school of art. Here the word *school* refers not to an institution of education but to a group of people who share beliefs and goals. Two clear examples of schools in art arose in Paris during the late 1910s and early 1920s when the dadaists and then the surrealists banded together and asserted their manifestos. Few playwrights or theatre people belonged to either school, but surrealist Antonin Artaud later had a great impact on the absurdist movement in the theatre. A clear example of playwrights forming a school occurred in New York during the 1930s, when leftist writers such as John Howard Lawson, George Sklar, and Clifford Odets drew together and discussed common aims.

Another major way to distinguish between plays has grown important in recent years—function. In conception and in actuality, how a play is meant to function and how it actually does function affects its nature. If a group of actors get together to create their own drama, they may begin with games or improvisations. Indeed, theatre in its most simple state is a game of make-believe played as a game by children. Some theatre, then, functions like a game and results in "scripts" that are quite effective for their given purpose. Other theatre functions like a ritual. The works of Jerzy Grotowski, a Polish director influential in the 1970s, are usually ritualistic. He and his company have often transformed old plays into new, more ritualized ones. Other play scripts are meant to function in other ways—for example, the plays written for outdoor pageantry, for puppet theatres, or for Broadway commercialization. Further functions might include instruction, religion, magic, or celebration. Various societies have used theatre in vastly differing ways.

The variety of drama written in the past is great indeed, ranging from the tragedies of the ancient Greeks to the imagistic pieces of the absurdists. The potential variety for drama in the future, however, is even greater. Each playwright needs to develop an individual sort of drama, unique in vision, material, structure, and style. The expectation of variety and originality, tempered by craftsmanship, establishes in a theatregoer a vigorous and open attitude for reading or seeing new plays.

KINDS OF THEATRE

This section examines different types of productions. It treats various sorts of contemporary theatre but leaves the historical review for later chapters. Here theatre is classified according to the people involved—their circumstances, objectives, relationships, and finances.

When faced with a new theatre experience, an observer might well ask: Who or what is responsible for bringing this production into being? What's truly original here? The play? The company? The space? Or the community? Of course, no single factor is responsible for any human action; always a complex of forces are at work. But the questions indicate the four factors most responsible for variations in kinds of theatre—the script, the theatre artists, the physical conditions of the production, and the social milieu in which the production occurs. Since the last section explored the various types of plays, attention is given here to the other three factors.

Regardless of which script is involved, theatre varies in subject, craftsmanship, manner, and impact according to the theatre artists involved. A play comes alive only through particular actors, and different actors create differing lives onstage. For example, the character of Hamlet is simply a literary personage existing only in words, or at most in the imagination of a reader, until an actor assumes the role of Hamlet and literally brings him to life. But the life that Laurence Olivier gave Hamlet is not the same life that Albert Finney gave him. Thus, when a particular actor plays Hamlet, the creation is unique and different from all other Hamlets. There is no ideal Hamlet, no perfect Hamlet, no definitive Hamlet, because there are only different Hamlets. The same applies to all characters in all plays. Thus, as casts change, so do plays change. Whole plays come to life uniquely in the work of particular production groups. The kind of theatre one group produces with a particular play is quite different from the kind of theatre another will produce with that same play.

The work of theatre groups varies not merely because of the different actors but also because of each group's aesthetic and practical objectives, talent level, amount of experience, internal relationships, and societal connections. Obviously, the objectives of a group affect their productions. For some groups, such as Broadway companies, the dominant objective is money. But for others, such as the professional repertory theatres in

Joseph Papp, head of New York's Public Theatre and producer of *A Chorus Line*

America's major cities, the main objective is producing good theatre. University groups have the complex objectives of educating students, furnishing theatre for a community, and providing a place for experiments. Off Broadway and alternative theatre groups often act as the principal innovators of new forms and as career ladders for young artists.

In every group some dominant person—usually a producer or a director—establishes aesthetic objectives for the production of each play. The group's talent level also affects production quality. The more professional the theatre organization, the higher the percentage of talented people it is likely to contain. But sometimes professional companies have relatively few talented performers, and occasionally a young company, such as an alternative theatre group or a university theatre, features a high percentage of talented actors. Talent exists everywhere, and one of the pleasures of going to see unheralded theatre productions is to discover new talents.

The level of experience in a company also affects the kind of theatre it produces. A company's experience can be considered in two respects: first, how many productions each of the individuals has participated in and, second, how long the company has been working together. The quality of experiences for theatre artists is often more important than mere quantity. An actor may participate in a large number of poor productions under weak directors and acquire bad habits, whereas under a wise director that same actor may grow significantly in only one or two productions. But, usually, experience counts in all the arts because so much of craftsmanship depends on acquiring skills through trial and error.

Internal relationships within a company also affect the final product on stage. Often an intimately shared sense of joy in group creativity gives an amateur or small theatre production a spirit missing in many professional productions. Indeed, the ego protectiveness in professional theatre is frequently harmful, impairing ensemble creativity. But sometimes excessive emotionalism can distort amateur productions. Still, the personal relationships between members of any theatre company affect their powers of creativity.

A theatre group's place in a community also makes a difference. Every company identifies itself and its mission in a social community not merely with its publicity but more significantly with its choices of materials and the quality of its productions. The relationship between a theatre group and its surrounding society becomes clear in how supportive or critical the group is of that society. The reverse is also true. The supportive or critical nature of a community's response affects every theatre company. Thus, each group reflects its enveloping society and to some degree affects it as well.

Any theatre organization arouses a particular set of expectations in the minds of its audiences before they arrive. Those can be altered or ad-

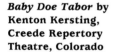

V I S I O N

Baby Doe Tabor by Kenton Kersting, Creede Repertory Theatre, Colorado

justed, but the theatre won't survive long if the expectations are ignored. If people arrive at a theatre expecting a good avant-garde performance and get a sentimental comedy instead, they may be too disappointed to return. Every theatre develops a reputation, which helps audiences know at least vaguely what to expect when they arrive.

The physical conditions of a theatre in which a production company operates profoundly affect the resulting performances. Rehearsal conditions make a difference to actors as they work, and performance conditions affect both performers and spectators. Even the arrangement of a theatre building makes a difference—particularly the proximity of the stage to the audience, the type of seats, the size of the stage and backstage areas, and the overall size of the entire complex. Every company must tune its productions to a certain physical size and shape. Particular sizes and shapes of theatres offer no automatic virtues. Neither newness nor luxuriousness of facilities insure good theatre, but neither do primitive or ill-kept theatres help art very much. The best theatre facilities are clean, functional, and comfortable for everyone.

Furthermore, plays function emotionally in ratio to full or empty seats. If all the seats are full—indeed, if there is a physical sense of people being crowded into the audience space—then the play is more likely to make a favorable impact on the entire audience. Thus the size of the audience itself becomes a significant physical condition in the production.

Shakespeare's *Hamlet* on a thrust stage, University of Evansville

The financial conditions of a production naturally affect the nature and kind of theatre that results. From the initial conferences onward, the director and designers work within a budget, and they adjust the physical details of the production to it. Few companies have unlimited budgets, and financial constrictions sometimes actually stimulate inventiveness. Jerzy Grotowski, a contemporary Polish director, preferred "poor theatre" during the 1970s, and he made it popular to eschew the unnecessary trappings of most bourgeois productions. Some sort of financial backing is, however, necessary for most theatre pieces, and often the lack of money seriously impairs the creativity of whole productions. From the type of scenery, costumes, and properties onstage, one can surmise what budget controlled the production's physical aspects. No doubt every theatre production is seriously affected in its specific physical details by an inadequate budget, without even considering the salaries for the artists. Whether the members of a company like it or not, financial conditions always make a difference in dramatic art.

The *conventions* of every theatre building also help determine the kind of performance that results. In this context, conventions refer to the built-in physical and social circumstances that affect audience response. The typical conventions in theatres mostly affect an audience's senses. A play usually occurs in a sound-insulated space separated from the interferences of everyday life. The common practice of maintaining a comfortable auditorium temperature illustrates how reasonable and necessary some conventions can be, but others are more arbitrary. Most theatres also have conventionalized seating—padded chairs facing the performance. In most theatres the performance space is separated from audience space. For vision, the seats are positioned so that spectators can easily observe the performance space; auditoriums are dark, but stages are brightly lit. Scenery and curtains usually hide the backstage and fly galleries. Conventions of time govern when the curtain rises, the frequency of intermissions, and production length. All these conventions may, according to habit, seem natural unalterable codes, but each is flexible and can be changed to alter the impact of a production.

The people in a theatre group also make a difference to the kind of art produced. The sort of human beings who comprise any theatre organization naturally affects the work of the company. The kind of theatre one sees on a particular stage reflects the personality of some contributors indirectly—the designers, for example, and it displays the personality of others directly—the actors, for instance. How strange to see an actor reveal the nature of his own self while portraying a character, but such revelations are there for anyone to see. In every art the creators reveal their deepest spirit in the work, and so it is in theatre. The most important quality that gets communicated in all art is the basic humanity of the artist. In a social art like theatre, the spirit of many different individuals and of the group as a whole comes into public view.

The human natures of the members of a theatre company are revealed in the performed play. Frequently, a theatregoer may be touched pleasantly by one production and repulsed by another, not so much because of the sort of play presented nor even because of the skill of the presentation, but because of the sort of people that the theatregoer meets within the production. The meeting between a person in an audience and an actor, though not directly personal, is far more intimate than many people realize. One of the unique characteristics of experiencing theatre is the intimate experiencing of life with other, often strange human beings. The people of theatre are living their very lives before an audience, and as their human natures stand revealed, the audience responds more or less positively or negatively. The inner natures of the individuals in any theatre make a profound difference in the kind of dramatic art appearing on that stage.

Not every manager, director, designer, or actor turns out to be a truly influential innovator, but every creative artist develops ideas, feelings, and intuitions individually. An amazing amount of innovative and original thought goes into the creation of even the most conventional theatre production. Every production, no matter how humble, achieves uniqueness. To recognize how each production resembles others is important for the sake of communication, but to discern the unusual qualities of each production arouses more excitement and satisfaction in a spectator. Watching any play with such an attitude should assure one of pleasure no matter what the level of artistic accomplishment. Creativity glistens as a special, live facet in every piece of theatre art.

In this world there is room for an infinite number of kinds of theatre. The more different kinds of theatre one meets, the greater will be the breadth of one's experience. Informed experience produces increased awareness, and sometimes even wisdom. No one need enjoy every kind of theatre, and certainly in each type the quality range of individual productions varies widely. Nevertheless, in each sort of theatre production in every locale, vital human energies are at work in a creative effort. One need only perceive them in order to understand and to experience the lives and intuitions of other people.

4 *Perception and Analysis*

Everyone possesses an internal scale of value for judging experiences. Without one, a person could not survive the challenges of life. Some values, such as those regarding honesty or friendship, operate generally in many phases of a person's life. Other values, such as those pertaining to excellence in art, are more specific. A scale of value in art is a system for analyzing and evaluating creative works.

Changes continually occur in one's scale of value. As time passes, everyone discards some values and adopts or refines others. But in art as in other spheres of life a willingness to learn and to change is a virtue. Some people develop frozen attitudes toward theatre; they "know what they like" and limit themselves too strictly to a tiny range of experiences. Others are more willing to explore the unfamiliar and to expand their tastes. Certain people, especially the young and the wise, are quite willing to consider value changes. This chapter sets forth a number of criteria that might become a part of anyone's scale of value for responding to theatre.

An audience in the Strand Theatre, Dorchester, Massachusetts

APPROACHES

Everyone responds to dramatic performances differently, and people need consciously to discern their own basic attitudes. Everyone carries a mental set of expectations. Usually people's initial attitude toward any theatre piece is positive or negative. With a positive attitude, a person is ready for sensitized perception and discerning analysis; with a negative attitude, a person gets ready to criticize. But anyone can learn to recognize value and quality in art without being negative. The negative, critical point of view is always that of an outsider; the positive, analytic viewpoint is ever that of the artist and a friendly audience. Any spectator can remain a skeptic by negatively observing the artwork, or that same person can enter the world of the artist by trying to experience the work and searching for the spirit of other human beings in it. Of course, even with a positive attitude one may discern weaknesses in an artwork but still enjoy it, whereas a negative attitude tends to destroy all pleasure. A positive approach offers far greater rewards.

Two basic intellectual approaches to art are the extrinsic, or Platonic, and the intrinsic, or Aristotelian. Plato believed art ought to have a particularly moral function in society and that drama should be ethically instructive. He concerned himself more with the effects of art on audiences than with the internal features of artworks. Aristotle thought the best way to know a work of art is to examine what brought it into being.

45

He suggested a causal method of analysis in order to realize the materials, the form, the style, and the purpose of each artwork. Both approaches can be valuable; both can furnish useful insights about art.

Throughout history serious thinkers have utilized one approach or the other, believing that drama should be written to instruct or that it should simply exist for its own sake. Playwrights, too, have adopted one attitude or the other. Most of them have chosen the intrinsic approach and concerned themselves with the action of the play more than with its effect

Hemingway by Sam Smiley

on society. Dramatists who take the extrinsic approach pay more attention to the messages of their plays and their effects on audiences. A theatregoer can naturally take advantage of information from both the Aristotelian and Platonic approaches, but most people find it useful to develop one dominant attitude, either the critical or the analytical.

Another essential pair of viewpoints in the realm of art are those of artist and audience. Obviously, any work of art is made by one or more artists and then viewed by one or more audience members. But some of the responses of both parties are not so obvious. About the artist's approach, three facts stand out. First, art is created less often for singular reasons than because a complex set of motivations impels the artist to self-expression. Second, while laboring to make an artwork, an artist acts as creator, but when the creative process is completed and the work finished, the artist suddenly becomes a viewer. Third, artists also enjoy the artworks of others. A significant portion of an audience in any realm of art is made up of artists.

Still, most theatre audiences are composed of people who like art but are not themselves artists. At one extreme are those who know nothing about theatre, who make no pretense about knowing, and who approach a performance with a kind of innocent willingness to enjoy whatever they see. At the opposite extreme among appreciative people are those audience members who are well-informed about theatre, who have seen many different performances, and who are more eager than ever to see a new one. Both sorts of people make fine audience members. Those who enter the theatre unaffectedly are as important to the nature of audience reaction as are the connoisseurs. Most audiences contain people who are neither totally new to the theatre nor confidently expert.

Most theatregoers are to some degree sophisticated. The word *sophistication*, used positively, means knowledge about and experience with art. In America today most audience members have some sophistication about theatre. Movies and television provide most people with experiences similar to theatregoing. Also, drama deals with life, so people naturally compare what they see on stage with their own real experiences. Because of theatre's life proximity everyone is potentially a good audience member regardless of one's relative measure of sophistication. Some people have never seen live theatre and do not wish to, but maybe they never had an opportunity early in their lives to see a theatre piece. Others have seen one or two plays and want to see no more; probably they didn't see theatre of very high quality. Of course a percentage of people in any community won't attend a theatre because of their entertainment habits, the expense, or their lack of motivation. Some people do not like creative things at all; they avoid paintings, music, books, and theatre alike. But most people enjoy good theatre when they have a chance to see it.

Three nonsympathetic attitudes toward theatre are common. Some people argue that theatre is a minority art that doesn't much affect the social community. They say more people see movies than plays. They also compare the viewing hours that Americans spend in front of television sets with the number of hours they spend in theatres. Certainly only a small percentage of the American public goes to the theatre, but the foregoing argument is loaded in favor of the mass media. Answers to the following questions might provide telling insights. What segment of the population attends the theatre? What educational level does a typical theatregoer represent compared with that of the average moviegoer or television watcher? Why do so many intelligent, well-educated people pay attention to drama? Why are society's leaders so aware of perceptive theatre? Such questions indicate that theatre, as well as the other arts, reaches those who lead the populace.

Another negative argument aimed at theatre has to do with its mo-

**Jeremy Irons and Glenn
Close in *The Real
Thing* by Tom Stoppard**

dernity. Some people contend that theatre is out of date. This accusation has a grain of truth. Theatre is indeed a handicraft pursuit in a mass-production age. The same can be said of all the fine arts. Excellent plays cannot be turned out at the rate of a hundred a day or a thousand per week. To prepare a performance takes from 50 to 100 people and about two months of steady work, and the resulting production can be seen by only a few thousand people. But the amazing fact is that theatre remains a personally creative occupation for many people. They love the handicraft involved. Mass production of theatre is impossible; yet modern technology has helped theatre in many ways, providing better lighting instruments, shop tools, scenic materials, sound amplification, and even building construction. Theatre is not technologically out of date; only its means of communication remains the same. Because it is always so alive, theatre displays most directly certain features of the spirit of humankind. Like the other arts, theatre won't really go out of date until humanity itself does.

A third negative accusation leveled against theatre is that as a business it is speculative and unsound. Most business people realize that investment in the production of a Broadway play involves a greater degree of risk than drilling for oil. Many older people advise young people that theatre isn't a good profession because it offers so poor a likelihood of making a living. It's all true. But to argue that theatre isn't a sound business enterprise is like arguing that a racehorse isn't a milk cow. One can't judge racehorses by how much milk they produce; so it is with theatre. After all, it's a fine art, and art's function has more to do with entertaining or sensitizing people than with producing revenue.

Nor is financial success a true measure of theatrical quality. Still, people have somehow come to judge the success of a play by the number of tickets it sells, by the amount of money it grosses, or by the length of its run. All these facts about a given production might hint that it has achieved a certain level of artistry, and such facts obviously indicate the popularity of the piece. But commercial popularity is neither a guarantee of artistry nor of the lack of it. People tend to judge plays by financial results because journalists can objectively report such information. But measuring success by box office receipts means that some works of high quality but minority appeal get overlooked. Fine plays with good casts sometimes close early on Broadway because after only a few performances ticket sales drop below a minimum number, and the show's producers end the project for fear of losing money. No simple method exists for judging the success of a production. But today's financial yardsticks mean little about the true value of art. Especially in the non-commercial theatres, ticket sales reveal far less about quality than does the total response of that particular theatregoing community.

Each person's approach to theatre, then, depends on certain significant mental attitudes. How one thinks of theatre in general dictates how one may react to a particular dramatic work. Human experience is as varied as the nearly infinite modes of human consciousness, and the ways people experience theatre is equally varied. Exactly how each person approaches an evening in the theatre makes all the difference. One can approach theatre as a business product, an item of entertainment to be paid for and consumed; or it can be approached as a work of art, a set of stimuli to be experienced and remembered. A person can approach theatre as an old-fashioned, minority art or as a vibrant, entertaining place where some of society's most imaginative and intelligent people gather to be stimulated. Anyone can choose to approach drama negatively as a critic or positively as one who enjoys and understands. One can adopt Plato's extrinsic viewpoint or Aristotle's intrinsic one. The choice rests with each individual. But whatever a person's approach, it ought to be at least partly conscious.

SUGGESTIVITY AND SIGNIFICATION

This section deals with two difficult questions. *What* does a drama communicate? And *how* does it communicate? No one can answer these questions perfectly or permanently. The potential variety of theatre is too infinite. But some ideas about *what* and *how* are useful. Later chapters, particularly Chapter 5 on playwriting, provide information about principles of dramatic structure, whereas the following discussion treats the function of drama before an audience.

A drama is an event performed by people for people. All concerned with living or witnessing the event are alive, and their experiences are real. For centuries the idea of pretense in actors and the idea of escape

Charlie's Aunt, **Brown County Playhouse**

49

Left: *Lady House Blues*
by Kevin O'Morrison,
University of Evansville

Right: *Fool for Love* **by**
Sam Shepard

for audiences have been overemphasized. In theatre whatever happens really happens! What actors and audiences experience, they actually experience. The artists enact a pattern of human life, highly organized and intensified, in a place where a group of people can see it at once. Thus, the artists of the theatre present something important, something worthy of attention, something that may affect the lives of the people who watch. Drama is life—selected, ordered, intensified. Drama offers real, live experience. It is a unique way of knowing about existence, a special way of experiencing and sharing life.

Drama, like other art, is meant to be suggestive. Most playwrights want their plays to stimulate the imaginations, feelings, and thoughts of their spectators. Theatre artists generally agree that performed plays ought to entertain, to enliven, and to challenge audiences. *Suggestivity* as a power in art means that an art object suggests different things to different people, that it has the power to trigger many physical and mental associations. In order to be suggestive, a drama needs both ambiguity and clarity. A play needs to be clear about the basic details of who the people are and what is going on. Also, the language needs to carry ideas and information clearly at some level or another. But if everything is too clear, too obvious, too predictable, then the play becomes dull. In all good art ambiguity is necessary. Plays need to suggest more than they say, to represent more than they are. Ambiguity in drama amounts to that mysterious element of life—the unknowable. When faced with controlled ambiguity in art, the intuitions of each audience member work independently and generate startling private responses. Every good piece of theatre contains a balance between clarity and ambiguity, and in that balance resides each drama's power of suggestivity.

A drama offers not merely experience but meaningful experience. But what a play means varies somewhat from person to person. Whenever the meaning of a play is under discussion, one should remember the three loci of thought in relation to drama. First, the playwright and other theatre artists want a play to contain and project certain thoughts. The artist thus intends a particular meaning. Second, the play itself contains particular thoughts; these can be spotted inside the play as dramatic materials. The artists' intended thoughts may or may not be there within the performed play; some of their thoughts probably will be there and some will not. Third, each audience member who sees a play undoubtedly has certain thoughts while watching it. The play suggests thoughts to a person, but often they are not precisely the same ones that it contains. The artist has intentional thoughts, a play has material thoughts, and an audience member has meaningful thoughts. In this special sense, artists do not make meaning, and artworks do not contain meaning. Meaning occurs in the minds of beholders.

Another way to consider a performed drama is as an object of emotional communication. As artists, playwrights observe or conceive an emotional experience in life. They focus their craft on that experience and intensify it. Theatre artists join a playwright in renewing the experience and bringing it to life over and over during rehearsals and performances. Finally, if all the details are right, an audience experiences approximately the same emotional experience the playwright perceived in the first place. For this process to occur, the artists involved must do more than merely copy life. They must find those significant details—artists often call them images—that best trigger emotionality in viewers. Selecting the right details and putting them in the right order are the most difficult actions in the process of creation.

Every drama contains certain *emotional powers*. Aristotle first discussed them in his *Poetics*. Defining tragedy, he mentioned the emotional powers of pity and fear. In order for a play to be serious in the special sense of tragedy, it must contain fearful situations and pitiful characters; and if the dramatist makes the situations fearful enough and the characters genuinely worthy of pity, then tragedy can occur. Emotional powers refer to emotive elements within a scripted play or a performed drama. They may also refer to the emotional potentials a play possesses for evoking certain feelings in an audience. If a tragedy contains pity and fear in the proper degree, then those who witness the tragedy may feel that same fear and pity rising within themselves. The basic emotional powers for comedy are ridicule and laughter, and for melodrama they are fear and hate. But each play has its own unique emotional powers. Part of the joy of seeing drama is to realize that feelings have arisen within oneself. Life without feeling would be a dull affair. Drama can intensify a person's feelings through the exercise of emotional powers. Thus, in a number of ways drama communicates by providing memorable life experiences.

ANALYTIC METHODS

In order to understand dramas either in text or in performance, some method of analysis is necessary. Analysis means careful examination, and it means separating a whole into parts and studying those parts and their relationships A number of analytic systems are available as critical aids to the serious student of drama, and the following section explores them. Everyone is likely to develop a personal system by eclectically choosing among the various methodologies.

Aristotle's method of dramatic analysis is one of the best. He was the first to discover or discuss many basic principles of drama, and even his terminology has persisted to our own day—as examples, such words as *action, plot*, and *character* are Aristotelian. But his method amounts to more than mere terminology. Using an intrinsic, causal method, he first asked: Why did drama come into being? He tried to discover what principles are most important in the formulation of drama, and he looked for those principles within plays themselves.

Most significantly, Aristotle asked four crucial questions about the causes of drama coming into being. His four questions can usefully be asked about any play. What are the *materials* of the drama? What is the *form* of the work? What is its *style*? And what artistic *function* does it

Left: Aristotle

Right: Karl Marx

fulfill? The materials of a drama are not only its words, but also the subject matter, events, people, and thoughts it contains. The form of a drama amounts to its overall organization, the sort of story it has, the way the action moves from incident to incident, or its pattern of change. The style of a drama is the manner in which the artist expresses himself, a manner more or less lifelike, more or less exaggerated. The function of a drama is best expressed by identifying what sort of play it is, what sort of experience it should give an audience. By asking Aristotle's four causal questions, anyone can employ his probing analytic method. Adequately answered, his questions can reveal the nature of any drama.

Aristotle also named six elements of drama: plot, character, thought, diction, melody, and spectacle. These, too, extend the analytic possibilities of his method. The chapter on playwriting explains these six elements in detail. But the following questions introduce the terms and show how each can be useful in analysis: *Plot*—how are the events of the play organized into a pattern of action? *Character*—what kind of people exist in the play, and how do they change or fail to change? *Thought*—what feelings and ideas rise in the minds of each character, and what ideas does the play as a whole suggest? *Diction*—what sort of language do the characters speak, and how do they express themselves emotionally? *Melody*—do the words sound natural in the mouths of actors, and does the dialogue have a musical flow? *Spectacle*—where is the play set, and does that place help bring on the happenings? Answers to such questions lead to revelations about the internal nature of a play.

Plato founded an approach to art that can be applied to drama. He stressed the imitation of essences, rather than the photographic imitation of sensory experiences. He wanted art to function well in society by teaching truths and ideals. According to Plato, art ought to be true, good, and beautiful. Some basic Platonic questions are: What is the essence of the particular drama? What is its vision? What concepts are at its core? How true is it, and what truth does it project? What sort of morality does the play advocate? What can a person learn from the play? Is it beautiful, and if so, how does its beauty appear?

German philosopher Georg Wilhelm Friedrich Hegel also established a methodology for societal as well as artistic analysis. His method is popularly called the dialectic. Formally, it features the thought pattern of thesis, antithesis, and synthesis. With this triad of concepts, Hegel stressed that one should look for forces that oppose each other, and for the resolution of their opposition. One way to apply Hegel's triad to dramatic analysis is to ask the following: What forces oppose each other in the play? What is the nature of the struggle? What is the outcome of the struggle? Which force wins and why? And what does the outcome mean?

Karl Marx was also a thinker whose influence was both political and cultural. Today's Marxian critics employ Hegel's triad, and they associate art with the social philosophy of dialectical materialism. They study drama as a reflection of the development of human history; thus the various characters in any play represent classes, segments of society, or social ideals. A key Marxian question might be, How does a drama reveal historical necessity?

Contemporary American critic Kenneth Burke established an incisive methodology for literary analysis, which is useful in dramatic analysis. In part, he put Aristotelian concepts into modern terms. Writing about the "dramatistic" nature of life and literature, he established a pentad for analysis: act, scene, agent, agency, and purpose. His questions can be asked about a play as a whole or about any unit of a play. What action is taking place? Where is it happening, and why does it occur there instead of somewhere else? Who makes it happen? How does that person make it happen? What is the purpose of the action?

Kenneth Burke also developed three other terms that, taken together, make up dramatic rhythm. He called them *poiema, pathema,* and *mathema*—purpose, passion, and perception. At the beginning of a play someone purposefully sets out to accomplish something. The person then goes through a series of experiences because of that intention. At the end, when the person accomplishes or fails to accomplish the established purpose, perception of the entire action occurs. In such a way, the dramatic rhythm of a play becomes clear.

Another way to approach art is to ask biographical questions about the nature of the artist's epoch, country, race, family, education, environment, friends, successes, failures, strengths, weaknesses, and peculiarities of body and mind? Such questions provide hints about why and how an artist made a particular work. Biographical materials, of course, provide more insight into the man than into his work.

Johann Wolfgang von Goethe, a German dramatist and poet, established another important set of questions that provide a basis for analysis. They are simple but most telling. Goethe suggested that to understand any work of art one should ask: What is the artist trying to do? How well did he do it? To what degree was it worth doing?

CRITERIA AND QUESTIONS

Perhaps all the methods stated above may seem overly complex when one sits down to enjoy a dramatic performance, and certainly enjoyment should precede and accompany all analysis. Nevertheless, anyone's pleasure increases with knowledge. Good questions help one to know what to look for in a drama. The commonsense approach to analysis is fine if one has some knowledge. Anyone, even a child, can experience a performed drama at a sensory level merely by watching and listening, but sorting out one's experiences and their significance requires mental perception. This section provides some further criteria for consideration and some stimulating questions.

Drama ought to be an intense life experience. The experience of drama is threefold. First, the characters experience the action of the play. Second, the actors experience the performance of the action. Third, audience members experience the enactment both with their outer senses and with their inner selves.

Drama should trigger both feeling and thought. At best, art impels audiences into states of emotion that arouse intuitions. For example an audience member can watch a well-performed drama and feel sympathy

**During *5th of July*
rehearsals, director
Marshall Mason (left)
talks with actors
Swoosie Kurtz and
Christopher Reeve and
with playwright
Lanford Wilson (right).**

for the characters who are experiencing emotions, and yet the observer
can retain a thoughtful perspective. The theatre offers an opportunity to
observe people having emotional experiences for the sake of others. It
urges an audience to empathize positively or negatively with characters
and to learn something in the process. In human responses to art, emotions function cognitively. People can realize some thoughts only because
of the stimulus of art. Theatre promotes sympathetic feelings along with
conscious consideration of the causes and the results of those feelings.
It permits audiences a chance to observe life minutely from a wise
perspective. An action happens, but not to them. They can experience it,
but they do not have to survive it.

When a performed drama fails to trigger any emotions at all in an
audience, the resultant absence of feeling makes bad theatre. Feelings
about dramas are similar to but consciously different from the same
feelings in life. In art, feeling is always controlled for the sake of knowledge and pleasure; in life, feeling is not usually controllable at all.
Without feeling, any art object is cold and empty; without feeling, theatre
is a blank. Feeling, intuition, and imagination are the special ways art
makes knowing possible.

Originality is in this century a major criterion for the judgment of art—
of drama. Every artist needs to be original, and audiences want to know
how a work demonstrates it. But the concept of originality can be applied

variously. A play can be innovative or revolutionary. A performance, too, can be original as when an inventive group of actors genuinely live through the ordeals in the action of a new play or when an old play is brought to life in a new way. In some respect the dramatic event should be new in material, form, style, or function.

The audience's desire for originality means they do not want fakes, forgeries, or copies. They want art that escapes the norm, avoids the commonplace, and shuns the conventional. But judging originality demands knowledge and requires experience with the art form. A performance that appears strikingly original to a 16-year-old may seem derivative to an experienced theatregoer. When anyone's standards become absolutely frozen, then that person can no longer admit genuine originality. In *The Act of Creation*, Arthur Koestler wrote that an artist is original when he escapes the ordinary and sets up a new sort of relevance. Original artists compel society to revalue its values. The best theatre artists impose new rules on the old game of drama.

Although people value the new in art, they also value the old. Part of the fascination of drama is to see how new actors, directors, and writers do the old things. People go to see Shakespeare's plays over and over in different productions. His plays are old, but like fine antiques they grow to be more esteemed each year. Not every novelty in art, however, is genuinely original, nor does every old play remain valuable. The enduring things in art are objects or principles that continue to function meaningfully for succeeding generations of living human beings. The old is often the out of date, but sometimes it becomes the classic. Although the former may lack contemporary value, the latter is a universal treasure.

The classic Greek virtues of *the good, the true*, and *the beautiful* can also become useful criteria for considering achievements in drama. Good art lives up to its potential and performs well what it is meant to do. Although any given piece may be positive or negative, good art celebrates the humanity of man. It helps preserve those patterns of behavior that humanity has learned are social necessities. Drama always stands as a behavioral model. Whatever suggestions theatre artists may intend, most people in audiences judge automatically that each character behaves

Joy Reilly as Jenny in *The Threepenny Opera* by Bertolt Brecht, Ohio State University

admirably or despicably. People learn behavior from good and bad models. Drama presents both, and it usually distinguishes between them. People need to consider what is good and what is bad in their society. Theatre identifies both.

The true in art can mean many things. Simply stated, every artist should tell the truth about the world as he knows it. If an artist sacrifices truth for the sake of something else, it shows—the work is hollow. Artists need to be honest about what they perceive, and they must invest their work with credibility so audiences, too, can believe it. In the world of art the fakes and phonies don't ordinarily last long. If authors write about something they do not know, audiences can tell they are faking. If actors don't understand the characters they are playing, audiences can sense something wrong. Truth in drama may mean verisimilitude, or lifelikeness. It may mean honesty in the artist. A play also may have aesthetic truth by achieving its potentials. Drama may present aesthetic truth by achieving its potentials. Drama may present factual truth about persons, places, or events. All these sorts of truth are major concerns of theatre artists.

**A scene from
The Insect Comedy
by Karel Capek,
production design
by Josef Svoboda**

As for beauty, everyone needs to develop attitudes that help identify what is beautiful or ugly in life and in art. Beauty does not necessarily mean pleasantness, sweetness, or joy—though it can include those qualities. Rather, beauty is a quality possible in nature or in a work of art. In a drama beauty means that anyone seeing it can sense its unity, its completeness, the appropriateness of all its parts, and the proper magnitude of the whole. A beautiful drama has in every part an essential rightness, and its structure is refined to fit its function. A tragedy ought to be a beautiful tragedy and be different from a beautiful comedy or a beautiful melodrama. Just as no one expects a beautiful girl to look like a beautiful horse, so no one should expect a beautiful musical to resemble a beautiful absurdist play. Any art object may possess beauty if all its materials work together in a harmonious pattern, expressed in an interesting but appropriate style, and fulfill the function for which the work as a whole was intended. Usually anyone can quickly see whether or not a painting has beauty. In the theatre the spectator must wait until the play ends. Only then can one know for certain. Because a staged drama bombards the spectator with so many visual and auditory details, the beauty of drama is harder to judge. Still, everyone must decide personally about the degree of beauty in any drama.

The best art is valuable. The best drama is worth something to people. But what? Value can be gauged in many different spheres. Seeing a play may provide a memorable experience; or it may give a person an insight to use in everyday life; or it may for a while lift a viewer out of a mundane mental state. Often characters in plays provide examples of behavior to adopt or to avoid. But more important, drama teaches awareness. From Shakespeare's *Othello*, for example, an audience can learn more about keeping one's eyes open than about the evil in one's friends. A great work of art is in so many ways a human treasure.

Images are another sort of treasure in drama. Images are among the best values of drama because a person can carry them away mentally

57

and remember them permanently. Furthermore, the sharing of the dramatic experience may be immensely valuable. Not often in life can people share with family and friends such intense experiences, whether comic or tragic, with the same pleasure as in the theatre. A drama's value varies with the performance's power and according to the mental state of the individual spectator. For many people the experience of great theatre is one of life's treasures because it can be shared joyfully and remembered fondly.

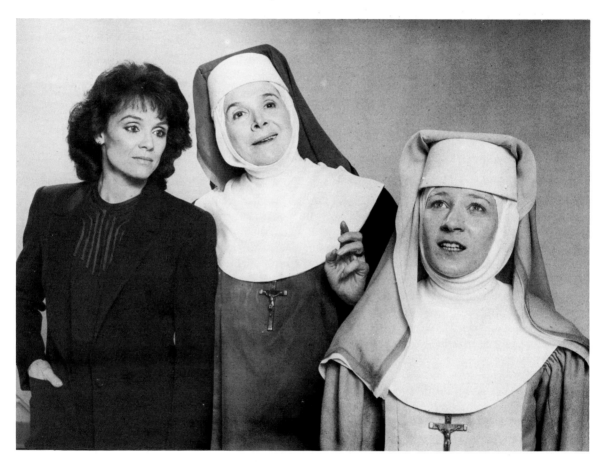

Agnes of God **by John Pielmeier**

What about success? Does the earning power or popularity of a play say anything about its value or its level of accomplishment? Yes and no! Success to an artist is making an art object that fulfills his intention. Successful plays can sometimes be performed unsuccessfully or vice versa. Success with audiences is something else again, because audiences differ. Too often in American society, success is measured monetarily. For many people, a successful play is one that runs a long time, makes a fair return on the investment, provides a profit for the investors involved, or makes some performer rich. But financial success occasionally comes to plays that are not good artistically, and it often fails to come to plays that are masterpieces. Also, Americans sometimes gauge success according to fame. Some people think that if a play becomes well known, then it must be good. Fame in contemporary society has more to do with publicity campaigns and journalistic values than with artistic quality. Success remains a relative criterion for evaluating art. To measure the success of a drama, a viewer should gauge its accomplishments in the various spheres of interest.

A concluding criterion for judging the worth of dramatic productions, or other art objects, is self-expansion. Does the experience of witnessing a performed drama affect the inner self of a viewer? Every human being consists of given physical elements, inherited characteristics, and acquired traits. Every person develops a persona by means of life experiences. The developmental process within a human being continues throughout a lifetime. The experiences a person has when contacting great or even good art positively expands the self. Drama can provide knowledge about people, places, and life situations. It can stimulate imagination, sensitivity, and intuition. In some people it even provokes self-understanding, awareness, and wisdom. Dramatic art is one of mankind's most highly developed ways to achieve self-expansion.

This chapter ends with a collection of questions for analyzing drama. Each item can be brought to bear on the analysis of a play or on the performance of it. The questions are grouped under the four causal headings of material, form, style, and purpose. The list is not exhaustive, but it should help anyone see into a drama.

Materials

1. What sort of details about human experience make up the play?

2. What is the play's central concern—the problem the characters deal with?

3. What is the subject? What information does the play give?

4. What situations exist in the play? What incidents occur?

5. Who are the people in the play? Where are they, and why do they stay there?

6. What basic thoughts occupy the mind of each major character?

7. What central thought does the play as a whole project?

8. What sort of language carries the drama?

Form

1. What is the play's action? What is going on?

2. How is the action unified—by story, thought, or image?

3. What is the form, the structure, or the organization?

4. Is the play a tragedy, a comedy, a melodrama, or a mixed type?

5. How does it arouse and fulfill expectations?

6. What sort of world does it create?

7. What is the basic situation, and how does it change?

8. What's the magnitude of the play and of the performance? Does the length seem to match the material?

9. What forces are in conflict in the play? Who wins? Why?

10. What is the play's story? Or why does it not have one? If it has multiple story lines, how do they intertwine?

11. Is the play always predictable? Or does it offer surprises? If it does, what is the nature of the best ones?

12. What are the play's climaxes? Are they accidents, discoveries, or decisions?

Style

1. What is the style of the play? How do the language and character behavior differ from everyday life?

2. Does the style of the performance match that of the play?

3. Is the style consistent throughout?

4. To what degree are the characters and their actions lifelike?

5. How poetic or prosaic is the play's diction?

6. Does the language sound right in the characters' mouths? Do the actors handle the words credibly?

7. Does the play happen in a place that stimulates the action?

8. Do the elements of scenery, lighting, costumes, properties, and makeup support the characters and the actions? Or do they call undue attention to themselves?

9. What word or phrase best identifies the overall style?

Purpose

1. What is the purpose of the whole drama?

2. What sort of experience does it provide?

3. What were the artists trying to do? How well did they do it? To what degree was it worth doing?

4. What sort of play is it supposed to be, and how is it supposed to affect the audience? Did it?

5. Did the audience remain attentive and responsive throughout?

6. What was the audience reaction at the end of the play?

7. What feelings did it arouse? How intense were they? How long did they remain?

8. What insight into life does the play provide?

9. As an entity, is the play good? How does it function in today's society? What behavior does it suggest?

10. Is the play true? How so?

11. Is it beautiful? How can its beauty be described?

12. To what degree is it original? What is traditional or innovative about it?

13. Is the play successful in the spheres of attendance, finances, audience response, and skill of performance?

14. Is the play clear?

15. Is it fun? In what way?

16. Is the drama itself a good experience to share?

17. How is the entire work self-expansive for the viewer?

Amadeus by Peter
Shaffer

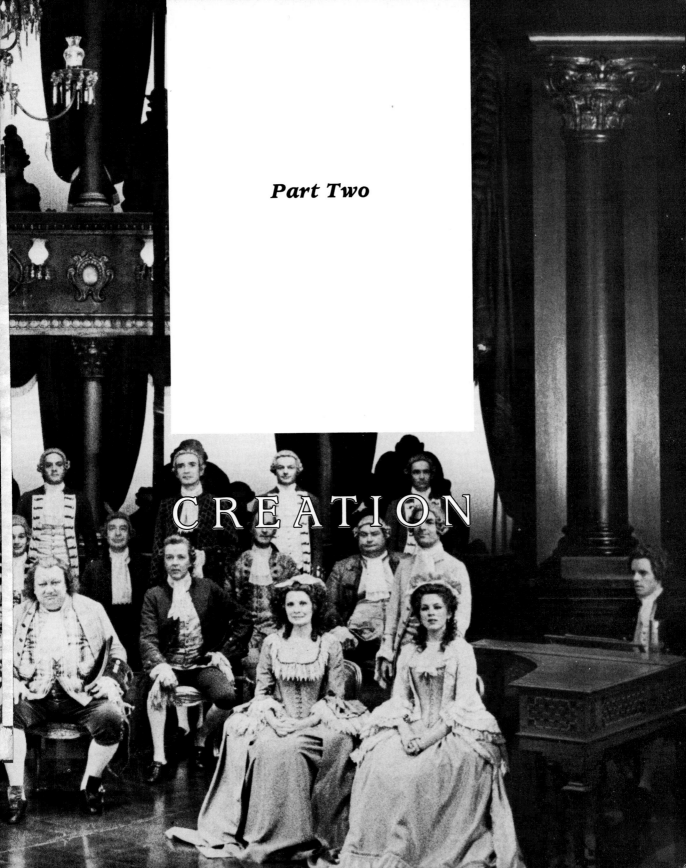

Part Two

CREATION

5 *Of Plays and Playwrights*

A playwright is a seer, a storyteller with special vision. Playwrights see into human existence and turn it into stories that actors will truly experience before live audiences. To dramatize life in this manner, a writer must develop skills in both literature and theatre, and must combine craftsmanship with artistry. Somehow a playwright has to develop the uncanny ability to see into the existence of people and spot the special moments, the significant turning points in human lives. By showing human changes and how people feel about them in story form, a playwright reveals the inner quality in human existence.

This chapter explains how playwrights try to give order to the chaos of life. It also describes a playwright's typical working process and sets forth some of the most functional creative principles writers employ. Finally, it defines the actual elements of a play. Every detail of this discussion emphasizes the living process of the dramatist.

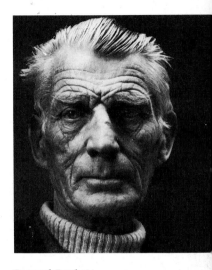

Samuel Beckett

THE PROCESS OF PLAYWRITING

To create plays worthy of production, a playwright perfects a vision, a way of seeing life. Writers thus combine a personal point of view about daily existence with a long-term philosophy of life. The process of developing a vision happens to some degree naturally, but anyone can modify it through education, conscious choice, and selected experiences. Some people call a writer's vision a perspective on life, and others call it a mental set. Leo Tolstoy, a nineteenth-century Russian playwright and novelist, wrote that a writer's particular vision makes the writer see and choose one character from a crowd, one event among many, or one thought rather than others. Each writer develops powers of judgment that govern this process of selection. Many observers of the drama argue that the strength of a writer's vision depends on the life-affirming attitudes that it displays.

Because each playwright views things differently, audiences are delighted. People go to the theatre not to see the same old world through ordinary eyes but to discover something special from a fresh point of view. Everyone wants to witness unusual events, to experience life in new ways. Audiences expect playwrights and their fellow artists to offer something different, original, or extreme. Therefore, artists need to foster their own special ways of responding to life, to develop personal techniques for creating. Every playwright needs to be bold enough to become truly audacious, because audacity is as necessary to originality as skill is to beauty.

Since each writer views the world from an individual stance and works in an individual way, generalizations about playwriting methods are never perfect. But most writers follow similar procedures in play composition. Certainly everyone who writes plays works through at least some of the following stages.

The process of playwriting begins before the work starts. Experienced writers call it a rising *creative compulsion*. Some sort of initiating spark, usually a feeling rather than an intellectual idea, occurs inside the artist. The writer realizes a readiness, a necessity for expression. The artist endures the routine of daily life and senses a growing urge to get busy, to work, and to respond to the universe. An inner compulsion to create, then, is the subjective drive that motivates a beginning.

With a feeling of inner readiness, the playwright suddenly finds a *germinal idea* and begins work. Sometimes the germinal idea comes easily, and sometimes it comes from a careful examination of the world. The writer sifts personal experience and the experiences of friends for the special moments, the unique experiences that can make a potential drama. Often a writer keeps a notebook with many ideas written in it; all writers keep such a notebook in their minds. Sometimes a new perception activates an old idea. Arthur Miller writes that his original idea for *Death of a Salesman* came from thinking about "the inside of a man's head." With a certain character in mind for a number of years, Miller suddenly realized that if he examined the inside of the man's head

Anton Chekhov reads a play to the Moscow Art Theatre company

carefully enough he would discover why a man would commit suicide. The germinal idea for *Blood Wedding* by Federico García Lorca was a newspaper account of the murder of a bridegroom soon after his wedding. Whatever the source, a germinal idea is some imaginative notion that provides the basis for a play.

Most writers claim that not just any idea will do for a play. A good germinal idea ought to have certain qualities. It should strongly command the interest of the writer. After all, the writer must be willing to

Left: Eugene Ionesco

Right: Jean-Paul Sartre

live with it for months or years while nurturing it into a play. Also an idea needs to contain the potentials for a special life excitement—for action. It must be an imaginative trigger for the writer's mind as he devises a pattern of human activity. A good idea ought to have a special intensity about it, the quality of making life feel more vivid. Furthermore, the idea ought to be different, strange, and original. Most important of all, a good germinal idea somehow has to penetrate human existence. It serves as a thoughtful stepping-stone into an unknown realm. With it a writer starts an imaginative quest for new meaning in life.

After selecting a germinal idea, the writer begins to make a *collection* of pertinent ideas, good characters, and significant information—a process that continues for weeks or months until the play is finished. Few, if any, plays are made up all at once merely in the author's imagination. All writers jot down ideas, and most plays demand at least some research. Before beginning the dialogue of a play, playwrights sit day after day thinking of ideas and images to add to their work. They may interview people who are similar to the characters. Occasionally, they may need to visit certain locales to see and absorb the atmosphere of a particular place. Feelings also add to their store of information about the people and the situation of the play. But the most important part of the collection process for any play is the careful consideration of all the possible events that could go into it. Only after thinking of all the possibilities for the

Left: Maxwell Anderson

Right: Arthur Miller

action can the author settle down to the difficult business of selecting specific scenes.

At some time in the process of composition most playwrights make a *rough scenario*, a plan for the action of the play. The writer tries to pound all the materials into some order, usually into some sort of story sequence. When assembling the materials for a play, writers struggle with ideas and characters, but when composing a scenario they wrestle with form. A rough scenario for a play may contain many different elements, such as a list of characters and a description of the setting. Most important, however, the writer needs to identify an action and to develop a story line. An action is the process of change that occurs throughout the play, and the story is the event-by-event process that leads to a major climax. Probably the most difficult and the most special aspect of writing plays is the development of an action.

The *final scenario* is a fuller treatment of the play, usually a detailed outline that guides the writing of dialogue. Most playwrights consider a scenario crucial to composition. It holds both the materials and the keys to their formation. Scenarios vary from writer to writer, but most are amazingly similar, consisting of a title, the given circumstances of time and place, a list of characters, a prose narrative of the story of the play scene by scene, and a working outline of many dialogue units. Scenarios are careful, concrete plans, sometimes a kind of short-story version of the play. To compose a scenario is arduous work; it shows the writer's discipline. Writers who try to get by without a scenario normally end up with a weak first draft and have to spend far more time in revision than if they start with a good plan. Since action is the chief ingredient of every play, a careful scenario concentrates on the action and usually saves months of revisions. Nearly any first draft of a play written without a scenario turns out to be merely a scenario in dialogue form. Dramatic composition demands intensive planning of a scenario.

For playwrights the thinking time is usually longer than the drafting time. All the early stages in the creation of a play—creative compulsion, germinal idea, collection, rough scenario, final scenario—normally demand more time of the writer than drafting the dialogue does. Ideas are hard to come by, and scenarios are difficult to write. Each of the predrafting steps often needs more than one version, and most require a period of time for gestation. During this part of the playwright's working period, he experiences false starts, changes, and surprising developments. The predrafting stage requires patience, discipline, and imagination as the chief companions to the writer's creativity. Finding and putting together all the many bits of material before the characters begin talking is the normal process of constructing a play.

Eugene O'Neill

Eventually the day arrives when the writer begins the *first draft*. Drafting means putting on paper the dialogue of the characters and the necessary accompanying stage directions. To draft a play is to pull the words, sentences, and speeches that the people say out of the mind of the playwright. The process is sometimes painful, sometimes fun, but nearly always it gives writers a sense of accomplishment as they work. The play begins to grow, take shape, and become real. The preliminary work pays off. If the writer has explored the subject, developed the characters, and established a strong line of action, then the dialogue usually flows freely. Somehow the characters seem to take over the writing and in a strange way write the play themselves. But even when the words come easily and well, a writer works meticulously. Most beginners try to do their drafting in a hurry; experienced writers know better and take their time. Getting the words as right as possible in the first draft is crucial to the development of the play as a whole.

After drafting a play, the dramatist faces an inevitable period of revisions. Even though every writer tries to get the first draft down as perfectly as possible, most plays require extensive rewriting. The period of revisions includes the testing and rewriting of everything that needs it—sentences, speeches, beats, scenes, and acts. A wonderful expression that playwrights use to explain what happens during the revision period is "to puzzle." A writer puzzles over every sentence, every speech, and every bit of action to get them just right. Revisions require a writer to sort through the work again and again. Most plays go through at least three full drafts before the writer is ready to show them to anyone else.

When the play reaches an acceptable condition, the writer is likely to show it to friends, to a mentor, or to a critic. Most playwrights get a group of actors together to read through the piece. All playwrights want and need feedback. Subsequently, even more revision normally occurs. The words of the play are worked through over and over, until they are as perfect for the writer's vision as can be managed. Only then will the writer have a "final" draft. The writer comes to believe that the play has been polished into as fine a condition as possible. But even this draft is final only in a temporary sense; it amounts to the version which the playwright can use for submissions. No play is totally finished until it goes on stage, alive. Theatre people other than the writer must give it that life.

After a play is written, it must go through a public process. The writer, who's been laboring as an artist, suddenly becomes a business person with a product to peddle. Sometimes with the help of an agent, the writer struggles to get the play into the hands of producers, directors, or actors who might put it on stage. Most writers have to endure the process of submissions, readings, rejections, and more submissions. Some authors are fortunately associated with a particular theatre—as is Lanford Wilson with the Circle Repertory Company in New York—and thus obtain production contracts more easily. But with luck every good play finds some producer or director who eventually accepts it with the intention of giving it a production.

For plays, production is crucial. Every play must be realized live on a stage before it actually exists as the sort of art object it's meant to be. A play is not really a play until acted before an audience. Even then it exists fully only during the time that actors give it life. The final stage of a play's development is thus a theatre company's creation of it. Succeeding chapters contain discussions of what actors, directors, and designers do for a play. But while they do their work, the writer often remains involved, especially in the first production. The writer cuts, rewrites, and polishes, maybe even writes whole new scenes. Finally, when opening night arrives and it all comes alive on stage, the play truly comes into being.

ELEMENTS OF DRAMA

The previous section identified the steps a dramatist may follow in writing a play. But what really goes on inside playwrights' heads? What

Tennessee Williams

do they do? Well, they construct plays. They build strange verbal objects out of the ideas, images, and wisdom of their minds. In fact, playwrights' minds tend to dwell on certain concepts as they work: situations, moments, structure, and action.

Both situations and events are important in a play. A situation in a drama, as in life, consists of certain circumstances and a set of relationships. When people get involved with one another, situations develop. A play is not, however, merely a situation. It is a pattern of situations broken open by events, or crucial moments. A playwright constructs a play by finding significant moments in human lives. Significant moments for drama are traditionally grouped under three headings: suffering, discovery, and reversal. Suffering refers to moments of deep feeling in a character; discovery is an internal change within a character, a passage from ignorance to knowledge; and reversal is any major change in a character's condition. In *A Streetcar Named Desire* by Tennessee Williams, Blanche tries to adjust to life in the household of her sister, Stella, and her brother-in-law, Stanley. She suffers emotionally; Stanley discovers her decadent past; and in a reversal of her expectations, he destroys her. At best, a play presents certain crucial moments in someone's life when that person's existence is defined.

Bertolt Brecht

Action, however, is the key principle of playwriting. While working on a play, a playwright's mind dwells on people in tense situations and on their crucial moments of experience as they try to survive. As the writer puts more and more such peak moments together, a structure begins to emerge, a pattern of progression that audiences can follow—a plot. Now the essence of a playwright's work is coming to light. Countless dramatists through the ages have used a special principle to make their plays coherent. They use this principle to lock characters, situations, moments, and structures together in comprehensible and interesting forms. The key ingredient that holds them all together is *action*. The hardest part of the playwright's real work is to recognize the potentials for genuine action in the play and to bring them out. Only action makes good drama.

Aristotle first identified the six key elements of drama that every playwright must handle. No one has offered a more useful description of the components of a play. But Aristotle's book, *Poetics*, is difficult to read, and the following discussion not only puts his concepts into modern words but also supplements his discussion with certain more contemporary ideas. The key elements are plot, character, thought, diction, melody, and spectacle. Aristotle's six elements have led writers ever since to concentrate on materials and organization, matter and form, and detail and structure. His approach to the principles of writing plays is called a form-matter approach.

Plot, the formative element in a drama, is organization. As the arrangement of all the other materials of a play, plot amounts to the architecture of the piece. A plot provides a play with unity, coherence, and wholeness. The most important aspect of plot is action, that pattern of human change that matters most to an audience. Some people call it the through-line of action, or the spine of a drama. To plot a play is to set up such a pattern, or sequence, of action. Most people, even those not expert in playwriting, sense intuitively what a play's action is. Action is "what's going on." A writer must plot the action and thus control the sequence of what happens. Unity, coherence, and wholeness are significant qualities of a plot. Action, form, and structure comprise the most important aspects of plot that a writer consciously thinks about.

What about story? Story offers one special way to make a plot. In fact most dramas have stories, but not all of them do. Every play has a plot, an organization, but not every play has a story. The following are the main principles that writers use to make stories:

CREATION

Sam Sherpard

Balance: At the opening of a play the forces or people are in a state of tensional equilibrium. To the degree that the opening situation is relatively static, it is balanced.

Disturbance: Something upsets the equilibrium in the world of the play and starts the action.

Protagonist: One character at the play's center actively tries to restore balance; it's the one who exercises the most willpower in causing events.

Stake: Throughout the play the protagonist (and often the antagonist) strives to obtain or preserve an important object, person, or idea.

Plan: The intentions of the protagonist amount to his or her plan when setting out to attain the stake. The plan comprises the intentionality of a play, and in any story, plans and intentions cause suspense.

Lines of action: The behavior of the protagonist and allies as they try to fulfill the protagonist's intentions constitute the line of action. The lines of action also involve opponents, chiefly the antagonist who tries equally hard to prevent the protagonist from achieving his or her objectives.

Obstacles: Anything that impedes the protagonist's line of action is an obstacle. Obstacles cause conflict. They are of four basic types—material things, people, inner traits, and chance.

Crisis: The most important story element of all, a crisis occupies a period of time during which two or more forces conflict and the outcome is uncertain. Without a series of crises, no story can happen.

Climax: A climax occurs the moment a crisis comes to a close when one of two contending people or forces wins.

Complications: A surprise, or any unexpected element—a person, a bit of information, or an accident—that changes the protagonist's line of action is a complication. When complications enter a story, they often become obstacles. Surprising complications create high narrative interest in stories.

Substory: Some plays contain secondary stories that focus on a minor protagonist and a limited line of action.

Resolution: At the end of a well-wrought play a final situation involving a new set of static relationships comes into being. Resolution at the end often amounts to a situation similar to the balanced one at the beginning.

Character is the second significant element of drama. Stories are about people. What the characters of a play think, say, and do make up that play's action. Plot stands as the first element in the dramatic hierarchy only because it is the formative element, but writers often concentrate even harder on perfecting characters. Because of a character's basic physical attributes and essential attitudes, each character has certain potentials. But the job of writers goes beyond understanding the people of their plays. They must devise patterns of action that call for overt behavior. For a character to be convincing, the audience must witness the character's behavior, not just hear about it. Macbeth may have the potential for murder when the three witches first speak to him, but he is not a murderer until he performs the deed. Well-written characters have six types of traits: biological, physical, dispositional, motivational, deliberative, and decisive. A character's inner nature shows especially in making choices, particularly ethical or moral ones. Character literally appears in the act of decision, and traits of a character come into being only through action.

The third basic element that a writer handles in writing a play is *thought.* In plays, thought can be considered in three loci, or places. Intentional thought about a play occurs in the mind of the playwright. Material thought exists within the play itself. Also, a play may stimulate meaningful thought in spectators. The three sorts of thought can be the same, but often they are not.

Understanding how thought operates *inside* a play requires attention

C R E A T I O N

Dario Fo

Left: David Mamet

Right: David Rabe

to the sensations, emotions, and logic of the characters. A playwright builds characters with thoughts; they are the materials of characterization. Material thought is anything that goes on inside a character, especially sensory experiences, emotional feelings, and logical reasoning. Although sentience, feeling, and logic are three important types of thought for building a character, writers utilize others as well—for example, memory, imagination, opinions, and dreams.

What about the philosophy of a play? Do playwrights speak to others by communicating their ideas through plays? Of course, they do. Every play can be taken as a meaningful speech. As a whole, each drama *says* something. Even plays written "neutrally" by their authors still make some sort of statement to the world. To understand a play's overall statement about life is to understand its signification, which means that through a play an audience member can come to understand an author's vision of human existence. One of the most effective ways to figure out the meaning of any play is to consider these questions: What are the forces in conflict in the play? Who wins or loses? Why? Once these questions are answered, an author's vision within a play becomes clear.

Diction is the fourth major element that dramatists employ when writing a play. Simply defined, diction refers to the play's words. Of course, everyone understands that to write a play means to put words on paper, to write dialogue. In this sense every playwright is a poet, a person who makes an object with words. Words are the chief materials that writers utilize in performing their creative work. At best the words of a play, like the words of a poem, express what a character is feeling and thinking. The most important overall function of words is to express the unknown in terms of the known. Since what is most difficult in this world is to know how someone else feels, thus the expression of feelings, sensations, and ideas amounts to the chief function of words in drama.

Many devices of the lyric poet are useful to a playwright. Most creative writers employ such devices as metaphor, simile, and personification. Metaphor is an imaginative figure of speech that every writer uses. A metaphor compares two things, showing how they are alike in only one respect. It tends to explain an unknown quality or feeling by comparing it with something concrete and known. For example, the American poet Ezra Pound was riding the Paris subway one day, and at one of the stops he noticed a beautiful face, then another, a beautiful child's face, and another. For hours he pondered how to express in an imaginative image what he had seen. Finally, he thought of an image and wrote a couplet employing it, comparing the face to petals on a black, wet bough.

Another aspect of diction is that playwrights usually compose plays in beats. A beat of dialogue corresponds to a paragraph of prose. It is a small unit of conversation that the writer controls. Often a beat amounts to a period of time when the characters discuss one subject before moving on to another, or it may be the time in conversation when one character drives the action until another interrupts and takes over. Some beats advance the story; others are devoted to character, mood, or thought. Each beat has its own structure, but most beats contain a stimulus, rise, climax, and close. The plays of Harold Pinter offer unusu-

Left: Lanford Wilson

Right: Beth Henley

ally clear examples of beat structure. Indeed, he calls attention to many of the beats in his plays by noting the places to pause. In all plays the principal device for rhythm in dialogue is beats.

The fifth major element playwrights employ in the composition of a play is *melody*. The concept of melody refers to the built-in sounds of the language of a play, the music of its words. As writers put down syllables, words, phrases, sentences, and speeches, they carefully control the sounds that the human voices of the actors will produce. They also utilize such techniques of sound association as repetition, assonance, consonance, and rhyme. Writers indicate sounds with words and make silences with punctuation marks. Punctuation in a play indicates the timing of a performance. But do what they may, authors can control the melodics of a performance only partially; the actors are in the position of rendering the sounds alive. The musicality of voice an actor employs when saying a line can indicate the meaning of the line. Melody in a play is a complicated matter, but one that writers attempt to control.

The final of the six Aristotelian elements is *spectacle*. A dramatist controls the essential visual ingredients of a play as much as the melodic or thoughtful ones. Spectacle refers to everything about a play that must occur visually. A playwright conceives the essentials of the spectacle, and then the production team—director, designers, technicians, and actors— furnishes the reality. The playwright usually conceives the place where the action happens and indicates the nature of the light, costumes, and properties required for the appropriate physical atmosphere and for the action that will occur in it.

Spectacle, however, means more than just the physical environment that the scenery and lights represent. The actors furnish the essential spectacle as they live through the characters' experiences. Actors physically enliven a play with their bodies, and an audience watches each physical nuance, every visual detail. All those physical details taken together—for instance, hand gestures, eye movements, nods of the head, walking, or tears—communicate the emotions of the play. Of course, the major pieces of stage business, such as stabbings, shootings, or love scenes, are crucial to maintaining the interest of an audience. No play can be duller than a great Shakespearean tragedy delivered by fine, experienced actors who merely stand around reciting the lines. Shakespeare was a master of stage spectacle, and his plays are more interesting when the actors are physically lively. All playwrights try to accomplish with the visual aspects of their plays that which is necessary and compelling.

The six basic elements, then, that every writer manipulates in writing a play are plot, character, thought, diction, melody, and spectacle. The application of each is potentially infinite in its variety. Each element stands for a group of principles that can help a writer in the process of creating a play. But none of these elements suggests rules for composi-

Left: Tina Howe

Right: Marsha Norman

**Playwright Clifford
Odets (right) rehearses
with Ethel Barrymore
and Cary Grant**

tion. There are none. Rules tend to limit creativity; principles liberate the imagination. The more knowledge playwrights have about the principles represented by these six elements, the more likely they will be able to employ their full talent as they write.

PRINCIPLES FOR CREATING

Writing plays demands more, however, from the writer than merely sitting in a room stringing words together. Poets and novelists create alone, maybe getting some useful suggestions from an editor, then revising, and finally publishing their words. Poems and novels do not go through the same socially creative process as plays. Typically, a playwright first sets a play down on paper as a solitary creative act, but before the play is finished it goes through a crucible of creative development.

The process of co-creativity, so central to the artistry of the theatre, is as significant to the playwright as to other theatre artists. The plays of most playwrights go through a developmental period that helps the authors perfect their dramatic powers. There is a significant difference between the manuscript version of most plays and the final version after a play has reached the stage in production. What happens is a testing and a refining process. Once a director, designers, and actors go to work on the play, many creative minds examine, test, and perfect every functional detail. Often the director and other participants will find a weakness in the play, perhaps a beat that could be eliminated or maybe an entire scene that needs revision. The skillful playwright sorts through the suggestions that the members of a production team make and then modifies the play. Sometimes, of course, a play suffers during a rehearsal period, but usually the play benefits.

For a playwright, a play's first director enacts several functions. The director responds to the writer about the script in three stages. First comes the prerehearsal period, when the director analyzes the play in detail. Then the director and the playwright normally work through the play slowly, identifying its strengths and weaknesses, exploring improvements the writer might make for the coming production. At the same time, the director utilizes the playwright's ideas to shape a production concept—a system of ideas necessary to develop the appropriate scenery, costumes, properties, lights, sound, and acting style for the production. Often the director is able to spot any serious weaknesses in the script, and if the playwright is wise, he or she makes revisions to overcome them. The designers are also studying the script during this preproduction period. Their imaginations focus on its visual rendering. They, too, sometimes contribute suggestions that, if the writer listens, may help the play.

The second phase of production is the rehearsal period. During this time the director starts bringing the play to life. While the director and the actors struggle daily with the particular moments of the play, the director is again likely to find details about the play that need the writer's attention. Sometime during most rehearsal periods most plays need cutting. Writers tend to include too much dialogue, too many words. An intelligent director can often cut a play more skillfully than the writer. This second stage of a director's work on the script also includes performances. While the writer normally attends some performances and becomes aware of audience responses to the production, both good and bad, a director usually takes an even more objective view of the strengths and weaknesses of the play. Especially in professional theatre, a director suggests script revisions to be made even after the play opens and plays to the public.

The third stage of work in which the director may join is the revision period that follows the first production. Most dramatists study their play in its first production and polish it even further. Again the director's notes and suggestions are useful to the writer. Certainly some directors working with new plays fail to understand them, misinterpret them, or request revisions harmful to the play. But for the most part directors are highly aware of theatrical values, and they usually offer sound advice on the pruning and polishing every play needs in its first periods of planning, rehearsal, and performance.

The time necessary to write, market, and develop a play is long indeed. Most full-length plays require from a few weeks to several months of steady writing. Then months or years are required for the marketing process. The production period itself may also be lengthy. The director and designers work on the play for several months. A cast rehearses from three to eight weeks. Then the performance of the play extends from an opening for a run of a few days in amateur theatre to months or years in the professional theatre. After the first production, provided the play is a good one, additional productions often occur. Eventually, most good plays are published. When the opportunity for the publication of a play presents itself, the writer is again tempted to review the play and polish it. After this long, arduous working period, some plays are finally published. Only with publication does a play become set with any permanence. Only then can it be said that the play has gone through the crucible of the theatre's developmental process.

Strangely, as with most works of art like paintings or pieces of sculpture, a play enjoys a life of its own. Once the author finishes it and hands it to others, at whatever stage of the process, these others take it and make it theirs. The actors think the play belongs to them. Whether or not the playwright attends rehearsals, the play comes to life through the actors. Only through them does it touch live audiences. Centuries after their composition, Shakespeare's plays continue their wondrous lives. Many other plays also have an ongoing existence. Some directors may cut a bit, add a line here and there, change a name or a reference, and thus alter a play. Furthermore, every subsequent company uses new concepts, sets, and business. Nevertheless, with all good plays the essential soul, the spirit of the play, persists and continues to work a lovely magic on audiences.

Wendy Wasserstein

EVALUATING THE WRITER

Every paragraph in this chapter can furnish ideas for judging a play. But the most important criteria are *action, perception, reality,* and *emotion.* Does the play have an action? Is something going on that an observer can notice and care about? Action is a pattern of human activity involving change. A good action is apparent soon after the start of the play, and it persists clearly until the end. If an audience ever wonders what is going on, or if its interest lags, then probably the action is weak. Also the best actions in plays have unity and completeness. When everything fails to hold together, or when the ending hangs inconclusively, then the action

Anton Chekhov and Leo Tolstoy

is poor. To find the action of a play ask: What is going on? How did it start? How does it end? How are the people or their circumstances different at the end than at the beginning? Action is the heart of a play.

What significant perceptions does the drama reveal? What image of the world does the play present? What types of people appear, and what is the nature of their inner experiences? A playwright's attitudes about the characters are revealed as they are permitted to state their convictions about life. The author's perceptions about the world are evident in how everything turns out. Every play articulates a morality. Every comedy, tragedy, or melodrama states in essence how the world was, how the world is, or how the world will be. More significantly, every play implies how the world ought to be. Of course, each drama makes its message clear in a different way, but always the basic moral vision of the author is the soul of the work.

Does the play establish a reality? What is the nature of the world that the play depicts? To what degree is the reality consistent and credible? Audiences permit authors to establish their reality in any imaginative world they wish, as long as they follow through in a consistent manner. Whatever degree of stylization or distancing from everyday life the play may entail, an audience will probably accept—provided that the world of the play in some way illustrates, reflects, or reveals the world as human beings actually live it. Audiences like temporarily to believe in the worlds of *Peter Pan* and *The Wizard of Oz* as much as or perhaps even more than they do the more realistic worlds of *Who's Afraid of Virginia Woolf?* and *Cat on a Hot Tin Roof.* A play need not be realistic, but it must provide a credible and consistent reality that is worth knowing. The living body of every play is its reality.

To what degree does the play arouse emotions? If a play is dull and boring, if it does not reach out and touch the audience, then it doesn't work—at least not for that particular audience. A good play deals with emotions in the characters; it gets them into emotional situations, so that they suffer. When the people in a play have extreme emotions—fear, sorrow, hate, joy, and the like—the audience members tend to feel for the characters or feel against them. Viewers may sympathize or not, but in response to a good play they always empathize with or "feel for," others. What most people want from drama is feeling. They want characters to care about. They feel for the characters as the latter endure experiences and express feelings. Drama at its best offers meaningful and emotionalized experiences. In a sense, an audience member lives through the experiences of a play along with the characters. The degree to which this happens varies from piece to piece, but in the best dramas this emphatic experiencing always occurs. If a play makes a viewer feel something, then it is good. If it causes the viewer to feel deeply, then perhaps it is great. In any play, feeling is the spark of life.

Ultimately, each person must respond honestly to each drama for himself. Perhaps an experienced observer can help a novice identify action or the lack of it, but everyone knows when nothing is going on in a play. Each audience member responds to some perceptions in a play and not to others. So each must eventually judge the nature and consis-

CREATION

William Shakespeare

tency of the reality which a work depicts. Most important, each individual alone knows what emotions a given work arouses within the self. Thus, the beauty of a play, or the lack of it, is a personal response to the drama itself.

What every dramatist faces while searching for dramatic action are the facts of human existence. How can any person penetrate the baffling questions of life on this earth? But the dramatist must try. The world's chief mysteries are the writer's concern. For example, if someone is living an upright, honest life and suddenly suffers misfortune, why should this be so? Why does evil sometimes come to good people? Why do ordinary, decent human beings sometimes hurt others? Ultimately, how does any particular person face death, the passing of loved ones, or the fateful end of one's own life? Such are the questions of serious plays. But other fascinating questions animate adventure stories and comedies. In adventure stories, how can people cross a desert, attack an island, escape an evil spell, or overwhelm a terrorist? As for comedy, what happens to an innocent who prefers chocolates rather than bullets for a battle, to a twin mistaken for his brother, or to a young male student who must masquerade as a friend's maiden aunt? Each day a writer must face life's ultimate realities, be they serious, adventuresome, or comic.

All playwrights are artists, some greater and some lesser in skill, stature, or popularity. Playwrights, however, must not only come to know the nuances of human existence, but also they must perfect their craft. To become a master in any art takes a lifetime; as the old saying goes: "The lyf so short, the craft so long to lerne." Playwrights are creators of actions, images, stories, and characters. They tend not to be great philosophers offering unique ideas or theoretical concepts; rather, they probe the quality of contemporary life and offer sensitive responses to the world in their time. Their work depends on the sensitivity and clarity of their vision. Playwrights, along with other artists, are the antennae of the human race. By listening closely to the best playwrights of this or any other age, one can learn some truths about the human condition. When artists falsify what they know to be true about humanity or about themselves, then their art is immoral. When playwrights look at the world and tell what they see by composing dramas with action, perception, reality, and emotion then they create valuable pieces of art. When that happens, the world is a better place. A playwright's art expands the world.

6 *Directors in Action*

Theatre demands both private and public creativity. Poems and paintings are made in solitude, but dramatic art is impossible without the shared creativity of people working together. Although a playwright's initial work is done alone, once the author carries the play script into a theatre building, the co-creative process begins. At that moment a director becomes central to the final stages of the process that brings a play to life onstage. As a playwright's creativity is for the most part solitary, so a director's creativity is mostly social. A playwright creates with ideas, images, and words; a director creates with actors, designers, and technical people. The act of playwriting is private; the act of directing is public.

CREATING WITH OTHERS

A director acts as catalyst to the theatre's social creativity. Playwrights can make scripts; actors can bring them to life without a director; but directors are the sensitive experts of human process who translate inert literary objects into live theatrical events. Playwrights are not usually adept at the craft of directing. Most dramatists do not direct their own plays because they realize a director's creativity added to their own usually means a far richer production. A rehearsal period is a time of struggle that playwrights do not always like. Actors often resent someone who pushes them toward preconceived characterizations, but they need someone to hear them, watch them, and help them develop a character. The best directors are men and women of theatrical experience and discrimination who can encourage actors and coordinate the work of other artists. In the best contemporary theatre, both the playwright and the director stand as significant creators.

Every work of dramatic art has at least two visions, that of the playwright and that of the director. The writer uses vision to bring the play into being, and that vision remains indelibly stamped on it. A perceptive reader can usually find a playwright's vision within the play itself. But when engaging in the process of bringing a play to the stage, a director imposes another vision on the written drama. Speaking simply, the playwright looks at the world, perceives something about it, and puts that down in dialogue. A playwright's vision says, in effect, "The world is like this." The director's vision says, "Here's an unusual piece of drama, and we are presenting it in a unique way." When the two visions are complementary, the result is dynamic. But if the director's vision violates that of the playwright, the results can be confusing. When a director has no

Vsevelod Meyerhold

83

**Director Mike Nichols
receiving a Tony Award
from actor Anthony
Quinn**

vision at all, theatre is usually a bore. A writer's vision focuses on the
world, a director's vision on theatrical enactment.

A play is inert until a director and actors give it life. Dramatic literature
exists on the printed page, but drama as art only appears on the lighted
stage. Because a play is only one factor in a finished drama, different
directors handle a given play in differing ways. But a director's work is
for most audience members the least apparent of any of the theatre's
creators. Perhaps the director's touch is hard to spot because a director's
job is to excite, select, and balance the work of others. Audiences notice
little of a director's achievement except through the work of others. But

the following discussion reveals how anyone can learn to identify the director's hand.

A theatre director bears the heavy burden of having the central responsibility for everything the audience sees and hears. An old saying in the theatre goes like this: "if things go well, the playwright and the actors get the praise, but if things go badly the director gets the blame." A director's job is to see that everything is right—to be sure that all the other people create as well as they can and that they work smoothly together. Above all else, a director is an artist of human beings.

Occasionally, people speculate about whether or not directors are creative or interpretive. The answer, of course, is that they are both. Insofar as directors read and interpret a play script, their work is derivative. But when they take a play as one sort of material and add actors, lights, costumes, and settings as other materials, then they undoubtedly create as originally as any other artist. A director is the theatrical creator who carries all the responsibilities for perfecting the final work of art.

Many approaches can be made to the job of directing. In fact, all directors somehow perform the work in their own way. But some specific approaches can be identified. Some directors plan everything meticulously before rehearsals and design conferences begin. Others study the play but prefer to remain more open to the suggestions of others; they come to rehearsals prepared, but with nothing written out for execution. Still others, unfortunately, contribute nothing—neither homework before rehearsals nor stimulation during them. In any case, a director always establishes the way a company works, and directorial control or lack of it persists throughout the performances. In a fine work of theatre art, a playwright provides the material and the form, but a director provides the style. Style in theatre is the manner of communication. In this regard, a director plans, stimulates, and selects all the details of the performance.

Just as there are different kinds of directors, so are there different types of directing jobs. Although the work is often similar, a director faces one set of problems when handling a serious play and another set when dealing with a musical comedy. Many contemporary directors, such as Mike Nichols, work in more than one media. They may direct a stage play and then make a movie. Some directors in New York work in both television and the theatre. But the work of a film director is vastly different from that of a stage director. Although the film or television director still must handle people and stimulate them, the technology of the camera demands as much attention as the work of the actors. A film director sets actors into positions and gives them attitudes and bits of activity to perform while overseeing the photographing of them as objects. A television director is primarily concerned with calling camera shots in a control room. A stage director prepares actors during a long rehearsal period to perform self-sufficiently before a live audience.

The work of a stage director demands taste, energy, sensitivity, and discipline. Nearly anyone can undertake the job of directing a play, but few develop sufficient craftsmanship and artistry to do it well. The best directors today are neither lazy permissives nor insecure dictators. The best ones are the well-prepared, tolerant co-creators. While directing the

Director Tyrone Guthrie (left) in rehearsal

process of theatre creation, the most important quality for a director to possess is awareness. A director must attempt to see, analyze, and solve any problems that arise, and must try to anticipate others beforehand.

To trace the stages of a director's work is to understand the range of activities involved. The first problem for any director is how to get a job. Like other theatre artists, directors must sell themselves, not in the sense of self-prostitution, but rather by convincing those who control theatres

Left: Max Reinhardt

Right: Marshall Mason

of their ability to handle the work. An employer can see whether or not an actor fits a role or can read a writer's script. But good directors come in all sizes, ages, and personality types. Most producers hire directors only after they have seen their work. Therefore, directorial careers evolve slowly. Often people start as student directors of short pieces in university theatres, as workshop directors in repertory theatres, or as stage managers in professional companies. In most cases, directors begin their careers with modest productions and work up to more elaborate ones. The craft of directing takes a number of years to learn.

The training of a director requires several stages. Sometimes a person goes through them one at a time, but most directors experience them simultaneously. First, a director must have a sound, basic liberal education. The better a young director knows such subjects as psychology, history, languages, literature, science, music, and graphic arts, the more able a beginner will be to deal with creative and practical problems in the theatre. Second, a director should read plays—all of them. Of course, a director must know the plays of Sophocles, Shakespeare, Molière, and all the great established dramatists, but be should also know as many modern, contemporary, and manuscript plays as possible. It takes years to read all the plays, but it must be done in order to reach full knowledge of any given play a director may be called on to direct. Third, all directors need a theatre education. They must know how to act, design, build scenery and costumes, stage manage, and run props, lights, and sound.

Also, they need to observe the work of other directors. Some of that observation can come from classes, but mostly it comes from live work in the theatre in each of the production jobs. Fourth and last, a director must gain experience directing. Only by working day after day to solve a director's problems does a person begin to think like a director, and that is essential. But directors' development never stops, and everything they experience will eventually aid them in their art.

Play selection is every director's most difficult and most important task. When professional directors are asked to direct a play, they must consider whether or not they like the play before accepting. But directors who work as members of theatre companies, especially in repertory and university theatres, must continually face the problem of what play they ought to do next. Choosing the right play, naturally, affects the outcome of the production. Some plays interest a director creatively, other perfectly good plays do not. Some plays fit the available actor pool, others do not. Many plays are not right for a theatre's particular audience, budget, or technical facilities. Often a director must select a play that fits harmoniously into a season. In every case, when choosing a play, the director is selecting the life activity that a number of people will experience for many weeks. All directors continually search for good new plays or for potentially exciting old ones. Also, they remain constantly aware of not only what their audience wants but also what it needs. The choice of a play is never easy.

A director's next step is to work through the script, analyzing it. In the case of a first production of a new play, the director often labors over the script with the writer. These sessions contribute greatly to the quality of both the script and the production. The opportunity for a director to hear the playwright talk about the play helps provide beneficial insights. More often, a director must develop a new production of an established play without the help of the playwright. With no playwright available, the director must study the script alone and thoroughly digest it. Directors usually read a play numerous times and follow a careful process of analysis to discover all of a play's problems and potentials.

What results from a director's study of a script is a production concept. The director's concept consists of the central complex of ideas devised to control all the creative and technical work. A directorial concept cannot normally be reduced to one sentence, because it consists of many ideas and images. But the director must be aware of what ideas and images are the most important in order to communicate what is wanted to designers and actors. A director's concept often consists of these items: the play's action, subject, and central idea; its key emotion, mood, and audience effect; its principal style; and its important images, colors, and symbols. The best way to learn to identify directorial concepts is to witness at least two different productions of the same play. Watching Shakespeare's *Hamlet* in different productions would help one discover how two directors handle the same play script. A production concept is the key to well-coordinated theatrical productions. The strength and wisdom of the director's concept pervades all the details of every produced play.

After a director has devised a production concept, then the staff planning period begins. The director sets schedules and begins meeting with designers. For the designers of sets, lights, and costumes, a director's ideas about the production of the play are essential leads to their work. During the same period most directors meet with the producer and other business personnel in order to help lay out a promotional campaign. The better the planning on the part of the director, designers, and producer before the actual production period begins, the better will be the final product.

Also during the initial phase of the production the director must cast the play. Although directing calls for many abilities, a director's talent or lack of it becomes most apparent in casting. Casting includes the activities of finding, auditioning, and assigning actors to roles in the play. During auditions the director tests the voice, physical presence, imagination, experience, and raw talent of actors. Few directors cast merely on the basis of physical type, but every director pays attention to the physical appearance of actors in relation to the roles they may play. All directors tend to talk in their own terms about the practice of casting, but most respond intuitively to the process. Not only must directors choose each actor carefully, but also they need to be sure that their casts fit together as an ensemble. An oft repeated truism in the theatre states that if a director chooses the right play, that's half the work, and if the director chooses the right cast, 85 percent of the work is done.

How does a director cast a play? A director studies the characters in a play and then tries to find actors who fit the requisite physical and psychic qualities. While studying the play, the director develops conceptions of each character, identifying the given circumstances—age, weight, coloring, and the like—and the key quality in each of the characters. The quality is an intuitive matter, an inner reaction, a feeling for each. Then the director must look at a number of actors in order to locate at least two or more persons for each role who seem to project a similar set of given circumstances and a similar quality to the ones discovered in the play. By comparing actors, directors best perceive what qualities they really want. Often directors think of actors they know who would fit some of the parts in a play, and they try to interest them in participating. Also

Left: Andre Bishop

Right: Tom O'Horgan

A director and cast rehearse *Sunday's Child,* Long Wharf Theatre

most directors hold open auditions in order to find actors they don't know. Then they must consider the few final candidates for roles in the production. At that time they must test, consider, and decide which finalists to use. In making final decisions most directors pay special attention to experience and training, appearance and voice, and sensitivity and personality. Finally, it must be made sure that each actor fits with the rest of the group and is a person with whom the director can probably work well.

There still remains the challenging process of rehearsal. Some people may think of rehearsals as a dull grind leading up to the climactic excitement of opening night, but they are wrong. During rehearsals the people of the theatre engage in the basic creative process of transforming, unifying, and intensifying life. Theatre at its best is neither pretense nor mere show business. It provides an opportunity for people to cooperate during a rehearsal period and perfect a performance that they will live through again and again for the entertainment and enlightenment of audiences. The rehearsal process is not simple. Strangely, what happens in rehearsals cannot be forced or rushed. A growth process occurs— slowly. A director cannot be too easy on his cast or too dictatorial. The best directors nowadays work organically with their actors—suggesting and listening, prodding, and reassuring. American directors Mike Nichols and Marshall Mason are outstanding examples of such directors. For most stage directors, rehearsals are the most creative stage in the development of the production. Working with actors is what they like.

Most directors arrange rehearsals in about five segments. The first stage of rehearsals consists of readings. The actors familiarize themselves with the play, and the director discusses its divisions and objectives. The second stage of rehearsals involves blocking and "businessing," that is, devising all the movement necessary for the action. Also during this stage the actors memorize their words. The third stage of rehearsals is developmental; the actors test, select, and modify the precise details of behavior with which to bring the characters to life. The fourth stage is even more complex: the coordination of all elements on stage. That's when the director introduces more technical elements—scenery, properties, costumes, lights, sound—to the actors and helps them adjust properly to each new element. Simultaneously, the actors are usually on the verge of bringing their characters fully to life. This period is often tense but always exciting. When the director handles the coordination period well, the production elements blend into a work of art. Finally, come the dress rehearsals. They are the final rehearsals with all costumes, lights, sets, and props during the days just before opening night. That's when the fine tuning of all elements occurs. During dress rehearsals everyone commits some errors as the company finally establishes the precise patterns of the performance.

Despite the care that theatre artists give the preparation of a production, opening night remains something of a mystery. Not until that particular company performs the play live before an audience can anyone know for certain how it will go. But audiences are not merely testing agents. People go to the theatre for experience, for fun, for insight, and for sharing. Most opening night audiences eagerly enter the spirit of the work. The first night for most productions is one of excitement and high spirits, and if the play goes well, a night of joy. Even after plays open, some directors continue making adjustments to improve the production. No matter how much directors might like to assist during performances, however, their director's work occurs mainly during the rehearsals.

How do directors judge their own work? Most analyze their productions by critically viewing several performances and by inviting comments from trusted friends. Newspaper criticism is not often useful as most newspaper reviews are too brief. Also, some reviewers are not well informed about theatre, but of course others are quite astute. When directors look for feedback on the success or failure of their work, they look mainly to audiences. As directors stand or sit in a theatre with an audience watching their productions, they can tell both consciously and intuitively how the entire audience is reacting. Audiences clearly reveal their attention level and their emotional involvement; one need only to listen and watch them. Furthermore, rising or falling attendance as a play's run progresses tends to indicate the success or failure of the project. The final evaluation of directors' work, however, must occur in their own minds. At best, directors employ awareness of the most intense sort in response to their own theatre creativity. The pleasure of directors is to share the life experiences that the playwright discovered, that they themselves planned, that the actors brought to life, and that audiences enjoy.

THE DIRECTOR'S CRAFT

Just as a painter must learn to handle brushes and paint, so must a director learn the craft before becoming an effective theatre artist. But a director's tools and materials are less concrete than those of a painter. A director works with live people within a particular time span in a certain space.

The first essential for directing is the ability to create a good working atmosphere for the other theatre artists. In order to generate such an atmosphere, a director provides a place with enough space for the play's activity and with enough quiet for the actors' concentration. But more important than the physical surroundings is the psychological milieu established by the director. It should be one that makes the actors comfortable yet stirs them to creativity. The rehearsal situation should be controlled yet have enough freedom for inspiration to rise. If a director chooses skilled actors and gives them a good milieu to work in, then the play will soon come to life.

Second, every director needs to learn how to develop an imaginative production concept. He must understand the play, conceive an approach to the staging, and then communicate it effectively. The concept must be expansive enough to stimulate appropriate work from each actor and

Director John Malkovich (second from left) discusses George Bernard Shaw's *Arms and the Man* with actors Raul Julia, Glenne Headly, and Kevin Klein.

each designer, as they must ultimately bring it to life. Actors do not merely live roles; they also live directors' concepts. But no actors can do so without understanding what they should experience. Orson Welles provided a striking example of a concept when in the 1930s he decided to produce Shakespeare's *Julius Caesar* in modern dress, treating the spirit of Caesar in the play as contemporary fascism. Like Welles, every director uses a script to conceive an imagined world and, with his actors and designers, develops that world into reality.

The key consideration a director must hold in mind while working in design conferences and in rehearsals is the play's *action*. Everything must be tuned to what is going on. Whatever distracts the audience's attention from that, no matter how antic, causes confusion and eventual boredom. Uncontrolled distractions and excesses spoil a production. The action in *Death of a Salesman* might be stated like this: Willy Loman probes his memory and his present relationships to discover why he and his sons aren't a success. A director who thoroughly understands the action of a play can better marshal all the necessary details to activate it.

A good deal of a director's craftsmanship has to do with how rehearsals are handled and what is accomplished during them. A director should always come to each rehearsal well prepared. At first, the best preparation is a thorough knowledge of the play and a confident idea of the necessities for bringing it to life. After that a director needs each day to consider what problems should be handled at that rehearsal. Most important, a good director nowadays works organically, trying to promote creative exchange between director and actors and between actors themselves. Actors do not want to waste time on nonessentials, but they do want constructive suggestions and feedback. Furthermore, most theatre people have little tolerance for any company member who is allowed to break the accepted rules, such as being on time, memorizing lines, displaying temperament, or showing contempt for others. A director must insure that rehearsals have a sense of freedom within a disciplined environment.

The specific work of directors with actors varies greatly from production to production, rehearsal to rehearsal, and actor to actor. They may need to stage, to coach, to teach, or to counsel actors. Sometimes they stage a scene, carefully working out its movement, and then set the emotional tone or the tempo for the actors. Other times, directors must coach individuals, explaining how each cast member might best approach the enactment of one or more sequences. Occasionally in amateur productions, directors are required to teach actors about the craft of acting. Frequently they must counsel actors about personal problems they may have with the production, with other company members, or even with life outside the theatre. Unfortunately, too, a director must occasionally discipline an actor who disturbs the work of the group or even dismiss one who doesn't perform the work satisfactorily. But most director-actor relationships are good ones, and many close friendships arise between these artists of the theatre. One of the pleasures of theatre work is getting to know new and fascinating people. Certainly, directors need to be straightforward with actors, but they should also be levelheaded psychologists. To impel people into emotional states and to get them to transform themselves requires adroit leadership.

An explanation of a few basic principles of staging should help anyone better understand the process of directing. In order to stage a play well, a director utilizes stage space three-dimensionally. Every stage consists of actual space, not mere pictorial space. Movement within cubic stage space should stress all the dimensions. A director needs not only to meet the mobile and pictorial requirements of a particular play but also to utilize the particular stage to its fullest capacity. Every theatre's stage has unique physical potentials and limitations. The basic stage types are proscenium, thrust, and arena. This book's chapter on theatre architecture describes each of those types and other variants. With each stage configuration, varying principles of movement and picturization are necessary.

Certain principles of movement, however, apply to any kind of stage space. The basic movements are horizontal, vertical, diagonal, and curved. Figures 6.1–6.5 illustrate some basic principles of stage movement. Diagonal movements are the strongest, and they provide the most emphasis in the three-dimensional stage space. Curved movements also stress multiple dimensions, and they are the most lifelike. Horizontal movements are the weakest because they are the flattest and most repetitive. A good director consciously equalizes the four types of movement during the performance time, thus providing spatial and visual

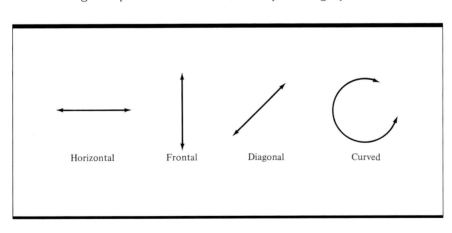

Figure 6.1

The basic lines of stage movements

Horizontal　　　Frontal　　　Diagonal　　　Curved

variety for the audience. The different kinds of movement also provide means for emphasizing or deemphasizing certain physical actions in a play. (See Figure 6.1.)

Other technical principles of staging are: actor body position, equal use of all the stage areas, and pictorial balance. The actor body positions are: open, ¼ right, ½ right, ¾ right, closed, ¾ left, ½ left, and ¼ left (See Figure 6.2.) The divisions of stage space are shown in Figure 6.3.

The basic element in every stage design is the floor plan. A play's

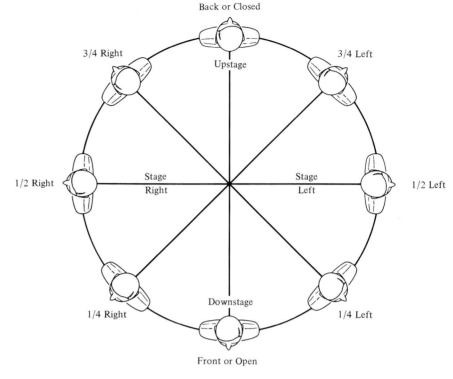

Back or Closed

Upstage

3/4 Right

3/4 Left

1/2 Right

Stage
Right

Stage
Left

1/2 Left

1/4 Right

Downstage

1/4 Left

Front or Open

Figure 6.2

**Actor body positions
onstage**

director develops a floor plan in cooperation with the scenic designer. The best floor plans begin with an action pattern that the director conceives while reading the play and studying its movement potentials. From the action pattern the director and the designer arrange forms, walls, and furniture to enforce the chosen flow of movement. Figures 6.4 and 6.5 show an action pattern and a floor plan for William Inge's play *Bus Stop,* from a design by Wes Peters.

A setting must also provide a functional and credible visual picture. The picturization of the play as developed from the floor plan is usually more the province of the scenic designer than of the director. A picture of what the stage should look like to viewers is called an elevation. This book's chapter on design explains the stage designer's work and mentions principles of pictorial composition. Nevertheless, once the designer arranges the stage picture, the director must approve it, since it is the director who must utilize the stage setting. The visual aspect of the set becomes a background for a constantly changing picture as the director arranges actors in pictorial compositions and moves them from place to place. A setting must work as an organic whole, establishing an appropriate spatial and visual milieu for the play's events.

A director also uses actors to make visual compositions within the stage space. Essentially, actor placement and actor movement are the dual phases of composition. When placing actors, the director carefully sets their body positions, their distances from one another, and their arrangement in patterns. When one actor is onstage alone, then the composition has the most significant relationship to the scenery. When two actors are onstage, then the distance between them is emotionally meaningful. In theatre terminology, playing level is when two actors stand in the same plane parallel to the audience. When three or more actors take stage, then a director's main compositional figure becomes the triangle. Thus, the director controls balance and focus to keep the production interesting and emphatic. Good directors make a drama visually compelling.

Each production a director puts together possesses special problems. Sometimes a fight, a murder, or a love scene must be staged. Certain types of plays call for special expertise. Musicals require an understanding of music and dance, even though a director may team up with a choreographer and musical director. When rehearsing plays like those of Shakespeare, the director must be able to coach the actors in reading poetic lines. With each play the challenges are new. For each drama a director applies old principles to new problems and sometimes new principles to old plays.

One other important matter for every audience member to think about is directorial ethics. Most theatre people agree that a director owes first allegiance to the overall production—that is, to making it as startling, entertaining, and perceptive as possible. But directors also need to deal honestly with a play; they should understand and project its spirit as best they can and not violate its basic nature. Some directors treat plays unethically. For the sake of making striking, newsworthy productions,

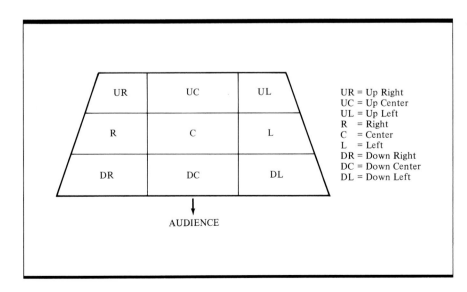

Figure 6.3

The divisions of stage space

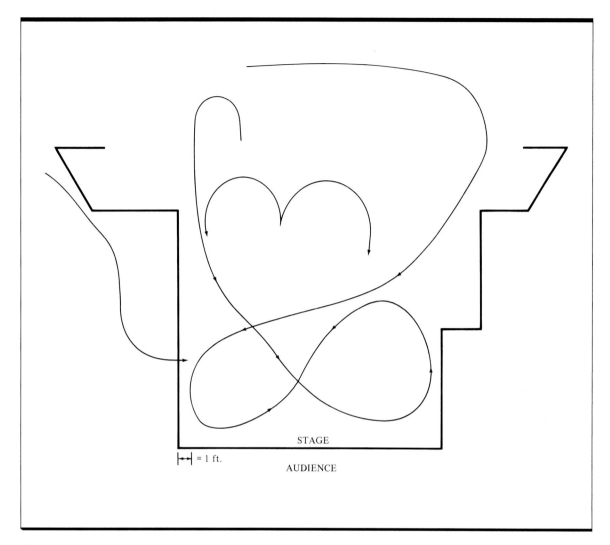

STAGE

|←→| = 1 ft.

AUDIENCE

Figure 6.4

Action plan for the Brown County Playhouse's production of William Inge's *Bus Stop* in a set designed by Wes Peters

they distort them. Others ruin plays because they fail to study them enough. All such circumstances are breaches of artistic ethics.

Directors also should treat their co-workers in an ethically humane way. They ought to respect actors rather than abuse them or manipulate them negatively. Similarly, a director's connections with designers and other technical people should not be exploitative. In every instance, a director ought to be a co-creator. Most audience members are unaware of bad directorial ethics, but with a bit of sensitivity and careful observation, an audience member can glean intuitive messages about the production from the performers.

To be an artist in the theatre, a director must first develop a craft. To those who ask if directorial technique might interfere with artistic inspiration, the answer is simple. For any artist, technique means creative freedom; craft often promotes a person's imaginative freedom. Tech-

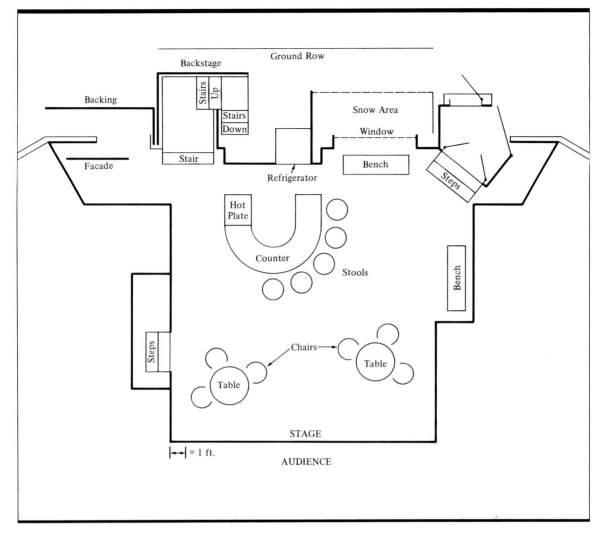

Backing

Ground Row

Backstage

Stairs Up

Stairs Down

Stair

Facade

Refrigerator

Snow Area

Window

Bench

Steps

Hot Plate

Counter

Stools

Bench

Steps

Chairs

Table

Table

STAGE

|←→| = 1 ft.

AUDIENCE

Figure 6.5

Floor plan of the set for the Brown County Playhouse's production of William Inge's *Bus Stop*, designed by Wes Peters

nique, however, must not become an end in itself, nor should it ever be repeated over and over for its own sake. Mindless technique and formulaic craftsmanship spoil art. Mechanical artisans turn out one meaningless replica after another. But only through the creative employment of good craftsmanship can a genuine artist produce a series of objects to treasure.

ANALYZING A DIRECTOR'S ARTISTRY

Untrained eyes cannot easily identify in a dramatic production the work of its director. Because the script exists in words and can be read outside the production situation, a playwright's work is readily apparent. Because the actual work of the actors and the various designers can be seen, their creative achievements can be studied individually. But good directors contribute variously to the work of all the other artists, so their work appears only in the work of the other artists. How can one analyze a director's artistry? The following questions lead to pertinent answers.

What is the play's central action? After the first few minutes of a production, an audience member should know what is happening and should never be in doubt about it until the end. These questions should help anyone discover the action: Who are the people? Where are they? What is happening to them? Why do they stay? Who is pressuring them? How are people changing or refusing to change? What is going on?

Do the physical elements of the production command visual attention? Naturally, most audience members watch closely during the first few minutes of a production because the novelty of the visual scene compels their eyes. But scenery and lighting alone cannot long maintain audience interest, especially not if they remain static. Visual movement, variety, and change are the factors that command and renew attention. The stage pictures that the director composes with the placement of actors should be fascinating, and the patterns of action that the actors follow on the stage floor should be dynamic and varied. One of the best keys to the judgment of a director's visual craftsmanship is to notice if each area of potential acting space is used about as often as any other area. A few other visual elements to watch for are the following: Do the lighting instruments have the angles and intensity to reveal the actors' faces all the time? Does the scenery make the actors easy to look at, or does it draw undue attention to itself? Do the costumes help the actors characterize their roles, or do the clothes appear out of key? Are all the colors apparently chosen for a connected purpose? Do the visual elements meaningfully relate to each other?

Can the audience hear each word from every actor? Nobody in any theatre audience should ever have to strain to hear or to wonder what an actor said. Excepting occasional lines intentionally muffled or overlapped, all the words ought to be clearly audible. Also the director needs to create an enfolding aural milieu for the play, sometimes with music but more often with silence.

What about the details of actor movement? Is there enough actor movement to lend the performances interest and reality? Are they doing something appropriate all the time, or do they sometimes just stand around? Do they walk aimlessly from place to place? Can the audience see the actors' eyes, or do they continually make the mistake of looking at the floor? Do they gesture too often, or do all their movements seem organic and well motivated? Every movement must serve a purpose, but lack of visual detail is simply boring.

Are the actors credible? This question about the acting is always crucial. From start to finish, the production ought to be believable. Given the particular world of the play and the degree of exaggeration established at the outset, a spectator should be able to believe whatever the actors do or say. The best actors—such British actors as Laurence Olivier and Ian McKellen or such Americans as George C. Scott and Kevin Kline—are able to perform unusual, exaggerated details onstage and make them credible. But whenever the actors appear to be phony, exhibitionist, or conceited, then theatre as art disappears. When an entire production is convincing, high audience involvement results, and that amounts to success in the theatre.

A number of critical questions that reveal a director's work should be asked after the play is over. What is the audience response at the final moment of a play? The quality of the silence or the amount of laughter as the lights fade onstage show the involvement of the audience during the play's significant final moments. Even how the spectators applaud reveals their basic attitudes. Also, audience members ought to note their own emotional response just after the play ends and the applause stops. Furthermore, the way an audience leaves the theatre shows its mood. After good productions most people experience a strong aesthetic response—an inner feeling of intensity plus a heightened sense of the reality of existence. Some experience of that sort means the production has stimulated one's body, feelings, and mind to increased awareness.

Was it the right play for the theatre to present? In the opinion of the audience member, should the theatre have bothered to present the play? Or would another have been more appropriate, meaningful, or entertaining? Sometimes the answer to this question needs careful consideration rather than snap judgment. Often a drama that is at first disquieting turns out to be a vivid memory. Not all plays are meant to be instantly pleasing or even stimulate audience euphoria. Drama deals with all sorts of human experiences, the grotesque and the beautiful, the sorrowful

Orson Welles (third from left) acts in his production of *Heartbreak House* by George Bernard Shaw

and the comic. If one goes to a theatre and gets the same experience as everyday life or the same experience he has had in a theatre before, then perhaps the theatre has failed in the realm of originality. At least an audience member ought to understand why the director chose to do the play.

Did the drama seem whole? Did all the pieces fit together? Or, in more complicated terms, did the production reveal its form? Every play possesses some ambiguity and leaves some questions unanswered. But

Director Charles Ludlam (right) acts in his product of *The Mystery of Irma Vep*

Des McAnuff and Peter Sellers

when the organization of the piece is right, then the materials, the details, and the bits come across as well unified. Everything works together. If the form is right, an audience member gets a sense of completion, a strange experience of satisfaction with how it all turned out, or even sometimes a gnawing dissatisfaction with the world. In every case the play should reveal its shape to those perceptive enough to look for it.

Did the play's audience grow? Over the length of the production's run, did more and more people attend? Or did fewer and fewer? The answers to these questions are not readily available to everyone, but that information often reveals the relative success or failure of the director's activities. Certainly, other factors may also affect the rise or fall of attendance, but increasing attendance or sold-out houses tend to demonstrate the appeal of a production and therefore its success with the available audience. Artists must certainly please themselves with their work, but they must also please others if their work is to have wide impact.

What does a person need to know in order to be a good stage director? Directors need to understand as much as possible about the theatre and about life. They also need to know about acting, design, and all the other technical phases of theatre production. The more expert they are in each area, the better their productions will be, because they can stimulate other artists. At rehearsals, a director must be an audience of one, responding to the trials and errors of the actors. Indeed, every director must become a master of process—the process of bringing a play to life as well as the process of making a live play a permanent part of the experience of those who witness it. With the play the playwright gives a heart to the production; the director's judgment gives it a brain. A director controls the living process of theatre creation.

7 Actors at Work

Acting is magic. It has a double power, attracting some people to perform and compelling other people to watch. First of all, it's fun—childlike perhaps, but enjoyable. Everyone does some acting while they're young, and there's a genuine sense of play in all theatrical performances. Acting comes, too, from the natural impulse in all humans to mimic others. Everyone learns patterns of behavior that way. But acting has even deeper roots in the religious rituals of primitive peoples, in the impulse to control existence. Everyone takes on more than one role each day—parent or student, employee or consumer, applicant or boss. But actors are especially awesome because they attract attention and because they really can change into somebody else.

This chapter deals with the world of the actor. It describes the four essential realms of an actor's existence: the connections between acting and life, the actor's work on self, the actor's work on a role, and the requirements of an actor's career.

ACTING HUMAN

Acting is natural to the creative life of humankind. Living somehow seems to demand that everyone must act during everyday life and certainly on special occasions. Some type of acting evidently existed early in the development of human culture. Near primitive campfires, people enacted events they had experienced or pretended events they hoped would come true. Anthropologists claim that *mimicry after* an event signals the beginning of theatre, and *ritual before* an event signals the beginning of religion. Actors in costumes and masks have always held magical powers over others. Enactment has a special place in most human societies. Drama, religion, and magic have always been closely related. No figures in human culture have more magical power over the imagination of others than actors with their strange enchantment of others. Persons who have the ability to transform themselves into someone else, to change their very nature, are at least fascinating, perhaps grotesque, and probably a little bit frightening. If such persons can change themselves, what might they become? What might they perform right before our eyes? Acting has developed over the centuries into one of the strangest and most complicated of human arts, and it demands creativity of the most intense sort, creativity with a person's very self.

Acting is easy, but it's hard. That sentence appears contradictory, but it well represents the many contradictions acting involves. To act is the simplest way for a human being to express creativity. You don't need any

Richard Burton in
***Hamlet* by William Shakespeare**

103

special equipment, and anyone can do it—to a degree. But it is the most difficult of all arts to perfect, because the actor has to learn to transform his or her very own inner self.

Anyone can act a little bit. Most people have some talent for it. Mimicry is a natural process that human beings develop for learning. But few people acquire the craftsmanship and experience to act well before audiences. Indeed, to act for one person is no great feat, but to act for a group is far more complicated. Still, nearly every child enacts many roles

Kevin Kline in Henry IV, Part I

during play—cowboy, nurse, engineer, clown, athlete. Most adults consciously change roles several times each day—traveler, worker, student, customer, family member—and each role has a different set of requirements for every person's daily performances. Everybody acts some while repeating a joke, relating a story, expressing a memory, or telling a lie. Acting is thoroughly human.

Beginners in the theatre think they can act about as well as anyone else. After all, they sometimes reason, a person only has to be natural, learn the lines, and move around the stage as a director dictates, all the while letting off emotion like some sort of personal steam. But genuine acting is more than that; it is a special transformational activity that not everybody is able to do.

The first thing to understand about acting is a fact most people can recognize but never stop to think about—the difference between acting and performing. Strangely, few people realize this essential difference. Genuine acting requires quite a different human action from performing. For the purposes of this discussion, the words *acting* and *performing* have special meanings. To act is both to involve oneself in a role other

Pygmalion **by George Bernard Shaw, Repertory Theatre at Christian Theological Seminary, Indianapolis**

than the normal ones of daily life and to transform oneself in that rare, magical manner that communicates directly to others. Performing, on the other hand, demands a different approach and a different set of skills. Performing is showing oneself, demonstrating one's ability or talent— perhaps singing, dancing, or telling jokes. Performing may be just as important a human endeavor for some people as acting is for others. But they are not the same. Acting requires a deep change in a human being.

THE DISCOVERY OF SELF

Constantin Stanislavsky, a twentieth-century Russian actor, separated the actor's training into the two categories of work on self and work on a role. He also helped the world of theatre realize that an actor needs to develop craftsmanship of two sorts: external and internal. He stressed that every actor needs what might be termed "personal craftsmanship" before even approaching a role, and even while rehearsing or playing a show, the actor needs to practice certain exercises in off-hours. Thus this section explains the necessities of an actor's training.

An actor's work on self can involve daily exercises, workshops, lessons, coaching, and classes. Whether alone, with others, or with a teacher, several sorts of daily or weekly exercises help an actor get ready and stay ready for the more creative side of actors' labor. The self-discipline required for actors to work privately is great indeed, because when they finish all the exercises, they have nothing really to show. Only the actors themselves, and maybe their acting teachers, can tell the difference. Still, many actors increase their skills markedly through careful training. Usually, such training is best accomplished under wise direction. Without some seasoned advice, actors often acquire bad habits.

The actor's work on self can be separated into two divisions: the physical and the psychological. Although the two are closely related, most actors benefit by focusing on one problem at a time. But everyone realizes that psychological work affects the physical and vice versa.

To point out that good actors do physical exercises to keep their bodies in shape does not reveal the variety of exercises most actors use. The bodily exercises they perform are not simply mechanical calisthenics to keep their muscles well toned. To develop suppleness and muscular control many actors also take dance. The disciplined training of ballet or modern dance pays excellent physical dividends. Furthermore, the varied skills an actor may gain in a jazz or acrobatic dance class may come in handy in some role. All dance training adds to an actor's abilities. Some actors, of course, prefer their own special kinds of workouts. Some go regularly to gyms or participate in such sports as handball, tennis, and basketball. Many actors nowadays are involved in running as a means to better health, weight control, good appearance, and even meditation. Some get involved in tumbling, circus, and acrobatics, although such pursuits are more specialized. Actors today are intensely aware of keeping their bodies well tuned for the expressive needs of their art.

For all actors, voice is another even more conscious physical concern. Without a healthy, responsive voice no actor has much of a chance for an artistic or professional career. Therefore, actors take great pains to develop their voices. Often they attend voice workshops and there learn a system of particular exercises that are well suited to their needs, and sometimes they also take singing lessons. Actors work especially hard on the four basic phases of vocal production and the practice exercises for each. When an audience member knows the four phases, then the quality of vocal work among actors becomes apparent.

The first phase of voice production is respiration. An actor needs particularly good control of breath. The air pushed out of the lungs forms the essential energy for vocal projection. Phonation, the second phase, produces voiced sounds in the larynx, or voice box. There the vocal cords respond to the air stream by vibrating and producing the voice. The third phase of voice production is resonation. The pharynx, the mouth, and the nasal cavities amplify the sound of the voice. The fourth phase is articulation, the final formation of human sounds in the mouth and the addition of certain noises to the voice. The main articulators are the tongue, lower jaw, teeth, and hard and soft palates. Most voice coaches today emphasize organic training, the involvement of the whole body. They help actors improve posture, muscle tone, and overall relaxation, and they encourage actors to concentrate on such things as deep breathing, avoiding tension, and placement of tones.

Most people can understand why actors need physical exercises for

Edmund Kean in Shakespeare's *Richard III*

flexible bodies and voices, but not so many comprehend the necessity for internal work. Often the imaginative exercises and theatre games that actors go through appear somewhat self-indulgent or ridiculous. It is often said that creativity cannot be taught—one is born with it or not. Apparently the saying is only a partial truth because many actors have learned how to increase their creative capacities in classes stressing imagination. Actors, and other creative people as well, benefit from working in a disciplined, conscious manner on such activities as concentration, relaxation, imagination, sense memory, image making, sensitivity, suggestivity, mind control, and freedom of association. All these are internal and can be practiced. Perhaps through internal exercises a person's innate capacity for creativity cannot be altered, but many actors have proved that such exercises help them fulfill their potential.

One of the best books on the techniques of internal work for actors is *To the Actor* by Michael Chekhov. In it he stresses the need for an actor imaginatively to place a power center in one's own body. The solar plexus is a natural center. While using it as an energy source, Chekhov suggests that the actor go through a series of mental and physical exercises. For example, he suggests the action of pushing a large rock, pulling a heavy wagon, or walking across a room and imaginatively filling the space. Throughout the book he argues convincingly for discipline, relaxation, and concentration. There are, of course, many wonderful acting teachers these days in professional schools and universities. The best way to understand creative exercises is to take or at least observe a good acting class. An actor's work on the inner self never ceases.

WORK ON A ROLE

The actor's art comes to fruition in rehearsal and performance. No matter how hard a person may work alone on acting skills, no matter what acting classes may offer, no actor can really practice the art without going on stage in a full production. As Stanislavsky pointed out, work on a role is the second major realm of the actor's effort.

Unless the actor holds a permanent position in a company, the first step toward creating a role is, of course, to audition and get a part.

Constantin Stanislavsky in *Woe to Wit* (left) and *The Lower Depths* by Maxim Gorki (right)

Attitudes and procedures for auditioning are treated later in this chapter. Here it is important to note that during the casting period an actor first gets strong impressions of the company and of the play. Good actors listen carefully and respond to director, script, and other actors. Auditions are not only a time for showing skills but also a time for positive attitudes and sensitive reactions. Auditions are seldom easy to endure because of the uncertainties and doubts they stimulate and because every actor knows that despite great willingness the chances of getting a part are slim. The actors who are most consistently successful are those who have trained themselves well and who possess a positive attitude toward the audition situation.

Once assigned a role, an actor must analyze the play by reading the whole thing through, identifying and tracing the action throughout. Like the director, the actor should make a personal analysis of the play to discover the essential features of its structure. Every actor ought to be able to tell the basic story of the play and know how his or her own character fits into it. But the actor's overall analysis of the play isn't complete before talking with the director. What the director thinks about the play's central action, its most essential subjects, its style, and the overall effect makes a great difference to the individual actor.

Next comes careful analysis of the actor's own role. Although overall analysis of the play is important, the actor's investigation of his or her particular role is the most demanding part of the analytical work. Some of the most significant elements are the given circumstances, the function, units and objectives, relationships, and the through-line of action. What are the given circumstances about the character—the simple facts of who, what, when, and where? How does the character function in the whole story—as hero, villain, or what? The character participates in what units, or scenes? Furthermore, within each unit why is the character there? What does he or she want? What are the character's intentions? What is his or her super objective, or overall goal? What are the essential relationships between the character to be played by the actor and the others in the play? What is the character's through-line of action? The last question is the most important, because the through-line controls all the rest. To find it means that the actor must understand what

**Actors read through
Distant Fires, Hartford
Stage Company**

the character is actually doing every moment during the play's action.

Another crucial concern of the actor is to memorize the lines of the role. It's never easy, and people take it for granted. Only beginners, ill-trained amateurs, or ignorant professionals fail to learn a play precisely as written. Only when the words are learned perfectly can the actor free his or her mind to concentrate on intentions and feelings. Memorization amounts to three processes—learning, retention, and recall. First, the actor must learn the words perfectly and be able to repeat all the lines without error. Second, after learning the lines, the actor must review them continually. Most actors go over all the words of their entire role at least once a day outside of the theatre. Third comes recall; the actor must associate the lines with responses to other actor's speeches, the actor's own movements, or other external factors. For every speech there ought to be a stimulus that makes the words leap to mind. Eventually, the process of recall is automatic, and the words of the character become habitual. In some amateur performances the participants cannot possibly act because they don't know their words perfectly. Memorization is a significant part of every actor's work.

The length of rehearsal period for a play varies from company to company and from production to production. Often because of union restrictions, professional companies in the United States utilize only three weeks. In other countries three months is more typical. University groups rehearse each production from four to eight weeks. Sometimes summer stock companies spend only one or two weeks in rehearsal. Regardless of the length of time available, a director normally divides the rehearsal period into parts, and the actor's work on a role corresponds roughly to the rehearsal divisions. Some sort of pattern for rehearsals such as the following is typical: (1) reading and analysis, (2) exploration and memorization, (3) blocking and business, (4) setting and polishing, and (5) technical and dress rehearsals.

Thus, after analyzing and while memorizing, the actor explores with the director and other actors the possibilities of movement and line readings. Some directors strongly suggest or even demand particular movement patterns in rehearsals. The movements that an actor makes are called blocking, and the more minute, lifelike moves or gestures are called "business." *Blocking* refers to where actors enter, walk to, and station themselves. *Business* consists of the movements of head, eyes, hands, arms—the concrete details. Eventually, an actor must set the blocking and business as surely and memorize them as perfectly as the words of the script. Inventive blocking and business bring a play to life.

A more difficult matter in acting is internal characterization, or self-transformation. Even to define this process of human personality change is difficult, but actually effecting such a transformation is nearly impossible. Yet, good actors accomplish it night after night. Acting goes beyond pretense. Acting is being. An actor does not simply go through the

Laurence Olivier in a variety of roles: *Richard III* (far left); Shylock in *The Merchant of Venice* (center, top); Lear in *King Lear* (center, bottom); and Archie Rice in John Osborne's *The Entertainer* (far right)

motions of a role. When acting at its best occurs, the actor's very self changes. Actors transform their own inner selves to experience the life pattern in a play, and they respond to certain stimuli as the characters they have become. Acting is living through experiences *as if* the circumstances of life are the same as those in the script. For an actor the process of portraying a role requires the moderation of one's habits of mind in order to have the genuine life sensations of the character. The foregoing explanation draws from the Stanislavsky system and from all other systems of acting. Good acting is not so much a matter of living a part as it is of altering one's own self and then going through an artistically created set of experiences. Acting is experiencing an artistic reality.

CREATION

Some of an actor's work on a role is public and some is private. The best actors put in a great deal of time working alone. An actor not only must accomplish the difficult task of memorization alone but also must think through all the possibilities of his role. Many actors write out biographies of their characters, and most write many notes in and out of rehearsal. Writing things down objectifies them. Actors also like to get on stage alone to walk and talk through their roles, trying out different possibilities. A lot of meticulous emotional work can happen only when the actor is laboring alone. Conversely, certain problems can be solved only in rehearsal under the scrutiny of a director and in connection with other actors. Most people know about rehearsals, but too many novices fail to realize the value of solo work on a role.

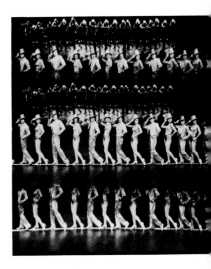

A Chorus Line

Even transforming the self is not the whole of acting. Another significant stage in the development of a role is connections with others: ensemble work. Properly understood, *ensemble work* refers to the living stimuli passed back and forth between actors as they rehearse or work through the play. The interchange amounts to a special sort of willing cooperation, a giving of energy and emotion. Actors often talk about the ability and willingness of particular members of their troupe "to give." A group of actors creating a play develop a special spirit of togetherness. That spirit must be generated first in rehearsals, or else it never can happen in performances. Ensemble acting is co-creation at its human best.

Other periods of rehearsal are for working and polishing the acting. In these times the company, individually and together, tries to speak and physicalize every speech in numerous ways. Each speech deserves more than one different attack before a solution is decided. Actors who set too quickly what they will do in a scene are likely to fail. Only after careful searching and only by intelligent choice can the best details of acting come out. To an observer, such rehearsals may appear slow, but they amount to a tough but fascinating portion of the actor's work.

The final steps of the actor's preparation for a role occur in technical and dress rehearsals. When technical rehearsals begin, the director turns his attention from the actors themselves more to mechanical problems. If the actors have prepared well, technical matters only stimulate their imagination and catapult them further into the world of the play. But during these rehearsals there are bound to be difficulties—a prop breaks, lights need adjustment, or costumes require refitting. Once technical rehearsals are completed, dress rehearsals begin. Ideally, every dress rehearsal is exactly like a performance. The rehearsals seldom get interrupted, but after each, many details are adjusted and many problems solved. One significant occurrence remains for each actor, and it usually happens during the final rehearsals, although sometimes it comes in the first performance—the final blossoming of the characterization. Suddenly the actor and character become one, a living creation. Only then does acting in the true sense of the word really happen.

With the beginning of performances, the actor's fullest creativity and some of the most intense life experiences begin. An actor creates in two ways, which might be called generative and regenerative. The actor assembles the details of a role during generative rehearsals and then lives through the role during the regenerative performances. Both the generation and the regeneration are, though different, creative. When the production goes well, acting is a joy. The reasons are many and have to do with self-fulfillment and communion with others. But when a production goes badly, acting can be very painful. Fortunately, even when overall productions are weak, most actors get a positive feeling from their work. In performances, acting has a strange ritualistic aura for the actor, and most actors experience a feeling of magical power over an audience. Acting is one of the most immediately rewarding of human arts.

Stage fright needs a special note at this point, because so many young actors worry about it, and all actors probably experience it sometime. "Stage fright" usually refers to such overt symptoms as butterflies in the stomach, sweaty palms, cold feet, and yawning. All these symptoms are physical, of course, but psychological fear causes them. As always with fear, stage fright arises because of the unknown. An inexperienced or half-prepared actor is more likely to have stage fright than an experienced or well-prepared actor. In fact, the better the actor's preparation, the less stage fright he is likely to have. In many companies, on opening night no stage fright occurs at all in any of the actors—excitement and a sense of anticipation, yes, but no fear. Opening night means heightened energy because the opening of a new show is a climax. It marks the end of the generative work of rehearsals. Actors with good training and experience worry little about stage fright and talk about it even less.

Sometimes during performances another problem arises for many actors—how to take criticism. During rehearsals an actor becomes accustomed to the comments of the director, and most directors warn actors not to pay attention to the comments of anyone else during this time. But when performances begin, so do critiques, public and private. Every creative artist necessarily holds his work out to the public, and some people quite normally like it and others just as normally do not. Both attitudes can be troublesome. Some unknowing actors find unsophisticated compliments hard to take; some inexperienced actors expect everyone to say something nice. Too much praise can damage the performance of some actors, because they suddenly begin to see themselves as more important than they are. Often actors must also face negative criticism. They should have prepared their roles well enough to believe in them despite any negative comments. Only with the advice and consent of the director should an actor make modifications in his or her performance. Actors learn through experience to take both accolades and slams with a grain of salt. They should listen more to the community of opinion in response to their work than to any single person.

During the run of a play, a production normally gets better and better, provided the director continues to watch and make suggestions and provided the actors take their work seriously. Each actor should pay

Jessica Tandy and Hume Cronyn in *The Gin Game* by D. L. Coburn

attention to audience responses, and often the actor can alter timing slightly to stimulate the audience more surely. Sometimes rhythms change or even bits of business. Scenes or speeches may even get rewritten if the director and playwright think alterations are necessary. The actors get more accustomed to one another, because, somehow, knowing a fellow actor in rehearsal is one thing, whereas knowing the same actor under the scrutiny of the public eye is quite different. During performances the quality of the acting is likely to improve as long as the actors are convinced their creative work is fresh and positive. For amateurs, who normally play only for short runs, each performance is an adventure. For the best professionals, retaining freshness time after time is not difficult at first. But after thirty to ninety performances, the key problem of acting changes. By then all the lines and moves have become so habitual that each actor must concentrate on retaining freshness. Too often even seasoned professionals fall prey to stale performances. At this point in the run of a show, a director often returns to rerehearse scenes and sharpen everyone's attitudes. Despite all the problems, the time of greatest excitement, creativity, and fun for the actors is the time of performance; that's when actors come to life.

WHAT ABOUT A CAREER?

Besides the artistic work, actors must also deal with complex career problems. Every actor's career is different. Therefore, generalizations about the business of acting are difficult. But young actors can benefit by learning about the typical stages in an acting career, the facts of job hunting, and the circumstances of the American theatrical marketplace.

Most acting careers go through at least four stages. First, as an untrained amateur, the actor needs good teachers and the chance to act in any production at all. Early roles are likely to be small, but the actor simply needs time on stage. College theatre departments are good places to begin. The second stage in an acting career is the developmental stage. Here, actors often hit a plateau when their experience fails to match what they know or think they know. Apt places for working through this stage are graduate departments in large universities, summer stock companies, and semiprofessional groups. Third, an actor who has survived long enough to pass through the first two stages now needs professional seasoning. Often this means finding jobs in small professional groups, in touring companies, or perhaps even in television. In each stage the actor usually must start at the bottom again with small roles and work up to larger ones. The actor who continues to survive eventually passes into the fourth realm of steadily working actors. It contains a rather small group of artists with generally excellent capabilities, but anyone who works hard enough and long enough can get there. Also, it takes a little luck.

Some basic facts about acting careers come as answers to the following questions. For a career does an actor have to go to New York? Yes and no. There are more jobs for actors, more productions going on in the confines of New York City than anywhere in the world. Most professional companies go there for casting because the talent pool is so large. But young actors have the most success getting work in New York after they have training and experience enough to make them genuinely professional in their craftsmanship. Careers often start and grow outside of New York, but the best ones usually demand some time there.

Does an actor need an agent? In New York and Los Angeles agents are generally necessary. How does an actor get an agent? The best way is to be recommended by another working actor associated with that agent. But there are other approaches, too. Young people often put together showcase productions Off Off Broadway for the sake of attracting the attention of good agents. How does an actor get a job in professional repertory companies, alternative theatres, and summer stock? By auditioning! As the beginning actor grows in experience, he learns more and more about the how and when of auditions.

What's the key factor in getting started in an acting career? It is contacts. All actors depend totally on the people they know for information and recommendations about work in the theatre. The greater the number of solid contacts an actor can establish the better. Contacts come in strange ways. Sometimes a friend of a friend can help. Often the very people an actor works with in one production become the ones who can help him or her find work a year or two later. Good contacts are one of the keys to a successful acting career, and for the actor who looks for them good contacts are available everywhere.

What about unions? Generally speaking, theatre companies fall into one of two broad categories: professional and amateur. A professional company is normally one that employs members of Actors' Equity Association or apprentices. Of course, some nonprofessional theatres pay actors modest salaries, but most do not. Nearly all film and television actors, other than students practicing in university situations, are paid, and most are members of the Screen Actors Guild (SAG) or the American Federation of Television and Radio Artists (AFTRA). Often, for a novice, union membership appears to be a catch-22. The young actor can't get hired as a nonunion member, and he can't join a union without having a professional job. Most unions purposely establish barriers to membership in order to protect its members from overwhelming competition. The truth is, however, that when a young performer has the talent, gifts, or connections to be hired professionally, the unions are not difficult career barriers. For a given production or season, each professional company can hire a quota of nonunion actors, and when they are hired, those actors may earn points toward union membership or else may be required to join immediately. Appendix I of this book lists the various theatrical and film unions and their addresses. Most of the unions have membership information available.

go Buchanan

An example of an actor's photo and résumé

Julie Harris, Ethel Waters, and Brandon de Wilde in *The Member of the Wedding* **by Carson McCullers**

As young actors contemplate a career, they need to make a careful self-analysis. Certain personal qualities are essential for any actor who wants to work successfully in the theatre. A novelist must sell a book, a painter a painting, and a musician his skills with an instrument. But, in a unique manner, actors must sell themselves; so every actor needs to take a long look at the self he or she is trying to sell. Some of a person's qualities can perhaps be adjusted—for example, losing weight—and others acquired—for instance, learning to move freely—while others cannot be altered—basic body type. Some people consider actors to be ego-centered. Self-contemplation is essential for every actor, but, of course, conceit is not.

What is acting talent? And who has it? Certain factors are good indicators—appearance, voice, sensitivity, discipline, self-confidence, friendliness, grit, intelligence, and imagination. The more striking an actor's appearance, the better, but every actor needs to consider what roles he or she is physically suited to play. Also, the actor needs a good basic voice. Sensitivity is the ability to feel for others; without this capacity few actors do well. Discipline refers to the person's willingness to work long hours for little pay. Self-confidence is essential because the actor is so often under the scrutiny of directors and audiences. An actor also needs to be friendly and able to live easily with many other people. Grit refers to the quality necessary to keep going even when one's career seems impossible. What about intelligence? Some directors say they do not like actors who intellectualize too much, and some good actors did not make very good grades in school. But creative intelligence never hurt any actor, and worldly wisdom never hurt anyone. Imagination is essential, of course, especially for self-transformation and the manipulation of emotional life. All these things and more amount to acting talent.

An acting career is always unpredictable. It is unique among all human pursuits especially in terms of pay, unemployment, permanence, and security. Actors the world over, indeed all theatre artists, tend to work hard for relatively little pay. Sometimes they must hold another job for enough money to survive, and they often work at other jobs between roles in theatre. Today television, radio, and films furnish a large part of most actors' incomes. By combining theatre with media and activities some actors earn a good living, and a few even become wealthy. But unemployment is a frequent fact of life for actors. There is no tenure in theatre, no permanence. In an actor's world, security does not exist. Indeed, many an actor's career is short, since looks, personalities, and fortunes change. By middle-class standards an acting career is no career at all. Perhaps that explains the shocked faces of so many parents when sons or daughters announce their intentions of becoming actors. Nevertheless, the personal, human rewards for living a life of human development in pursuit of a special sort of living creativity are worth the struggle, the impermanence, and the insecurity. Actors have to keep moving—looking for work, finding a new company, or touring. They move from role to role and place to place. Actors are contemporary gypsies, and their careers are as fleeting as life itself. Perhaps therein lies the excitement and value of being an actor.

The final consideration about acting goes beyond the actor's concentration on self, the work on a role, or the difficulties of a career. Ultimately, acting is special because of the connections between acting and life itself. There is a direct relationship between an actor's life experience and abilities as an actor. Just living provides an actor with what Tyrone Guthrie, a famous British director, called "weight on stage." The more varied and extensive an actor's life experiences, the more credibility, maturity, and truth he brings to the roles he plays. Every actor, of whatever age or level of experience utilizes his or her own life experiences—sensations, feelings, and thoughts—in order to create roles in the theatre. Each actor's experiences are different, and for each actor the manner of storing or using those experiences is different. Thus, generalizations about how actors utilize life experiences never seem to work for every one of them. But somehow the actor takes a role in a play, learns the essential circumstances from a director, and then combines role and circumstances with self in a strange, creative amalgam. The mixture occurs psychologically, is revealed physically, and suddenly comes into being before an audience. Every actor draws from real life to make a special life, a new life, a life more real and more intense when he or she steps onto the stage. Acting is life intensified.

Actors simultaneously transform themselves and open their own persona to public view. Using playwrights' and directors' guidelines, actors imagine themselves changed, and for a time onstage they do indeed transform themselves internally and externally. Still, when genuine actors take the stage, somehow they reveal the very core of their being—if they are acting as best they can. When an actor shows off, it's obvious, and most audiences do not like it. But when an actor holds back, is afraid, or puts up internal barriers, fewer people can tell what's wrong, but even unsophisticated viewers can notice a difference. During a performance an actor's attitude toward people and toward life itself get exposed clearly and surely. Every actor must learn to be open and honest. People in audiences have spent all their lives learning how to read other people, and they respond to the actor's very being. The live communication between actors and audiences is special. It never happens in a film or on television, but it always occurs in the theatre. Actors are the life of the theatre, and their encounter with audiences is the key to its wondrousness.

The Maids by Jean Genet, Indiana University

8 The Scenic Artists

Theatre at its best requires the efforts of many different artists, and some of the most important ones provide the visual and aural elements of a production. Many talented designers work in the theatre creating the scenery, costumes, sound, and lighting so necessary for a play to come to life. But when talented artists gather to work on a single project, they face problems of communication and focus. How can each aspect of a production be designed, constructed, and added so that the whole appears to have a single vision? In theatres in most of the world, directors still act as the key coordinators, but in Europe contemporary theorists have developed the concept of "scenography," the work of achieving artistic unity in theatrical productions.

This chapter examines the particular functions, special talents, and individual work of the various theatre designers. It examines the co-creative process by which their separate efforts are brought together, and it provides some principles and criteria for evaluating their work.

STAGE AND COSTUME DESIGNERS

Sometimes in European theatrical productions a master designer, or scenographer, is responsible for all the elements of visual and aural design. But in most American productions the work of designing stage sets, properties, costumes, makeup, lighting, and sound is divided among several people. Sometimes because of an individual's talents or because of budget limitations, one person takes on two or more of these functions. Often a scene designer also plans the properties, a costumer oversees the makeup, and a lighting designer attends to the sound effects. This section and the next introduce the work of each kind of designer separately, and the two sections briefly explain the activities required of the many technicians and crew people who help any theatre production come into being.

A scene designer, in cooperation with a director, envisions the stage setting for a production, plans it, and oversees the work of bringing it into being. The process of visualization usually begins with an analysis of the play and the generation of mental images associated with a play's environment and its required actions. The designer refines the images into an overall vision of the setting and then makes sketches and eventually renders them as drawings, paintings, or three-dimensional models. Next come working drawings that detail the construction of each requisite item. Working closely with a technical director, the designer helps supervise the construction of the whole setting and in the case of small

Stage technicians prepare the set for Shakespeare's *Love's Labor's Lost*, Yale Repertory Theatre

119

**Jo Mielziner's scene
design for *Winterset* by
Maxwell Anderson**

theatre companies actually helps build it. The technical director, or TD,
of most theatres is in charge of all shop construction and is a person of
significance to the entire operation, especially in his multiple functions
of budgeting, purchasing, organizing, and supervising. If detailed painting is required, the designer often does the job. In late technical and
dress rehearsals, the designer joins the technical director in looking after
final details, adjusting the setting to the other elements of the production,
and making sure the run crews execute the scene shifts properly. In
technical and dress rehearsals and in performances, these crews, under
the direction of the stage manager, shift and maintain the scenery and
properties.

The stage setting ultimately makes a symbolic impact on audiences,
and with that in mind, the scene designer must consider broadly both
the style and the type of setting that might best serve the play. The style
of the setting has to do with the way it creates the reality of the places
in the play. It may offer the illusion of a realistic locale, for example, two
back porches with a bit of yard separating them for William Inge's play
Picnic; or it might be quite abstract and nonillusory, perhaps a mere set
of platforms for a production of Shakespeare's *Hamlet*.

Most stage settings contain some degree of abstraction, some use of
suggestion, if only in the selective treatment of detail. How scenery is
generally executed varies greatly. Some common types of sets are box,

fragmentary, constructivist, symbolist, distorted, painted, or minimalist.

Although a designer employs numerous design principles while devising a setting, the most important one is the transformation of space. Because a stage is primarily a place for actors, a magical space in which certain acts occur, the designer needs somehow to transform it into a fitting symbolic environment. Other design principles serve that one. The designer marshals concepts of line, mass, form, shape, texture, color, and motion, all for the sake of the symbolic transformation. If the design works, the spectators are immediately convinced, the atmosphere seems right, and their attention easily focuses on the actors. When the design doesn't work, then nothing seems visually right about the production.

Scene design also has a practical side. A designer must be a master of materials, tools, and budgets. For example, he must be able, when desirable, to make full use of hard scenery (wood, metal, plastic) or soft scenery (cloth, rope, scrim). He needs to be mindful of the potentials of traditional and modern tools, understanding the effects possible with such materials as wood, conduit, or Styrofoam. Every setting also has a specific budget, and the designer must be able to conceive all that's required and have it completed within the specified financial limits. Perhaps most important, the designer needs to be adept at designing settings that the available work force can execute in the time available.

The properties designer is usually responsible for all of a production's portable items, particularly the furniture and the specific things that the actors handle. In most productions a properties master must find—borrow, buy, or rent—the required items. For example, a play by A. R. Gurney, Jr., called *The Dining Room* needs a dining room table, chairs, buffet, and six place settings. But sometimes a production requires unusual properties that cannot readily by found. In that case, a designer may have to envision, sketch, and make drawings for the construction of a particular item. For example, Dario Fo's play *We Won't Pay! We Won't Pay!* requires a coffin, and if it can't be found, then the production company must construct it. Properties requirements vary from production to production, but always someone must be responsible for finding or constructing them. The key principles for properties are credibility and functionality. Because in theatre each detail is so important, every

The properties shop of the Guthrie Theatre

Ming Cho Lee's stage design for *Electra* by Sophocles

prop must be just right or the entire production may suffer the loss of audience acceptance. Ultimately, each prop becomes a symbol, not only representing a thing, but also suggesting other visual or emotional values. For example, the box of gold in Molière's *The Miser* is his treasure chest, but it also suggests excessive materialism or perhaps awe-inspiring greed. Thus properties often carry an unusual burden of signification.

A costume designer faces many problems similar to the others as well as some unique ones. For the costumer a mastery of universal design

Bus Stop by William Inge, Brown County Playhouse

factors—such as line, mass, texture, value, and color—is essential. But three concerns of the costume designer are particularly crucial, and all three have to do with the actor. First, a costume assists an actor in the creative transformation of a person into a character. The costume provides the actor with heightened visual transformation, because all the details of dress together makes a symbolic impact on a viewer. Second, each costume profoundly affects the movements of the actor. Every item of dress encourages or forces the actor to move in a certain manner. Third, each costume must somehow blend with all the other design elements, achieving the desired degree of harmony. Costumes transform, affect, and integrate the actors. Functionally, each costume works *with* the actor.

When a costumer studies a play, certain key questions lead to functional and appropriate design decisions. What are the given circumstances of time, place, and milieu for each character? What are the character's physical characteristics—sex, age, size, and manner of moving? What are the character's psychological and emotional traits? What is his or her function in the play? Also some extrinsic questions are necessary. How should each costume be coordinated with the rest? How will it blend with the other visual factors, especially the setting and the lighting? Which actor will play the role? All these questions and more need to cross a costumer's mind.

Most plays demand that a costume designer be aware of the social factors of clothing and of the history of human dress. In most human societies, clothes for a certain occasion tend to signify a person's sex, occupation, personality, independence, and status. The modifications in human dress from century to century, even from decade to decade, are significant. Even though spectators are seldom experts, costumes are one of the best indicators of the period of a play, and in most audiences there are some viewers who know historical details. Of course, most designers take liberties with historical accuracy for the sake of symbolic visual effect and a concern for contemporary taste. Often stylization or exaggeration of line, color, or detail is necessary in a given design. Nevertheless, each costume designer must carefully consider clothing theory and historical accuracy of dress.

Specialists in the area of costuming distinguish between costume designers and costumers. The former is concerned mainly with the design process, and the latter with costume construction and maintenance.

For the costume designer, the design process has many complex stages. After analyzing the play and hearing a director's suggestions, the designer conceives each costume, renders a costume plate to illustrate it, and usually supervises its acquisition or construction. Sometimes costumes can be purchased, borrowed, or rented. Most theatres collect old clothes for use in plays, and they also store the costumes made for each production in order to use them again in the future. But in many

A costumer builds a costume

Costumes by Robbie Stanton for *The Madwoman of Chaillot* by Jean Giraudoux

cases a costume must be constructed. Then a costumer must find or make a pattern, purchase appropriate material, cut the cloth correctly, fit the costume, and sew the whole thing together. If costume crews are available, then usually the costumer supervises the work. Each costume must, of course, be fitted to the particular actor; fitting is not merely a matter of tailoring but a process of interaction and character development with the actor. It is a time when the costumer and actor are co-creators. Then during dress rehearsals and performances, crew people must see that the costumes are kept clean and neat. When the production is over, the costumer oversees the final cleaning and return or storage of every piece. The entire process is long and difficult, but without costumes actors would make a bare impact indeed.

Makeup is usually necessary in the theatre for two reasons, because the intense lighting makes anyone's skin look pale, and because most actors wish to transform themselves visually into the characters they play. Since stage actors become quite expert in makeup techniques for themselves, in realistic modern plays no makeup designer may be necessary. Each actor merely talks with the director or costume designer about the appropriate color and style of makeup to be applied. Sometimes, however, makeup is more complicated and actual designing is necessary. In that case the costume designer or a makeup specialist designs the requisite makeups and renders them on charts or color plates. Always in dress rehearsals someone needs to check the appropriateness of each actor's makeup.

THE ELECTRONIC DESIGNERS

Because lighting is one of the wonders of the modern stage, lighting designers have become ever more important to the theatre. For nearly two thousand years, producers had to depend on the sun to illuminate their productions, and so from ancient Greece to Elizabethan England plays were offered mainly in the daytime. Eventually, candles, torches, and gaslight came into use; as a result many theatres burned down. Today, modern electronic technology provides ever increasing potentialities for the generation and modulation of light. Some of the highly functional items of equipment in modern theatres are high-intensity spotlights, color media, projectors, and computer-controlled solid-state dimmer boards. Special-effects machines create such visual images as moving clouds, rainbows, or abstract shapes.

Because both the stage setting and the costumes need illumination, a lighting designer must work in close association with the other designers. Furthermore, because among all the design elements the lighting is the most mobile, the director is also highly involved. The lighting designer, then, not only needs to be good at his or her own craft but also must understand the other areas. Also, the lighting designer should be able to communicate with the other members of the production's conceptual team. Most important, he or she must concentrate the mobility and expressiveness of light on the actor in the production space. Light is crucial to human awareness of the three-dimensional nature of space, and it is equally crucial to perception of movement within that space. In the theatre, light even has the power to suggest time and its passage. The lighting designer can significantly affect the flow of audience attention and feeling.

Similar to the other theatre artists, lighting designers must command both the craft and the aesthetics of their art. First, they must know enough about electricity and the equipment to utilize it well and safely. They must then think of such traditional lighting factors as direction, intensity,

Josef Svoboda's production design for *Owners of the Keys*

125

and color. Some of the other major concerns of the lighting designer are clarity, visibility, pattern, integration of areas, movement, rhythm, mood, time, and overall impact. They must remain mindful of the effect the lights are having on the planes, textures, and colors of the settings and the actors in costume. Also, for each play the lighting designer must take a unique approach, occasionally approximating everyday life but usually working more imaginatively.

The procedure of a lighting designer often includes seven steps: analysis of the play, conceptualization of the design, development of a light plot, writing the cues, preparing and hanging the instruments, setting intensity levels, and blending the lighting with the other production elements. Often the designer helps oversee or train the crew people who hang the instruments and operate the lighting equipment during the run of a show.

Basic lighting equipment includes instruments, battens, color media, and dimmers. Instruments come in many sizes and serve many functions; some of the most common types are spotlights, projectors, area lights, and strip lights. Spotlights have a housing, a lamp, a reflector, and a lens. Battens are long pipes, suspended at various places in the theatre, on which lighting instruments, curtains, or scenery can be hung. Some battens are permanently mounted above or behind the audience; more mobile ones are normally placed above, behind, or at the sides of the stage. A color medium is any transparent material used for filtering stage light. Although colored glass is used in some strip lights, most instruments employ gel, a transparent sheet of plastic, or cellulose acetate, dyed with color. Although cheaper than glass, gel is more perishable, but most designers prefer gel because it is readily available. Many different types of dimmers are in use today. For theatre purposes, a number of them are put together in a bank. A plugging panel provides the designer with the opportunity to regroup instruments during the course of a production. Dimmer boards, of course, provide operator control of individual dimmers or groups of them.

Most of the sounds in nonmusical theatre productions come from the actors, but often plays call for incidental music or for atmospheric sound effects. Naturally, a staff of vocal and instrumental experts bring their artistry to bear on musical productions. But for straight plays a specialist in sound must often design one or more tapes to be used with a production. Occasionally, the sound designer and the director enlist the aid of a composer and live musicians to help create a sound track. Sometimes one of the other designers, often the lighting designer, takes care of the planning and execution of sounds for a production. But most theatres employ a specialist in sound equipment and resources.

Sound designers face multiple problems. In the first place, they must be well-acquainted with sound equipment, not only that which the particular theatre owns but also with what better units—such as preamplifiers, tape decks, or speakers—might be borrowed, rented, or bought. In addition, they ought to be well-acquainted with resources for music and sound effects. They need to know many different musical styles, periods, and artists. Some plays call for classical orchestral music, others for

A lighting control board, Long Wharf Theatre

popular or contemporary music. Sound designers must also be inventive enough to find or create unusual sound effects, such as thunder, gunshots, trucks passing, wind, chickens crowing—whatever the production needs. In some cases they have to solve electronic problems, and in others they must deal with problems of acoustics. Inventiveness is a key quality for those theatre people who work with sound.

Following a design procedure similar to the others and in concert with the director, the sound specialist studies the entire production and fulfills

A sound designer at work

its required or suggested needs. He or she must also study the play, decide upon the noises or melodies to be employed, devise and record them, write the cues, prepare the equipment, set volume levels, and fine tune all the sounds during dress rehearsals. One or more operators then take over the task of running the sound equipment during production time. In addition, sound crews are often responsible for documenting the production by recording one or more performances, and they must maintain the electronic system within the theatre by which cues are broadcast in various areas of the theatre building. Thus the work of sound specialists in the theatre is most complex.

Ultimately, the effectiveness of recorded sound as a production element depends largely on the equipment available to the designer. Sophisticated sound equipment is more and more common today. Contemporary electronic innovations have made it more possible than over before to record, to reproduce, and to control sounds with increasingly good fidelity. Part of the sound designer's job is to try to avoid distortion and electronic noise in the sound system. Some of the basic items of sound equipment are microphones, preamplifiers and mixer-amplifiers, power amplifiers, loudspeakers, tape recorders, and turntables. Many theatres also have such items as patch bays, equalizers, reverberation devices, digital sound mixers, and synthesizers. The sound designer should be expert with each of these pieces of equipment.

The two foregoing sections have focused on the designers of settings, properties, costumes, makeup, lighting, and sound, but other creative people are often needed in technical production. For example, theatre companys frequently employ engineers and technologists to solve problems about the construction or execution of devices for use onstage. Often the people who build the sets, props, or costumes are as creative—certainly they work as hard—as those who design them. Many specialists contribute to the overall production, such people as graphics designers who create posters and program covers, photographers who take publicity and production shots, pyrotechnic experts who handle fires and explosions, and even shoemakers who create special footwear. The variety of artists who create the visual and aural milieu of a production is endless.

THE CO-CREATIVE PROCESS

Theatre requires the talents of many specialized artists, but all of them focus their efforts on the final product: the play as actors experience it before an audience. The best theatre people know that the result of their combined labors is always greater than any of their individual contributions, and they are willing to create together—cooperating, integrating, and blending. But when a production works, somehow everyone is still

A stage crew constructs a set

able to achieve personal goals and to attain an inner sense of personal fulfillment. When talented actors, designers, and technicians work harmoniously together under intelligent leadership, the results are aesthetically rewarding to all concerned. This section traces the necessary co-creative process.

A director usually develops a concept and with a producer coordinates the work of all the designers, shop supervisors, technicians, and crews, so the entire production projects a singular vision of the play. It's the director's job to make sure the final product has unity, variety, appropriateness, and the desired aesthetic effect. A production manager arranges a series of meetings and individual conferences to influence, encourage, or modify the work in each of the technical or design areas. Some directors insist that their ideas for each of the areas be strictly executed. But the best contemporary directors trust the talents of their designers and work more cooperatively with them. When genuine co-creativity occurs, theatre is likely to be at its best. As the leader of the production group, the director is particularly responsible for analyzing the play and establishing the basic interpretative approach for everyone. He also determines many of the basic requirements in each of the areas. All the director's ideas about the production, taken together, make up the director's concept, which should be the key to the entire production.

In early production meetings the director sets forth the concept, and the designers explain their ideas. Often useful discussions take place in which new ideas are generated, changes made, and difficulties identified. Some typical concerns of the group might be the range of colors to be used in the designs, the method of making transitions between scenes, and the schedule for planning and executing each production element. The early production meetings are normally held long before the actors go into rehearsal or the crews begin construction. A great deal of careful planning must first take place.

Next comes a period of research, thought, and innovation. The director and each of the designers have probably done some research even before the meetings begin, but now they focus on and share certain of the most useful sources. Several intermediate production meetings occur in which the director asks for progress reports and the group attacks problems of common concern. Many individual conferences take place as well between the director and each of the designers, and also among the designers themselves. As they work, the designers often compare notes and exchange ideas. Most theatre directors and designers have had experience in several, if not all, the other areas, and so the exchange is often advantageous. A group of creative minds should together be able to generate more useful ideas than could a single individual.

Each of the artists, however, must finally sit down in solitude and render a design. That process naturally demands both craftsmanship and skill. Usually the design work results in such items as sketches, render-

Director Michael Blakemore (left) discusses the Broadway production of Michael Frayn's *Benefactors* with actors Sam Waterson, Glenn Close, Simon Jones, and Mary Beth Hurt

ings (color plates or models), and working drawings (perhaps patterns or plugging charts). Then the director must eventually approve the design in each area before any work can begin. Each of the designers must know the detailed plans of all the others. Without continual communication and overall cooperation, a production with a singular vision is impossible.

Next, during the construction period, many other people become involved. In the areas of scenery, costumes, and lighting, a group of people is necessary. How many people work on properties and sound depends on the size of the theatre. In major professional companies every technical area has a construction head and a working crew, but in many noncommercial theatres one person handles props and another takes care of sound. Most theatres have a technical director who is in charge of construction in the scene shop. He or she takes the plans of the scene and property designers and with the help of construction crews executes them, eventually putting the whole setting together onstage. Then, in most instances, the scenic designer and a special crew paint the set. Costume shops also have costumers (supervisors), specialists, and crews. Few human endeavors are so strangely rewarding as joining with others to help create a production. In some small companies everybody pitches in on all the jobs—actors work in the shops and technical people sometimes perform. In any case, most construction periods seem all too short, and the final deadlines always arrive too soon.

In technical rehearsals the various pieces of the production are put together for the first time. The intense and often frenetic work of coordination happens in a rush. The set is finally up and usually being painted. The final versions of the properties appear. During several intensive sessions the cues and levels are set for lights and sound. Also some new members of the production group gather; these are the "run crews," the people who will shift the scenery, look after the costumes, help with costume changes, set out and put away the props, operate the lighting board, and run the sound equipment. All the designers come to see that their particular functions are fulfilled, that their realms of design work satisfactorily. Many final adjustments have to be made—in everything. Although the director remains in control, at the time of technical rehearsals a stage manager takes immediate charge of actors and crews. That leaves the director free to oversee the coordination of all the practical and artistic elements. During this period tempers are sometimes short, and everyone's inner tensions seem to rise. But the climax is near.

If the technical rehearsals are effective, and if each of the construction crews meets its deadline, then dress rehearsals are the time for fine tuning everything. In every dress rehearsal the production should look and sound as much as possible as it will opening night. Most important, during these rehearsals every artistic element, every technical detail must be right for the actors who have to live in the set, move in the costumes, handle the props, and respond to the lights and sound. Most productions go through several dress rehearsals, at least three or four. Usually the first one is fairly uncertain and filled with mistakes, with actors not concentrating and crews missing cues. But in a carefully planned production, the final dress rehearsal usually turns out to be good. Often for the final dress rehearsal the director even invites a few friends to give the actors a hint of an audience. Still the tension is mounting and the excitement growing, because opening night looms only 24 hours away. That's the climax toward which everyone works.

Opening nights in the theatre are always exhilarating. Before the curtain rises, the run crews are busily efficient, and the stage manager intense. The designers and construction crews are mostly worn out and

An opening night at the Metropolitan Opera

perhaps already working on another production. But the actors are full of energy and excitement. How about the director? Well, the director usually feels suspended. After assuring and reassuring everyone for weeks that his or her concept will work, now the director faces the time of truth. Only when an audience arrives, witnesses, and responds can anyone tell for certain about the quality of the production. Fortunately, most audiences are marvelously sympathetic, or else they wouldn't be there. Even for productions that aren't so good, opening nights are mostly happy climaxes to all the work. During the run of the show, the actors get over their nervousness, adjust to the audiences, and usually improve. The running crews get the routines of the show down pat, and if all goes well, the production gets better and better. The final performance is a climax, too. When the actors experience the play for the last time, it's an occasion for celebration, but it's a little sad, too, because the time has come for the whole thing to disappear and become merely a set of memories.

Even after the final performance, though, the work isn't over. There's still the "strike." After the final curtain falls or the final blackout takes place, then working crews strike the set, take down the lights, and prepare the costumes for cleaning and eventual storage. In amateur companies everyone pitches in to help; actors and technicians join up to tear it all down. Some of the props, a few items of scenery, and most of the costumes go into storage, but everything else gets dismantled or thrown away. Nothing looks so empty as a stage after the set has been struck and everyone is gone.

Fortunately perhaps, by the time the final performance of a production occurs, most technical theatre people are already involved with new projects. The designers and construction crews who work for an entire season with a company always have another show to plan, another set of plans to execute. Indeed, those people must take care to organize their work over the months so that it won't overwhelm all those involved. Nevertheless, the work still seems endless, and the new deadlines draw near. One fact about theatre production persists through it all, the one circumstance that's always true—other people are always there. Only in the theatre, perhaps, do so many different designers, technicians, actors, and crews work together so intimately and so intensely for artistic ends. Theatre's special circumstance is co-creativity.

EVALUATING THE RESULTS

What are the major criteria for evaluating a production's visual and aural aspects? It's easy enough for anyone to watch a play and say, "Oh, I liked the setting, but I didn't like the costumes." Or perhaps someone else exclaims, "The lighting was good, but the music was awful." Audience members naturally have a right to their opinions. Such remarks

Guys and Dolls

133

indicate a general response, but not a profound one. Such reactions don't really explain much about the speaker's evaluation of the production. What are the reasons for liking or not liking any aspect of a production? In the process of living, each person acquires a store of ideas about and experiences with art. Whether or not they realize it consciously, this mental collection of sentiments becomes the key to their reactions.

To complicate the matter further, art makes a dual impact on human beings. It is discursive and nondiscursive. Those words explain how art communicates with people. Discursive communication means the conscious or logical transfer of information. Nondiscursive communication means emotional or intuitive suggestion. Most dramatic art is a combination of the two. Plays contain discursive expression so that audiences can follow the story, understand a scene, or comprehend a speech. But productions contain even more nondiscursive expression in the ambiguous hints about human feelings. Spectators or critics can analyze discursive features of theatre with some ease, but the nondiscursive factors are more difficult to analyze. The visual and aural aspects of any production tend to be planned discursively, but they make an impact nondiscursively. Nevertheless, such qualities as ambiguity and suggestivity can be identified and to some degree understood.

Some of the chief criteria to apply to the work of the scenic artists are unity, functionality, magnitude, and appropriateness. Are all the elements unified? What are the keys to the unity? If everything blends well, what factors are responsible—color, texture, mass, rhythm, or what? Does each element function properly by providing what is essential for the actors? Is there anything unnecessary or nonfunctional? Does each item have the proper magnitude (size or emphasis) in relation to itself, to the other elements, and to the actors? Does anything attract undue attention? Is any detail harmfully out of proportion? Finally, and most important, what is the quality of beauty that results in the whole work of art? What emotional responses does it engender? How do each of the elements contribute or fail to contribute to the overall effect?

Basic questions about the scenery have to do with its design and execution. Did the scenery create an effective environment for the action of the play? Could the play have happened somewhere else? Was the scenery believable, abstract, or good? Did the scenery come to be symbolic of the play's action or circumstances? Was all the stage space utilized effectively? Was the floor plan reasonable and functional? To what degree were diagonals and curves emphasized in the channeling of the actor movements? Or did the setting force everything to look flat and less interesting? Was color employed emotionally, and did the colors go well with the costumes? Were there any interesting textures, and how much variety was apparent among them? Did the furniture look right, or was it merely the aged "stuff" of amateur theatre? Were the properties handled by the actors credible? Ultimately, did the setting sometimes disappear because it was so well unified with the action?

Criteria for evaluating the costumes and makeup can begin with an estimation of their overall impact. Taken as a group, did the costumes seem to belong together? In what ways were all the costumes visually

**Left: *Arms and the Man*
by George Bernard
Shaw, University of
Evansville**

**Right: *Tango* by
Slawomir Mrozek,
University of Tulsa**

related to each other—in period, color, texture, line? Was each outfit appropriate to the play's circumstances and to the particular character? Simply speaking, were they credible? But were they also imaginative? How? What factors were repeated in several or most of the costumes? Did the costumes affect the actors' movements appropriately—especially the men's trousers and jackets, the women's skirts, and the entire cast's shoes? Was any makeup noticeable? If so, was it supposed to be obvious, like a clown face, or was it just poorly executed? Did the makeup do its job and cause everyone's skin color to look natural in the production's lighting? Were all the actor's eyes carefully made up and thus easy to see? Were the costumes and makeup handled so that eventually they became an integrated and inconspicuous factor in the overall production?

What about the lighting? Lighting makes an intense emotional impact on most people. After a good production, it's often difficult to remember or to explain the effect of the lights. But some questions are good to keep in mind. Did the lighting add to the overall emotional power of each scene? Was the intensity of light balanced well in each scene? Was it varied throughout? Were the actors' faces always clearly illuminated? Did the lighting mold the space and emphasize its cubic volume? Or was it insufficient and pale? Or was it generally so bright that everything looked flat? What about the color of the lighting—too cold, too rich, or just right? Did the lighting make the colors and textures of the costumes and scenery more vivid or muddy? Consider the movement of the lighting. Did the fades up and down call undue attention? Were any mistakes discernible? Were the blackouts the right length, not more than 10 or 15 seconds apiece? And, finally, did the lighting create an satisfactory and suggestive visual atmosphere for the action?

Regarding the sound, one can begin by noting the proportional use of music and environmental sound effects. Judging their effectiveness means asking first about credibility. Was any sound effect phony? Were

Talley's Folly by Lanford Wilson, Wabash College

any of them late or early, or were they all right on cue? Did the music begin at appropriate places? Were all the sounds played at an effective level of loudness? Or did they call undue attention to themselves by beginning at the wrong time or by being too loud? When played before, during, or after a scene, did the music effectively match and support the emotion? Should there have been sound when there was silence, or the other way around? Taken together, did the sounds make an organic effect that harmonized with the whole performance?

A production's overall finish is another matter to note. Although some of the considerations of finish aren't direct results of the scene designers' work, the following matters affect the scenographic impression of the entire performance. Errors in finish are sometimes less the fault of the director than of crews responsible to the designers. Did the production start on time? Were the blackouts quiet, or could actors and technicians be heard stumbling around in the dark? Were the auditorium and the stage clean? (Some sets are supposed to look dirty, but not filthy.) Did all the elements seem finished? Or did some features look only half-done? (Some sets are supposed to suggest more than they show, but what they show should look right.) Were the properties really the right ones or obviously faked? (In comedies, "fakey" props are often part of the fun, but sometimes they just indicate a lazy prop crew.) Ultimately, did every visual and aural element seem somehow to fit into the whole? Did the production have an appropriate "feel" of finish?

The visual and aural world of each play offers artistic opportunities for people with various abilities. All the designers must become adept at handling many traditional design factors, but, of course, each of them needs special skills. For instance, scene designers need the talents of both painters and sculptors along with the crafts of carpenters and metalworkers. Costume designers need an imaginative sense of fashion, and control of style in its many guises. Lighting and sound designers must keep up with the frequent electronic advances of modern science. Nowadays they are all doing more and more of their work on computers. Indeed, contemporary technology constantly provides new materials and devices which inventive designers utilize in dramatic productions. But most significantly, the designers and technical workers join the director and actors to comprise the special co-creative group—the artists of the theatre.

CHAPTER 9 *Musicals Alive*

From the early 1930s to the present, musicals have persisted as one of the most popular types of theatre, and they have developed as a sophisticated dramatic form. Few commentators have adequately expressed the reasons for the growth of musicals in form and in vogue, nor have many theatre observers written about musicals except for reviews and historical summaries. Many theatre people consider musicals as mere popular entertainments rather than as legitimate works of art. Although some musicals may be more show business than art, the question remains—what is the art in musicals?

Audiences throughout the United States and other parts of the world flock to musicals more readily than to most other kinds of theatre. To see people respond to well-produced musicals is to realize their potential for stimulating pleasure. A musical represents a kind of theatre unlike any other. Musicals are also indicative of the startling diversity of theatrical types. During the twentieth century, talented writers, composers, and performers have shown that musicals can be marvelously creative. Also, audiences know that such melodic productions hold a special delight for most human beings. Musicals can be as artistic as any other form of drama, but their material, form, style, and function are unique.

Joseph and the Amazing Technicolor Dream Coat

In order to treat musicals in a thorough if introductory manner, this chapter is divided into four parts. It first sets out a brief background of musical theatre of the past and describes the various sorts of musicals on stage today. Next it explores the creative work of the people behind the scenes. The discussion then turns to the activities of the various performers in musicals. Finally, the chapter presents some principles of dramatic form and style in musicals and identifies some of the most frequently used principles of music and dance.

Whenever considering musicals seriously, any observer must keep in mind that the best musicals in the theatre are not mixtures; they are compounds. Some musicals simply mix drama, music, and dance, but the best ones do more than that. A mixture consists of two or more components that, though combined, retain their separate existence. A compound also contains various components, but they are made to become a well-blended, unique substance. This chapter deals with those musicals that are artistic compounds of drama, music, and dance.

ORIGINS AND VARIETY

From the beginnings of theatre, music and dance have always appeared in combination with the dramatic elements. The classic Greek tragedies, such as those of Aeschylus, when originally performed contained generous amounts of instrumental and choral melody plus choreographed movement. So it was with the origin of comedy. The plays of Aristophanes contained ample music and dance to keep audiences entertained. From ancient Greeks to contemporary Americans, theatre artists have seldom hesitated to blend musical and dance elements into their productions.

To understand the various types of musicals that have appeared and continue to appear in theatres, certain terms are useful. Each term represents a particular combination of the three basic elements—dialogue, song, and dance. A *variety show* is a collection of acts performed during one time span; it has little unity in material, style, or form. A *revue* is an episodic series of sketches (short humorous dialogues) with songs and dances thrown in; its unity is usually stylistic rather than formal. A *musical play* is a conventional drama in which music is used only occasionally. A *musical comedy* is a comedy, usually a farce, with a formal plot and numerous songs and dances that contribute to the development of that plot. Today the term *musical*, used as a noun, means any well-developed drama that uses songs and dances to advance a plot, develop characters, and express feelings; it may be comic, sentimental, or even serious. American theatre artists in particular have developed the musical into a significant form of dramatic art.

Use of the term *musical comedy* to label mixed stage pieces first

Sunday in the Park with George

occurred in America in the early 1870s. E. E. Rice, who created both the text and music of *Evangeline*, wrote that he hoped his production would "foster a taste for musical comedy." George Edwardes, manager of the Gaiety Theatre in London, called his 1893 production of *A Gaiety Girl* "a musical comedy," hoping to distinguish it from the previous burlesques he had produced. Most authorities name *The Black Crook*, which opened on September 12, 1866, in New York, as the first significant American forerunner of what is now musical comedy. It was a fairy tale extravaganza that mixed ballet, spectacle, and operetta, and it set the precedent for the Broadway "leg show" in which the unclothed feminine figure became a central attraction. *The Black Crook* ran for 16 months, was revived often, and toured the United States for more than forty years.

Gypsy

Historians of the theatre usually cite several minor kinds of theatrical entertainments as the forerunners of contemporary musicals: these were extravaganza, pantomime, variety, minstrel, burlesque, vaudeville, follies, farce-comedy, and operetta. During the nineteenth century most of these types were occasionally called musical comedy. An extravaganza, developed especially in France, was originally an imaginative spectacle featuring elaborate sets, costumes, and dances. Pantomimes were popular for a time in England and on the continent; they were elaborate productions without words. Variety, another sort of mixed entertainment, contained dialogue, song, and dance routines.

The minstrel show, one type of variety entertainment, reached a peak of popularity just before the U.S. Civil War. Ed Christy established its three-part structure. In part one came the traditional minstrel olio section of variety entertainment. In part two the fantasia, or free-for-all, featured individual performers and specialties. During part three the performers burlesqued the show's previous materials. Most of the people onstage wore burnt cork on their faces and pretended to be blacks. Minstrel shows persisted in America until the 1930s.

Burlesque refers to several sorts of theatrical shows. At first, it meant a parody or farcical enactment of some well-known play, poem, or novel. John Brougham was a nineteenth-century American writer of burlesques. During the 1860s and 1870s in England and then in the United States, burlesque came to mean a show with girls in scanty costumes who sang and danced plus stand-up comics, often in baggy pants, telling sexual jokes. The female striptease routine did not become one of its principal features until the 1920s in America.

Vaudeville also has a long, complex history. According to David Ewen in *The Story of America's Musical Theater*, vaudeville started in the olio section of minstrel shows when certain cast members were starred in song and dance routines. As a special branch of theatre, Tony Pastor brought vaudeville into vogue in America in the 1860s through the 1880s. Although Pastor was the so-called father of vaudeville, the first known use of the term was on February 23, 1871, in Louisville, Kentucky, when a troupe called itself Sargent's Great Vaudeville Company. Probably the most significant development in theatrical production resulting from vaudeville were the productions of Florenz Ziegfeld. Drawing ideas from American vaudeville and from the *Folies Bergère* of Paris, he organized superb shows—American extravaganzas really—and called them "follies." During the first thirty years of this century, the *Ziegfeld Follies* became legendary.

Farce-comedy, deriving from the Roman comic playwright Plautus, became in the 1870s a common sort of popular entertainment in Great Britain. The Vokes family of England and an American troupe called Salsbury's Troubadours introduced the idea of combining comic plot and variety specialty numbers. In contrast to the comic operas of England, France, and Austria, these shows contained more dialogue and farcical action.

During the 1880s and 1890s European operettas, comic operas, and *opéras bouffes* dominated the American musical stages. Americans enjoyed the fantasy worlds and high spirits of the works by Jacques Offenbach, Johann Strauss II, and especially W. S. Gilbert and A. S. Sullivan. *H.M.S. Pinafore* by Gilbert and Sullivan was perhaps the most popular of all. Opening in America in November of 1878, it became the hit of the era. In one season 90 different companies throughout the country presented *H.M.S. Pinafore*. It was responsible for bringing a large, new American audience into theatres—especially women and children. Before then, most American families did not consider theatre respectable, but Gilbert and Sullivan's productions proved that stage presentations could be wholesome entertainment.

The operettas also led American librettists and composers to copy their success. Two of America's earliest comic operas were Willard Spencer's *The Little Tycoon* and Reginald de Koven's *The Begum*. Victor Herbert, who was the first significant composer for the American musical stage, wrote many beloved operettas, such as *Babes in Toyland* (1903) and *Naughty Marietta* (1910). The primary era of operetta popularity came to a conclusion with the works of Sigmund Romberg, who composed such pieces as *The Student Prince* (1924) and *The Desert Song* (1926). The era of operettas established in American theatre the idea that an evening's entertainment could contain a dramatized story with song, dance, comedy, spectacle, burlesque, and production numbers.

Artists in this country, however, wanted to perfect a distinctly American identity in musical entertainment. Operettas remained too European for many American tastes. The first to give the musical stage a New World identity was George M. Cohan. In the early 1900s his energetic musical productions included *Little Johnny Jones* (1904), *Hello Broadway!* (1914), and *Little Nellie Kelly* (1922). In Cohan's productions the subjects, characters, and idioms were distinctly American. The racy humor and driving tempos are still a part of American show business. Other composers began to develop their own spirit. Composers Jerome Kern and Irving Berlin brought American musicals into even higher repute. Kern developed scores for *Mr. Wix of Wickham* (1904), *Show Boat* (1927), and *Roberta* (1933). Berlin composed such shows as *Watch Your Step* (1914), *Annie Get Your Gun* (1946), and *Call Me Madam* (1950). George Gershwin is another famous American composer of musicals—from *La La Lucille* (1919) to *Porgy and Bess* (1935).

During the early twentieth century certain patterns for musical comedies became traditional. Despite the arbitrary procedures, many of the results were entertaining. The period saw such musicals as *Sally* by Jerome Kern, *Good News* by De Sylva, Brown, and Henderson, *Anything Goes* by Cole Porter, *Oh Kay!* by George Gershwin, and *A Connecticut Yankee* by Rodgers and Hart. The formulas of the early period of musical comedy even produced *Annie Get Your Gun* by Irving Berlin, *Kiss Me, Kate* by Cole Porter, *Guys and Dolls* by Frank Loesser, *Wonderful Town* by Leonard Bernstein, and *The Pajama Game* by Richard Adler and Jerry

Show Boat

Ross. Thus, traditional musical comedy grew into a permanent genre of American theatre.

Periodically, throughout the country, some writers and composers, however, sought to escape tradition and produce musicals more unusual in nature. Writers made a conscious effort to treat earthy subjects more truthfully and from new viewpoints. Directors tried harder to make the new musicals more organic than typical musical comedies. Composers wanted their music to be more integral to the whole. Playwrights and composers attempted to unify everything. They wanted every song, dance, comedy routine, and production of the overall drama to fit together. Among the originators of the "new" musical were Richard Rodgers and Lorenz Hart, with *On Your Toes* and *Pal Joey,* and Jerome Kern, with *Show Boat* and *Music in the Air*. In 1931, *Of Thee I Sing*—written by Morrie Ryskind and George S. Kaufman, composed by Ira and George Gershwin—won the Pulitzer Prize; it was the first musical to receive such high artistic recognition. Other significant productions of the 1930s were Berlin's *Face the Music* (1932) and *As Thousands Cheer* (1933). Ballet was first used as an integral element in *On Your Toes* (1936), a musical written by Rodgers and Hart; also, their *Boys From Syracuse* was the first musical based on a Shakespearean play.

The first choreographers to stage entire productions were George Balanchine and Agnes de Mille. Their names stand out in the mid-twentieth

143

century as innovators who made dance an organic part of musicals. In the last half of the century, more and more choreographers are also directors—Jerome Robbins (*West Side Story*), Michael Kidd (*Li'l Abner*), Bob Fosse (*Redhead*), Gower Champion (*Bye Bye Birdie*), and Michael Bennett (*A Chorus Line*).

Oklahoma!, produced in 1943, marked the maturation of the American musical. Drawing from the play *Green Grow the Lilacs* by Lynn Riggs, Rodgers and Hammerstein wrote the book and music for *Oklahoma!* Rouben Mamoulian directed and Agnes de Mille choreographed it. Each of them—Riggs, Rodgers, Hammerstein, Mamoulian, and de Mille—made unique contributions to the production. In *Oklahoma!* all the elements blended into a dramatic unity that was thoroughly entertaining. Rodgers and Hammerstein developed the potentials of musicals even further in such hit productions as *Carousel* (1945), *South Pacific* (1949), and *The Sound of Music* (1959).

Of course, many artists besides those named contributed to the growth of the musical. During the span of the twentieth century, musical scripts have improved dramatically—especially in the use of motivation and story. Stylistically the productions have improved in credibility and spectacle. Among the most important musicals since *Oklahoma!* are *Street Scene* (1947) and *Lost in the Stars* (1949), both composed by Kurt Weill; *The Most Happy Fella* (1956), by Frank Loesser; and *West Side Story* (1957), by Leonard Bernstein. The musical became even more eloquent

Oklahoma

with *My Fair Lady* (1956) and *Camelot* (1960), both by Frederick Loewe with book and lyrics by Alan Jay Lerner. *The Man of La Mancha, The Fantasticks, Oliver, Brigadoon, Hello, Dolly!, Mame, Cabaret, Fiorello,* and *George M* are also notable. *Hair* caught the spirit of the 1960s, and *Annie* was one of the strongest hits of the 1970s. In the 1980s, some of the noteworthy musicals are *A Chorus Line, La Cage aux Folles, 42nd Street,* and *Big River*. The musical persists as a powerful and unique theatrical form.

BEHIND THE SCENES

Musicals, like other sorts of drama, are created in three stages. A few creative men and women find and develop original ideas; a larger number of people gather to rehearse and build the show; and a specialized group performs it. All three stages in a musical's development require shared creativity. In stage one, at least one person and usually more are involved in bringing a book, lyrics, and music into being. Stage two demands the work of directors, designers, technical crews, and performers. In stage three the actors, singers, and dancers join forces with the run crews to recreate the show for each performance.

The whole thing begins when someone gets a germinal idea. Sometimes an expert in musical productions conceives an absolutely original idea, but more often today the basic idea for a musical occurs when someone spots an already existing drama or other piece of writing that can be transformed into the book for a musical. For example, *My Fair Lady* came from George Bernard Shaw's play *Pygmalion*. Such musicals as *The Fantasticks, Hello, Dolly!,* and *Kiss Me, Kate* also came from plays. Some musicals even came from films; examples are *Applause, Little Shop of Horrors,* and *Promises, Promises*. Novels and stories provide materials for some—such as *Cabaret, Oliver,* and *Camelot*. A few even originate in comic strips—such as *Li'l Abner, You're a Good Man Charlie Brown,* and *Annie*. *Godspell* and *Jesus Christ Superstar* grew out of the Bible. Some are based on biographies; *Gypsy* was about Gypsy Rose Lee, *Funny Girl* about Fanny Brice, and *George M* about George M. Cohan. A few start with an original idea never before dramatized. Alan Jay Lerner conceived *Brigadoon*, Michael Stewart *Bye Bye Birdie*, and Stephen Sondheim *Company*.

A dramatist writes the basic script for a musical, called the book. Whether based on someone else's story, play, or biography, the dramatist still must perfect a plot, develop characters, express ideas, write dialogue, and describe spectacle. The changes that a dramatist makes in transforming a novel into a musical book are extensive because the magnitude and means of expression of the two media are so different. A writer who conceives an idea and writes it from scratch may be more totally original, but his creativity is not necessarily greater. Award givers today have overstressed the idea of adaptation as being only semicreative. A dramatist is someone who takes materials, any materials, and develops them into fresh dramatic form, and that is what the writer of a musical book must accomplish. A dramatist, then, is responsible for developing the dialogue and stage directions for a musical.

The lyrics sometimes come from the hand of the writer of the book, sometimes from the musical composer, and occasionally from a person who simply serves as lyricist. For *Brigadoon* Alan Jay Lerner wrote both the book and the lyrics. Jerry Herman created the music and lyrics for *Hello, Dolly!,* and Joe Darion wrote only the lyrics for *Man of La Mancha.* Just as the writer of a musical's book must know and use principles of playwriting, so the writer of the lyrics must know and use the principles of lyric poetry. The lyricist sometimes writes the words before the music is composed, but most often he or she is well acquainted with the story and with each song before starting to develop a specific lyric. The lyricist writes the poetry.

The composer of a musical is, of course, the person who creates the music. He or she is responsible for the songs and the development of the entire score. The composer must work closely with the dramatist and the lyricist to be sure the music fits well. All these original artists adjust their work to achieve a good blend. Sometimes the composer also acts as musical arranger, but often an arranger orchestrates the musical compositions for the instruments the production group desires. The composer makes the music.

The producer is sometimes thought of as only a business manager, but for a musical the producer is usually involved in the entire process and from start to finish frequently provides creative ideas. Indeed, some-

Stephen Sondheim

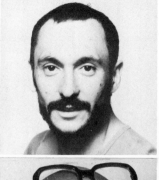

Well-known directors of musicals: Tommy Tune (left); Michael Bennett (center, above); Harold Prince (center, below); and Bob Fosse (right)

times a producer envisions the original idea for the project. Sometimes, too, the producer simply handles the company's money and organization. In every case the success or failure of any major social undertaking, such as a professional musical production, depends on leadership, organization, and financial expertise—the special realm of the producer. Some outstanding producers of musicals are David Merrick (*Carnival*), Saint Subber (*Gigi*), and Harold Prince (*Cabaret*). The producer runs the whole show.

A director coordinates all the creative elements of a musical production. He or she draws together the creativity of the writers and musical composers, the designers and crews, the choreographers and dancers, and the singers and actors. A director must develop a production concept and make sure that everyone's work contributes harmoniously to the whole. After going over the script with the writer, the director prescribes requirements to the designers, approves the ideas of the choreographer and musical director, and finally rehearses the actors. Directors must be dynamic creators and adroit psychologists. Handling a company of creative people during weeks of intense work is probably the most difficult job of all. The director puts the show together.

In addition to the overall director, a musical production usually also has a musical director, who has the responsibility for organizing and rehearsing all the musical elements of the production. Those working closely with the musical director are the rehearsal accompanist, the singers and chorus members of the cast, the conductor, and the performance musicians. In amateur groups the musical director usually acts as conductor, but in professional companies another person serves that function. The musical director takes the work of the composer and arranger to the performing musicians and rehearses with them. In order for the music and dance to grow together as the production develops, the musical director and choreographer must cooperate well together.

The choreographer for a musical is the creator and director of the dances. In creativity and originality, the choreographer often matches the contributions of the dramatist and the composer. The directorial involvement of the choreographer is as demanding as that of the stage director or the musical director. More and more in contemporary musicals, dance is so integral a part of the whole that nearly the entire show appears to be danced. Productions such as *Hair* and *A Chorus Line* are good examples of the masterful contribution of choreographers. Some superb choreographers, such as Tommy Tune and Michael Bennett, also direct the overall production. Other notable choreographers are Michael Kidd, Bob Fosse, and Onna White. Choreographers are responsible for all the dancing in a production and also any movement set to music or rhythm; they control all the acting in the medium of dance.

As many designers are necessary for a musical as for any other theatrical production. Different designers normally create the settings, costumes, properties, and lights. The work of these people when designing musicals is essentially the same, but the style is often different. For musicals, visual spectacle is perhaps even more important than it is for nonmusical dramas. Scene designers must usually produce more sets, which are more elaborate, and more difficult shifts of scenery. Costumers must dress characters in believable clothes and in striking outfits that permit the freedom of limbs necessary in dance. For musicals, properties are no more or no less complicated than for straight plays. But musicals often require more elaborate lighting. Especially in musicals, theatre technicians must be as creative as other members of the company. Some people get more recognition than others, but without skilled crews no musical could take stage. Everyone contributes significantly to the final product.

Richard Rodgers and Oscar Hammerstein III

The work of conceiving, formulating, rehearsing, and building a musical is as complex a social activity as any in human society. The range of skills and creativity is wide indeed, and much of the hardest work happens behind the scenes before opening night.

THE PERFORMERS

The people who glow in the limelight and smile to the applause are the performers, and they deserve it. Not only do the actors, singers, and dancers of musicals have to create in cooperation with the director, the dramatist, and the composer, but also they have to utilize their selves. For a performer to be great or even good in musicals, many skills are necessary. For musicals, most actors today must also sing, and most singers must also act. Skill in the two activities does not develop at the same time. Although most performers are better at one than the other, the great performers in musicals can do both. There is also dance. Developing all three skills is even harder, and few performers do all three equally well. Fortunately, most musicals provide some opportunities for specialized work in acting, dancing, or singing. As a show is developed, the writer, composer, director, and choreographer work together to make sure that each role can conceivably be played by the kinds of performers available. In most professional productions, those people polish each role in order to fit the person who has been cast. If a leading lady is an excellent singer, then the songs are geared to her talent. Whatever work occurs during preparations and rehearsals, the performers are the ones both in the spot and on the spot. They have to create the show afresh each night.

Acting in musicals demands the same sort of internal and external work as acting in any other sort of theatre production. The chapter on acting presents the major considerations, but some special problems arise in musicals. First, musicals are more presentational than most regular stage plays. That means the dialogue scenes are more turned toward the audience, presented more "out front," physically and psychologically. Songs and dances are still more presentational. Another special problem for actors in musicals is making broader transitions. Not only must actors change emotionally from one mood to another as the musical moves along, but also they must make stylistic transformations from dialogue into song or dance and back again. All the acting must be compelling and thoroughly lifelike within the world of the production. Musicals appear phony when the style of the songs and the dances is too far removed from the style of the acting in the dialogue scenes. For actors in musicals, the balance of psychological life in the three realms—dialogue, song, and dance—is of special concern. All must be lived conjointly and credibly. Some of the leading musical actor-dancer-singers of the last few decades are Julie Andrews in *My Fair lady*, Richard Kiley in *Man of La Mancha*, and George Hearn in *La Cage aux Folles*. Other great performers of the American musical stage have been Gwen Verdon, Ethel Merman, Vivian Blaine, Alfred Drake, Mary Martin, Carol Channing, John Raitt, Gertrude Lawrence, and Joel Gray.

CREATION

Cats

Dancers are also significant performers in musicals. Some of the stars of musical theatre dance nearly as well as they act or sing. But the skilled dancers in most musicals are not usually the major actors or singers. Dance is such a demanding art that a performer must have special talent and training in order to be good enough to perform the routines that contemporary choreographers devise. In most musicals certain dance numbers are specialties calling for virtuoso acrobatic, ballet, jazz, or modern dancers. The range of dance is wide indeed. Two shows may require quite different skills. A few dancers rise to stardom as musical performers, and some become choreographers and directors. Ray Bolger is a famous dancer who became a star, as did Cyd Charisse and Gene Kelly. Gower Champion, Jerome Robbins, and Tommy Tune are well known director-choreographers who began as performing dancers. The world of dance has contributed many skilled performers to musicals.

Music is naturally another art that has contributed greatly to musical theatre. Many composers, conductors, and performers from the world of music have also made theatrical appearances. Singers like Florence Henderson, who have talent for acting as well, are in demand. There are never enough good voices for the theatre. At one time musical theatre called mainly for musical performances of a rather simple and obvious sort. This fact is no longer true. Great indeed are the performance skills required of the singers and instrumental musicians in works such as those of Leonard Bernstein or Stephen Sondheim. Even such a contemporary piece as *Hair* demands singers of talent and skill.

The ideal performer for musicals is a person who can act, sing, and dance equally well, and who has developed skills to a satisfactory level in each art. But to take part in a musical means that the performer must combine acting, singing, and dancing in a unique way. Good actors do not necessarily act well in musicals, good singers often fail in musicals, and good dancers may or may not dance appropriately. The strange psychological work of the actor must be combined with the presentational bent of the singer and with the kinesthetic skills of the dancer. The most important quality of all is to be able to sell a song, a dance, or a scene. The crucial work of creativity for performers in musical theatre is to be able to project a self that is transformed in keeping with the world of the drama. But even beyond craftsmanship, a great musical performer must have an open and energetic spirit.

THE FORM OF MUSICALS

The pleasure of seeing and hearing a fine musical is unique. A good musical has its own magic. It beguiles the senses and touches the spirit. No other theatre experience is like it. A musical induces feelings of sympathy and joy that seldom occur in everyday life. This summary of some aesthetic principles in musicals provides information for an understanding of the difficulties in creating musicals.

The materials of musicals is life seen through a theatrical glass. Many of the same human experiences that straight dramas deal with also appear on the musical stage. During the last 40 years, musicals have treated many subjects—from the lives of Fiorello La Guardia, Gypsy Rose Lee, and George M. Cohan to the life of Jesus. In most, love is perhaps the dominant concern. Musicals have dealt with erotic love, romantic love, young love, and even religious love. Because musicals tend to be positive views of human life, romantic materials work well in them. But some musicals, such as Stephen Sondheim's *Company* or Howard Ashman's *Little Shop of Horrors*, puncture romantic views of life. But compared with most straight plays, the situations and events of most musicals are more simplified. The characters are usually less detailed but more striking. The thoughts, though fewer, make their impact more obviously. Sometimes the materials of musicals come directly from life, but most often they come from other, established dramatic or literary works.

The form of musicals varies, of course, but the best ones have strong stories with progressive action. The unity of good musicals today is most striking as well-integrated scenes of dialogue, then song, and then dance blend together into an aesthetic whole. Writers and composers work for unity of action and mood, although variety and change do occur within established limits. Suspense remains a significant principle in the best musicals. Causality of action appears frequently in the story lines. Somehow expectation is aroused and then fulfilled in every sort of musical, and the variety of pattern is nearly infinite—from small musicals like *The Boy Friend* to fully developed ones such as *My Fair Lady*, from the air of

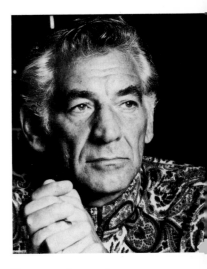

Composer Leonard Bernstein

romanticism in *The Fantasticks* to the spirit of rebellion in *Hair*. Bertolt Brecht and his associates created one sort of musical with *The Threepenny Opera*, Anthony Newley another sort with *Stop the World—I Want to Get Off*, and Stephen Sondheim another with *Company*. Strangely the most significant feature of form in a musical appears to be the creation of a special world. The world of each musical is unique, inviting, and—when the artwork is right—enjoyable.

The style of musicals demands a special manner of expression. By comparison with nonmusical dramas they are generally more presentational, more audience-directed. They tell a story with more externals of physical action and song. The style is less verbal. Musicals have more conventions; for example, audiences accept the possibility that songs and dances can occur regularly in the world of the play. The performers in musicals usually demonstrate a greater variety of skills than those who appear in straight plays. But the most striking facet of style in musicals is the triple expression of emotion. The characters express themselves in words, in song, and in dance.

Each musical has its own aesthetic goals. Although the same may be said about any drama, the overall purpose of musicals as a type is the arousal of positive social emotions. Musicals provide appealing sensory stimuli to both the eyes and ears of spectators. Their stories present characters that tend to arouse interest, then sympathy, and finally intense concern. The audience at a musical expects pleasure, and so it cooper-

Guys and Dolls, with **Sam Levine and Vivian Blaine**

ates with the performance most fully when all the stimuli converge in a special sense of joy. Most musicals are positive in nature; few negative ones have been successful. They usually contain positive emotional powers and arouse positive emotional responses in sympathetic audiences.

Critics, philosophers, and even many theatre people have failed to recognize that musicals occupy a special realm in the theatre. In fact, they are a species of dramatic art as unique as mimetic, didactic, or imagistic drama. The artists of musicals are hammering out a theory of musicals, and it is time that thinkers recognize the extent of their work. Musicals are special dramas that contain dramatic actions, songs, and dances blended creatively into a unified whole. They are distinct in form, material, style, and purpose. In an artistic musical, all the components work together, and each is made more telling because of the proximity of the others. Musicals are not so much a mixture of other arts as a unique compounding of disparate elements of entertainment into one work of art. The emotional effect of a successful musical is special. To experience a fine musical is to feel the happiness of the human community.

CREATION

The Moscow Art
Theatre production of
The Lower Depths by
Maxim Gorky, 1902

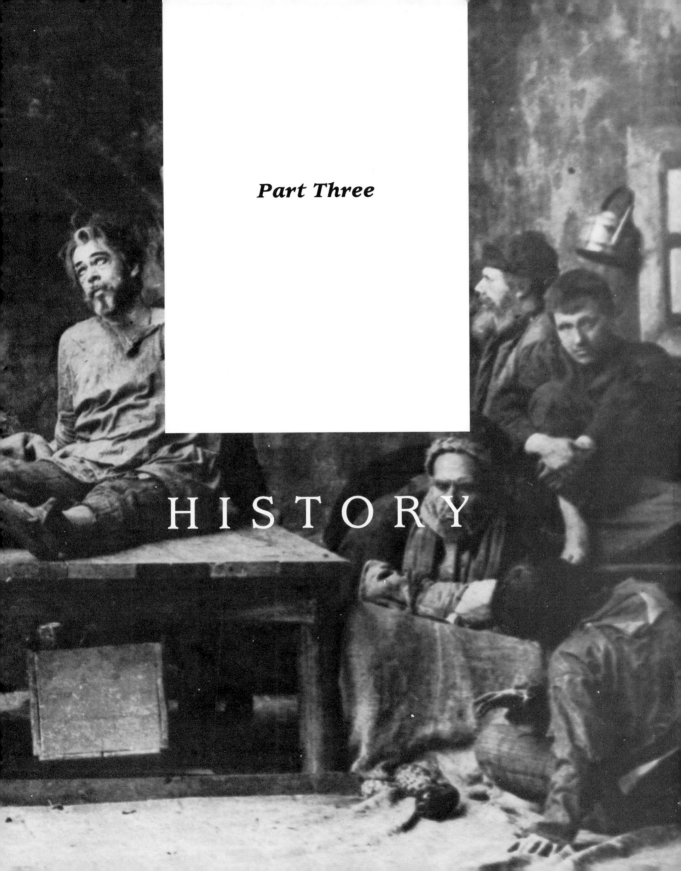

Part Three

HISTORY

CHAPTER 10

Classical and Medieval Drama

Anthropologists suggest that even in the earliest stages of human cultural development people performed some type of drama. In the beginning, theatre probably served religious or educational purposes, but it has always been entertaining. When a primitive man reenacted for his family the experiences of a hunt after the event, he educated them and delighted them with his version of adventure. But when he acted out a hunt before the event for the sake of having good fortune, he then created a religious ritual. Thus, before human beings developed a written language, they passed stories of gods and feats of bravery from one generation to another. They did so through storytelling, acting, song, and dance. Even today Native Americans perform ceremonial songs and dances much as they did centuries ago. Also the impulse to mimic others appears to be natural to human beings. Such basic impulses in people helped bring theatre into being.

This chapter introduces some of the leading theatrical figures of the ancient Greek theatre of Athens, of the Roman Empire, and of Europe in the Middle Ages. Although the birth of drama has no definite date, the history of dramatic art usually begins with Greek and Roman theatre. The first famous Greek playwrights wrote during the fifth century B.C. for the annual festival of Dionysus in Athens. The Romans patterned their theatres after the Greeks, but they lacked playwrights of stature. Theatre in western Europe declined during the Roman Empire (27 B.C.–A.D. 476), almost disappeared for about four centuries, and then revived in the Catholic Church in the Middle Ages. Ritualized theatre occurred in the Byzantine Empire (A.D. 300–1453), and under religious supervision, medieval theatre flourished from the tenth through the fifteenth centuries.

GREEK THEATRE AND DRAMA

The people of Greece founded Western civilization, established its first important democracy, and produced the first playwrights. Greek civilization began about 1500 B.C., and it soon developed a number of independent city-states. Of those, Athens grew to be the most well known.

In 510 B.C. Athens became a democracy, and the Athenians emerged as the most prosperous and enlightened people of the world. Women, slaves, and foreigners, all of whom were denied voting rights, however, outnumbered the voting citizens. The Greeks treated slaves well and often permitted them to earn their freedom, but women for the most part were expected to stay at home. Although boys attended school from age 6 to 16 or older, girls learned to read, write, and play musical

157

**A Roman tragic fresco;
Museo Laterno, Rome**

instruments in the home.

Athens experienced its Golden Age during the fifth century, especially under the rule of Pericles, who reigned 460–430 B.C. During that time the average citizens of Athens probably attained a higher level of cultural sophistication than any other society before or since. During the Classical Age (c. 500–323 B.C.), Athens produced the finest and most original drama of ancient times. In the fifth century, many important intellectuals emerged—such as the historian Herodotus and the mathematician Euclid—but two outstanding philosophers, Socrates and Plato, set the intellectual standards for the century. During the Golden Age of Greece, theatre reached its first climactic development. At that time the three great Greek playwrights—Aeschylus, Sophocles, and Euripides—wrote their tragedies.

The first official record of drama in Greece occurred in 534 B.C. when Thespis won the prize for the best tragedy presented at the City Dionysia, a major religious festival held in Athens. Until the innovations of Thespis, plays were simply narratives that a chorus and a leader presented through song and formalized dance. Thespis receives credit for adding the first lines for an actor impersonating a character and for being the first to perform them. Unfortunately, none of Thespis's plays have survived, but historical records indicate that he traveled in a cart from town to town and performed his plays. In honor of Thespis, actors are sometimes called thespians.

Although the Greeks held festivals honoring many gods, only during festivals honoring Dionysus, the god of wine and fertility, did they perform plays. They even built special theatres for festivals in celebration of Dionysus, the son of Zeus, the greatest Greek god, and Semele, a mortal. Greek mythology tells of Dionysus's birth, murder, dismemberment, and rebirth. In honor of Dionysus, four festivals occurred that related to the four seasons of the year. The ceremonies honored Dionysus's birth, and at the same time the Greeks prayed for fertility and abundant crops.

Greek theatre reached a peak of excellence during the fifth century B.C. in Athens at the City Dionysia, where drama was introduced earlier. Held annually in the spring, the festival lasted several days. On the first day, a long procession took place with dances, and it came to a climax with the sacrifice of an animal (often a goat) and the presentation of other gifts to the god Dionysus. On the second day, contests occurred for dithyrambs, presented by groups who sang and danced. Dithyrambs were wildly emotional choric hymns in honor of Dionysus. On the third day, acting companies presented five comedies. Days four through six were devoted to tragic poets, and each of them got one day on which to present three tragedies and a satyr-play. On the seventh and final day, the city government presented awards to winning tragic and comic writers, choruses, and—later in the century—actors.

Greek audiences were enthusiastic supporters of the drama festivals. They arose at dawn and took their food for the day to the theatre. Entire families and people from all classes attended; even prisoners were released to see the plays. Originally everyone got in free. Later the government initiated a slight fee of two *obols*. But those who were too poor to pay got in free. The front row contained reserved seats for dignitaries, but all other seats were taken on a first-come-first-served basis.

The word *theatre* derives from the Greek *theatron* ("seeing place"), the area where the audience sat and watched. As many as 14,000 Greek spectators sat in a semicircle of marble or stone seats built on a natural hillside, affording excellent sight and acoustics. In early Greek theatres the chorus and actors performed below the audience in a circular space called the *orchestra*. In the center of the orchestra sat the *thymele*, an

Models of the ancient Greek theatre at Delphi and the Temple of Apollo

altar for religious ceremonies. A wooden *skene*, or scene building, stood at the back of the orchestra to house the actors and to serve as a scenic background for entrances and exits. Some scholars believe there was a raised stage area in front of the skene that actors also used, and gods and heroes could speak from the top of the skene. The Theatre of Epidauros near Athens had an orchestra 67 feet in diameter. By 350 B.C. the Theatre of Epidauros definitely had a raised stage, a *proskenion*, on which the actors performed.

Because the Greek playwrights presented their dramas outdoors between dawn and dusk, they used no artificial lighting. Also, they employed minimal scenery and props, but costuming was often elaborate. The deaths of characters took place offstage, but the bodies were often wheeled in on a special platform (*ekkyklema*). A crane device (the *mechane* or *deus ex machina*—translated "god from the machine") allowed gods to appear and disappear as if from the heavens. Most of the Greek plays occurred in only one place, so scene changes were not often necessary. Historians speculate that the ancient producers employed painted panels (*pinakes*) and revolving triangular prisms (*periaktoi*) with three different scenes.

In the fifth century B.C. the playwright, the state, and a *choregus* collaborated on the production. Playwrights submitted scripts that were selected for production almost a year in advance. The state furnished the theatre, salaries, and costumes for three actors in a tragedy or for five actors in a comedy. A *choregus*, a wealthy citizen· appointed by the government, contributed the rest of the expenses. Each *choregus* produced a lavish or a skimpy production, depending on his generosity. He paid for training the chorus, their costumes, musicians, extra actors and their dress, and the scenery. The poet not only wrote the script but also directed the actors, composed the music, and usually acted in the drama. A poet's salary is unknown, but he probably did not earn enough from playwriting alone to live. Small festivals, however, throughout the Greek state produced some of the plays after the City Dionysia.

Masks constructed of linen, cork, lightweight wood, and possibly leather, were an impressive and vital part of each production. Because actors often doubled or tripled roles and because young men played the female parts, masks helped distinguish the characters. Since the distance was great between the stage and the back rows, the masks were large and covered the entire head. They featured stylized hair, beards, and decorations. Especially after the fifth century, dramatic masks were larger than a human face, and they had large mouth openings so that actors' voices would project better. Productions late in the fourth century utilized masks with high headdresses in order to give each character a more striking appearance. The individuals in the choruses of Greek tragedies probably wore masks that matched. For example, the masks that the chorus used for Aeschylus's play *The Furies* depicted underground spirits of vengeance with writhing snake heads; they were so hideous that when they first appeared, some women in the audience miscarried. The chorus's masks for comedy represented various birds, animals, or whatever the play called for. After the fifth century the makers of tragic and comic masks employed more exaggerated facial expressions.

Information concerning Greek costumes comes mainly from scenes painted on ancient vases. The members of each tragic chorus probably dressed alike, and the people in comic choruses wore more varied costumes that coincided with their masks—often birds, animals, or insects. Tragic actors wore a tunic (*chiton*), a short cloak (*chlamys*), or a long cloak (*himation*), and most of their costumes were embroidered. The sleeves were long instead of the customary sleeveless Greek tunic. The comic actors wore grotesquely padded outfits. Worn over flesh-colored tights, their tunics were purposefully too short or too tight. Comic male characters often wore an exaggerated red leather phallus. Satyr actors probably wore a flesh-colored suit and a goatskin loin cloth with a phallus attached in front and a tail in the rear. Presumably, tragic actors wore a soft, high-topped boot, but some comedians may have gone barefoot.

Partly due to the large theatres and the masks actors wore, Greek acting was reputedly rather simple and expressive but not realistic. Although few facts remain about individual Greek actors, the Greeks did not allow women to appear on stage. Tragic actors were in great demand and received good wages. Playwrights chose actors especially for excellence of voice, because they had to project their words through a mask to a large outdoor crowd. In tragedies, actors moved in a stately, formalized manner and used only broad gestures.

As acting became more popular, the Greeks held contests for actors as well as playwrights and choruses. The playwright usually acted in his drama until about 468 B.C., when Sophocles decided to employ a third actor and not act himself. Also about then, a governmental decree established a limit of three actors for tragedy and five for comedy. Since the same actors appeared in the playwright's five plays and portrayed both male and female roles, they played many different characters. Naturally, some actors are reported to have been more emotional than others.

A large chorus of singers and dancers slowed productions but enhanced the spectacle of Greek plays and served as a dominant production factor. The chorus usually entered after the prologue and remained on stage until the end of the play. Early tragedies probably had 50 choral members. During Sophocles' time the chorus consisted of only 15. The amount of money spent on the production showed in the elaborateness of the chorus's costumes and masks. The chorus usually entered singing and dancing in unison. Sometimes, however, the chorus split into two groups and performed by turns. Choruses sang, chanted, or spoke to the accompaniment of a single flute, similar in sound to a modern oboe or clarinet. At times, musicians used other instruments for special effects. The musical mode of these productions was probably more Oriental than Western.

In Greek plays the choruses set the mood and often interpreted or commented on the action. Usually supporting the protagonist, the chorus supplied a background of emotion for the actors or served as spectators encouraging reactions in the audience. The chorus leader sometimes spoke lines separately from the chorus body by acting as spokesman for the group. In tragedy the *stasimon*, or choral ode, remained dignified and was delivered or sung along with expressive, though stylized, gestures. For comedies and satyr plays, choruses danced and sang in a more varied and lively manner.

The Greek theatre produced three famous writers of tragedy: Aeschylus, Sophocles, and Euripides. In the fifth century B.C., the Golden Age of Athens, many poets wrote tragedies, but only 31 plays by these three authors exist today. Tragedy used stories from history or myths that everyone in the community knew. Myths are stories or legends handed down from one generation to another. Homer's *Iliad*, an account of the Greek war with the Trojans, and his *Odyssey*, about Odysseus's return from the Trojan War, remain good examples of myths. To compose a tragedy, an ancient Greek playwright freely interpreted myths, changing characters and events to suit his vision. Violence filled the plots, but murders occurred offstage because of the religious association of the theatre and production difficulties. Onstage, messengers and chorus members gave detailed narrations of the violent scenes.

Most tragedies consist of five structural parts. The *prologue* sets the mood and explains important events that occurred before the action of the play. Then the *parodos*, or entrance of the chorus, establishes the proper mood. The main action develops through *episodes*, or action scenes, interspersed with *stasima*, or choral odes. The plays end with an *exodos*, a concluding scene in which all characters and the chorus depart.

The first Greek playwright whose plays still survive is Aeschylus (525–456 B.C.). Born into a noble family, he was a respected citizen of Athens and a hero of some battles in the Persian Wars. His main contributions include adding a second actor, reducing the importance of the chorus, and increasing dialogue to elevate drama above mere rituals with song and dance. He won 13 playwriting contests, but he received his first award at age 41. Besides acting in his own dramas, Aeschylus created startling production effects when he directed his plays. He stressed lavish spectacle and designed unusual costumes and choral dances. He supposedly developed the Furies' masks previously mentioned and sent horse-drawn chariots on stage.

The plays of Aeschylus deal with moral, religious, and political problems pertinent to the Greek people. He wrote about the decisions and fate of characters involved with the gods and the destiny of the community. One of his dramas, however, *The Persians* (472), is based on the historical Battle of Salamis, in which he had fought. His poetry stresses the miseries rather than the glories of war. The only extant Greek trilogy, the *Oresteia* (458), belongs to Aeschylus. In the three plays of that trilogy—*Agamemnon, The Libation Bearers*, and *The Furies*—he tells the story of the house of Atreus. In the first play, Agamemnon returns from the Trojan Wars and Clytemnestra, his wife, murders him. In the second play, Orestes, Clytemnestra's son, kills her. In the third play, the Furies persecute Orestes, and Athena finally pardons him. *Prometheus Bound* (probably written after 468) utilizes another myth, and it is part of an Aeschylean trilogy whose other plays are missing. Aeschylus probably wrote 90 plays, but only 79 titles and 7 complete plays have survived.

Sophocles (c. 496–406 B.C.) achieved the greatest popular success of

Aeschylus

the three tragic poets. During his lifetime he was Athens' most esteemed playwright and a leading citizen. As a boy, he was considered handsome and a good dancer, lyre player, and wrestler. Coming from a wealthy family, he received the best available education. Sophocles then served in public office as a foreign ambassador. In 440 he became a military commander. When he was about 90, he wrote his last play, *Oedipus at Colonus*.

Sophocles' main contributions include introducing a third actor, inventing painted scenery, and fixing the chorus at 15 members. He made drama more structured and less a spectacle. Whereas singing and chanting occurred during half of Aeschylus's *Agamemnon*, less than a third of Sophocles' *Antigone* utilized the chorus. He wrote each play of a trilogy as an individual unit instead of using the same theme for three dramas. Seven tragedies and part of a satyr play remain from the approximately 125 plays he wrote. Sophocles won 24 prizes; in his first victory he bested Aeschylus in 468 B.C.

The plays of Sophocles present stronger relationships and characterizations than those of the other writers of classical tragedy. He developed complex plots that built to heightened climaxes. Sophocles' best-known plays, *Antigone* (c. 441), *Oedipus Rex* (c. 430–425), and *Electra* (c. 418–410), depict a person struggling against fate, suffering against the odds, yet facing defeat with dignity.

Aristotle, the famous Greek philosopher and dramatic theorist, drew

Sophocles

his definition of the tragic hero from Sophocles' leading character in *Oedipus Rex*. He described the tragic hero as "a man who is highly renowned and prosperous and just, whose misfortune, however, is not brought upon him by vice and depravity, but by some error of judgment or frailty." (*Poetics*, Sec. 1453a, II.5–10.) In the play, Oedipus unknowingly kills his father, becomes king of Thebes, and innocently marries his mother. Years later, after they have four children, a plague strikes the city. To cure the plague the murder of the old king must be revealed. When Oedipus discovers he is the guilty party, Jocasta, his wife and mother, hangs herself, and Oedipus blinds himself with her gold brooches. Then he banishes himself from the kingdom, leaving his children with Creon as ruler. The psychologist Sigmund Freud's famous Oedipus complex derives its name from Sophocles' drama; it implies a son opposing his father and being unwholesomely dependent on his mother.

During his lifetime, Euripides (c. 480–406 B.C.) gained the least popularity of the three authors. To his fellow citizens he appeared to be an antisocial recluse out of tune with his time. Euripides took no active part in Athenian political and social life. He trained as an athlete and a painter before rejecting those occupations to become a writer. Many Greeks thought his plays depicted dangerous ideas and questioned traditional values. Euripides advocated elevating the status of women, yet most of his female characters aren't particularly likeable. Historians believe he suffered through two unhappy marriages. He voiced criticism of his society in plays that presented antiheroic characters opposed to slavery and war. Because of his unpopularity, in 408 B.C. he left Athens to live at the court of Archelaus, king of Macedonia.

More plays of Euripides exist today than those of any other ancient Greek playwright. Of about 92 plays, 17 tragedies and the only complete satyr play, *Cyclops*, survive. But Euripides won the fewest awards—four. His tragedies tell about war, women, and religion; they depict violent, pitiful, and agonizing situations. *Medea* (431) describes the cruel revenge of a scorned woman who kills her husband's new wife and her own children to make Jason, her ex-husband, suffer. *The Trojan Women* (415) condemns the suffering and barbaric atrocities of war.

Some critics consider the plays of Euripides artistically inferior in dramatic construction. But one leading authority, H. D. F. Kitto, explains that he wrote his plays for didactic purposes and crafted them most skillfully. Euripides often stressed character over plot. He also used more realistic detail in character, dialogue, and costume than the other tragedians. Euripides initiated the third form of drama, between tragedy and comedy, and probably his influence later resulted in the development of pastoral drama and melodrama. But instead of concentrating on romance, he described the emotions of hate and revenge that characters in love can express. He wrote dialogue exchanges showing realistic relationships between two people, whereas Aeschylus and Sophocles described the relationship of man and gods or man and the universe. Eleven of Euripides' dramas start with a character's monologue instead of a choral song. A majority of his plays end with the appearance of a god in the *deus ex machina* informing the audience of the final outcome and arguing for the central idea of the play. Euripides was the last great playwright in the Classical Age.

During the fifth century B.C. each writer of tragedies produced one satyr play. A day at the festival of Dionysus started with three tragedies and ended with the shorter, satiric satyr play. Structured like tragedies, the satyr plays revolved around a chorus of satyrs, half-goat and half-man characters. Giving the appearance of being naked on top, they wore a sheepskin loincloth with a phallus in front and a tail in back. Satyr plays parodied the mythological gods and heroes that were treated seriously in tragedies. The production contained wild dances with obscene language and gestures. The only complete extant satyr play is Euripides' *Cyclops*. The short satyr plays provided comic relief in a day filled with long tragedies.

In 487 B.C., about fifty years after the first contest for tragedies, Greek comedy became officially recognized as part of Greek dramatic festivals. A comic writer only produced one play for the contest, whereas a tragic poet wrote three tragedies and a satyr play. The word *comedy* derives from the Greek words *cosmos* and *ode* meaning revel song. During one day of the festival five different writers presented five comedies. The festival at Lenaia paid more attention to comedies than the City Dionysia. These humorous plays written before 400 B.C. are now called Old Comedy. They satirized Athenian political, social, and moral life. Their stories did

Above: Euripides

Left: Terracotta statuettes of Greek actors

not come from myths but made fun of current events and people. The plots focused on a central characters' ridiculous embroilment with a problem. For example, in Aristophanes' *Lysistrata*, the women decide to go on a sex strike, refusing to sleep with their husbands, until the men stop the Peloponnesian War.

The actors in Old Comedy usually portrayed aristocrats, slaves, or important Greek citizens. Such comedies often used five actors, instead of the three typical in tragedies. Although cast sizes varied, 24 members made up the Old Comedy chorus. Male comic actors wore tight-fitting clothes, padded stomachs, and a phallus. When called for, the chorus wore elaborate costumes and masks representing birds or animals. The poetry, acting, music, and dance created an atmosphere of farce and fantasy.

Aristophanes

Comic structure differed somewhat from that in tragedy. The plays started with a *prologue* in which the leading character conceived a ridiculous solution to a problem. Second came the *parodos*, or entry of the chorus. Next was the *agon*, a dialogue debate about the pros and cons of the absurd solution and the final adoption of it. Then in the *parabasis*, the chorus directly addressed the audience and made fun of important people, audience members, or certain issues that the playwright wished to express. A series of *episodes* then took place, in which the idea for solving the problem was exercised. The play concluded with the *komos*, or *exodos*, the final feasting and celebrating.

The only complete extant Greek comedies of the fifth century belong to Aristophanes (c. 448–380 B.C.). Eleven out of about 40 of his plays remain. An aristocratic conservative, Aristophanes believed some Athenian people and ideas were leading Athens to ruin. So many of his plays satirize corrupt Athenian politicians through exaggerated characterization. Some of them are mythical burlesques or parodies; others are fantasies; and still others comment on society, war, and politics. Aristophanes wrote on a variety of topics: *The Clouds* (423) attacks the education and morals of the sophists (professors and philosophers of the day); *Lysistrata* (411) is a farce about war; and *The Birds* (414) satirizes political philosophy. His plays achieved popularity for their witty dialogue, keen satire, and musical parody. He did not feel confident about staging his own plays, so he usually turned them over to another director. His son, Araros, supposedly supervised the presentation of the last one or two. But in *The Knights* (424) Aristophanes wrote such a strong attack on the militaristic demagogue, Cleon, that no actor would play the role, so Aristophanes played it himself.

The Hellenistic Age (323–30 B.C.), which starts with Alexander the Great's death and ends with the incorporation of Egypt into the Roman Empire, followed the Classical Age of Greece. The new era produced several notable writers of comedy and at least one great philosopher. Hellenistic culture consisted of a mixture of Greek and Oriental elements. Macedonia, ruled by King Philip, lay north of Greece and possessed the same race and language. When Philip died, his son Alexander, who was only 20, was prepared to rule the kingdom; because Aristotle, a famous philosopher (384–322 B.C.), had tutored Alexander through his teenage years. Alexander soon became known as one of the world's greatest military commanders. He conquered Greece, Egypt, Syria, and Persia— which included present-day Iran, Iraq, Turkey, and part of India. In his brief reign, Alexander the Great spread Greek culture into every land he conquered. He moved the center of learning from Athens to Alexandria in Egypt. Alexander built theatres and libraries, and his scholars collected and saved many of the scripts of the fifth-century Greek tragic poets.

Aristotle, Alexander's old teacher, has remained even more influential in the modern world, since many of his ideas have retained their value. During the fourth century, Aristotle wrote about many subjects including science, metaphysics, and dramatic poetry. He exercised great influence on modern thinking.

Aristotle's father was a friend and physician to the king of Macedonia; therefore, his boyhood was spent at court. At age 17, Aristotle went to Athens to study philosophy with Plato. He stayed there for twenty years as pupil and teacher until Plato died in 347. Then Aristotle went to the court of Hermias on the Mysian coast of Anatolia. He married Pythias, the niece or adopted daughter of the ruler Hermias; according to Aristotle's will, he left a son and a daughter from his marriage. In 342 Philip II, then king of Macedonia, brought Aristotle to court to tutor his 13-year-old son, the future Alexander the Great. When Alexander became king, he gave Aristotle a large sum of money to set up his own school in Athens to teach Greek scholars. After the death of Alexander in 323, Athenians harbored anti-Macedonian feelings, and Aristotle fled for his life to the island of Euboea. He died there a year later at the age of 62.

Aristotle's most significant contribution to the world of theatre is his famous book *Poetics*. It is a valuable book about drama and explains the principles that an artist uses to make the best kind of tragedy. He made up no rules, but he simply reflected the result of his careful study of the great classical tragedies. The most important principle he uncovered is the principle of action. Aristotle believed the best plays feature a dramatic action, a pattern of human change. He also analyzed the components of drama carefully and identified six qualitative elements: plot, character, thought, diction, melody, and spectacle. Many thinkers have interpreted Aristotle's principles, and some writers have attempted to overturn his principles. But Aristotle managed to write perhaps the first and most pertinent book to explain how drama, all drama, really works.

The Hellenistic period saw changes in theatre structure and performances of tragedies. The stage was elevated 8–13 feet; and probably the orchestra ceased to be used. After the fifth century, Greek drama remained popular, but the performances declined in quality. Costuming for tragedies included high headdresses, padding, and thick-soled boots.

New Comedy, a fresh form, took precedence over tragedy and Old Comedy. Writers of New Comedy dealt with the middle class, and they composed plots that were more about love and family relationships. Although still written in verse, their dialogue sounded more natural. The chorus took a more minor position by merely singing between the five acts. Actors portrayed stock characters like romantic young lovers, comedic servants, courtesans, domineering parents, and swaggering sol-

**Greek comic actor
seated on altar**

diers. Costumes and masks became more realistic. The writers of New Comedy enforced a startling change from the traditions of classical drama.

Although about 70 authors wrote New Comedy, only one play, *The Grouch*, by Menander (c. 342–292 B.C.) has survived. Menander lived in Athens as a cultured, sophisticated gentleman who liked women and society. He wrote plays for an educated, leisure-class audience interested in comedy of manners. Out of 105 plays, one complete drama and parts of three others were discovered in Egypt in the twentieth century; Menander's *The Grouch* was found in 1957. Since he won only eight contests, Menander may not have been the most popular writer of the Hellenistic age, but he was probably the most skillful. His comedies became models for Roman writers, and his influence appeared even in the writings of Shakespeare and Molière.

THE ROMAN STAGE

The Romans patterned their theatre after the Greek models and developed a greater variety of performances. But Roman drama never equaled the stature of Greek drama of the Golden Age. Romans excelled in warfare, government, and engineering, whereas the Greeks flourished in art, literature, science, and philosophy. While Greek drama emphasized man and his relationship to the gods as depicted in Greek mythology, the Roman audience demanded more robust entertainment. Dramatic performances during the Roman Republic (509–27 B.C.) were more refined than during the Roman Empire (27 B.C.–c. A.D. 476), when all power lay in the emperors' hands. Later, as the Roman world declined, so did its taste in entertainment. Theatrical emphasis changed from flamboyant comedies to gruesome tragedies and obscene mimes. People preferred entertainments like violent gladiator fights, chariot races, and animal battles. Only works of three authors are extant—the third- and second-century B.C. comedies of Plautus and Terence and the first-century A.D. tragedies of Seneca.

Although Rome was founded in 753 B.C., it didn't become a republic until 509. The wealthy aristocratic citizens at first dominated the government, but gradually the common citizens gained more governing power. Rome became the leading city-state of the Italian people and started its conquest of neighboring states. But the people became divided between a wealthy class and a class of poor peasants. Civil war erupted and two brilliant statesmen—Julius Caesar and Augustus Caesar—saved Rome from internal destruction. In doing so, however, they changed the system of rule from one focusing on a senate to one headed by an emperor. Julius Caesar started reforms to help the common people, but some statesmen felt he was too powerful, and in 44 B.C. they assassinated him.

The first ruler of the Roman Empire was Caesar's nephew Augustus. Under his rule (27 B.C.–A.D. 14) Rome lived in peace and prosperity. Augustus promoted learning, patronized the arts, and beautified Rome. Trajan (98–177) expanded the Roman Empire to its greatest extent. After A.D. 180 Rome began to decline, and by 476 northern barbarians had overrun it.

Roman drama began in the third century B.C. Livius Andronicus, performed the first regular Roman play in 240 B.C. Andronicus, who many scholars believe was a Greek slave, translated and performed Greek tragedies and comedies. After various other entertainments such as chariot races, music, and dance were established, drama started at the Roman religious festivals. Each festival occurred for the worship of a different god. *Ludi Romani*, the oldest official festival, was held in honor of Jupiter, but five other important festivals honored other gods. Traveling companies also performed plays for public and private consumption.

The Roman drama festivals were major social occasions. The state or a wealthy citizen paid the festival expenses. Usually a producer took over the production, bought a script, and paid the various members of the company. Roman playwrights were not so closely connected with the productions as were Greek authors.

Citizens of all classes attended the plays free of charge. Most seats were assigned on a first-come-first-served basis, but senators probably had a special reserved section in the orchestra. Roman women also attended dramas. The audience loudly expressed their favor or disfavor. The spectators went in and out freely to get food, to see a gladiatorial contest, or to watch jugglers and acrobats. Performances continued all day, and comic mimes occurred between plays.

During the Republic (509–27 B.C.) the Romans constructed open-air theatres in desired locations and demolished them after a festival was over. In Rome about five festivals took place each year. Because each festival dedicated offerings to a different god, a separate theatre was built for each. Typically in these festival theatres, they built temporary bleachers for the audience around a semicircular orchestra. A long, narrow stage, rose about 5 feet above the orchestra. Unlike the Greeks, the Romans avoided hillside theatres and erected scaffoldings instead.

Roman designers probably built and demolished more than 500 theatres before Pompey ordered the construction of the first permanent theatre in 55 B.C. Eventually, during the Empire, the Romans built about 125 permanent theatres. Remnants of these buildings exhibit lavish Roman architecture. In a typical theatre of the period, the auditorium and stage formed one building that seated 10,000–15,000 people; some may have held as many as 40,000 spectators. The audience area was arranged in a half circle around a circular orchestra, where special groups sometimes sat or where unusual performances, such as water ballets or animal fights, took place. Behind the orchestra, the stage rose 5 feet, and it measured 20–40 feet deep and 100–300 feet wide.

A roof covered the stage and aided the production in many ways. Mainly it helped acoustics, but also it protected the elaborately painted background, the *scaenae frons*. This permanent setting was two or three stories tall and lavishly decorated with columns, porticos, niches, and statues; it contained three to five entrances. Settings for comedies called for a street scene, and tragedies used a palace or temple. But the facade remained the same, and the audience used their imagination. Probably the producers placed *periaktoi*, three-sided scenic units, at each end of the stage. By revolving the *periaktoi*, various painted scenes would appear at each side of the stage. Between 133 and 56 B.C. the Romans introduced the first curtain in front of the stage. It was called the *auleum*.

Roman comic actors employed masks made of linen and painted a flesh color. The open mouths aided the actors' projection. Attached wigs of hair represented different characters: white for old age, red for slaves and rogues, and black for youth. Plays based on the Greek used Athenian costumes. Comedies about Roman life adopted a short Roman tunic, possibly covered with a cloak, or toga, and flat sandals or soft slippers.

Roman comedy achieved far more popularity than Roman tragedy. Two types of comedies were written: those based on Greek plays (*fabula palliata*) and those based on Roman material (*fabula togata*). Only scripts of the former survive, and they imitated Greek New Comedy with two changes. Characters often broke into song, and a flute player accompanied a majority of the dialogue scenes. Roman comedy also eliminated the Greek chorus. The stories followed those of Greek New Comedy depicting everyday domestic affairs and misunderstandings of the upper middle class. The characters represented stock types with few respectable female roles. The Roman period of dominance lasted over nine hundred years, but the only important playwriting occurred in the years A.D. 240–75 B.C. The comic playwrights Plautus and Terence wrote the only extant Roman comedies.

After trying various occupations, Titus Maccius Plautus (c. 254–c. 184 B.C.) started writing plays at the age of 45. Some sources describe him as a man with a paunch, red hair, and big feet. In addition to being the most popular Roman comic writer, he acted in and directed his own plays. Although he freely adapted the Greek New Comedy for a Roman audience, he also influenced the writing of dramatic comedies for many centuries thereafter. Shakespeare, for example, patterned his *Comedy of Errors* after Plautus's *Menaechmi*, and Molière modeled *The Miser* after *Pot of Gold*.

Plautus's boisterous farces told complicated stories of young lovers, intrigue, mistaken identity, and misunderstanding. He utilized many traditional characters from Greek comedy, but he added just as many innovative Roman characters. Although he wrote in verse, he used a colloquial vocabulary, and his dialogue often had a lifelike ring. He employed a great variety of rhythms and meters. Some of his typical characters include young lovers, the old miser, the braggart soldier, pimps, courtesans, and comic slaves. Plautus's plays mixed dialogue with lyrics. About two-thirds of his comedy consisted of words recited to the rhythm of pipes or a flute. The 21 surviving plays of Plautus depict blustery stock characters in romantic farcical situations of revelry and trickery.

Publius Terentius Afer (195 or 185–159 B.C.), known as Terence, wrote more subdued, romantic comedies that appealed more to the Roman

The Roman theatre at Orange, France

aristocracy. Born in Carthage, North Africa, and brought to Rome as a boy, he served at first as a slave. His master recognized his talents, educated him, and eventually freed him. Supposedly on his way to study drama in Greece, Terence was lost at sea. During his short life he wrote six plays, all of which have survived.

With one exception, Terence modeled the stories of his plays after Menander's comedies. For example, Menander's play *The Arbitration* sets a pattern for Terence's *The Mother-in-Law*. Terence wrote complex plots featuring refined characters, and he emphasized romance between nice, young couples. In response to the influence of his aristocratic friends, Terence focused his plays on an upper-class father, a son, a young girl, and a devoted slave. Music accompanied only about half of Terence's pieces. Although he lacked the farcical, boisterous humor of Plautus, he influenced later playwrights. He might be credited with the invention of comedy of manners. A better craftsman than Plautus, Terence never achieved the same popularity during his lifetime.

Roman tragedy differed from the Greek by concentrating on gruesome violence, flamboyant characters, and striking spectacle. Actors wore long gowns, elevated boots, high headdresses or wigs, and large distorted masks—all of which bear similarity to the later Greek tragedies. The cumbersome costumes and headpieces created a slow, exaggerated acting style. Producers often resorted to mass spectacles involving live chariots and marching slaves to hold the audience's attention. Cicero complained about tragic theatre in 55 B.C., because the actors were lost among the six hundred mules on stage. Roman tragedy never equaled comedy in popularity or quality. Authors wrote tragedies from 200 to 75 B.C., but none of their plays survive.

Lucius Annaeus Seneca (4 B.C.–A.D. 65) wrote nine surviving tragedies during the Roman Empire. Born in Spain of an eminent Roman family, Seneca studied philosophy and rhetoric in Rome. He became famous as a dramatist, orator, satirist, philosopher, tutor, and statesman. His political life had its ups and downs because of charges brought against him that may not all have been justified. At one time Seneca was a tutor to Emperor Nero and helped him organize an efficient government. Then on a charge of conspiracy with Piso, Nero ordered Seneca's suicide in A.D. 65; for a Roman emperor to order political suicide was a common practice of the period.

Seneca's tragedies are closet dramas. He wrote them to be read aloud but not produced on stage. In the first century A.D., oral readings of drama and poetry were popular entertainments. Seneca's tragedies contain elaborate speeches, moral philosophy, strong emotions, and horrifying deaths, plus ghosts and witches. Although not a great playwright, some of Seneca's ideas (such as elaborate speeches and using ghosts and witches) influenced Renaissance and Shakespearean tragedy. His plays are organized in five acts with choral interludes. They contain violent scenes that would be difficult to produce live on stage. In his play *Thyestes*, the central character dines on the limbs of his own children and views their severed heads. Seneca based most of his plots upon Greek tragedies, but he wrote in original Latin meter. Many of Shake-

**A Roman terracotta
mask for tragedy**

speare's central characters bear similarities to Seneca's. The latter's characters possess an obsession—revenge for example—that leads to their destruction. Seneca's dramas reflect the fears of his time—instability of power, anxieties of rulers, forces of the supernatural, and injustices to humankind.

During the Empire, the Roman audience possibly lost interest in tragic drama for two basic reasons. First, few good writers tried their hands at writing tragedy, and the rules for composing tragedies were too restrictive. The result was boring plays. Also, audiences had become accustomed to witnessing more sensational entertainments such as gladiatorial battles, animal baiting, and chariot races. After 29 B.C., evidently no Romans wrote new tragedies for stage production.

In ancient Greece, acting was a respected profession, but the Romans considered actors to be lower-class citizens. A few Romans achieved fame and fortune through acting. But many actors, especially the mimes, were slaves. In spite of their lowly profession, however, actors often received public praise, gifts, and special services. Men played all the roles in comedies and tragedies, but women appeared on stage for the first time in mimes. Using masks, a troupe of 3 to 6 actors often played 10 or 12 roles in one performance.

Qualifications for a comic or tragic actor differed. Comic actors portrayed stylized characters like courtesans, cunning slaves, young men,

173

or braggart soldiers. They needed expressive gestures and nimble movements. Burdened with high shoes and large masks, tragic actors were selected for broad gestures and emotional range. Actors probably exaggerated their gestures and movements, because the theatres often held 14,000 people. Trapeze artists, jugglers, and sword swallowers competed for audience attention, but regular actors were classified as tragedians, comedians, mimists, or pantomimists.

Quintius Roscius Gallus (d. 62 B.C.), commonly called Roscius, gained popularity, social prestige, and fortune as an actor. One of the few Roman actors to perform in both tragedy and comedy, he founded a school of acting and taught natural, skillful hand gestures. He also wrote a comparison of acting and oratory. Roscius carefully worked out each role and planned his gestures with credibility in mind. The famous orator Cicero became a friend of Roscius, took lessons from him, and even defended him in a lawsuit with a famous speech, *Pro Roscio Comoedo*. Emperor Sulla gave Roscius a gold ring and the rank of knight. Roscius reportedly became so wealthy that he acted without pay. His reputation as the most famous Roman actor carried over to the early nineteenth century when American actors wanted billing with names like "The Young Roscius" or "The Ohio Roscius."

Performances of comedy and tragedy competed with other theatrical and many nontheatrical presentations. Romans produced oral readings, *fabulae Atellanae*, mimes, and pantomimes. Sometimes they flooded the amphitheatre for sea battles, or *naumachiae*, with slaves on ships fighting to the death. The *fabula Atellana*, was a short farce with stock characters. The improvised plots exaggerated events of daily life and burlesqued myths. Actors portraying fools, hunchbacks, and old men required stylized costumes and masks. Roman farce reached a peak of popularity during the first century B.C., at which time they had written plots with stock characters similar to the Italian commedia dell'arte of the sixteenth century.

Pantomime (*fabula saltica*) became another substitute for tragedy. More or less a narrative dance, Roman pantomime probably was a precursor of what moderns know as ballet. Often a single actor-dancer, aided by change of masks, silently danced and gestured all the roles of an entire drama. This type of mimist usually wore a long tunic similar to the tragic actor's and a mask with a closed mouth. Accompanied by various musical instruments, a chorus narrated a story concerning mythology or history with an emphasis on love. Such elaborately staged storytelling became popular among the Roman aristocracy.

Also during the Empire, mime (*fabula riciniata*) replaced comic drama. The common people chose mime theatre, which probably began in the Roman world before A.D. 211. Most mimes were short plays with some scenery and costumes. Actors wore makeup and wigs in place of masks. Because of the roles, they were chosen for their sexual attraction or grotesquerie. Women first appeared on stage in mimes, and some became mistresses of prominent men. But the caliber of actors was generally lower than in other types of theatre. The stories concerned everyday life from a comic or satiric viewpoint. Starting in the first century

B.C., some simple plots with abrupt endings were written down. A majority of their plots revolved around adultery or violent acts. During the Empire, mime became more elaborate and obscene. Actors engaged in sexual acts and actual violence on stage, and they often ridiculed the Christian sacraments. The opposition of Christians to theatre probably originated in reaction to such performances. But mime persisted and became the favorite theatre of Rome until the theatres were closed in the sixth century.

A famous mimic, Theodora, married Justinian I, emperor of the Byzantine Empire. Born and reared in Constantinople, Theodora supposedly started her stage career as a child and then became a noted courtesan. A small, pale woman, Theodora possessed a beautiful figure and face. Justinian fell in love with her, and in A.D. 523 he persuaded his uncle, then emperor, to repeal the law forbidding senators and actresses to wed. When his uncle died four years later, Justinian and Theodora became the sole rulers of the Roman world. She was about 24 years old and Justinian about 44. She greatly influenced him, and because of her courage, firmness, and intelligence she helped him preserve his crown. After her marriage, Theodora became a strongly moral person, and among other social deeds she developed restorative homes for prostitutes. Delicate in health, she died in A.D. 548.

As Rome declined, so did its theatre. Pressure from Christians closed most theatres from the sixth to the tenth century. Ironically, the Catholic Church was largely responsible for reopening theatre doors.

THEATRE IN THE MIDDLE AGES

The Middle Ages span the period between the fall of the Roman Empire (A.D. 475) and the formation of modern European nations. Although the Renaissance started in Italy around 1300, the medieval period lasted from about the year 500 to 1500. In the early Middle Ages, European countries lacked strong, central governments, so little kingdoms sprang up and fought each other. But one great leader arose—Charlemagne, called Charles the Great, and he became king of the Franks from 768 until 814. A strong leader and ardent Christian, he built a dynamic empire and established schools to teach Greek and Latin to both lords and peasants. In 800 the pope proclaimed Charlemagne emperor of the Holy Roman Empire.

Feudalism, a system of landholding and social classes, established economic, political, and social order from the ninth through the fourteenth centuries. Since kings were figureheads and the lords kept fighting each other for land, small landowners needed protection. They gave their land and services to a powerful lord in return for protection from robbers and other warring nobles. In the eleventh century the lords started building stone castles instead of wooden stockades for protection. Feudalism created peace and order, and it established three distinct classes of people. The nobility included the large landowners and the knights; small landowners became vassals; and those without any land were serfs, or peasants. Feudalism started to break down in the fourteenth century.

Medieval society from the tenth through the fourteenth centuries revolved around the Catholic Church, and nearly everyone in Europe was Catholic. People led a harsh existence. They accepted the Church's interpretation of God, and they thought of paradise as a heavenly life hereafter. Their religion certainly helped make their everyday life more bearable. Monks and nuns, who could read and write, kept alive the spirit of education and art. Both the nobility and the peasants owed allegiance to the all-powerful Church. Although most people were extremely poor, the wealthy Catholic Church built elegant Gothic cathedrals, such as Notre Dame, built in Paris from 1163 to 1330. The Church decorated its cathedrals with the finest art—stained glass, sculpture, and paintings.

The Crusades, a series of holy wars lasting from 1096 to 1290, strove to rescue Palestine and the tomb of Christ from the hands of the Turks, who were Moslems. Approximately 3,000 knights and 12,000 infantrymen marched in the first Crusade, which recaptured the Holy City for a short time. Eight Crusades, including the Children's Crusade, spanned three centuries. Many lives were lost, but the Holy Land still belonged to the Turks.

The power of feudalism and the Church declined somewhat from 1300 to 1500. Trading brought about by the Crusades helped towns spring up, and towns took power from the feudal lords. Craftsmen formed guilds to protect their interests. To become a member of a guild took three stages of training as apprentice, journeyman, and master. The masters ran the guilds and influenced city governments. During the twelfth century, universities appeared and replaced the monasteries and clergy as educators.

In the first four hundred years of the Middle Ages, probably no plays were written. Yet wandering bands of mimes, jugglers, and minstrels kept the art of theatre alive by performing at festivals and weddings. Between the sixth and tenth centuries, the Church forbade acting, and continuous injunctions were posted against theatrical performances. Because most people could not read, the early scop and gleeman (c. 650–1066) handed down literature. The scop composed poems and told Germanic legends at court; the gleeman, a wandering entertainer, usually sang others' poems to the accompaniment of a harp. In England, the earliest known Christian poet, Caedmon (c. 670), composed beautiful verse from Biblical tales and later became a monk. Legend also says that King Alfred the Great of England (849–c. 899) disguised himself as a gleeman, entered a Danish enemy camp, learned their battle plans, and thereby launched a surprise attack.

Greek theatre started in religious festivals, Roman theatre ceased because of conflict with the Christian church, and medieval theatre revived again inside churches. During the tenth century, churches started producing dramatic interludes as a part of their services. The first dramatized episode probably occurred at Easter in about 925. From then until 1250, tropes—dramatic interpolations into religious services—occurred inside church buildings. A choir chanted the early tropes in Latin. Later, priests wrote more elaborate Latin dialogues and composed special music for them. By the thirteenth century, completely developed plays appeared in vernacular, or the native language, which the congregation could understand. These liturgical dramas, connected with a church service, enacted only stories from the Bible. For example, at Christmas came the Nativity story and at Easter the Resurrection. Priests and choirboys acted out the dramas.

As the plays became more complicated, the stage space expanded from the church altar to the long, massive sanctuary. Medieval churches were built in the form of a cross. Along the aisles, various *mansions*, or scenes, were set up. Each mansion represented a different locale: one might be a throne for Pontius Pilate's house, and another a table for the Last Supper. The area in front of and around the mansions served as a general acting area, called the *platea*. As the play progressed, the actors and audience moved from one mansion to another. Some of these pageant dramas, which brought the stories of the Bible to life, were given in churches even into the sixteenth century.

From the fourteenth to the sixteenth centuries, drama changed immensely, and churches withdrew their complete power over productions. About the year 1200, plays started being performed outside as well as inside churches, but little is known about the productions until 1350. Sets became more elaborate and performances moved from the church steps to the marketplace. The clergy rendered the tasks of writing, producing, and acting to various trade guilds, or professions. Thus medieval religious drama came to its peak in the period from 1350 to 1550.

An English pageant wagon for a Corpus Christi play

The most widely produced kinds of medieval dramas were the *mystery*, or cycle, plays. Probably the name derives from the French word *mystère*, meaning "trade" or "craft," since professional guilds produced the plays. Also the Latin *ministerium* means "service," and the mystery play grew out of the liturgy. A mystery, or cycle, play consisted of a group of one-act plays, based on Biblical stories or characters, strung together in a sequential cycle. The complete English cycle of plays depicted a history of the world from the Creation to the Last Judgment. Often God and the Devil were two of the characters. The strong theme of man's salvation and redemption from hell held the plots together. The cycle might start with God creating the world and its people; a play about Adam and Eve followed; next in the cycle came the story of Cain and Abel; and so forth. Most of the mystery, or cycle, plays are simply structured and feature conventional characters. Their authors remain unknown, since the clergy first wrote them, and guild members and other laymen later rewrote them. But some of the best mysteries contain good poetry, suspense, and pathos. The cycle pageants no doubt produced a lasting impact on their audiences.

In England the Corpus Christi religious festival presented an outdoor drama honoring the sacraments of the Last Supper. The festival, held in the late spring, started with a procession and religious ceremony. Performances of the cycle plays took place on movable wagons in various parts of town. The Corpus Christi cycle told the whole emotional history of man's fall and his redemption through the goodness of God.

The Corpus Christi festival changed drama in England and other European countries. First, it established a movable pageant wagon that could travel from town to town. Second, it placed all of the production in the hands of the trade guilds. Each guild produced a play that in some way fitted that guild's occupation. For example, the bakers performed the Last Supper, the goldsmiths directed the Magi Bearing Gifts to the Christ Child, and the shipbuilders presented the Building of the Ark and the Flood.

The Second Shepherd's Play, a clever farce combining the Biblical and the modern, is the most famous medieval cycle play. It is the thirteenth play in the Wakefield cycle, which contains 32 plays. In the first part, a man steals a sheep and unsuccessfully tries to pass it off as his wife's new baby. In the second part, the shepherds journey to Christ's manger.

Another cycle drama that originated in the thirteenth century is the passion play. It deals mainly with the Crucifixion and Resurrection of Christ. The most famous one is still produced by local inhabitants in Oberammergau, West Germany. Beseiged by the plague in 1633, Oberammergau vowed that if the plague ceased they would enact the passion of Christ every 10 years. They were spared, and the inhabitants combined two Augsburg cycles from the fifteenth and sixteenth centuries to form their drama, which is still performed once every decade. *The American Passion Play* in Bloomington, Illinois, recaptures the power of medieval drama each year at Eastertime. This production utilizes some of the old medieval effects with Christ ascending into heaven and walking on the water.

The ascension scene in the *American Passion Play*, Bloomington, Illinois

Another form of religious drama, the *miracle* plays, told about saints or martyrs of the Church and used mainly non-Biblical materials. They started during the twelfth century and displayed real and fictional miraculous deeds of popular figures like St. Nicholas, St. George, and the Virgin Mary, who was extremely popular although not actually a saint.

When churches turned over the production of plays to the cities, performances moved to a platform in the town square or on movable wagons. The fixed stages presented more lavish sets than the movable wagons. Cycle plays demanded more scenery than short, simple plays. The Biblical mystery and passion plays called for scenes in heaven, earth, and hell.

A wagon stage usually contained two mansions, or sets. When these sets were no longer needed, workers drove the wagon away and replaced it with another; or the wagons could be set up in a circular arrangement. The guildsmen often drove wagons to various parts of one city or to various cities for performances. Heaven, earth, and hell needed to be on different wagons.

Fixed stages contained extremely elaborate mansions. A typical setting for a cycle play might consist of the following mansions (starting at the audience's left and moving to the right): Paradise, Nazareth, the Temple, Jerusalem, a palace, the Golden Gate, the sea, and Hell. On the left appeared a beautifully decorated Heaven; on the opposite side of the stage, Hell often looked like the mouth of a fire-breathing monster, and it was called the "Hell mouth." An acting area surrounded each mansion. Behind the mansions stood a painted curtain representing the sky. Realistic special effects employed many people to operate the pulleys and ropes. Hell usually emitted smoke and fire from its monsterlike mouth. Trapdoors enabled people to disappear and reappear. There were mechanical animals and flying angels. Sometimes rain fell and lightning appeared for the scene of Christ walking on the water, and the boat often rocked on real water. When Christ ascended into heaven, clouds opened revealing angels while Christ rose into the air. In 1501, Mons, in Belgium, produced the most elaborate cycle play, using 67 mansions.

The sets for these plays were spectacular, but the costumes usually showed less ingenuity. The churches furnished robes for such figures as Christ and the angels, who usually had wings. Saved souls wore white and damned souls black. Important characters carried an identifying emblem. Ordinary characters wore contemporary clothes of the period; therefore, Roman soldiers appeared in medieval armor. Satan and devils dressed in imaginative costumes and masks. Satan often appeared in a horrible mask and a hairy coat, and carried a staff and a padded club to beat actors or rowdy audience members. In addition to fearful masks, the devils displayed wings, claws, beaks, horns, and tails. Their masks, probably constructed of papier-mâché, often held hidden devices that belched fire and smoke. No positive record of masks exists, but written

Mansions in the Valenciennes *Passion Play*

reports indicate that the devil wore a black mask, while God and Christ wore gilt masks.

Until the late fifteenth century mainly amateurs acted in plays. The clergy acted inside the church, and craft guilds took over when drama moved outside the church. Actors probably received wages according to the dignity of their parts. In England, men and boys portrayed all the roles, often doubling in parts, whereas in France some women and girls participated. Many plays required singers and musicians. In the twelfth and thirteenth centuries plays called for about 20 to 30 actors, but from the fourteenth to the sixteenth centuries lavish productions required many more actors. Approximately 150 actors played 350 roles in 1501 in the elaborate Mons production. Individual plays were usually rehearsed only two to five times. The Mons performance, lasting four days, required only 48 rehearsals.

The medieval audience for the guild productions stood in the street or peered from windows or roof tops. Special bleachers existed only for the rich or elite. By the fifteenth century, however, workers built temporary scaffolds for the lavish productions. In most cases, seats were unreserved and admission free.

When theatre moved outside the church, various types of secular or nonreligious drama achieved popularity. Especially in England and France, the morality play served as a bridge between religious drama with Biblical characters and secular drama concerning ordinary men. These didactic plays, which preached a certain idea or moral, flourished from 1400 to 1550. The central character, Man (usually called Mankind or Everyman), fought a battle between personifications of good and evil to determine which would gain control of his soul. The plays were allegories containing single-faceted characterizations of the seven virtues, the seven deadly sins, Death, the Devil, or other abstractions. Most plots dealt with the spiritual trials of an average man during his lifetime. Later, morality plays evolved to cover various themes of education, political satire, and scientific discoveries, such as the earth being round. Some plays even employed didactic themes favoring the Protestant or the Catholic point of view; such themes were particularly popular during the Reformation.

Everyman (c. 1500) is perhaps the best and the most well-known of all the morality plays. Probably written by an anonymous English author (although some claim it is a translation from the Dutch), the play describes man facing his death alone. On the way to his grave, Everyman can find only one former companion, Good Deeds, who will accompany him to the judgment seat of God and plead for him. Some of the characters who reject him are Strength, Beauty, and Discretion. During the course of the play, Everyman realizes that his past life relates to his salvation.

Other types of secular drama began to appear late in the Middle Ages— folk dramas, mummers' plays, and farces. Folk drama, a form of pure entertainment, actually contained more dancing and games than drama. Local talent performed folk plays in connection with rural festivals on village greens. Few plays were written down, but two examples that

1545 : HANS . SACHSN. ALER·51·IAR

Hans Sachs

survive are *Robin Hood and the Sheriff of Nottingham* from England and *The Play of Robin and Marion* (c. 1283) by France's Adam de la Halle. Mummers' plays achieved popularity because masks and costumes disguised the actors. Usually performed in a king's or noble's banquet hall, the entertainment concluded in a dance. Mummers' plays were the forerunners of English masques and Italian *intermezzi*.

During the thirteenth century, medieval theatre artists developed farce. It started in France and Germany, and it spread quickly to England as well. Farce achieves humor through exaggerated situations and imperfect characters. Medieval farce depicted the failings of humankind—like cheating and marital infidelity—and showed its ridiculous behavior in any given situation. From the beginning, horseplay, or broad physical humor, was an essential ingredient of farce. France produced one extremely popular, although anonymous, farce entitled *Pierre Pathelin* (c. 1470). The plot involves a lawyer, Pathelin, who tricks a merchant out of some material by pretending madness. Later Pathelin defends a sheperd on charges of stealing sheep, and he gets cheated out of money himself.

Germany produced the most prolific poet and dramatist of the sixteenth century—Hans Sachs (1494–1576). His most famous plays are short farces. The son of a tailor in Nuremberg, Sachs became a master shoemaker and a mastersinger, who toured most of south and central Germany. Richard Wagner's opera *Die Meistersinger* (1868) glorifies Hans

Sachs as a touring singer. Early German farces called Shrovetide or carnival plays centered around a *Narr*, or fool. This character developed into Hanswurst in the eighteenth century. Sachs's farces described local people and used homespun humor. His characterizations, natural dialogue, and clever verse supported his themes of morality and humanity. In 1550 Sachs established the first German theatre in Nuremberg in a deserted Catholic church. By 1580 he had established a nonprofessional German theatre which consisted of simple but entertaining productions.

In England, John Heywood (1497– c. 1580) turned the "interlude" into a professional form of drama and utilized professional actors. Originating as a short, entertaining sketch, the interlude developed into a nonreligious farce with a small cast. Heywood left to posterity six interludes that are short, farcical dramatic dialogues, or debates. Heywood's interludes form a bridge between medieval drama and Elizabethan comedy. They contain medieval humor, Renaissance secular traits, and Reformation satirization of corruption in the Church.

Nonreligious morality plays and interludes brought about the rise of the professional actor. By 1500 many professional troupes attached themselves to the households of kings or nobles, and sometimes the troupes toured. During the span of the Middle Ages, however, most actors were amateurs.

Greek, Roman, and medieval dramas were mostly religious in philosophy or celebratory in emotion. A majority of the plays didactically presented a closed, God-centered vision of the universe and of human existence.

Governments or religious orders financially supported Greek, Roman, or medieval theatre as social festivals or celebrations on special occasions. Greece produced the first important playwrights—Aeschylus, Sophocles, and Euripides—and the philosopher Aristotle. The Romans founded their theatre on Greek models. Romans built striking outdoor theatres, but they failed to leave much worthwhile drama. Medieval religious drama started in the Catholic Church, and later, laymen took over productions. Soon nonreligious plays and professional actors emerged. The decline of the feudal system, the Reformation, a renewed interest in classical learning, and the withdrawal of financial support for theatre paved the way for the new Renaissance drama.

11 The Renaissance in Italy, Spain, and France

The Renaissance in Europe lasted from the fifteenth through the seventeenth centuries. The movement began in Italy and spread to the other European countries. The word *renaissance* means rebirth, and the cultural Renaissance was a rebirth of learning and creative activity founded on the principles of humanism. Based upon ideals of dignity, freedom, and equal law, humanism exalted the reason and the free will of all people. Artists began to create for personal pleasure, not merely to satisfy God.

Four important ingredients contributed to the energy of the Renaissance. First, the art of the early Renaissance evinced a Greek and Roman classical influence, while that of the later Renaissance produced an elaborate baroque style. Second, intellectual and creative people shifted their focus from matters of religion and salvation to the importance of each individual human being in daily life. Third, the new spirit of intellectual freedom and Gutenberg's invention of the printing press in 1455 led to a change in education. People suddenly wanted to read and write in their own language and to develop their own culture. States founded great libraries, and scholars expanded their interests to the affairs of the world. Fourth, adventurers expanded the world geographically, while thinkers advanced it scientifically.

The Renaissance began in Italy because that peninsula was central on the trade routes from Asia and Africa; also, it was the seat of the Roman Catholic Church. Florence and Venice, the trading ports and cultural centers of Italy, brought in the wealth necessary for important leaders to make changes. Wealthy and intellectual Italians encouraged commerce, social contacts, and the development of education and the arts.

During the Renaissance, Italy and France developed a neoclassical style of drama based on the classics. Those two countries rebelled against medieval drama; whereas Spain was at first influenced by medieval drama but later formed its own style. Each country had its own period of world dominance, and strangely the outstanding periods for theatre in these countries partially coincided. Italian artists contributed elaborate scene designs, and Italian actors developed the commedia dell'arte. Spain produced its own great drama, especially the works of Lope de Vega and Calderón. France saw the rise of neoclassical playwrights—Corneille, Racine, and Molière—and baroque staging.

THE RISE OF ITALIAN DRAMA

The Italian Renaissance produced various forms of dramatic entertainment. Its architects built enclosed, classically designed theatres with

185

proscenium arches, and spectacular scenery, painted in perspective. During this era acting once more became a profession. Unfortunately, no Italian plays of great stature came to the fore. Various courts and academies produced royal processions, street pageants, *intermezzi*, pastorals, operas, neoclassical revivals, and formal pieces. Perhaps the most important Italian innovation in theatre occurred during the sixteenth century in small professional groups that performed the informal and popular commedia dell'arte, a type of comedy that came to exert great influence

fuoa mia.   Bernoualla   Che buona mi sa

Commedia dell'arte players, etching by Jacques Callot

on European drama.

Similar to the medieval interlude, the Italian *intermezzi* consisted of comic performances given between the acts of a serious drama or opera in the late fifteenth and early sixteenth centuries. Music, dance, and special effects were the main ingredients. During the 1570s the *intermezzi* achieved greater acclaim than the plays themselves, but by 1650 they had disappeared.

Pastoral drama, which flourished in the sixteenth century, combined classicism and romanticism. The stories always occurred in a rural, natural setting. They combined romance, nature, and poetry in an escapist drama about shepherds and shepherdesses with satyrs and nymphs. Pastorals were extremely popular in high society, and aristocratic women liked to act in them.

The only original Italian Renaissance contribution to theatre literature was the development of opera in the 1590s. Opera started as an attempt to create a drama with music and dance based on Greek mythology. As designers and artists built ornate Italian theatres and introduced elaborate settings and special effects, opera flourished.

Some of the elements that encouraged the Renaissance as a whole also hindered the development of a new, individual Italian drama. The educated elite and the leaders of the academies, frowned on the employment of common language in drama; they preferred more formal drama in Latin. Until the sixteenth century few people could read Greek, so the major influences on Italian drama were the Roman plays.

Many comedies and tragedies produced in the early Renaissance were the original scripts of Terence, Plautus, and Seneca. Adaptations in Latin of the Roman dramas were performed; some translations into the vernacular were made; and finally original plays were written in the native tongue. The latter dramas were based on the Roman concepts, thereby creating a neoclassical drama. The main Greek influence in Italy came with the translation of Aristotle's *Poetics* in 1498. Italian theorists began to stress the three unities of time, place, and action, and insisted that playwrights should write plays with those principles in mind. Humanists stressed Aristotle's concept of imitation of action, but they misinterpreted him also to mean imitation of classical authors. Thus they tended to impede originality in playwriting.

Italian neoclassical comedies contained romance, intrigue, kidnapping, and the discovery of long-lost relatives. Lodovico Ariosto wrote the first comedy in Italian, *La Cassaria* (The Casket). Niccolò Machiavelli, a notable writer, politician, and thinker, wrote the popular *Mandragola* (c. 1513–1520). It used a favorite comic theme of infidelity; an old jealous man is tricked into approving a sexual relationship between his young wife and a young man.

Most Italian neoclassical writers based their tragedies on Seneca's. They used revenge, ghosts, horror, and narration instead of tragic action. They

The Bogus Bride by James Fisher, Wabash College

187

structured their tragedies like the Greek classics, but they wrote them in mediocre poetry. Giangiorgio Trissino (1478–1550) was the author of the first imitation of a Greek tragedy written in Italian—*Sofonisba* (1515). Italian comedies contained more literary value and reflected contemporary life better than the tragedies. The Italian Renaissance playwrights failed to produce any lasting drama. They placed too much emphasis on imitating the Latin plays, and they lacked imagination and skill as playwrights. They were also curtailed by the performances of amateur actors before limited audiences of princes, nobles, and popes. The general populace never saw the productions.

Between the late fourteenth and late sixteenth centuries, however, Italian drama initiated some improvements. In place of stock, stylized characters, the plays featured characterizations with more individuality. These later Renaissance Italian dramatists broke from medieval drama by separating drama, state, and Church.

Italian architects and scene designers revolutionized the theatre. In the late sixteenth century, the Italians built permanent indoor theatres with proscenium arches. Designers concentrated on detailed perspective sets and hidden, mechanized scenery changes.

The Roman architect Vitruvius greatly influenced the Italian theatres built for formal drama. Most theatres used U-shaped seating with the center of the U as a pit. Managers sold the center area as standing space for elite critics or admiring young gentlemen, and sometimes actors used it during a performance. The general seating space was arranged, as in Greek and Roman theatres, in a semicircle. After 1637 those who paid the highest ticket prices got to sit in boxes that were placed around the walls in tiers of two or more. Servants and members of the lower classes usually sat in a gallery above the boxes. The stage was elevated and level across the front, but it raked sharply upward in the back. Little room existed in the stage wings, but space above and below allowed for scenery storage and changes.

The oldest surviving Renaissance theatre is the Teatro Olimpico, built in Vicenza in 1580–1584. The seats were arranged in a shortened semicircle. The stage had a permanent background similar to the Roman theatre, but the five arches remained open with permanent street vistas behind them in three-dimensional perspective.

The Teatro Farnese built at Parma in 1618 contained a new innovation that exists in most theatres today—a permanent proscenium arch. The decorated arch focused central attention on the stage and hid the edges of the scenery or any machines from the audience's view. Spectators sat in a horseshoe arrangement with raised seats.

Renaissance scene designers conceived elaborate and realistic stage sets. Court architects were the main set designers, but famous artists like Raphael, Michelangelo, and Leonardo de Vinci also created some designs. The designers painted sets in detailed perspective with many three-dimensional features.

Sebastiano Serlio (1475–1554), an Italian architect and founder of the classical school of architecture in France, published an influential book on stage design—*Architettura* (1545). In it he explains three types of

SCENE TRAGIQUE

A setting for tragedy by Serlio

classical settings for comedy, tragedy, and pastoral plays; and for many decades other designers closely followed his prescriptions. The comedy setting consisted of a permanent street scene with citizens' houses and shops. Serlio recommended a street scene of palaces for tragedy. The pastorals depicted a woodland scene with country cottages. To create a completely perspective illusion, Serlio proposed the stage floor be painted in squares diminishing in size toward the back. To increase the illusion of distance, the stage was raked, sloping upward at the back, and the top, rear flats sloped downward toward the floor. Painted houses made of canvas and wooden frames were set on the stage. The upstage houses appeared smaller than the downstage ones.

Nicola Sabbattini (1574–1654) published the *Manual for Constructing Theatrical Scenes and Machines* (1638), which discusses various methods of changing scenery, especially scenic wings. He recommends that angled wings be set up parallel to the proscenium in groups, with each group extending a little further onstage as they progress toward the back of the stage. Each group should consist of the same number of side wings, one behind the other, as there are scenes in the play. To change scenery, workers merely pulled the first set of wings offstage, revealing a new set on which was painted a different scene. The painted back scenes, consisting of two large flats that met in the middle, were changed in the same manner.

The Italian designers also introduced borders, or pieces of cloth that extend across the top of the stage. Painted like part of the scenery, borders block the audience's view of the above stage by hiding lights and special effects.

Because the elaborate scene changes took place in full view of the audience, many stagehands were required to change simultaneously the wings, back flats, and borders. By the early seventeenth century, the angled side wings were replaced by flat wings. In the 1640s, Giacomo Torelli (1608–1678) improved scene changing with his invention of the chariot-and-pole system. Slots were cut in the stage floor to correspond to each wing and back-scene position. Under the slots, tracks ran parallel with the front of the stage. Poles thrust through the stage floor were attached to casters, or chariots, that ran on tracks under the stage. Wings and back scenes were attached to the poles. Pushing the chariots toward the center of the stage brought a new set onto stage, while pulling back moved the set offstage. Eventually, Italian designers attached all the scenic pieces to a windlass, enabling one man to change an entire set by turning a crank.

Elaborate Renaissance productions demanded spectacular special effects. One of the most popular effects was the *glories*, wooden platforms concealed by clouds that flew people through the air by means of pulleys, ropes, and cranes. Trapdoors for the appearance and disappearance of characters or scenery were effective. Fire, smoke, and sea scenes re-

A sixteenth-century Italian stage design by Peruzzi

mained popular effects.

In this period, designers utilized many oil lamps and some candles to create the lighting effects. Chandeliers usually hung in the auditorium near the stage. Other lights hidden behind a parapet across the front of the stage served as footlights. Oil lamps behind the proscenium arch and above the painted wings furnished further illumination.

Costumes for Italian Renaissance productions were elaborate in style and color. Costumers naturally adapted classical styles for Roman and Greek dramas, but they used distinctive dress of the period for contemporary dramas. They strove to enhance the visual impact of each production through the use of elaborate dress on as many characters as possible. For example, even servants were dressed in silks rather than rags.

Actors of the formal Italian theatre were amateurs. Gestures, movement, and speech were supposed to be realistic. Most of the acting occurred downstage because the actors appeared too large against the upstage perspective scenery.

Formal theatre existed for the Italian elite, but in the middle of the sixteenth century *commedia dell'arte*, which means "comedy of professional artists" became the popular theatre for the common people. Traveling groups of players improvised the words and action from scenarios, which were plot outlines without dialogue. They used mostly stylized characters in farcical situations. Commedia thrived in Italy from 1550 to 1750, and its influence spread to the rest of Europe. Commedia troupes performed in marketplaces, fairs, courts, and occasionally formal theatres. Most often these companies set up temporary performance facilities. They normally constructed a simple platform with an area beneath or behind for costume changes, and they hung a cloth drop behind the stage. They used simple furniture such as tables and chairs and numerous props.

The comic actors of the commedia portrayed type characters with set names in their improvisations. Almost 800 scenarios that give bare outlines of commedia plots still exist. The head of the company outlined the characters and action for each performance. The actors then improvised the dialogue and business as the drama progressed. Originally, particular actors devised the stock characters. These originators established a character's personality traits, costume, and mask. An actor often played the same role for a lifetime. When another actor assumed the role, only minor changes were made.

In commedia productions specific bits of comic business that proved popular with the audience were called *lazzi*. These were incorporated into the scenarios and used over and over. Bits of pantomimed action found in American vaudeville and burlesque shows are similar to *lazzi*. Also some of the classic film comics such as Charlie Chaplin, Abbott and Costello, and the Three Stooges are perhaps related to commedia performance style.

Most troupes contained seven men and three women who could play the parts of lovers, masters, or servants. One or two sets of lovers, who usually went by their own names and acted in a more realistic manner, formed a stabilizing contrast to the stylized master and servant roles. The masters usually consisted of two old men and a soldier. One of the old men's parts was Pantalone, who might be a money-minded merchant, a duped husband, an irate father, or a ridiculous lover. He later appeared as a character in some of Shakespeare's plays and as Molière's *The Miser*. Dottore, the other old man, was a doctor of law who interfered in other's business, or perhaps he was the father of a lover. Capitano was a braggart soldier, sometimes a lover, and usually a coward.

A comic scene with commedia dell'arte characters

Excellent comedians and expert dancers or acrobats portrayed the servants, or *zanni*. Arlecchino started as a stupid servant; later he became Harlequin, a buffoon and clever servant who wore the famed diamond-pattern costume. Pedrolino, another servant, became the French Pierrot with white face and loose white costume. Pulcinello turned into the English hunchback Punch. There were other servant roles, and sometimes the Capitano, or Scaramouche, behaved like *zanni*.

Stereotyped masks and costumes complemented the commedia dell'arte style. Usually made of leather, masks covered the whole face, half the face, or just the eyes. Arlecchino, or Harlequin, eventually wore a black half mask with his red, blue, and green patterned suit. Pulcinello sported a hook nose and humpback. Pantalone wore a brown mask with a large curved nose and a gray beard, red breeches and vest, a long, black coat, and a cap. Dottore wore a long black professor's cap and gown and a dark mask with red cheeks and a short beard. Capitano carried a huge wooden sword and wore a long-nosed mask with a swaggering moustache. The lovely ingénue and her handsome young lover were costumed in lavish contemporary dress without masks.

The heart of commedia descended from generation to generation in families of actors. Children endured rigorous training to replace their elders. These early professional actors were intelligent as well as accomplished artists in song, dance, acrobatics, and spoken dialogue. They were often proficient in other languages and traveled to courts and theatres in foreign countries. The companies bore attractive names like the Gelosi (the Zealous), the Accesi (the Inspired), the Fideli (the Faithful), and the Desiosi (the Desirous).

The Gelosi was one of the most famous of the commedia acting companies. Francesco Andreini (1548–1624), its leader, could speak five languages, and he was an accomplished musician and writer. At the request of Henry IV, Francesco took his company to Paris in 1600. In the productions, Francesco portrayed a popular Capitano. His wife, Isabella (1562–1604), was the company's brilliant and beautiful leading lady. A published poet, she also spoke four languages and could sing and dance most gracefully. One of their seven children, Giambattista Andreini (1578–1654), became the famous French actor Lelio.

While the Italian Renaissance failed to produce any plays of permanent importance, its artists proclaimed the importance of man and art. They managed to reawaken society's interest in theatre, even though the Church still opposed the profession of acting. The success of commedia dell'arte with its clever, professional actors and actresses spread to other countries. With the aid of Italy's finest artists, the formal Italian Renaissance theatre developed elaborate scenery and lavish theatres.

THE GOLDEN AGE IN SPAIN

Spain's Golden Age of power and influence occurred from about the middle of the sixteenth to the middle of the seventeenth centuries. Spain's Renaissance developed from essentially medieval ideas. In 1492 Spain sent Christopher Columbus to discover the New World. History shows Spain to be the greatest world power during the reign of Charles V and of his son Philip II. Charles V (1516–1556) made Spain the most powerful nation in the world by 1550. Philip II, born to Charles V in 1527, ruled from 1556 until his death in 1598. Philip tried to win worldwide power for Spain and for the Roman Catholic Church. Under his rule, Spain acquired its greatest strength and widest geographical boundaries.

Internationally influential and incredibly wealthy, Charles V and Philip II encouraged all the arts. Similar to England and France, Spain's greatest period of dramatic literature (1580–1680) started during her period of world dominance. Spain produced two great playwrights during this period, Lope de Vega and Calderón.

Spanish drama developed special characteristics under the combined influence of Moorish and Catholic cultures. After the power of Rome declined in the Middle Ages, most of Spain—except for a portion of the north which the Catholics retained—came under rule of the Moors in 711, and Moslem religion prevailed. Around 1200 the northern Catholic forces began to drive out the Moors. El Cid was one of the great Catholic heroes in the conflict. In 1492 King Ferdinand II and Queen Isabella conquered Granada, the last Moorish stronghold. Spain eventually evicted all the Moors, and at the same time the rulers expelled all Jews. The Moorish culture gave Spaniards a strong attitude toward personal honor and the respectful treatment of women, and the Catholic influence gave them a deep faith in God and the Church. Both of these characteristics appear in Spanish Renaissance drama.

Probably because the Spanish people were so concerned about the place of the Church in their own country and in their colonies, religious drama provided the principal material for theatre at a time when most of Europe had lost interest in it. From 1550 until 1765 Spain developed her own style of religious drama. The best Spanish playwrights of the period wrote *autos sacramentales*, religious plays associated with the Corpus Christi festival concerning the power of the Church's sacraments. *Autos* combined the characteristics of the medieval cycle and morality plays. The playwrights, however, created sacred events allegorically rather than literally. Death, Jealousy, or Pleasure—allegorical characters—appeared in the same play with human and superhuman characters. The devil often took the form of a Moor or a pirate.

At various places in the major Spanish cities, actors presented the *autos sacramentales* on pageant wagons called *carros*. Similar to English pageant wagons, the *carros* had wooden frames covered with painted canvas. Some of them were even two stories high, and the upper story could open to reveal a scene inside. Some *carros* contained machinery for flying set pieces or actors from the lower level into the upper one. At first two *autos* were used for each play, and later the number increased to four.

Besides religious plays, dramatists also wrote full-length secular plays, known as *comedias*, of which they composed two types. Some were based on classic Roman models, but the most popular type were the "cape and sword" (*capa y espada*) plays. They featured minor nobility in stories of love and adventure. These secular plays could be comic, tragic, or a combination of both. Most contained three acts and were episodic in structure, and few obeyed the neoclassical rules of unity. *Comedias* flourished from 1550 to 1700.

Lope de Vega (1562–1635), whose full name was Lope Felix de Vega Carpio, was the most important and prolific playwright of Spain's Golden Age. Lope wrote at least 1800 plays, of which more than 450 survive. Also he composed many volumes of verse and prose. He evidently wrote some plays in 24 hours and an average of 20 pages every day of his adult life.

Lope's personal life was also astonishingly filled with romance and adventure. Born of peasant parents in Madrid, he received a university education, but he left his studies to fight in an expedition against Portugal. In 1588 he was banished for eight years from Madrid for criminal libel against one of his mistresses. A few months later he eloped with Isabel de Urbina, daughter of a herald in the court of Philip II. Then he sailed with the Spanish Armada, the fleet that set out to fight England. When the Armada was defeated, he returned to Valencia to live out part of his exile writing plays. After his first wife died, he married Juana de Guardo in 1598, but he spent more time with Micaela de Lujan, an actress. Although he was an unfaithful husband, he demonstrated great interest in his many legitimate and illegitimate children. Eventually, he turned to the Church and took the priest's order in 1614, but he brought scandal to the priesthood by his continual passionate affairs.

Lope de Vega constructed many kinds of plays in various verse forms. Most of them ignore the classical unities, mix tragedy and comedy, and end happily. He brought the cape and sword play into prominence and thereby influenced the future writing of Spanish playwrights. *Madrid Steel* (1603), *A Certainty for a Doubt* (c. 1625), and *The Gardener's Dog* (c. 1615) remain popular cape and sword plays. They contain elements of action and suspense, intrigue, mistaken identities, and themes of love and honor in the exploits of the aristocracy. Lope also wrote about historical legends and peasants. *The Sheep Well* (c. 1614), remains his most famous and perhaps his best-written drama; in it a group of Spanish peasants revolt against their feudal lord.

Most of Lope de Vega's plays contain the same basic themes and situations with somewhat stereotyped characters, but his colorful, adventurous romances held the audience's attention. Often compared to Shakespeare because both authors wrote in a similar form at the same time, Lope lacked Shakespeare's master craftsmanship and insight into humankind. Lope's plays, however, depict an adventurous spirit and self-confidence important to the Renaissance movement and indicative of the author and the Spanish Golden Age.

When Lope de Vega died, Pedro Calderón de la Barca (1600–1681), known simply as Calderón, became Spain's most popular playwright. Of his approximately 200 plays, 100 survive, of which 80 are *autos sacra-*

Lope de Vega

195

mentales. Calderón also wrote numerous *zarzuelas*, secular musical entertainments, for the court. He used characters and action in a variety of verse forms to accentuate his themes of love, honor, patriotism, religion, and philosophy. The son of a government official with a dictatorial temper, Calderón's early works show the effects of family life through abuse of paternal authority. He received a university education and entered the service of the constable of Castile. In 1623 he started writing plays for Philip IV, and in 1636 the king knighted him for meritorious service to the country. In 1651 he became ordained as a priest and stated that he no longer wanted to write plays. The king, however, commanded him to write for the court theatre.

Calderón wrote his best secular works between 1622 and 1640. During that time he wrote both cape and sword plays and more serious dramas. His *comedias* depict a clash of values: honor in conflict with love, ambition with loyalty, and peace with justice. His two most famous secular dramas are *Life Is a Dream* (c. 1636) and *The Mayor of Zalamea* (c. 1642).

After 1652 Calderón wrote only for the royal court. Spanish court theatre combined drama, dance, and music in tales about classical mythology and ancient history. The short, light musical comedies came to be called *zarzuelas* because they were performed at the royal hunting lodge, La Zarzuela. These sketches encouraged the rise of opera in Spain, but they also led to a decline in nonmusical drama. Calderón's numerous *autos sacramentales* contributed to the Counter-Reformation movement. His religious plays tell about the conversion and martyrdom of the early saints. He wrote his best *autos* late in life, and they dramatize the fall and redemption of man.

In Spain the first public theatres—called *corrales*—appeared about the year 1520 and were temporary structures. The Corral de la Cruz, built in 1579, was the first permanent theatre in Madrid. *Corrales* were similar to the English inn theatres.

A typical Spanish inn converted into a *corral* was three stories high and built around a rectangular courtyard. Only men stood in the *patio* area or sat on a few rows of benches near the stage. The elevated and curtainless stage stood directly opposite the tavern, or *alojería*. Stairs led above to the gallery for women, the *cazuela*. Directly above the *cazuela* was a gallery for important city officials, and above that another gallery for clergymen and intellectuals. Along the two sides of the courtyard were roofed platforms with benches; these units were called *gradas*. On the first level behind the *gradas* were *aposentos*, actually rooms or windows of the surrounding inn. Above this were two more floors of *aposentos*, or railed boxes, from which special people could view the play. In 1574 roofs appeared over the *corral* stage and by 1617 over the whole building.

Public and court theatre behavior differed. The audience that gathered for productions in the Spanish *corrales* was rowdy and made a lot of noise. The people ate and drank during the performance, and they used whistles and rattles to demonstrate their feelings about the presentation. The court audience behaved in a more dignified manner. The kings paid playwrights and hired professional troupes to stage many lavish plays.

The Corral de Comedias at Almagro, Spain

King Philip often demanded that actors perform at his court on such short notice that they had to cancel public performances. Circumstances such as those precipitated the decline of the public theatre.

Spanish theatre settings and costumes have always been elaborate. During the Golden Age, theatrical producers in Spain used different types of staging for the three different places of performance: the public theatre, the outdoor wagons, and court theatre. Staging for the *corrales*, or public performances, resembled Shakespeare's Globe theatre productions. They took place on a raised platform that had no front curtain. Simple set pieces were used to represent such places as a garden or a

197

room in a castle. Later trapdoors, painted flats, and machinery for moving objects were added. The religious productions, were similar, but they were more elaborate. The court theatre, however, employed the most ornate costumes and scenery. In 1640, Italian architects completed the first Spanish proscenium-arch theatre in the king's palace, where lavish, baroque productions took place.

To compensate for the lack of scenery, Spanish actors in all productions wore elaborate costumes. With few exceptions, actors used contemporary clothing for all plays; their dress suggested little in the way of historical accuracy. *Autos* and court productions were costumed far more lavishly than those in public playhouses.

Women performed in Spain as early as the fifteenth century, but they were not officially licensed to appear on stage until 1587. Spanish actresses often received criticism for their immoral dancing and sometimes for their daring costumes. In 1599 the Royal Council decreed that actresses could not perform at all unless their husbands or fathers were in the company.

Although Spanish actors did not have a high social rank, they were better off than their French contemporaries. Spanish actors worked long hours and were usually paid by the single performance, or else they had a share in the company. Troupes sometimes received an extra allowance for travel or to perform *autos*. A typical day for a Spanish actor of the period would involve these activities. He probably studied his role from 5 to 9 A.M., rehearsed until noon, performed in the afternoon until 7 P.M. in a public theatre, and appeared again at court during the late evening hours. All actors had to be able to sing, dance, and play a musical instrument.

From 1650 onward, Spain's economy, politics, and culture declined. No dramatists wrote plays of significance after the death of Calderón in 1681, until the twentieth century.

NEOCLASSICISM IN FRANCE

Italy greatly influenced the French Renaissance and its theatre. Henry II, who ruled France from 1547 to 1559, married Catherine de' Medici from Italy. Upon Henry's death, Catherine was placed in a position of power and influence throughout the lives of their three sons: Francis II (reigned 1559–1560), Charles IX (reigned 1560–1574), and Henry III (reigned 1574–1589). Also Cardinal Richelieu and Cardinal Mazarin strongly advanced Italian culture and neoclassical drama while they were chief ministers from 1624 until 1661. Under Louis XIV's rule, France became the cultural center of the world. Molière and Racine became France's greatest playwrights. Later in the period, theatre and costume designers employed an ornate, baroque style.

French theatre in the Renaissance developed slowly. Two circumstances that hindered its progress during the early sixteenth century were religious wars and a theatre monopoly in Paris. Civil War between the Protestant Huguenots and the Catholics raged between 1562 and 1598. Henry IV, a converted Catholic, instigated peace between the religions with his Edict of Nantes in 1598, thus creating a more stable French society. Beginning in 1402, the Confrérie de la Passion, originally an amateur company that later became professional, established a monopoly on all theatrical performances in Paris that lasted until 1598.

Through the second half of the sixteenth century, French theatre developed more rapidly. In 1548 the Confrérie built a new theatre, the Hôtel de Bourgogne. It was the first Parisian theatre built since ancient times, and theatre productions took place in it until 1783—for 235 years. It held

Troisième Journée.
Le Malade imaginaire, Comedie representée dans le Jardin de Versailles devant la Grotte.

Dies tertius.
Ὁ Κενόνοσων, feu Æger imaginarius, Comœdia acta in hortis Versaliarum ad fores Cryptæ.

A performance of *The Imaginary Invalid* at Versailles, 1647

about 1600 spectators in the pit and the galleries around the walls. Staging was similar to the medieval mansions, with various acts placed along the sides and back of the stage. In the 1550s the first plays in French began to appear. In 1577 the famous Italian commedia dell'arte company Gelosi performed with great success at the French court. Also the Confrérie began to lease the Hôtel de Bourgogne for the productions of visiting troupes.

During the seventeenth century, France became the most powerful European nation and encouraged creativity in drama, literature, art, and architecture. France fought for the Protestant cause in the Thirty Years

War (1618–1648). The French also participated in the age of discovery by establishing trading posts for fur in countries throughout the world. Also during the 1600s the French kings established absolute rule, which aided the arts but eventually led to the downfall of monarchy in France and a lessening of France's influence throughout the world.

The first professional playwright in France was Alexandre Hardy. His tragicomedies were popular from 1597 to 1625. Valleran LeComte's troupe, Les Comédiens du Roi (The King's Players) performed most of Hardy's plays in the Hôtel de Bourgogne. This group dominated theatre from 1598 until 1612.

Farce with a commedia influence was the most popular entertainment at the Hôtel de Bourgogne from 1612 to 1625. During this period, three actors portraying farcical commedia characters dominated the theatre. Henri LeGrand enacted Turlupin, a character similar to the commedia Brighella. Hugues Guéru portrayed Gaultier-Garguille, and for a trademark he wore a pointed beard and a black cap. To play Gros-Guillaume, Robert Guérin whitened his face and emphasized his portly stomach by wearing two belts, one above and one below.

The dramatic style called neoclassicism dominated the French stage during the period 1625–1660. From 1624 until his death in 1642, Cardinal Richelieu was the real power behind young Louis XIII's crown. Richelieu encouraged the Italian idea of writing and staging drama, and in 1641 he built the first Italian-style theatre in his own palace. His influence was the primary force that impelled France toward a neoclassical theatre.

Neoclassical critics established strict guidelines based on classical models for all plays. A play had to be composed of five acts. The characters should exhibit universal rather than individual characteristics. The unities of time, place, and action were important. Each play should have one principal action that ought to take place in 24 hours or less. The play should have verisimilitude, the appearance of reality, and violence should not occur onstage. Furthermore, each play should teach a moral lesson, with rewards for proper behavior and punishment for anything improper, and of course all plays should be entertaining for the audience. Tragedy had to deal with characters of nobility and important issues; it should be written in lofty and poetic language and end unhappily. Comedy was required to treat middle- and lower-class characters involved in domestic and private affairs; the style was appropriately ordinary speech with a happy ending. Only tragedy and comedy were acceptable forms of drama.

Pierre Corneille (1606–1684) popularized French neoclassical tragedy. Born in Rouen, he studied law in a Jesuit school, but after seeing the actor Montdory perform, Corneille decided to write plays. In 1637 he wrote *The Cid*, one of the most famous of all tragicomedies. At first it aroused extreme controversy and changed his whole career. The play dealt with honor and love, but it was a tragedy with a happy ending. Cardinal Richelieu called upon the French Academy to judge the play. The Academy, which consisted of the 40 most important literary men in France, praised *The Cid* for the ideals in it that were neoclassical and censured it for those that were not. This criticism so shocked Corneille that he quit writing until 1640, at which time he returned with true neoclassical tragedies and comedies. Three of Corneille's best neoclassical tragedies are *Horace* (1640), *Cinna* (1640), and *The Death of Pompey* (1643). They have a strong central character who chooses death rather than dishonor. The characters are simple, but they become involved in complex plots. Although never wealthy, Corneille was successful and honored throughout his life.

From 1625 to 1660, French theatrical production blossomed with the work of a number of outstanding actors and designers. Bellerose and Montdory were the stage names of important French actors. Bellerose (Pierre le Messier), a dignified comic and tragic actor, brought increased social prestige to the acting profession. Montdory, whose real name was Guillaume des Gilleberts, was a favorite of Richelieu. Montdory was an emotional actor with a declamatory style. He had to retire early because he developed a paralysis of the tongue. Theatres changed about 1641 when Italian scenery appeared. Cardinal Richelieu's Italianate theatre (later named the Palais-Royal) had a proscenium arch and flat wings. About 1630, the French government began to subsidize theatre. The new funds encouraged elaborate productions and helped improve the social and financial situation of theatre artists.

Under the absolute rule of Louis XIV, France became the cultural center of the world. Although he inherited the throne in 1643 at the age of 4, Louis actually reigned from 1661 to 1715. The Italian-born Cardinal Mazarin controlled the government for him from 1643 until his death in 1661. In 1682 Louis moved to the magnificent Palace of Versailles with all the leading noblemen. His reign was a golden age for art and theatre, and he called himself the Sun King. Louis XIV's extravagant lifestyle matched baroque design. In the baroque style, columns and arches were festooned with garlands, carvings, and paintings. Noblemen wore embroidered coats and powdered wigs, while noblewomen dressed in jeweled robes and high headdresses. The Palace of Versailles, which took 32 years to build, was lavishly decorated with fountains, formal gardens, mirrors, mosaics, and tapestries. Theatres and stage productions of the time were equally elaborate.

Jean Racine (1639–1699) wrote at the peak of French neoclassical tragedy. Orphaned when young, Racine was reared by his grandparents who sent him to an austere Catholic religious sect for education. Instead of becoming a priest, Racine decided to enter the theatre, where he successively fell in love with two beautiful actresses. Thérèse Duparc was Molière's leading actress until 1667, when Racine convinced her to join the Bourgogne troupe. She played Racine's leading female roles until her death in 1668. After 1670, La Champmeslé, Racine's new lover, played the leading female roles in his plays. Racine and Molière became enemies over the issues of Mlle DuParc and a play of Racine's that Molière directed. Racine had other enemies in the theatre, and so he retired in 1677. He then became historiographer to Louis XIV and married Catherine de Romanet, with whom he had seven children.

Racine brought French neoclassical tragedy to its highest accomplishment. He wrote his best tragedies between 1667 and 1677, and perhaps

Jean Racine

the most highly respected is *Phaedra* (1677). Although his plots are relatively simple and feature strict unity of time, place, and action, his characters are complex. After Racine's retirement from the theatre in 1677, tragedy declined in France, and it has never regained such eminence.

Playwright Jean-Baptiste Poquelin (1622–1673) took the stage and pen name of Molière. He achieved fame as the best French author of neoclassical comedy. The son of wealthy parents, he grew up in Paris and received an excellent education. He renounced his right to take over his father's position as upholsterer of the royal household, and at age 21 announced he would become an actor. A year and a half later, his father bailed him out of debtor's prison. Since the French theatre seemed to lack good plays, Molière started writing his own. He aspired to be a tragic actor, but because of his voice and stature he succeeded instead in comic and farcical roles of the henpecked husband, sick man, and foolish bourgeois.

As a person Molière was strong, warm, loyal, courageous, and humane. He headed an acting troupe and directed his own plays. At age 40 he married an 18-year-old actress, Armande Béjart, either the younger sister or daughter of Madeleine Béjart, with whom Molière also had a close relationship. He and Armande had three children (one daughter survived). Armande played the heroine in Molière's plays. His marriage was not altogether happy, because Armande continually flirted with other men.

Molière's famous comedies of social satire and characterization are successfully performed today. He wrote and acted with simple, natural diction and with more credibility than most actors of the period. Whether in prose or verse, his comedies depict a double vision of right and wrong, normal and anormal. Many of his character ideas came from commedia dell'arte. He also wrote about 40-year-old men marrying 20-year-old women. While Molière suffered much illness and probably died of tuberculosis, he made fun of illness and doctors. His most famous comedies, which contain humorous observations of characters and manners, are *The School for Wives* (1662), *The Misanthrope* (1666), *The Miser* (1668), and *The Imaginary Invalid* (1673).

In 1673, during the fourth performance in the lead role of *The Imaginary Invalid*, Molière experienced an internal hemorrhage, but he managed to finish the performance. Friends rushed him home, but he died within a few hours. Acting was still frowned upon as a profession. Near death many actors denounced their profession, so they could receive the final sacraments and a formal burial. Molière had no time to do so; he was buried without ceremony, after nightfall, in unconsecrated ground.

Until the middle of the seventeenth century, European playwrights received a specified amount of money for their plays. Later, they were given shares for the initial run of the play; then they received no further money.

Baroque designers dominated the French stage from 1660 to 1700. In 1674, Louis XIV appointed Jean Berain (1637–1711) to be his chief designer. Berain conceived baroque costumes and sets for opera, court festivals, and public ceremonies. His settings featured elaborate special effects and complicated decor. A Berain costume consisted of fabric embroidered with gold and jeweled ornamentation, tassels, fringe, floating veils, and high headdresses. Berain's designs also influenced the excessive ornamentation of rooms, furniture, and everyday dress. After Berain died, his son Jean carried on his work.

Actors supplied their own costumes, which were usually contemporary clothes. The classical hero, however, wore the *habit a la romaine*, which looked something like Roman armor with boots, a plumed headdress and a full wig. Also Indian, Near Eastern, and classical characters wore fancy costumes but not in the contemporary style.

In 1689 the Comédie Française acquired a new home, the remodeled Etoile tennis court. The auditorium held about 2000 spectators in a standing pit and two levels of 19 boxes in a horseshoe shape. The stage was elevated about 6 feet. Five rows of benches were located on either side of the stage, but the spectators who sat in them often hindered actor movement. The stage was 41 feet deep and 54 feet wide, but the audience on stage reduced the acting space to about 15 feet in width. Operas performed there used elaborate productions, but straight plays usually called for single sets with flat wings, so emphasis was on the actor, not the scenery. Overhead lighting and footlights consisted of candles and oil lamps.

Molière as Julius Caesar in Corneille's *The Death of Pompey*

From 1660 to 1700, acting also reached a peak of perfection. At the time of Molière's death in 1673, Paris boasted five professional acting companies. In 1680, when the Comédie Française was formed by a merger of two other troupes and given a monopoly on all drama in French, it became the world's first national theatre. Thus by 1697 the Comédie Française and Lully's opera company were the only professional companies left. The Comédie Française had shareholding members (*sociétaires*) and members paid to perform minor roles (*pensionnaires*). Women of the troupes shared equal rights and pay. A company probably had 50 or more plays in its repertory.

In those days, actors tended to play the same type of role for years and were paid according to their importance. Actresses played prominent roles, but men using a falsetto voice often portrayed character women. Some of the most famous actresses were Madeleine Béjart, Armande Béjart, Mlle DuParc, Mlle Desoeillets, and Mlle Champmeslé. Most of the tragic acting at the Hôtel de Bourgogne tended to be declamatory, but Molière's company strove for a more credible style. Michel Baron (1653–1729), whom Molière trained, became the leading tragic actor of the late years of the century. His work was said to be unusually natural.

The Renaissance movement, from the fifteenth into the seventeenth century, started in Italy and spread to the rest of Europe. While Italy failed to produce any plays of permanent importance, its artists proclaimed the importance of humanity and art. The dynamic works of the commedia dell'arte introduced and developed professional actors and overcame the inhibitions of the medieval church. With the aid of Italy's finest artists, the formal Italian Renaissance theatre developed elaborate scenery and lavish theatres.

Spain's greatest era of dramatic literature (1580–1680) closely coincides with her Golden Age of world dominance. Spain continued interest in medieval religious drama through the *autos sacramentales*. But the greatest Spanish playwrights, Lope de Vega and Calderón, also wrote popular cape and sword plays. They rejected the Italian neoclassical style and developed a secular Spanish drama about honor, romance, and action.

Italian theatre greatly influenced the French Renaissance movement. France's best playwrights wrote between the years 1637 and 1677. Corneille and Racine composed neoclassical tragedies, while Molière wrote and acted in the popular comedies about contemporary life. Under the colorful monarch Louis XIV, France developed the first national theatre in the western world, the Comédie Française. Although Italian staging arrived earlier, by the end of the seventeenth century elaborate baroque staging became dominant.

12 Shakespeare and the Renaissance in England

England's Renaissance period (1485–1649) produced one of the world's greatest playwrights, William Shakespeare, and one of the most influential and longest-ruling monarchs, Queen Elizabeth I. The daughter of Henry VIII and Anne Boleyn, Queen Elizabeth ruled England from 1558 to 1603, England's golden age. This partially coincides with England's great period of literature and drama (c. 1585–c. 1610). During Elizabeth's reign, many important dramatists appeared, and managers constructed a new kind of theatre building.

The English Renaissance started about 1485 when the War of Roses, the 30-year bloody battle for the crown between the House of York and the House of Lancaster, ended with the death of Richard III and the ascension of the Tudor king Henry VII. About this same time, people began to publish books in English instead of Latin. Oxford scholars, who had studied in Italy, introduced humanism, and they rekindled interest in the classics. Henry VIII, who reigned from 1509–1547, married six times during his lifetime and thus caused a break with the pope in Rome. Eventually the Protestant Reformation in England broke the power of the Catholic Church and helped pave the way for a drama that differed from the religious medieval plays.

Discovery and exploration under Elizabeth I created a new wealthy class of merchants and rulers who supported artists and writers. Sir Walter Raleigh sent expeditions to colonize America. England and Spain fought the battle of the Armada over conquests of land and wealth and over religious differences of English Protestantism versus Spanish Catholicism. As commerce flourished, the middle class became more important and the standard of living grew higher.

John Lutz in *Hamlet*, University of Evansville

EARLY DRAMA

English drama of the early Renaissance showed a strong classical influence. Many plays were produced in Latin. The first example of a native English comedy was *Ralph Roister Doister*, written by Nicholas Udall between 1534 and 1541. University students, lawyers, and choirboys performed much of the drama produced between 1550 and 1585. Plays were usually performed at the universities or the Inns of Court in London, but some performances took place at royal courts. Lawyers studied and resided at the Inns of Court, where Queen Elizabeth sometimes attended their productions.

From 1559 to 1583, Queen Elizabeth preferred the court performances of a group of choirboys, the Children of the Chapel Royal. The choirboys mainly acted interludes, but later Ben Jonson and other playwrights wrote scripts for them. The Chapel Royal and other choirboy companies rejected the classical plays and produced a more open and free drama with emphasis on light romantic comedy.

A new form of drama emerged in the 1580s with three important dramatists: Christopher Marlowe, Thomas Kyd, and John Lyly, who were England's first professional playwrights. They combined the classical concept with medieval clowns, stage action, and subplots to produce an original English drama.

Before Shakespeare the best writer of tragedy was Christopher Marlowe (1564–1593). Educated at Cambridge University, he wrote *Doctor Faustus* (c. 1588). Marlowe developed the historical play, perfected blank verse, and built his dramas around a strongly motivated character. He became especially well known for the magnificent poetic dialogue in his plays. A freethinker, rebel, and drunkard, Marlowe was killed in a tavern brawl before he reached 30.

At that time Thomas Kyd and John Lyly also achieved popularity. Kyd (1558–1594) brought the revenge play to high acclaim with *The Spanish Tragedy* (c. 1587). Influenced by Seneca, Kyd pioneered in the bloody revenge, ghosts and suspenseful plot structure with strong reversals that also appear in Shakespeare's *Hamlet*. Government officers arrested and tortured Kyd because of his agnostic views about Jesus Christ. He was also dismissed from his theatre company and died in poverty. John Lyly

The Globe Theatre, Bankside, London, 1593

(c. 1554–1606) refined comedy with prose and added romance and pastoral settings, as in his *Love's Metamorphosis* (c. 1590). His dramas contain mythological themes and were mainly written for choirboy companies, but they influenced Shakespeare's *A Midsummer's Night Dream* and *As You Like It.*

Opposition from the Puritans, local governments, and some townspeople hindered the theatrical climate. Local governments opposed professional performances because large crowds spread the plague and caused

Left: Christopher Marlowe

Right: The Swan Theatre, London, 1596

thievery, fights, and small riots. Some townspeople felt the afternoon performances distracted people from their work or from religious services. With pamphlets and sermons, the Puritans attacked professional theatre for its "vice and folly." The Puritan opposition finally won the battle in 1642, and the government temporarily closed all theatres.

Queen Elizabeth, a theatre enthusiast, fought the Puritan antitheatre movement by placing English theatre under central government control. She improved the quality of plays in 1559 by banning medieval cycle plays and forbidding playwrights to write about religious or political topics. In 1572 Queen Elizabeth's official recognition of actors as professionals, instead of vagabonds or rogues, encouraged the theatre as a profession. She cut the number of acting companies by allowing only noblemen above the rank of baron to maintain a troupe. But the queen legally sanctioned the acting profession by allowing other companies to obtain a license. Previously, if an actor was not employed as a servant to a nobleman, he was subject to punishment.

In 1574 Queen Elizabeth vested all authority to license and censor plays, actors, and anything connected with the theatre in the Master of Revels. Sometimes, however, the government closed theatres because of the plague or for other reasons. Although government control restricted English theatre in some ways, the power of the queen ultimately helped keep the theatre going in spite of the opposition of the city government and the Puritan leaders. In 1574 the first professional company, The Earl of Leicester's Men, was licensed.

Prior to 1576 professional companies acted mainly in inn yards and banquet halls or on village greens. London had many inns built around square open yards surrounded by upper galleries onto which the bed-chambers opened. A stage could be improvised at one end and the lowest balcony used for the upper stage. An audience could stand in the yard, and higher-paying members could sit in the other balconies. Eventually some inns erected permanent stages with resident companies. London was the theatre center, but traveling companies often performed in inns of other English cities.

PRIVATE AND PUBLIC THEATRES

At least nine public theatres and seven private theatres were built between 1576 and 1642. Public playhouses held 1500–3000 people, and they were unroofed. All public theatres were built outside the city limits on plans similar to the inns, but they may have varied in shape from octagonal to round or square. The private theatres were enclosed and seated about one-fourth to one-half as many people on benches. The admission cost for public theatres such as the Globe, where Shakespeare worked, was about half the price of private theatres such as the Black-friars. The Children of the Chapel Royal and other child acting troupes performed in the indoor private theatres, churches, or courts. After 1608 children's companies lost popularity, so adult companies played in private theatres in the winter and in public ones in the summer.

The Fortune Theatre is the only period theatre whose actual dimensions are known; it was 80 feet square. The unroofed part of the Fortune contained a pit, or yard area, where the main audience stood on three sides of the stage, which rose 4 feet to 6 feet from the ground and was partially or wholly covered with a thatch roof. The stage was about 43 feet wide and 27.5 feet deep, with trapdoors for grave scenes and special appearances or disappearances.

Little definite information exists describing the exact appearance of the Globe Theatre, in which Shakespeare produced his plays. It was probably circular or hexagonal on the exterior. The first Globe Theatre, built in 1599, burned in 1613. Like the square Fortune, the Globe had trapdoors in an elevated stage, covered with curtains or wood, around which the audience could stand on three sides. The ceiling above the stage, commonly called "the heavens," probably was painted in a similar manner and contained a trapdoor. Above the ceiling a roofed hut housed special sound effects and machinery for raising and lowering actors and scenery, like cloud-wreathed thrones. Flags flew from the hut on the day of performances, indicating the type of play, and a trumpeter blew to signal the start of the play. Rebuilt on the same site, the second Globe lasted from 1614 until it was pulled down in 1644. The interior was decorated more elaborately than the original, and the roof was made of tile.

The wooden building of the Globe contained three circular tiers of galleries that tightly housed 3000 spectators. Higher-paying clientele sat on benches or stood in the galleries. Possibly some people sat on or above the stage. Little is known about the "tiring house," the area directly behind the stage, probably used for storage and dressing rooms.

Historians differ about some of the rear stage components of the Globe Theatre. The back of the stage probably contained two large doors with windows above. J. C. Adams's reconstruction of the Globe depicts a permanent "inner stage" between the doors, covered by curtains that could be opened for certain scenes. Adams also shows a balcony acting area directly above on the second level with a railing. C. W. Hodges argues that a removable pavilion on the main stage was used for acting space; balcony scenes took place on top and curtains could be opened below for discovery scenes. Because of the restricted sight lines in Adams's plan. Hodges argues that if there was not a removable pavilion, at least the upper and lower "inner stages" were thrust out from the back facade. Because of existing evidence, most scholars are more closely aligned with the Hodges theory. Some drawings show a third-story "inner stage" for a few acting scenes, but if it existed, it was probably used mainly for the musicians.

The indoor, so-called private theatres were open to the public. The first Blackfriars Theatre, built in what was originally the great hall of a monastery, opened in 1576 as the first private theatre. The Children of the Chapel Royal, a boys' company, performed there until it closed in 1584.

Above: The Globe Theatre, Bankside, London

Left: Three clowns in Shakespeare's *Much Ado about Nothing*, Indiana University

James Burbage built the second Blackfriars in 1596. The King's Men, Shakespeare's company, started performing at the Blackfriars after 1610. Until that time, private theatres only housed boys' companies. Although the second Blackfriars seated only about 500, the seating and stage arrangements were similar to the Globe. Backless benches added to the pit area enabled the entire audience to sit down. One to three levels of side galleries and some private boxes housed part of the audience.

Public, open-air Elizabethan theatres used little scenery and no front curtain. Shakespeare's *Antony and Cleopatra*, for example, has 43 scenes, but when originally staged, the production probably did not pause between scenes. The actors' entrances and exits in different acting areas and levels kept the play moving. Because the producers used so little scenery, audiences had to use their imaginations. Signs naming places of action were sometimes posted on the stage. Set pieces like thrones, beds, trees, and city gates were sometimes utilized. Perhaps some simple mansion sets similar to those used in medieval times were placed on stage. Scenery could be stored and brought up from below, and space existed under the roof of the main stage area for ropes and pulleys to raise or lower small set pieces from or onto the stage.

Open theatres like the Globe did not need lighting because the plays took place in the afternoon, but indoor, private theatres like the Blackfriars used candles or lanterns. In both theatres, actors bringing candles or torches onstage signified a night scene. Because of the minimal scenery, costumes and music were important to the creation of spectacle. Plays used integral songs and dances and sometimes had interludes and concluding dances. Colorful banners and musical flourishes greeted the entrances of royalty and generals. Costumes were lavish, but they were not always authentic for the period of the play. Most actors wore elegant, contemporary clothes of the Elizabethan period that were appropriate to the importance of the character. Fairies, ghosts, and witches had specific costumes, and Roman characters wore Elizabethan dress with a cloth draped over it. Often wealthy patrons donated costumes to theatres.

ACTING TROUPES

An actor's life was busy, but if he was successful, he could become wealthy. Most actors studied voice and movement. They often were required to sing, dance, fence, and perhaps play a musical instrument. In productions the actors spoke eloquently, and many of them had to play multiple roles. The actor rehearsed in the morning, acted in the afternoon, and performed at court or learned lines in the evening. Sometimes his company toured other cities. Hamlet's famous lines of advice to the actor indicate that the later Elizabethan acting style was more natural than exaggerated. Because the theatres were relatively small, the actors could hold the audience's attention with emotional speeches and specific movement. Although the plays contained elaborate language, the acting style of the age featured lifelike behavior and detailed dramatic action.

Adult professional acting troupes depended at least partially upon the support of a beneficent noble, one who also gave the company his name.

The Earl of Leicester, for instance, licensed in 1574 an important company headed by James Burbage. From about 1583 to 1593 Queen Elizabeth kept a troupe at court called the Queen's Men. Companies changed their name when they changed patrons. William Shakespeare and Richard Burbage worked for the Lord Chamberlain's Men, who under James I became the King's Men.

Companies consisted of 10 to 25 men; no women performed on the English stage at that time. Several members were shareholders, who selected and produced the plays, and they divided the profits according to the number of shares they owned. Other members were hired for about two years. If the company lacked funds to build or rent its own theatre, it sold "householder" shares to owners who were repaid one-half the gallery receipts. In addition to money obtained from patrons and the sale of tickets, companies rented their theatres to other performers. They also sold beer, ale, wine, apples, and nuts at the performances. The professional companies performed a large repertory and changed plays often. Plays were repeated several times during a season until the audience no longer demanded them. During the peak years a good company probably performed as many as 214 days a year. Every actor specialized in certain roles.

Each company used three to five boy apprentices who played female and child roles, although men probably played the older female comic roles. An apprentice started at age 6–14 and remained until he became

Above: Richard Burbage

Left: *The Tempest* by William Shakespeare, University of Evansville

213

18–21 years old. Each boy apprenticed with one actor, who paid his room and board and trained him in the art of acting. The company paid the adult actor when the apprentice performed. At the end of his apprenticeship, the boy could become a full-fledged acting member or enter another profession.

Some companies were made up entirely of children. These companies were choirboys at court chapels or town cathedrals. A choirmaster directed them, charged admission, and retained all the profit. In return, the boys received a good education. Choirboys usually performed before an educated and cultured audience, such as the Queen's court. The best troupe was the Children of the Chapel Royal, later called the Queen's Revels.

One of the most distinguished actors of the Elizabethan age was Richard Burbage (c. 1567–1619). He came from a theatrical family; his father, James, was an actor and built the first permanent theatre in London. Richard Burbage later built the Globe Theatre. By the age of 20, Richard Burbage had earned his place on the stage. Many critics considered him the greatest English actor of the period. Although short and stocky in physical stature, he exhibited great energy and considerable performance power, but he could also work subtly as well. Excelling in tragedy, Burbage first played the roles of Hamlet, Romeo, Macbeth, Othello, and Lear. Also an accomplished painter, some authorities credit him with creating a famous portrait of Shakespeare. Burbage died a wealthy man. Other famous actors of the time were William Kempe, Robert Armin, John Lowin, and Nathan Field.

SHAKESPEARE AND OTHER ELIZABETHAN PLAYWRIGHTS

The world's most famous playwright, William Shakespeare (1564–1616), lived during the English Renaissance period. He was a man of extraordinary genius as a dramatist and poet. From 1590 until 1613 he wrote 38 plays for the Lord Chamberlain's Men, later called the King's Men. He also acted minor roles. He was successful enough as a man of the theatre to purchase shares in the acting company, interest in theatres, and property in Stratford-upon-Avon.

Few records of Shakespeare's life exist, partly because he did not write about himself. Baptized on April 26, 1564, in Stratford-upon-Avon, near the Forest of Arden, Shakespeare was the third child of eight for Mary Arden and John Shakespeare. One of his brothers, Edmund, also became an actor. His mother came from a family of distinction, and his father was a glover whose prosperity declined when Shakespeare was about 13. As a boy, Shakespeare received a proper Latin-oriented grammar school education, but he was one of the few popular playwrights of the period who lacked the funds to attend Oxford or Cambridge. In 1582, at age 18, he married Anne Hathaway, eight years his senior. In May 1583, they had a daughter, Susanna, and about two years later twins, Hamnet and Judith. Hamnet died in 1596. Like most women of her class, Anne did not read or write and stayed home in Stratford when Shakespeare went to London.

William Shakespeare

From 1585, when Shakespeare's twins were born, until 1592, when Shakespeare emerged as an actor and rising playwright in London, almost nothing is known about his life. Historians conjecture that he started working as a teacher in a country school and then joined a traveling theatre company and went to London. It is known, for instance, that Lord Leicester's Men passed through Stratford in 1587.

Although Shakespeare's plays appeared at court and elsewhere, he wrote only for the Burbage company. That group was probably the best and most popular company in London, and so Shakespeare's plays were well acted. He received enough pay as a playwright and actor to purchase an interest in both the Globe and the Blackfriars theatres. In 1597 he bought New Place, one of the largest homes in Stratford. Eventually he acquired other properties there. After about twenty years of writing, in about 1610, Shakespeare left London to spend most of his last years in Stratford with his wife and married daughters. Some reports say Shakespeare became ill from drinking too heavily with Ben Jonson and the poet Michael Drayton. At any rate, he was ill and hastily made out a will. Shakespeare died at the age of 52 at New Place, on or around April 23, 1616, and his family buried him in the chancel of the Stratford parish church.

Although Shakespeare took ideas from other plays, history, mythology, and fiction, he formulated his own unique type of drama. He used lines of verse set in iambic pentameter, a variety of well-rounded characters, and interwoven plots to create dramas of value and meaning. Shakespeare's comedies, tragedies, and histories show the Renaissance man struggling with himself and against the powers of the universe. Shakespeare's humanistic plays prove the nature of man and the meaning of existence. Unlike classical plays, Shakespeare's dramas presented scenes of action set in many places over an extended period of time. His characters enact violence on stage rather than merely describe it. Shakespeare's plays continue to be popular because of their great insights into human nature and their author's strong command of the poetic language.

A few critics once claimed that Shakespeare did not write these plays and attributed them to various other authors. These claims, generally considered false, occurred mainly because: (1) little is known about Shakespeare's life; (2) he lacked a college education; and (3) no manuscripts exist in his writing. Shortly after Shakespeare's death, his friends published a collection of 36 of his comedies, histories, and tragedies. This *First Folio*, published in 1623, came from previous singly published editions of the plays. Also a book entitled *Shakespeare's Sonnets* appeared in print in 1609. Listed chronologically, the following plays represent Shakespeare as one of the world's finest writers: *Richard III, Taming of the Shrew, Romeo and Juliet, A Midsummer Night's Dream, As You Like It, Julius Caesar, Twelfth Night, Hamlet, Othello, King Lear, Macbeth*, and *The Tempest*.

Playwrights usually wrote for a certain company, but they could sell

A setting by Inigo Jones for the masque *Salmacida Spolia*

individual plays to any company. The writer was paid a certain fee for his play, and sometimes he received the proceeds beyond a specified amount for a certain performance. Around 1630 the playwright received a weekly salary for a certain number of plays each season in addition to a benefit performance. The Master of Revels reviewed each play for morally, politically, or religiously objectionable material. Playwrights helped at rehearsals, and many of them also acted in the company. After the playwright was paid, his play became the property of the acting company, who usually kept only one complete copy.

Another influential Elizabethan playwright, Ben Jonson (1572–1637), excelled at comedies and court masques, but he also wrote tragedies and poetry. His intense life fluctuated between periods of fame and glory and those of poverty and sickness. Born after his father's death, Jonson served as a soldier, bricklayer, and actor before becoming a playwright. Jonson once killed an actor in a duel, but he escaped hanging. He was in and out of prison for dueling, for disfavor caused by his writings, and for nonpayment of debts. But in 1616 Jonson became the first poet laureate of England under James I and published the first collection of his plays (previously only poetry was published). On his death in 1637, he was buried in Westminster Abbey.

Famous for his social satires, Jonson also wrote plays for a children's company and most of the court masques during the reigns of James I and Charles I. Some of his plays were produced by Shakespeare's company, where occasionally he acted. Jonson started writing in the 1590s, about the same time as his friend Shakespeare. His most famous plays are *Every Man in His Humour* (1598), *Volpone* (1606), *The Alchemist* (1610), and *Bartholomew Fair* (1614). He drew characters based on exaggerated human behavior. Through satire Jonson tried to ridicule and thereby correct the vices of his time, particularly vanity and greed. Although he did not attend a university, Jonson was recognized as one of the greatest intellectuals and literary men of the English Renaissance.

Other significant playwriting contemporaries of Shakespeare are John Marston (1576–1634), Thomas Dekker (c. 1572–c. 1632), Thomas Heywood (c. 1574–1641), Cyril Tourneur (1579/80–1625/26), and Thomas Middleton (1580–1627). Their plays concentrate on complex characters and perceptive insights into human nature and actions. Their characters struggle with forces of good and evil in an action that shifts rapidly in time and place. Like Shakespeare, their poetic imagery is based on humanistic ideals.

JACOBEAN AND CAROLINE DRAMA

Plays written during the reigns of James I (1603–1625) and his son Charles I (1625–1649) are sometimes classified as Jacobean and Caroline, labels derived from the names of the respective rulers, who were from the house of Stuart. From 1610 to 1642 the most popular dramas were tragicomedies with happy endings and romantic tragedies with unhappy endings. Skilled playwrights stressed the shocking and spectacular over the revelation of man's importance in society.

Francis Beaumont and John Fletcher formed a famous writing team. They collaborated between 1608 and 1613 to compose such popular tragicomedies as *Philaster, A King and No King,* and *The Maid's Tragedy.* When Beaumont quit writing, Fletcher collaborated with other authors and wrote his own plays, such as *The Scornful Lady.* These typical plays of the 1610–1642 period were extremely popular at court and influenced Restoration drama. Other important writers during this period of English drama were John Webster, John Ford, Philip Massinger, and James Shirley.

Under the Stuart rulers James I and Charles I one of the most popular forms of entertainment was the lavishly produced masque. Masques first appeared in 1512 under Henry VIII in the form of a masked ball. Mainly performed at court in banquet halls, the masque resembled the Italian *intermezzo.* Masques were produced for social occasions, usually to honor some member of the royal family or an important visitor.

Masques emphasized dancing, lavish costumes, and spectacular scenery. The cost far exceeded a regular production of a play by a professional company. Experienced actors and trained musicians performed some roles, but courtiers performed the nonspeaking dance roles and comprised the majority of most casts. Even women of the court appeared in masques; otherwise during this century, they were not seen on the English stage. The grand masque dances were usually all male or all female. Ladies and gentlemen of the court wished to look their best in elaborate costumes of gold and silver. The scenery often involved striking transformations.

The poetry of a masque, however, was relatively unimportant to its spectacle. But because of the prestige such productions offered, many leading playwrights wrote masques. Ben Jonson completed 32, but he quit in 1631 because he felt his eloquent poetry was lost among the elaborate scenery and costumes. Poets wrote short scripts (8–12 pages) with mythological characters—such as Diana, Neptune, and Oberon—or allegorical characters—such as personifications of Reason and Love. The plot usually honored a person or occasion by comparing them to mythological characters or stories. Titles of two masque extravaganzas are *The Masque of Beauty* and *The Masque of Oberon.*

Ben Jonson wrote and Inigo Jones (1573–1652) designed the most famous masques of the period. Jones, founder of English classical architecture as well as a scene and costume designer, studied perspective scenery in Italy. Designers often based masque settings on medieval models, until 1605, when Jones and Jonson did their first production together on an elevated stage with Italian perspective scenery.

In 1622 Jones designed the Banqueting Hall of Whitehall Palace in distinctly Italian style. Most of the Stuart masques were performed there, using a proscenium arch, painted perspective backdrops, and angled wings—a significant change from the relatively simple Globe Theatre. Jones's scenery became increasingly complicated and expensive to build. Various productions had a flaming hell, a great rotating globe, and a cloud machine that moved onstage. Eventually, Jones introduced England to all of the Italian Renaissance scenery innovations, such as flat wings and rapidly changing scenery. In 1629–1630 Jones converted the Cockpit at Court into an indoor theatre. He willed his papers to John Webb, who became a leading Restoration scene designer and architect.

Masques contributed little of literary value to the theatre, and they detracted from the imaginative tradition of Shakespearean scripts. But, Inigo Jones established a new trend in theatre design and staging. His masque productions influenced English scene design toward perspective settings and proscenium arches. Masques paved the way for opera, pantomime, and ballet.

James I and Charles I wanted to rule England as absolute monarchs. During their reigns England established colonies in North America. At home Charles spent a great deal of money entertaining his court with masque performances. In 1629 Charles even dissolved Parliament and tried to rule alone. But the English people wanted a voice in their country and fought back in the Civil War of 1642. The parliamentary army of Puritans, called Roundheads because of their short hair, eventually defeated Charles I and his Cavaliers.

Extravagant productions of masques enraged the Puritans, who had always opposed theatre. Since British royalty supported the theatre companies, the Puritan Parliament used the Civil War of 1642 as an excuse to close theatres and forbid all play production. In 1644 the Globe was pulled down. After Charles I was beheaded as a tyrant and traitor in 1649, some actors fled with the court to France, where they could perform. English theatres did not reopen until 1660 with the return to power of Charles II.

England's greatest era for playwrights occurred from 1585 to 1610, during which time more eloquent drama was written perhaps than at any other time in history. The three-sided open-air Globe Theatre was adaptable to quick-changing scenes. Excellent dramatic literature and actors of stature attracted an audience from all classes of society. During Queen Elizabeth's reign, England perfected a national theatre of lasting importance. Drama changed during the Jacobean and Caroline periods, but Inigo Jones established new innovations in theatre design that paved the way for Restoration drama.

CHAPTER 13 The Rise of National Theatres

The end of the seventeenth century saw a new social freedom, and with the eighteenth century came the Enlightenment. People demanded changes in politics and society. Some countries like France and the United States had violent revolutions for the sake of freedom. People of the lower and middle classes came to dominate the aristocracy. During England's Restoration period at the end of the seventeenth century, producers presented the English version of neoclassical plays. But the Enlightenment brought changes to the theatre. David Garrick introduced a more realistic acting style to England. Italian designers contributed elaborate baroque theatrical settings. Germany's golden age produced a strong national theatre and two outstanding playwrights, Goethe and Schiller. Theatre finally got under way in America. Everywhere actors became more respected. In the eighteenth century, permanent professional theatre finally came into being.

Thomas Betterton (left) as Hamlet

THE THEATRE OF RESTORATION ENGLAND

After the Puritans beheaded Charles I in 1649, England declared itself a commonwealth, a republic without a king or a House of Lords. Parliament governed until 1653, when Oliver Cromwell declared himself Lord Protector; he ruled as a dictator until his death in 1658. The Puritan government tried to stop all theatre. Society once again considered actors to be rogues and vagabonds, and for minor offenses some actors were imprisoned and flogged. The government even destroyed most of the theatre buildings. No one wrote new plays, and the quality of production fell.

The Restoration period spans from 1660 to about 1700. After Cromwell's death in 1658, his son tried to rule and failed. So in 1660 England called Charles II, a Stuart, to govern the country, and he did so until his death in 1685. Because rule by monarchy was reestablished in England, the period following 1660 is called the Restoration. During this era English society saw a marvelous restoration of trade, science, and culture.

Upon the death of Charles II, his brother James II came to rule from 1685 to 1688. But when James tried to force Catholicism on England, Parliament deposed him and chose James II's Protestant daughter Mary and her Dutch husband, William of Orange, to govern. They ruled jointly as William III (reigned 1689–1702) and Mary II (reigned 1689–1694). But most of the power remained in the hands of Parliament through a new Bill of Rights, which also barred Roman Catholics from the throne.

During the Restoration period, the theatre became a social gathering place for the wealthy. Common people did not attend the theatre. The king usually sat in the royal box directly opposite the stage, or sometimes he held special performances in one of the court theatres. The aristocracy acquired French habits and attended the theatre mainly to be amused. Refreshments were sold. The audience often behaved rudely, and spectators sometimes had disagreements with actors.

The Restoration period saw the development of neoclassical drama in England. During the reign of Charles II, nicknamed the Merry Monarch,

Goethe acting in his play *Iphigenia in Taurus*

popular drama usually conveyed tales of the aristocracy in comedies of manners, while heroic tragedies possessed more neoclassical concepts. The tragedies utilized themes of love and honor reminiscent of the Spanish cape and sword dramas.

The two best English tragic playwrights of the period were John Dryden and Thomas Otway. From 1668 to 1688 John Dryden served as poet laureate and royal historiographer. Dryden's most famous tragedy, *All for Love* (1677), retells Shakespeare's *Antony and Cleopatra* story in blank verse and according to neoclassical rules. Thomas Otway wrote the tragedy *Venice Preserv'd* (1682). Unfortunately, his literary success did not bring him prosperity, and he spent the last years of his life in extreme poverty.

William Congreve

The crowning achievement of Restoration playwrights was, however, their development of a type of drama called comedy of manners. As the sentiment of England's aristocracy turned against Puritanism, the sexual mores of the upper class grew self-indulgent and loose in order to express freedom. Comic playwrights wrote drama that depicted the excessive behavior of the aristocratic class; thus the characters—fops, high-spirited ladies, fanatics, fools, and conceited wits—mirrored England's Restoration society. The plays exaggerated life to entertain the audience.

Some of the leading writers of Restoration comedy were George Etherege, William Wycherley, and William Congreve. Etherege, creator of the comedy of manners, wrote flippant plays about seduction and arranged marriages. *She Would If She Could* (1668) and *The Man of Mode, or, Sir Fopling Flutter* (1676) are characteristic of his work. William Wycherley wrote satirically about illicit love and the battle of the sexes in *The Country Wife* (1675) and *The Plain Dealer* (1676).

Perhaps the most brilliant craftsman of Restoration comedy, William Congreve (1670–1729), managed the new theatre in Lincoln's Inn Fields for a time. In 1695 his popular play *Love for Love* opened there. *The Way of the World* (1700), his last play, contains some of the best comic dialogue and most clear-cut characterizations of the period. Congreve became discouraged over the nonpopularity of this play and the criticism he received on the morality in his plays, so he gave up the stage and spent the last 29 years of his life writing poetry and serving in various government jobs. Congreve left his fortune to the Duchess of Marlborough, by whom he had a daughter.

Most playwrights did not become wealthy from their plays. During the Restoration a playwright might hold a share in an acting company in return for writing three plays a year, or he might receive a fixed salary from a company. Whenever a playwright associated himself with a specific company, he then usually wrote roles for particular actors or actresses. After 1680 playwrights were usually paid by a benefit performance. They received the proceeds (minus the house expenses) of a designated night's performance or sometimes several nights' performances.

Three important theatres were constructed in London during the Restoration: the Drury Lane (1674), the Lincoln's Inn Fields (converted from Lisle's Tennis Court in 1661), and the Dorset Garden (1671). They combined Elizabethan and Italianate features. Christopher Wren evidently designed both the elaborate Dorset Garden in 1671 and the simple Drury Lane in 1674. Also Charles II commissioned John Webb, who had worked under Inigo Jones, to redesign two court theatres, the Cockpit and the Great Hall. Theatres seated up to 650 people. The audience sat in the pit, boxes, or galleries in front of a proscenium-arch stage. The most expensive seats were the first-level boxes. After 1690 some spectators sat on the stage.

England introduced some innovations to theatre buildings that the rest of Europe did not have. They utilized a large apron, an acting space in front of the proscenium arch with an entrance door on each side and boxes above the doors. Actors used the two apron doors mainly for most of their entrances and exits. The stage apron extended about the same distance in front of the proscenium as the depth of the stage proper behind the proscenium. In the Drury Lane, for example, the proscenium divided about a 34-foot-deep acting space in half. Most Restoration stages raked slightly upward toward the back. The Dorset Garden contained an elaborately decorated proscenium and a half roof over the apron. Statues and busts added ornamentation throughout.

The Restoration period also introduced scenery and lighting practices quite different from those of the Elizabethan age. The neoclassical idea that specific time and place were unimportant led to the use of stock scenery. Producers built general settings, such as a palace interior, a garden, a prison, or a palace exterior. Little is known about Restoration set designers or builders because easel artists painted the scenery for high prices. Producers used the sets frequently in various plays over a period of years. A green baize carpet covered the stage floor during tragedies to protect the costumes of the characters who died on stage.

Workers changed the scenery in full view of the audience, but the productions did not stop for scene breaks. Settings consisted of wings, borders, and shutters—two flats pushed together at the back of the stage. Stagehands moved the flats, which were set in grooves in the floor. Performances took place in the afternoon, so little lighting was needed. When necessary, chandeliers filled with candles lit the stage and auditorium. By 1673, footlights of either candles or oil lamps came into use.

A combination of realism and convention existed in the popular stage effects. Books, tables, and chairs were often painted on the scenery, but when characters were shot, the audience liked the appearance of real blood. Producers used fireworks and smoke along with fire-painted scenery. Lightning and thunder effects also came into play. Traps in the stage floor for graves and disappearances and flying apparatus for characters such as witches remained popular.

Costuming consisted mostly of contemporary clothes and wigs of the Restoration period. Leading characters in comedies wore particularly elaborate costumes. Actresses in tragedy usually wore black velvet with a long train. Leading characters in historical plays often wore special costumes. Henry VIII was costumed like Holbein's famous portrait of the king. Hamlet usually wore black, and Macbeth dressed in an English army officer's uniform. Classical heroes often wore a costume with a

Anne Bracegirdle as the Indian Queen

breastplate, short tunic, and helmet called the *habit à la romaine*. Actors also dressed in a costume *à la Turque*, which consisted of a turban and baggy trousers for Near Eastern characters, while for similar roles, actresses merely added a feathered headdress.

During the Restoration period, attitudes and practices in regard to acting changed. Actresses appeared on the English stage for the first time in the 1660s, so playwrights began to place more emphasis on female roles. A company consisted of about 35–40 people. Actors usually entered a company on a probationary status. Davenant and Killigrew ran an actors' training company in the 1660s and 1670s. For wages actors received shares in the company, but a manager actually paid the actresses. The best actors earned a good income. They supplemented their performance salaries with gifts and tutoring. A manager owned shares and could sell or mortgage them to nontheatrical people to get money.

In 1660, foreseeing a revival of theatre, Sir William Davenant and Thomas Killigrew acquired patents from Charles II to manage the only theatres in London. This monopoly lasted until 1843 and deterred the growth of English theatre. After managing one company jointly, the men split into two groups. Davenant, who proved to be the better administrator, served as manager, director and playwright of the Duke's Company, which contained the younger players. Killigrew ran the King's Company, with more experienced actors. After Davenant's death in 1668, actors

Thomas Betterton and Henry Harris became the artistic directors of the Duke's Company. By 1682 Killigrew was in financial difficulties, and so the two companies merged into the United Companies. Christopher Rich, a business man who assumed control in 1693, managed the company so poorly that in 1695 Betterton led a revolt. He acquired a license from William III to form a second troupe that lasted until 1707. Other theatres were licensed to perform outside of London.

Thomas Betterton (c. 1635–1710) was the Restoration's greatest actor and an important theatrical leader. He began acting in 1660, and during his career he created about 130 parts, including most of Shakespeare's leading roles. His most famous portrayal in a wig and coat was Hamlet. Although Betterton could not sing or dance and was unimpressive in appearance, he received great praise for his acting. He was noted for staying in character and for exercising restraint, and he evidently had a powerful voice and was physically lively. Betterton's acting style would be classified as somewhat formal and elocutionary. He married a popular actress, Mary Saunderson, who became known professionally as Mrs. Betterton.

Three Restoration actresses achieved the most fame: Mrs. Anne Bracegirdle, Mrs. Elizabeth Barry, and Nell Gwynn. Mrs. Bracegirdle (c. 1663–1748) excelled in comedies with Betterton. Although not an extraordinary beauty, she radiated such charm and cheerfulness on stage that leading playwrights wanted her to play their roles. She evidently led a more austere life offstage than most of the actresses of the day, and in 1707 at the height of her career she retired from the stage. Mrs. Elizabeth Barry (1658–1713) specialized in leading tragic roles opposite Betterton. A beautiful woman with a full, clear voice, Mrs. Barry acted with dignity, softness, or whatever quality the character demanded. Nell Gwynn (1650–1687) grew up as a child of the London streets, but from 1666 to 1669 she was the leading comedienne of the King's Company. Both pretty and witty, Nell Gwynn performed excellently as a singer, dancer, and speaker of prologues and epilogues. She found particular popularity performing roles in romantic dramas. After a short acting career, she retired to be the mistress of Charles II, and bore him two sons. She persuaded Charles to make their oldest and only surviving son a duke. Beloved by the public, Nell Gwynn supposedly remained faithful to Charles even after his death.

Nell Gwyn

EIGHTEENTH-CENTURY ENGLISH DRAMA

Political, social, philosophical, industrial, and artistic changes in the eighteenth century created the Age of Enlightenment. This movement of thought and belief developed from interrelated conceptions about God, reason, nature, and man. The Enlightenment strove to prove that the right reasoning would bring true knowledge and lead mankind to happiness and good fortune. This period lasted from about 1687 until 1789. During this time, the most educated people in England and throughout the world became interested in humanitarian ideas, especially those concerning nature, philosophy, and social problems. People came to respect science and logic as never before. Leaders wanted welfare for all human beings, religious tolerance, prison reform, better public health, and treatment for the sick and insane. Literature became important. During this century England began its industrial revolution.

The English philosopher, John Locke, provided an important theory of the social contract between the people and the government. According to Locke, men possess certain natural rights to life, liberty, and property. If a government does not protect these rights, then the people have a right to establish a new government. His ideas appear prominently in the U.S. Constitution and Declaration of Independence, and they played an important inspirational role in the American Revolution.

Throughout the century more and more people came to live in elegant homes, and many tried to dress more fashionably. Men wore extravagant bright-colored silk coats, waistcoats, breeches, and long, curled wigs. Women appeared in elaborate headdresses or high pompadours and hoopskirts. Social life centered around the coffeehouses where educated people met and discussed philosophical, economic, and social issues. As the century wore on, feelings of sentimentality began to rise, and the century ended with a romantic revolution, in which emotion overtook reason.

During the eighteenth century, England remained a democratic nation with a royal leader. When King William died in 1702, Anne, the second Protestant daughter of James II, became queen. During her reign, in 1707, England and Scotland united into a single kingdom called Great Britain. After Anne died in 1714, the English monarchs participated only minimally in the government. George III, who reigned from 1760 to 1820 treated the American colonies badly, and he was partly responsible for losing them during the American Revolution.

Theatre changed with the times. Authors could earn a living from the general public, and they no longer had to depend on the generosity of the aristocracy. Businessmen wanted to laugh and cry in one evening at the theatre; so drama turned to the middle class, and England built the nation's public theatres.

During the eighteenth century a performance lasted from three to five hours and might include in the following order: music, a prologue, the full-length play, variety routines with acrobats and trained animals between the acts of the play, an afterpiece (a comic opera, farce, or pantomime), and a final song and dance. Performance time gradually changed from mid-afternoon to about 6:30 P.M. Actors usually performed in the play and in one or more of the extra acts.

Although audiences behaved with more dignity than in Shakespeare's day, they still applauded favorite scenes and booed or hissed at the ones they disliked. Sometimes the audience protested something strongly enough to create riots. Seating in the playhouses was not democratic. The aristocrats sat in boxes, the middle class in the orchestra and the first gallery, and the lower class and prostitutes sat in the upper gallery.

Few playwrights could survive on play royalties, so not many succeeded financially. Usually when a theatre company produced a play, the manager paid the author a set sum. Sometimes writers received proceeds (minus house expenses) on every third night of the initial run of a play, but most plays did not run more than three nights. A playwright could sell a copyright for a play for 14 years and then renew it once. He did not receive a royalty for each production.

The Licensing Act of 1737 hurt playwrights because it reduced the demand for new plays. The Drury Lane and Covent Garden remained the only theatres that the government licensed to operate throughout the century. Other unlicensed theatres performed plays until Prime Minister Walpole became upset about certain political satires. Thus he devised the Licensing Act of 1737, which required licensing of any play by the Lord Chamberlain and authorized only theatres in the area of London designated as the City of Westminster. This act severely restricted the market for plays and their production.

Nevertheless, the eighteenth century produced a new kind of drama dealing mainly with contemporary middle-class life. Some of the earlier plays of George Farquhar, such as *The Beaux' Stratagem* (1707) and *The Recruiting Officer* (1706), and Sir Richard Steele's *The Tender Husband* (1705) were similar to the Restoration comedies. The new sentimental comedy veered from neoclassicism and achieved the most acclaim.

Colley Cibber (1671–1757) is credited with starting the new comedy about middle-class protagonists with domestic themes and scenes of pathos leading to a happy ending. Already an actor when he married in 1693, Cibber decided to write plays and act in them to earn more money.

A riot at Covent Garden, 1763

Riot at Covent Garden Theatre, in 1763. in consequence of the Managers refusing to admit half-price in the Opera of Artaxerxes.

In 1696 he wrote *Love's Last Shift*, which established him as an important leading actor and the first sentimental comic playwright. In 1704 he wrote *The Careless Husband* for Anne Oldfield and himself. At different times, Cibber successfully acted and managed the Haymarket and Drury Lane theatres.

Eighteenth-century comedies are called sentimental because the characters are unnaturally good and their problems are easily solved. These comedies stressed warmth and kindliness, and most of them lacked humor. But Oliver Goldsmith (1730–1774) and Richard Brinsley Sheridan (1751–1816) spiced their plays with wit and ridicule of manners. They were probably the most skilled English playwrights of the entire eighteenth century.

Goldsmith's most famous play was *She Stoops to Conquer* (1773). The play's hero thinks he is stopping at an inn, when he is actually staying at his fiancée's home. The characters have humor and humanity. It is one of the few English comedies frequently produced from its own time until the present.

A dramatist, poet, novelist, essayist, and journalist, Goldsmith grew up in Ireland. The son of Rev. Charles Goldsmith, a poor minister, young Oliver was ugly, undersized, and pockmarked. After attending Trinity College in Dublin, Goldsmith became a playboy. He gambled away his uncle's money that was intended to send him to law school. He took a walking tour of European countries and in 1756 landed penniless in Dover. Choosing to reside in London, he soon began work as a hack writer. He met important people, such as actor David Garrick and painter Sir Joshua Reynolds. Because of his talent and industry, Goldsmith's literary and financial situations soon improved. In 1762 he started writing essays successfully. Next he turned to poetry, the novel, and in 1768 his first play. He like finery and extravagance, and in spite of his high income he seemed always to be in debt. His writing career lasted for about 15 years before he suddenly died in 1774 of kidney failure.

Richard Brinsley Sheridan only wrote a few plays, but two of them, *The Rivals* (1775) and *The School for Scandal* (1777), made him famous. When *The Rivals* first opened in 1775, it was unsuccessful, and so Sheridan revised the play, hired a new actor for the lead, and held a second performance 11 days later. This time the play succeeded very well. Sheridan's best work combined sentiment with wit and provided good entertainment. Typically, *The School for Scandal* ridicules affectation and pretentiousness. Besides being a playwright, Sheridan was a Whig politician, adviser to the Prince of Wales (later George IV), and an excellent political orator.

Born in Ireland, Sheridan grew up and was educated in England. Frances Sheridan, his mother, acquired some fame as a playwright; his father Thomas wrote the *Pronouncing Dictionary*. In 1773 after his marriage to Elizabeth Anne Linley, a soprano, he turned to the theatre. Garrick encouraged him to take over the management of the Drury Lane in 1776. In 1780 Sheridan became a member of Parliament, and from then on he spent more time on politics than drama. In 1791 he helped finance the rebuilding of the Drury Lane Theatre, and he did so again in 1809 after a fire. In 1812 he lost his seat in Parliament and no longer had income from the theatre, so he died with creditors hounding him.

Also during the eighteenth century, ballad operas, comic operas, burlesques, and pantomimes grew in popularity. Most of the librettos were satirical. John Gay's *The Begger's Opera* (1728) caricatured Sir Robert Walpole and satirized operatic style and middle-class sentimentality. Two centuries later Bertolt Brecht based his famous *Threepenny Opera* on Gay's play. Later comic opera developed original music and more sentimental plots. Burlesque was a satirical play without songs. Sheridan's *The Critic* (1781) remains an excellent burlesque about authors and critics. The popular pantomime was a combination of silent, comic episodes with commedia dell'arte characters and serious scenes about classical mythology using dialogue and song. Pantomimes were a spectacle with music and lacked any literary value. Famous for his portrayal of Harlequin, John Rich (c. 1682–1761) created about 20 pantomimes under the stage name of Lun.

Tragedies about contemporary subjects never achieved the same popularity as comedies. Tragedy underwent similar changes in subject and style. Stories about the aristocracy, history, or mythology gave way to those about the middle class and everyday life. In 1731 George Lillo (1693–1739) wrote *The London Merchant*, the first and perhaps best domestic tragedy in English. After the middle of the century, tragedy declined even more in popularity. Most of the tragedies presented during the century were distorted versions of Shakespeare's works.

The eighteenth century gave more acclaim to its actors than its playwrights. Usually the leading actor of a company also functioned as its manager. The actor-manager staged and starred in most of the company's productions, and he profited the most. Two such leading men were Charles Macklin and David Garrick.

In 1750 two acting styles dominated the English stage—oratorical romanticism and realistic romanticism. Until 1740 most actors recited their lines in a monotonous declamatory or musical cadence with exaggerated gestures, but then Macklin and Garrick introduced a more realistic approach. Most acting was played downstage with the actor facing front. After a speech the actor usually moved to the right. Important speeches were presented with vocal vehemence, drawn-out pauses, and startling movements. Macklin and Garrick tried to change the actor into the character, and they insisted that their actors read the lines as each character would actually experience them. Perhaps their acting might not be considered realistic by today's standards, but their acting style amounted to a drastic change for the period.

Companies performed in a repertory system, offering different plays on succeeding nights. Actors had to know the lines for any role they were assigned on 24 hours notice. Garrick played 96 roles. If assigned a character, the actor played that part as long as he stayed with the company; age had little bearing on assignments. When one actor left a role, a new actor often took over the same interpretation and pattern of stage movement as the previous actor. Rehearsals usually lasted about three hours a day for two weeks. Since Garrick's method differed, he sometimes

Mr. and Mrs. Barry in
Venice Preserv'd

rehearsed eight weeks.

Actors' income varied considerably according to the roles they played, but generally their salaries increased during the century. A leading actor could be under contract for five years, but a lesser actor usually found employment by the season. Actors also received money from a benefit performance that might vary from a small amount to more than they earned for the entire year.

Although many actresses achieved popularity in eighteenth-century England, five women stand out. Early in the century, Anne Oldfield (1683–1730) was considered the finest actress. A beautiful woman with a sparkling personality, she played both comic and serious roles. Later, critics considered Kitty Clive (1711–1785) the best comic actress of the day. She played opposite David Garrick for 22 years. Although temperamental, she was a skilled comedian and singer. Susannah Maria Cibber (1714–1766), the daughter-in-law of Colley Cibber, often played Garrick's tragic leading lady. She left an impossible husband to join Garrick's company, and she overcame a singsong manner of speaking to become an accomplished actress. Mrs. Hannah Pritchard (1711–1768) played Lady Macbeth opposite David Garrick, and he refused to play the role after she died. She was considered the best tragic actress of her time. Garrick's early love and mistress was Peg Woffington (c. 1714–1760). Considered witty and intellectual, she was somewhat affected as an actress. Too impulsive

231

and independent to marry Garrick, she left his company in 1749 when Garrick married another woman.

Several leading actors of the time came from Ireland. Barton Booth (1681–1733) started acting in Dublin, moved to London, and from 1713 to 1727 helped manage the Drury Lane Theatre. Poor health forced him into an early retirement, but he is remembered as a good declamatory tragedian. Perhaps the most famous oratorical actor was James Quin (1693–1766). Noted for his slow, melodious voice and sawing body gestures, Quin played numerous Shakespearean roles, notably a fine Falstaff in *Henry IV, Part I*. A large man, Quin had a strong voice. He began his acting career in Dublin, and in 1714 he moved to London and worked at the Drury Lane. He served as actor-manager for John Rich from 1718 to 1734 and then returned to the Drury Lane. An excellent swordsman, Quin once defended the stage with his sword against rioters at the Lincoln's Inn Fields Theatre. Another Irish actor of note was Spranger Barry (1719–1777). As the romantic lover only, Barry outshone Garrick. Barry's wife, Ann, acted in serious roles opposite her husband.

Also from Ireland came Charles Macklin (1699–1797). He started a new, realistic trend in acting with his portrayal of Shylock in Shakespeare's *The Merchant of Venice*. From about 1734 to 1743 Macklin served as actor-manager of the Drury Lane. A tempestuous man, he was constantly involved in lawsuits and disputes.

David Garrick (1717–1779) became the preeminent English actor of the period. He appeared taller than his 5 feet 5 inches, and he played a wide range of comedies and tragedies. Delivering lines in the spirit of the character, he revolutionized the acting style of his day, changing it from a declamatory method to a sort of realistic romanticism. In addition to acting, Garrick worked as dramatist, poet, producer, manager, and adapter of plays. His father, Peter, served as an English army officer but was descended from French aristocracy. Garrick grew up in Lichfield with six brothers and sisters. He traveled to London with Samuel Johnson and started out as a wine merchant. Through such theatre acquaintances as Charles Macklin, he became interested in theatre.

Garrick's acting career started in a small theatre in 1741 when an actor playing Harlequin became ill, and Garrick spontaneously replaced him.

David Garrick

In the same year at the Goodman's Fields Theatre he played the role of Richard III, and thus Garrick became famous at the age of 24. The managers of the Drury Lane, who had earlier refused him, offered him for the 1742–1743 season the largest salary ever proposed to an actor. Within a span of seven months, he performed 18 different characters in repertory. Possessing great versatility, Garrick could act comedy and tragedy equally well. He was known for his expressive, dark eyes, mobile features, swarthy complexion, broken tones of utterance, and graceful gestures. Garrick believed in good voice production, but he opposed bellowing and overexaggerated movement. He felt the best way to build a characterization was to study human nature. For example, in order to play King Lear, he studied the behavior of a friend who had gone mad. When Garrick retired in 1776, he presented a series of farewell performances including some of his most famous roles—Hamlet, Richard III, and Lear.

As manager of the Drury Lane for almost thirty years (1747–1776), Garrick brought that theatre financial success. He selected both plays and actors with care. Garrick rewrote Shakespeare's plays to restore more of the originals and to eliminate some of the additions of the Restoration managers. He also wrote several original plays. He rehearsed his casts longer, brought them together as creative ensembles, and stressed a realistic acting style. In 1762 he removed the audience from sitting on the apron and tried to reform their behavior. When he renovated the Drury Lane, he cut down the size of the apron, enlarged the auditorium, and moved the orchestral musicians down from the gallery.

In private life Garrick fell in love with actress Peg Woffington, with whom he lived from 1742 to 1745. Perhaps because she was independent, unfaithful, and extravagant, they did not marry. In 1749 Garrick married Eva Maria Veigel, a Viennese opera dancer. She retired from the stage, and they had a happy marriage but no children. Suffering from kidney trouble, Garrick became ill and died in 1779. He is buried in Westminster Abbey at the foot of Shakespeare's statue.

Eighteenth-century theatre arrangements were similar to those of the Restoration. Most theatres had an apron in front of the stage, plus a pit, boxes, and galleries. The stage size, however, increased, and the apron diminished. The main change occurred in the size of the auditorium. In 1700 the Drury Lane seated 650 people, but in 1790 it housed 2300. Again in 1793 the Drury Lane was rebuilt to house 3600. Built in 1732 to replace Lincoln's Inn Fields, Covent Garden held about 1300, but by the 1780s its capacity had increased to 2500, and in 1793 it accommodated 3000. Other important theatres were the King's Theatre and the Haymarket.

After 1765, when Garrick returned from Europe with innovative ideas, he ordered new sets built for his productions. He so influenced other managers that scenery in most English theatres became more specific. Scene painters joined theatre staffs. After 1749 theatre administrators even brought famous painters from Europe to do their scenery. For instance, Philippe Jacques DeLoutherbourg came from France in 1771 to design sets for Garrick. DeLoutherbourg got away from the parallel wings and created more realistic settings. He insisted that all the set pieces for one play be painted by the same person, and he perfected special machinery for such atmospheric effects as rain, hail, and gunfire. Lighting also improved during this period, and by the middle of the century the sidelights reflected down from behind the wings; the footlights were often lowered below the stage level.

THE BEGINNINGS OF AMERICAN THEATRE AND DRAMA

Early Spanish, French, and English settlers brought theatre to North America. In 1598 a Spanish captain wrote perhaps the first American play, a brief *comedia*, and presented it with amateur actors in the vicinity of modern El Paso. In 1665 William Darby wrote probably the first American play in English, entitled *Ye Bare and Ye Cubb*. About 1700 Richard Hunter petitioned for permission to produce plays in New York City. Governor Robert Hunter wrote *Androborus* in 1714, and it became America's first printed play. During most of the eighteenth century a number of British actors and companies toured North America. These actors found some financial success, but they endured numerous hardships. The adversity they faced came from physical conditions and societal attitudes. Many American churches, especially those in Massachusetts and Pennsylvania, opposed the theatre. Some local governments, too, restricted theatre productions. New York passed a law forbidding theatre in 1709, and from 1751 to 1791 Boston prohibited stage plays.

The American colonial theatre began in earnest during 1716 with the construction of a theatre in Williamsburg, Virginia. In August 1749 Walter Murray and Thomas Kean began America's first professional theatre in Philadelphia on Water Street. They also performed in New York City and Williamsburg. In 1752 Lewis Hallam brought his wife, their three children, and ten adults from England to start professional theatre in the colonies. When Hallam died, his wife married David Douglass, another English actor, who kept the troupe touring until the Revolution. Following British patterns, Douglass built important theatres in Philadelphia and New York City. At the Southwark Theatre in Philadelphia, he produced *The Prince of Parthia* (1767) by Thomas Godfrey, the first play written by an American to be performed professionally.

At the outbreak of the Revolution in 1774, the Continental Congress issued an interdict against stage shows. For the next eight years, theatre remained alive in America mainly because of the British army. The actors were usually British soldiers and their women, including a few performers from the disbanded Douglass company. Throughout the war British troops and colonists alike attended New York productions. Also during the war, Mercy Otis Warren and other Americans wrote satirical patriotic plays not meant for the stage, but those works kept the American dramatic spirit alive.

After the American victory in 1783, theatre began to revive. Although a number of theatres were built, theatre management was not a dependable business, as John Henry, Lewis Hallam, and Thomas Wignell discovered. Several American actors, such as Joseph Jefferson I, rose to prominence. Royall Tyler, a lawyer who had graduated from Harvard, wrote *The Contrast* (1787), America's first comic play on a native subject. A social comedy filled with witty speeches and farcical scenes, *The Contrast* established several character types—for example, the Yankee country bumpkin—and it remained the best American comedy until the middle of the nineteenth century. From the end of the war until 1800 several authors contributed to the establishment of several other original American character types in addition to the Yankee—especially the Indian, the Negro, and the Irishman.

William Dunlap, whom many call the father of American drama, became the first professional playwright in America, and his varied career lasted through 1832. Born in 1766, his family moved with him to New York City in 1777, and there he became excited about plays. After seeing *The Contrast* in 1787, he began writing dramas himself. He composed a total of 53 plays, including comedies of all sorts, ballad operas, Gothic melodramas, translations, adaptations, and romantic tragedies. His most well-remembered play, still occasionally produced today, is *Andre* (1798). It tells the story of a British messenger who met Benedict Arnold and then was captured and hanged by Americans. Early in his career Dunlap realized that a playwright had little chance for success without access to a theatre, and so he became a manager. Beginning in 1798 he managed the Park Theatre in New York, but in 1812 he gave it up. His greatest success as a manager came with productions of European melodramas, especially those by Kotzebue and Pixerecourt. Perhaps Dunlap's best gift

The first Chestnut Street Theatre in Philadelphia, 1794

to American culture was his book *A History of American Theatre* (1832). It remains a valuable document about the development of American drama in the late eighteenth century.

EIGHTEENTH-CENTURY EUROPEAN THEATRE

Although French theatre reached a climax of quality at the end of the seventeenth century, other countries still looked up to France as the political and cultural center of the western world. The country produced such notable eighteenth-century philosophers and writers as Denis Diderot, Voltaire, and Jean-Jacques Rousseau. They stimulated the Enlightenment by arguing strongly for ideas of freedom and equality. By 1763 France had lost its dominions in America and its power in India. Still France helped America in its revolutionary struggle with England (1775–1783). Then another political and social upheaval occurred with the French Revolution of 1789–1799. The people of France rebelled against monarchical absolutism; they overthrew the government and beheaded many aristocrats. By the end of the century Napoleon Bonaparte, a great military genius, came to dominate French government.

The French playwrights of the period reflected the desires of the cultured, educated middle class. Although the early tragedies imitated Racine's and Molière's neoclassical plays, writers began to utilize ideas about religious tolerance and societal reform.

The principal serious French dramatist of that time was Voltaire (François-Marie Arouet, 1694–1778). After the production of his first tragedy in 1718, he was acclaimed as Racine's successor and adopted the pen name Voltaire. Since he wanted to become the greatest French author, he supported the causes most appealing to the middle and working classes. He fostered religious tolerance and humanitarianism. When Voltaire became interested in England's freedom of thought, he learned English and went to England to study Newton and Locke. Throughout his life he was in and out of favor with the French crown and in and out of exile.

Voltaire wrote poems, scientific books, important French historical studies, and 53 plays. *Candide* (1732), a short novel, is probably his most famous work. His best play, *Zaire*, was produced in 1732. Voltaire tried to reform the French neoclassical play. He only succeeded in limiting the amount of violence and adding ghosts, crowds, and more spectacle to dramas. After 1760, audiences booed his plays off the stage, and managers refused to produce some of his works. In his last plays he returned to strict classicism, but his philosophic ideas interfered with the stories and characterizations. Although his work had great impact on the eighteenth century, his plays are of little interest today.

Denis Diderot (1713–1784) advocated that tragedy and comedy should be augmented by two *middle genres*—sentimental comedy and domestic tragedy. The leading characters in these plays were members of the emerging middle class. Diderot wrote some domestic tragedies classified as *drame*, serious plays that do not fall into the traditional tragedy category. He also strove for more realism in acting and staging.

Mlle Clarion crowns Voltaire

The best French playwright of the eighteenth century appeared late in its span. Pierre Augustin Caron de Beaumarchais (1732–1799) wrote the most noteworthy and popular comedies of the period—*The Barber of Seville* (1775) and *The Marriage of Figaro* (1784). Gioacchino Rossini and Wolfgang Amadeus Mozart later made them into operas. These dramas reflected the rebellious feelings of common people toward aristocratic society that were soon to stimulate genuine revolution. The plays of Beaumarchais contain social criticism against the nobility and feature a good deal of witty dialogue.

Beaumarchais, a political adventurer and financial entrepreneur, became a writer by chance. He started out as a watchmaker, like his father. By 1764 he had married a wealthy widow, acquired the status of a noble, become a financier, and amassed a fortune. In 1777 he founded a society to secure royalties for playwrights. As a result, in 1791 France passed the world's first law concerning royalty payments. Working for the French government, Beaumarchais even spent ten years as a secret agent. In this connection he managed to contribute a great deal financially to the cause of American independence. When the French Revolution broke out, he attempted to help the revolutionaries, but he narrowly escaped the guillotine and was exiled. Beaumarchais returned to Paris a few years later to find his mansion ravaged and his wife and daughter living in poverty. He died three years later while trying to restore his fortunes and return to literary and political work.

Parisian theatres of the eighteenth century seated the audience as close to the stage as possible. Wealthy people sat in the three tiers of boxes at the sides of the stage, and a large number of people stood in the pit. By the time of the Revolution, managers had modernized most of the theatres, providing larger stages and better scene facilities. They also placed benches in the pit area and tried to increase both seating capacity and sight lines.

Scene designs and costuming modes of French theatres affected practices in the rest of western Europe. In 1759 when managers banned audience members from sitting on the stage, more elaborate, baroque scenery began to appear. In the 1750s some actors and such authors as Voltaire and Beaumarchais encouraged more authentic costuming, but it never became realistic.

Two actresses and one actor from the Comédie Française—Mlle Clairon, Mlle Dumesnil, and Henri-Louis Lekain—were the most famous French players of the century. Claire Hippolyte Clairon (1723–1802) acted in classical tragedies with carefully planned and subdued emotion. She performed in a manner similar to Garrick. After 1766 she retired and began to train other actors. Clairon, a beautiful woman, received more praise from Garrick and Voltaire than did her rival, Dumesnil. Acting on inspiration with strong emotions of passion and fury, Marie-Françoise Dumesnil (1713–1803) once kept an audience in tears for an entire

A baroque scene design by Giuseppe Galli Bibiena

Voltaire play. Henri-Louis Lekain (1729–1778) is counted the greatest French tragedian of his time. Although uninteresting in appearance and voice, he strove for more realistic acting and became director of the Comédie Française. Lekain campaigned to banish spectators from the stage and contributed to the reform of more authentic costuming.

The theatre of eighteenth-century Italy, although not as noteworthy perhaps as those of England and France, made several significant contributions. During the course of the century Spain, Austria, and France ruled various parts of Italy. At the end of the century, Napoleon assumed control. A few Italians held enormous wealth, but workers and peasants still lived in tenements, hovels, or caves. Like their counterparts throughout Europe, poverty-stricken Italians began to demand liberty and equality.

As during the Renaissance, Italy's greatest contribution to theatre lay in its outstanding scene designers. Several Italian families produced baroque designers who lived in various locales in Italy—families such as Bibiena, Mauro, Quaglio, Galliari, and Fabrizio. They designed for many theatres throughout Europe.

From 1690 to 1787 at least seven different members of the Bibiena family designed lavish, baroque sets, mainly for operas. Bibiena designs often utilized ornate columns, curved arches, and stairways with a feeling of massive, spaciousness in which the actor seemed almost lost. They painted the proscenium, so that their settings appeared even larger and more removed from the ordinary theatre atmosphere. Ferdinando Galli Bibiena (1657–1743) initiated the use of a more sophisticated perspective system for painting scenery. He used two or more vanishing points at the sides of the stage rather than just one at the center rear of the stage. His angle perspective changed the center of attention from a single vanishing point in the center to the whole stage, thus implying a continuation of the set offstage on both sides. His brother Francesco was also a designer. Ferdinando had three sons who became prestigious designers—Alessandro, Giuseppe, and Antonio. The most distinguished artist of the family, Giuseppe, had a son, Carlo, who carried on the family tradition.

Another Italian designer, Filippo Juvarra (1676–1736), made other influential changes in scene design. He veered away from Bibiena's massive, baroque settings, and his later designs appear to be more early rococo with light and airy spaces projecting a cool, uniform, and revealing light. Later in the eighteenth century, light and shadow became more important than specific detail. A rebellion against the baroque style inclined designers toward romanticism. Gian Battista Piranesi (1720–1778) projected an interest in Roman ruins and contemporary prisons in his many etchings and scene designs.

Although opera received the most attention in Italy, Carlo Goldoni (1707–1793) made some significant contributions to Italian comedy. A practicing lawyer, he started out writing scenarios for commedia dell'arte troupes. He made some changes away from commedia by freeing actors from wearing masks and developing a more sentimental comedy. Following Molière's example, Goldoni created a comedy of character with moral and fairly realistic tones. He wrote prose and verse in Italian and French.

His most famous play, *The Mistress of the Inn* (1753), demonstrates, that he was better at writing female characters than male ones. *The Fan* (1764) and *The Servant of Two Masters* are two other plays by him. In his plays Goldoni, a bourgeois himself, favored the middle and lower classes over the nobility. Because of his success at writing sentimental comedies, Goldoni was Italy's leading playwright of the period.

Throughout the fifteenth and sixteenth centuries disunity and religious wars ravaged Germany and kept the country in a backward socioeconomic condition. The Renaissance first affected Germany in the sphere of religion. The Protestant Reformation and The Catholic Counter-Reformation superseded interest in the arts. At the time, Germany was divided into two main parts—a large northern area called Prussia and a smaller southern portion named Bavaria—plus several other small kingdoms.

In the mid-eighteenth century, Prussia became a leading power of Europe under King Frederick the Great. He ruled from 1740 to 1786 and devoted the first half of those years to warfare. By conquest and diplomacy Frederick doubled Prussia's size and made it into a first-class power. He spent the last half of his reign on peace and recovery, education and industry. An enlightened ruler, he fostered music, art, and literature. Himself an author of poetry and history, Frederick was the last great monarch of western Europe.

German theatre managers made perhaps more changes during the eighteenth century than did theatre leaders in most other European countries. In the early 1700s German performances took place in makeshift theatres. The plays were mostly comedies based on commedia dell'arte improvisations. They used exaggerated characters, vulgar dialogue, and violent action. The productions were for the most part poorly acted. During the early part of the century, a famous German clown character named Hanswurst appeared in most of the plays.

In the 1720s Johann Christoph Gottsched (1700–1766), a literary theorist and critic, and Carolina Neuber (1697–1760), an actress, collaborated to improve German theatre. They strove to eliminate the Hanswurst burlesque improvisations. Gottsched tried to develop a German theatre based on the French neoclassical plays. Carolina Neuber and her husband Johann headed their own acting troupe. She tried to elevate theatrical performances. She held strict rehearsals for actors and insisted that they memorize their parts instead of merely improvising them. The collaboration of Gottsched and Neuber, lasting from 1727 to 1739, marks the turning point in the history of German theatre and the beginning of modern German acting.

Germany's first important playwright was Gotthold Ephraim Lessing (1729–1781). Outside of Germany he became best known as a critic. Lessing led drama away from French neoclassicism toward the English drama of the period. In response to the new spirit of freedom sweeping through Europe, Lessing employed more middle-class subject matter and sentimental themes. His most popular play, *Minna von Barnhelm* (1767), is a comedy. In 1767–1768 Lessing wrote important essays and criticism about the Hamburg National Theatre, collected under the title *Hamburg Dramaturgy*.

From 1767 to 1787 an important German literary movement arose. It was called *Sturm und Drang* (Storm and Stress). With new creative and political ideals, the Sturm und Drang dramatists revolted against eighteenth-century rationalism. They composed new works that at first shocked their German audiences. The movement produced two of Germany's greatest authors—Johann Wolfgang von Goethe and Friedrich Schiller. Only Goethe's first play, *Götz von Berlichingen* (1773), and his novel *The Sorrows of Young Werther* (1774) and Schiller's early plays *The Robbers* (1782), *Fiesko* (1782), and *Intrigue and Love* (1783) are in the Sturm und Drang style.

Johann Wofgang von Goethe

Other than those few early works, Goethe and Schiller considered themselves authors of classicism. The years 1798 to 1805 represent the peak of the classical age in Germany. By adopting certain principles of classical thought, authors in this period believed in the employment of poetic language and historical detail in literature. They strove for idealism by harmoniously balancing intellect and feeling. Humanity, the individual person, freedom, and morality became supremely important. Working together as director and author at the Weimar Court Theatre, Goethe and Schiller developed the famous "Weimar Classicism." They believed drama should strive to transform ordinary experience and set forth ideals. Goethe and Schiller used harmonic verse and structural patterns with matching movement and gestures on stage to achieve grace and dignity.

Many critics consider Johann Wolfgang von Goethe (1749–1832) Germany's greatest writer. Perhaps he would have been even more well known as a playwright had he not also been such a fine novelist, poet, lawyer, critic, journalist, philosopher, educator, theatre manager, painter, and statesman. Following in his father's footsteps, Goethe received his doctor of laws degree in 1771. He loved literature, and so in 1773 he published his first play and a year later his first novel. He served as a statesman for 11 years, and from 1786 to 1788 he resided in Italy. There he studied the classics and then returned to Germany a renewed and changed artist devoted to classical writing. Although Goethe had many romantic involvements, he did not marry until age 57.

Goethe was appointed director of the Weimar Court Theatre in 1791. When he started working closely with Schiller, they created the Weimar Classicism. The two men made Weimar the cultural, intellectual, and theatrical center of Germany, and they brought it fame throughout the world. Goethe served as the theatre's director for 26 years. He created many innovations, including a code of rules for acting, and worked hard to improve the acting troupe through strict rehearsals, interpretation, and correct use of voice and action. His productions were not realistic, as he strove to take the audience beyond ordinary life through harmony and grace in the production. Schiller contributed classical plays for Goethe to direct. When Schiller died in 1805, Goethe lost some of his interest in the theatre. He resigned as director in 1817, and the theatre group soon lost its creative power and popular appeal.

Goethe wrote many important works, but *Faust* remains his theatrical masterpiece. Goethe took the legend of Faust, who sells his soul to the

Friedrich Schiller

Devil, and made a tragedy of personal experience and high poetry that is universally appealing. Faust learns that pleasures are not happiness and that man finds salvation in striving for fulfillment. Goethe's plays show his genius and great poetic talent, but they are probably not so actable as those of Shakespeare or Molière. His works contain great poetry and thought-provoking symbolism. They utilize stories about human beings striving to perfect themselves as more humane creatures. They defend peace, home, and domestic virtues. Although Goethe himself wrote classical drama, he contributed ideas to the romantic movement, which rose to importance after 1798.

In addition to his activity as a playwright, Friedrich Schiller (1759–1805) wrote poetry and literary theory. Schiller came from a poorer family than did Goethe. The Duke of Württemberg separated him from his family to educate him as a military medical officer. When the Duke forbade him to write plays, Schiller left his medical post and spent seven years struggling to earn a living as a writer. In 1790 Schiller married Charlotte von Longefeld, with whom he had two sons and two daughters. In his second year of marriage he became ill from overwork and thereafter had continual health problems.

Schiller's early tragedies deal with political oppression and the tyranny of social convention. His first play *The Robbers* (1782) is a milestone in the history of German theatre. It reveals how a young man is wronged and becomes an outlaw, but eventually realizes that lawlessness does not bring freedom.

Like Goethe, Schiller turned from the Sturm und Drang movement in the 1790s to classicism. From 1798 until 1805, with Goethe's encouragement, Schiller wrote a series of classical drama that placed German drama far ahead of contemporary drama in the rest of Europe. His best plays are poetic tragedies about liberty and humanism. His Wallenstein trilogy (1798–1799) tells about the Thirty Years War. *Mary Stuart* (1800), *The Maid of Orleans* (1801), and *William Tell* (1804) are more psychologically oriented stories of downfallen famous people in times of crises. All of Schiller's plays demonstrate how the human spirit—its inner freedom and striving for integrity—triumphs over adverse circumstances. Schiller possessed a magnetic personality, while Goethe appeared somewhat aloof. The two men created an important national German drama and some of the best plays in Germany's theatre history.

From 1787 until 1819 the most popular playwright in Europe and perhaps the world was August Friedrich von Kotzebue (1761–1819). Kotzebue began writing when he was a law student, and eventually he wrote over 200 plays and several novels, as well as historical and autobiographical works. His plays appealed to the public, and many of them are translated into English. He wrote a variety of farces, verse plays, and historical and domestic dramas. Companies in many countries performed his works throughout the nineteenth century, and his plays greatly influenced writers of nineteenth-century melodrama.

Kotzebue lived in Weimar at different times, but he did not get along with Goethe. He entered government service and traveled back and forth between Germany, Russia, and France. At one time he served as director of the German theatre at St. Petersburg in Russia. Upon returning to Germany, he published writings that made some people consider him a Russian spy. Thus, in 1819 a radical student stabbed Kotzebue to death.

The Hamburg National Theatre (1767–1769) was Germany's first attempt to have a permanent, subsidized, nonprofit theatre. The company hoped to attract the best actors and playwrights, but Lessing's theatre journal, *Hamburg Dramaturgy*, was the company's only lasting contribution. Despite its failure, the Hamburg company made the public aware that Germany needed national theatres.

The first state-supported theatre, the Gotha Court Theatre, was founded in 1775. Konrad Ekhof, the most highly respected actor at that time, staged the plays. He brought in good actors, but he did little to encourage the new drama. When Ekhof died in 1779, the theatre closed. In 1776 the second national theatre came into being. The Imperial and National Theatre was commonly called the Burgtheater after the building in which the troupe played. State-supported, permanent buildings, in various cities continued to be built throughout the last part of the century. By the 1790s there were more than 35 permanent acting troupes in Germany, among which Goethe's Weimer company was probably the best. But by 1825 the Burgtheater had assembled the finest acting company in Germany.

Eighteenth-century Germany produced a number of fine actors. Konrad

Ekhof (1720–1778) worked especially hard to improve the quality of acting in his country. His style was even more natural than Carolina Neuber's. Ekhof tried to represent each character's feelings, sufferings, and changing moods through speech and gesture. He acted with the Hamburg National Theatre and spent the last three years of his life in charge of the Gotha Court Theatre.

Probably the most outstanding actor of the period was Friedrich Ludwig Schröder (1744–1816). His mother, Sophie Schröder, was an actress, so Friedrich started acting when he was 3 years old. He acted about 39 new roles each year, thus performing in over 700 roles in his lifetime. By 1780 he was acknowledged as Germany's greatest actor. He created the Hamburg school of acting and production. Schröder strove for realism and distinction between the characters and the setting. Goethe's Weimer classicism opposed Schröder's performance style.

In addition to being an actor, Schröder was a theatre manager and playwright. He wrote, translated, or adapted 28 plays. Schröder managed the Hamburg National Theatre from 1786 to 1798 and lifted the company to greatness. His best years as an actor were from 1780 to 1798, when he retired at the height of his career. Living in one of the most formative periods in the evolution of German theatre, Schröder improved the level of both acting and management.

After Schröder retired, August Wilhelm Iffland (1759–1814) became the leading German actor. He left his parents at age 18 to join the Gotha

A production of _Wallenstein_ by Schiller

Court Theatre and study acting under Konrad Ekhof. Also a popular manager and playwright, Iffland acted in his own domestic dramas and sentimental comedies. Although not a romanticist, he influenced the movement. From 1798 to 1811 Iffland served as manager of the Berlin National Theatre.

Until about 1765 and the advent of permanent theatres, most performances occurred on makeshift platforms. Then German cities built theatres generally like those in the rest of Europe, with a proscenium arch and boxes at the sides. With permanent theatres came more historical scenery and Italian staging. By the 1790s Germany had at least 35 permanent companies, and the plays required more complex settings. Designers set up doors and windows between wings to establish a more realistic set. Scene painting improved, and machines provided special effects. By the 1770s individual costumes for characters such as monks and knights grew to be popular, but generally costuming meant using clothes of the sixteenth century or possibly togas for some classical plays.

Restoration England developed a comedy of manners depicting the excessive behavior of the aristocratic class. Some important theatres were built in England, and the acting style appeared oratorical. With the eighteenth-century Enlightenment, sentimental comedy dealing with the middle class appeared. David Garrick stood out as the most innovative actor-manager, and he strove for a more realistic style of production.

The first theatre in colonial America was built in 1716 at Williamsburg, Virginia. The first American playwright was William Dunlap.

In the eighteenth century France began to produce neoclassical drama. Later the country became more interested in the middle class and in building theatres. After the French Revolution, the new government restored the actor's right to Christian burial.

Italy's greatest contribution came from families of baroque scene designers like the Bibienas. Carlo Goldoni wrote many sentimental comedies.

During the eighteenth century, German theatre developed from a rather primitive state to a high degree of accomplishment. Temporary stages, improvised Hanswurst comedies, and bombastic acting characterized the early years. Germany's best minds—such as Goethe, Schiller, and Schröder—labored to create a German national theatre of professional caliber. German theatre had its own spirit, flavor, and freshness, similar in many respects to the Shakespearean period in England. The government built many state-supported theatres, and with new approaches toward discipline, harmony, and realism, the acting profession became important throughout Germany.

14

The Nineteenth-Century Spirit

The nineteenth-century spirit stressed individuality and adventure. In thought and deed, the intellectual leaders of the nineteenth century emphasized the importance of the common person and the perfectibility of every human being. Leaders in all fields attacked frontiers with more energy than ever before. Some sought adventure in the earth's remaining physical frontiers, and others sought it in the exploration of using natural resources in industry. The scientific method began to dominate thought, and the industrial revolution occurred in the United States and England. The late eighteenth-century political revolutions in France and the United States took deep root, and the desire for equality spread throughout those countries and affected many others. Common men and women were for the first time in history considered important, and the novels and plays of the period reflected that sentiment. The theatre of the century in all its phases stressed the value of the individual during life's marvelous adventure.

This chapter specifically treats European dramatic art from 1800 to 1870 and American theatre for the entire nineteenth century and the first 15 years of the twentieth, but the discussion naturally refers to some incidents of earlier or later periods. It explores the impact of the broad cultural movement called romanticism on the theatre. Next comes a section on a new form and style of drama that blossomed during the century—melodrama and the well-made play. The chapter then explores the birth and development of American theatre and drama. The theatre of the nineteenth century was perhaps more vital than its drama, and many of that century's tendencies and innovations have proved to be significantly influential during the twentieth-century.

Adah Isaacs Menken as Mazeppa

ROMANTICISM

During the first half of the nineteenth century, the romantic movement dominated the world of art, touching the theatre as deeply as it did poetry and painting. The thinkers who fostered romanticism opposed the strict, reasonable rules of neoclassicism. The romantics doubted that logic could provide all the answers to life's problems, and they argued that natural instinct in each person more dependably provides directives for action. Shakespeare supplanted the Greeks as the favorite model of romantic playwrights. The romantic movement evolved slowly, of course, first rising in Germany, then in England, and last in France. Many traits of romanticism appear in other ages as well. Shakespeare and other Elizabethans used some of them, and romanticism has in some ways

Edwin Forrest as Shakespeare's Richard III

persisted throughout the twentieth century.

A few essential ideas gave the romantic movement its energy. Some were negative and others positive. The romantics distrusted reason, which they thought could not explain all of human experience. They opposed the established social order and believed that any person, rich or poor, could rise to great heights. They claimed that truth exists most clearly in the great variety of creation and that universal human experiences were the ones most worthy of poetic investigation. They often turned to medieval subjects. Many romantics took up the religious concept of pantheism, a belief that God exists everywhere and that all beings are a part of him. They thought every man should strive to understand existence, but because of God's greatness, only he can understand everything. Furthermore, to the romantics the secret of creating beauty lay in genius. They thought that each artist should search for natural forms and use models provided by the "noble savage," or simple peasant. The romanticists believed the best art resulted from creative activity that was free from all restraint; the later rise of modernism with its artistic explorations drew great strength from this romantic attitude. Finally, the romantic writers rejected classical rules and concentrated on feelings in their work.

Romanticism first appeared in Germany during the late eighteenth century. Romantic writers used the works of Shakespeare for inspiration and the early dramas of Johann Wolfgang von Goethe and Friedrich Schiller as models. Although Goethe considered himself a classicist and believed in the "maxim of objective treatment in poetry," he also realized sentiment was important in his work; in fact he began his writing career as a protoromantic and then later turned to classicism. Still, Goethe's *Faust* became a paradigm for later romantics. Schiller, who always worked subjectively, developed many features of romanticism, as in *The Robbers* (1782). The critic August Wilhelm Schlegel became the most important German in the romantic movement when he set romantic theory against classicism. Schlegel emphasized mood, character, and feeling, and he argued that plot is merely a technique for arousing interest. His attitudes have influenced poets, playwrights, and critics even into the twentieth century. Schlegel especially influenced Samuel Taylor Coleridge, a leading English poet and romanticist. Some of the dramatists who wrote romantic plays in German were Heinrich von Kleist, Franz Grillparzer, and August von Kotzebue. By the mid-nineteenth century the best German writers rejected conventional romanticism and began to create dramas with a new consciousness. Writers such as Georg Büchner with *Danton's Death* (1835) and Friedrich Hebbel with *Maria Magdalena* (1844) were forerunners of modernism.

England produced some of its best poets during the nineteenth century, such romanticists as Lord Byron, Samuel Taylor Coleridge, John Keats, Percy Bysshe Shelley, and William Wordsworth. But these poets wrote mostly closet dramas, pieces intended to be read rather than performed. Lord Byron was perhaps the best dramatist among them, and many of his plays were produced with success after his death. Sir Walter Scott, the well-known romantic novelist, also composed a few plays. The most notable British romantic dramatist of the period was James Sheridan Knowles. He wrote such plays as *William Tell* (1825) and *The Hunchback* (1832). They feature strong stories and vivid action.

What England lacked in dramatists during the first half of the nineteenth century, they made up for in actors. Some of the greatest British actors flourished at that time. John Philip Kemble became a leading actor-manager at the Drury Lane Theatre, and later he made the Covent Garden into the best theatre in London. He and his sister, Sarah Siddons, were known for their detailed and dignified classical performances, especially during the first fifteen years of the century. George Frederick

Cooke and Edmund Kean challenged the classical manner of acting with the "new" romantic style. Cooke was particularly well known for playing villains, such as Iago in Shakespeare's *Othello*. Kean also preferred villainous characters. During his period of popularity, from about 1815 to 1830, Kean lifted the romantic style to high perfection by stressing feeling and going to any lengths to convey emotion.

Later in the nineteenth century the British tradition of fine acting continued. William Charles Macready took over as the leading British

Left: John Philip Kemble

Center: William Charles Macready

Right: Henry Irving

tragic actor in the 1830s and 1840s. Audiences admired him for his detailed characterizations and restrained manner. As director of major companies in London, Macready began to insist on careful rehearsals. With meticulous attention to all details, he even planned the blocking for each of the actors in his productions. The greatest British actor during the last part of the nineteenth century turned out to be Henry Irving. Particularly good at developing the physical characteristics of a role, Irving always found gestures that effectively communicated his inner feelings. As manager of the Lyceum Theatre, he chose Ellen Terry as his leading lady. For a number of years they made a starring duo of great vibrancy.

Romanticism flourished later among French writers than among the Germans or British. The empire of Napoleon with its imitation of Rome stressed classical values, and perhaps for that reason romanticism appeared onstage later in France than in Germany or England. Influenced by Mme de Staël and Stendhal, Victor Hugo wrote a fiery preface to his play *Cromwell* (1827) that turned out to be the most influential declaration about romanticism among French dramatists. Essentially, he called drama the highest form of artistic expression and Shakespeare its greatest practitioner. Hugo called for a drama that paid as much attention to the grotesque as it did to spiritual ideals. The explosion of French romanticism came with the production of Hugo's drama *Hernani* (1830) at the

Comédie Française. The play violated most of the neoclassical rules and aroused controversy and near riots in its audiences. For the next twenty to thirty years romantic drama dominated the French theatre. The best romantic plays came from the pens of such playwrights as Alexandre Dumas *père*, Alfred de Vigny, and Alfred de Musset.

England was not the only country to produce fine actors during the nineteenth century; the Parisian theatre developed such outstanding performers as Talma, Lemaître, and Coquelin. François-Joseph Talma, who came to prominence during the reign of Napoleon, was France's leading actor during the early years of the century. He considered himself a romantic, but he performed mainly in neoclassical plays. Known for detailed study of characters, he was able to combine great feeling with vigorous action. The two other truly great French actors of the century were Frederick Lemaître and Constant-Benoit Coquelin. Lemaître, probably the best-known French actor of the romantic movement, was trained in both classical and popular theatrical traditions. Lemaître specialized in inventiveness, and he seldom failed to astonish and delight audiences with unusual stage business and emotional effects. Coquelin came to the stage later than Talma and Lemaître. The most famous character that Coquelin originated was the title role in the neoromantic play *Cyrano de Bergerac* (1898) by Edmond Rostand. Coquelin excelled in virtuoso performances that called for unusual vocal and physical technique; he played many of the leading roles in the plays of Molière and Shakespeare.

Sarah Bernhardt

Above: Eleanora Duse

Right: Charles Kean

Two European actresses began their careers during the nineteenth century and rose to the very heights of theatrical renown—Sarah Bernhardt and Eleanora Duse. Madame Sarah, an eccentric but talented performer, came to prominence in 1862 at the Comédie Française. Known for her dark eyes, slim figure, and musically resonant voice, Bernhardt created such flamboyant characters as Camille, Tosca, and Phaedra. Her offstage life became the stuff of legends, especially when she toured the United States and supposedly demanded payment in gold and slept in a coffin. Eleanora Duse, who came from Naples, became an international star like Bernhardt, to whom she made a striking contrast because of her quiet intensity and reclusive behavior. After achieving fame, she traveled throughout the world performing in Italian plays by Gabriele d'Annunzio, her lover, and in works by Dumas, Ibsen, and Strindberg. Duse, like Stanislavsky in Russia, led the way toward quiet, intense, realistic acting that was to become the staple of the twentieth century. She, too, toured widely in the United States and died in 1923 in Pittsburgh.

During the nineteenth century many fine writers appeared in Russia despite strict censorship under the czars and the later social upheavals. Romanticism appeared in Russia in the works of Alexander Pushkin, especially in his well-known play *Boris Gudonov* (1825). Nikolai Gogol, a dramatist of the mid-century, achieved even more lasting renown with a significant forerunner of realistic comedy—*The Inspector General* (1836). In the 1850s Ivan Turgenev became Russia's leading author, and when

in the 1860s he decided to live abroad, he became world-famous as well. In 1850 Turgenev wrote *A Month in the Country*, his most famous play, but it wasn't staged until 1872. Another outstanding writer of comedy in Russia was Alexander Ostrovsky. He was actually Russia's first professional playwright, and the first to devote himself exclusively to writing drama. Composing at least one new play a year, Ostrovsky wrote a number of outstanding comedies, such as *Diary of a Scoundrel* (1868).

Although romanticism as a literary movement lasted only for a relatively brief time in each European country, the romantic vision persisted throughout the century. Its pervasive attitudes rather characterize nineteenth-century strivings. The romantic view of life stresses the spirit of rebellion and a sense of adventure. It suggests that feeling may be even more important than reason in understanding human behavior, and in the creation of art it focuses on intuition and sentiment rather than analysis and logic. Even the stunning rise of modernism that began in the late nineteenth century could never have happened without the influence of romanticism, as it taught humanity the importance of each individual in the struggle for personal freedom.

MELODRAMA AND THE WELL-MADE PLAY

During the period when romanticism became dominant, a new form of play developed—*melodrama*. The word originally meant "melody drama," because producers used background music to reinforce the emotional appeals of most early melodramas. Melodrama became the most popular genre of the nineteenth-century theatre, and in more sophisticated versions it has remained popular on twentieth-century stages. Obviously plays like *The Passion of Dracula* or *Deathtrap* are melodramas, but so are such plays as *Look Back in Anger* or *True West*. Also, melodrama has become the major form of cinema. The James Bond or *Star Wars* films offer good examples of cinematic melodrama, but nearly all contemporary screenplays utilize features of the form. Also most dramatic programs on television are melodramas. All television adventure stories—especially those about detectives, policemen, or western heroes—are melodramas. Even soap operas, dealing with more domestic subjects, follow the melodramatic form.

Neither as serious as tragedy nor as light as comedy, melodrama concentrates on adventure and shows people trying to escape threatening predicaments. Although playwrights created dramas of an intermediate sort in every historical period, the form didn't blossom until the early nineteenth century. Authorities cite two originators of melodrama, a Frenchman named René Charles Guilbert de Pixérécourt and a German named August von Kotzebue. Written for people who could not read, their plays mixed suspense with comic relief, sentimental attitudes with sensational effects, and stereotyped heroes and heroines with dyed-in-the-wool villains. During the first quarter of the nineteenth century, their plays swept the world in popularity.

The form of melodrama demands a strong story line in which a villain threatens the well-being of sympathetic characters for the sake of some objective. The good people struggle to survive and to escape the threat. In the process, complications and surprises abound. The best melodramas have double endings in which the bad characters are punished and the good ones rewarded. For example: Dracula needs the blood of fresh victims in order to stay alive; the good characters attempt to find a way to escape him; and finally they destroy him and return the world to harmony. The materials of melodrama are the stuff of adventure stories—distant places, simple times, and clearly good or evil characters. The style of melodrama demands simple dialogue but sensational visual effects. The characters don't have to be articulate because their predicament is clear and their feelings readily apparent. The production effects are crucial, because to thrill the audience is the point of the play. The purpose of the whole is to arouse hate for the nasty characters and fear for the well-being of the nice ones. Melodramas are profoundly appealing, too, because their double endings of reward and punishment present an ideal system of justice not often found in everyday life. Ultimately, melodramas provide frightening and amusing stories that offer mass audiences a chance to escape humdrum daily existence.

Many skilled practitioners wrote the hundreds of melodramas that took the stage during the nineteenth century. Among them, the Irish playwright Dion Boucicault (pronounced 'boo-see-ko') achieved the most fame and fortune; indeed, he became the first dramatist in the English theatre to earn great wealth from his writing. Because his plays were so popular, he demanded and received a percentage of the gross income from every performance—an unheard of financial innovation for writers. Boucicault wrote such popular plays as *The Sidewalks of New York* (1857), featuring a tenement fire; *The Octoroon* (1859), containing the explosion of a ship; and *The Colleen Bawn* (1860), showing a near drowning in a cave. His plays skillfully blended sensational scenes with natural ones, odd characters with ordinary people, and tearful events with hilarious ones. Other well-known English writers of melodrama were J. B. Buckstone, M. G. Lewis, and Douglas William Jerrold. A number of Americans wrote popular melodramas, and they are discussed in the next section.

As the nineteenth century progressed, the writers of melodrama turned from tales about faraway castles in ancient times to stories about more familiar subjects, such as the evils of drink, contemporary murders, and social conditions such as slavery in America. Stage effects changed, too, and plays began to feature such scenes as horse races, train wrecks, and nautical disasters. The ethical subject matter of melodramas at first depicted vicious brigands attacking virtuous lords and ladies, but later plays came to deal with such matters as the struggles of ordinary people to avoid crime or escape alcoholism and of pure young women to remain that way. Although melodrama is often dismissed as good or evil, it has altered its ethics in nearly every generation. For example, in the mid- to late twentieth century, as traditional values were attacked, melodramas often turned ethical values around to make heroes out of such criminals as "godfathers" and bank robbers, figures who in the nineteenth century could only have been villains.

Along with the rise of romanticism and the development of melodrama,

A scene from *Uncle Tom's Cabin*

some dramatists devised the *well-made play*. The original French term, *la pièce bien faite*, referred to popular plays of the mid-nineteenth century—such as those by Eugène Scribe—that employed complicated, carefully worked out stories. The term is sometimes used negatively today to describe a play in which the author too obviously manipulates the story, or in which everything proceeds too logically and is wrapped up too neatly at the end. Scribe thought that the romantic writers stressed mood too much, and he wanted to develop contemporary stories, different from those used by Shakespeare and Racine. As a practical man of the theatre, Scribe assembled a set of techniques for playwriting to provide good stories on up-to-date themes. Plot mattered most. Knowing that common audiences responded well to vivid stories, Scribe wanted his plays to have plenty of action and intrigue. So he established a formula for narratives of all sorts—comedies, melodramas, and tragedies alike.

For thirty years Scribe dominated the French theatre with his 400 plays. Many of them came out of his "play factory," consisting of other writers who carried out specific jobs, much like the twentieth-century Hollywood writing committees. Some of Scribe's successes were *The Little Sister* (1821), *The Devil at School* (1842), and *Marco Spada* (1852). Alexandre Dumas *fils* pointed out the flaw in Scribe's dramaturgy: the lack of an inspirational idea, a basic philosophy. To Scribe a play is a play, some-

255

thing to be constructed according to a plan, not an artistic thing with an organic life of its own. Also, the French well-made plays of Scribe and others, such as Victorien Sardou, sacrificed detailed characterization for the sake of story complications. But the influence of the French well-made play of the mid-nineteenth century was great indeed, because of some of its worthwhile features. Later writers of realism—such as Ibsen, Strindberg, and Shaw—picked up some of Scribe's techniques. On the positive side, Scribe employed detailed exposition, careful foreshadowing, cause-to-effect scene progression, good crisis scenes leading to climaxes, strong suspense, and startling reversals. Great playwrights had used all these principles before Scribe, but he taught the world how to apply them to contemporary life.

Four special developments, then, of the early and middle nineteenth century prepared the way for the explosion of the modern theatre. First came the spirit of romanticism, which stressed the importance, perfectibility, and worth of all human beings, even common men and women. Second, actors went through several phases during the century, stepping from neoclassical dignity to romantic bombast and then to realistic reserve. Third, producers and writers together developed melodrama and placed increasing emphasis on realistic stage effects. Fourth, certain practical dramatists carefully assembled the dramatic principles necessary to make interesting the subject matter of ordinary lives.

THE GROWTH OF AMERICAN THEATRE AND DRAMA

From 1800 to the end of the Civil War in 1865, actors and actor-managers controlled theatre in the United States. In general, they tried to supply audiences with popular shows, especially sentimental and spectacular entertainments. The acting of the time was for the most part exaggerated and declamatory. During this period a trend began that still persists on American stages in the late twentieth century; producers in the United States strongly favored fashionable British plays over original American dramas. If American playwrights wanted to get produced, they were forced to imitate popular foreign works, write for a particular actor, or—like William Dunlap—become managers themselves. A few dramatists even wrote and acted in their own works. As a result of the prevailing conditions, the first half of the nineteenth century produced few notable American writers but many good actors.

Many American dramatists of the early nineteenth century, however, honestly attempted to write what they called a "national drama." With a wish to appeal to patriotic feelings of audiences, they drew upon American history for subjects, American political and social ideas for themes, and American types for key characters. Some plays were reactions to specific events. N. H. Bannister, for instance, wrote *The Maine Question* (1839) about a boundary dispute between the United States and Canada. Other plays treated politicians, and several dealt with America's past. One of the best American plays of the century was *Superstition* (1824) by James Nelson Barker, which treated intolerance in New England and the Puritan struggle against Indians. One of the most stimulating subjects to most Americans was war. Plays appeared about the American Revolution, the war with the Barbary states, and the War of 1812.

For serious plays, the best American dramatists before the Civil War were James Nelson Barker, John Howard Payne, Robert Montgomery Bird, and George Henry Boker. Each of these men wrote poetic tragedies in the romantic mode. James Nelson Barker, a government administrator from Philadelphia, wrote 11 plays, and *Superstition* was his best poetic tragedy. Utilizing complex but clear characters, Barker's play contains swift action and such scenes as an Indian attack, a trial, and an execution. An even more well-known American writer of the period was John Howard Payne; among other accomplishments, he wrote the famous song "Home Sweet Home." Payne first became a fine young actor in America and then traveled to England, where he had little stage success; so he turned to playwriting and became outstanding in that endeavor. He wrote more than 60 plays of various types. *Brutus; or, The Fall of Tarquin* (1818), which he wrote in England for Edmund Kean, was his best tragedy. Payne became the first American playwright to achieve great fame abroad.

The foremost writer of romantic tragedy in America was Robert Montgomery Bird. A scholarly but financially impractical man, Bird began a career as a physician and then became a playwright. But actors in general and Edwin Forrest in particular disillusioned Bird about the theatre, and later in his career he turned to politics and journalism. He spent the final years of his career as a novelist. Bird demonstrated considerable dramatic talent at writing fascinating situations, well-developed heroes, and the kind of declamatory speeches that actors loved. His best plays were *The Gladiator* (1831), an exciting story about Spartacus, and *The Broker of Bogota* (1834), a drama of intrigue about a middle-class man who suffers for the sake of his morality. Bird is best remembered for bringing romanticism to American poetic tragedy.

In *Francesca da Rimini* (1855), George Henry Boker wrote probably the best of all the American poetic dramas. The only American writer of the period with a reputation as a published lyric poet, Boker was able to fashion plays of dramatic merit, especially his masterpiece *Francesca da Rimini*. Unlike Bird, who concentrated on only one hero, Boker developed in his plays numerous fully drawn characters. The dialogue that he gave them was not only poetic but also witty and credibly emotional. *Francesca da Rimini* is the first play in English to dramatize the love story of Paolo and Francesca. In it, Boker was able to invest the lovers and the other characters with intelligence and wit, and he told the story with high suspense and careful irony. Several actors produced the play, but when Lawrence Barrett performed it in 1882, it achieved its greatest success.

From the beginning of the century, American playwrights showed a talent for writing comedy. Most of the American comic plays written then did not have very well-developed stories or characters. They were often episodic and featured many stereotyped characters, such as the Yankee, the Indian, the Negro, or the Irishman. The authors of these comedies meant them to be entertaining, and they wanted to satirize, to inform, and to moralize as well. Most of the plays contained numerous farcical scenes. Two comedies of the period stand out above the others. Anna

Cora Mowatt Ritchie's *Fashion; or, Life in New York* (1845) became a landmark in the development of American social comedy. With wit and irony, the play satirizes several social levels and concentrates on the relationship of individuals with society. The other great comedy of this period is *Rip Van Winkle*. Washington Irving wrote the original story in 1819, and several playwrights adapted it. But actor Joseph Jefferson III put together the best version and persuaded playwright Dion Boucicault to polish it; thereafter, between 1859 and 1905 Jefferson played Rip in literally thousands of performances. The play tells of an old Dutchman in the Catskill mountains who goes to sleep and wakes up years later, and the story contains as many elements of romantic melodrama as of comedy.

Another fine comic writer of the time was John Brougham (1810–1880). An Irishman turned American, Brougham was also an actor and a manager, but as a comedic playwright he composed 75 plays and staged most of them successfully. Many of his plays were farces, and some were burlesques that satirized the serious dramas of others. His best Irish plays were *The Irish Fortune Hunter* (1850) and *Temptation* (1856). Among his funniest burlesques was his put-down of Indian plays entitled *Po-Ca-Hon-Tas; or, The Gentle Savage* (1855).

Two uniquely American contributions to the theatre of the nineteenth century were the showboat and the minstrel show. In 1831, William Chapman first developed a genuine showboat, a "drama barge" on which

Left: Joseph Jefferson III as Rip Van Winkle

Right: Charlotte Cushman

his company played one-night stands on the Mississippi River. Due to his success, many others imitated his "Floating Palace," and all sorts of shows—from Shakespeare to Kotzebue—appeared on America's major rivers. The appeal of the showboat ended early in the twentieth century. As for the minstrel show, it began with T. D. Rice, who made performing in burnt-cork makeup popular. He developed his comic "Jim Crow" routine in 1828 by imitating a crippled black worker whom he had seen singing and dancing. A quartet called the Virginia Minstrels gave the first publicly produced minstrel show in New York In 1843. They sang, told jokes, performed skits, and danced; they accompanied their songs with fiddle and tambourine, bones and banjo. Although the minstrel shows reached their greatest popularity in the middle of the nineteenth century, they persisted well into the twentieth. The two best-known companies were E. P. Christy's Minstrels in the 1840s and Bryant's Minstrels, who had a run of 18 years from 1857 to 1875.

This country's most successful play of the nineteenth century was *Uncle Tom's Cabin*. Throughout much of the century, melodrama was consistently the most popular form of theatre, and by far the outstanding American melodrama was this story about love, religion, and slavery by Harriet Beecher Stowe. She published the book in 1852, and in the same year several stage adaptations of it appeared successfully in England and America. Mrs. Stowe always opposed the dramatization of her book, but because copyright laws were inadequate, she couldn't prevent stage versions of it. George L. Aiken, an actor, made the most successful adaptation. It ran for a record-breaking 325 performances in 1853, and for years touring companies presented the play throughout the nation. With genuine concern about the plight of the Negro in America, Mrs. Stowe meant the novel to favor the abolition of slavery. The play, too, damns the institution of slavery. The story features good characters—for example Eliza, Little Eva, and Uncle Tom—pitted against such villains as Simon Legree. A number of sensational scenes add audience appeal to the sentimental story. Eliza, for instance, escapes across an ice-filled river as bloodhounds pursue her. Producers added music and other entertaining features, but the play's principal appeal to Americans came through its strong and topical story.

The best and most popular American actors of the period were Junius Brutus Booth, Charlotte Cushman, Joseph Jefferson III, and Edwin Forrest. Strictly speaking, Junius Booth was British, but after traveling here in 1821, he became Americanized and remained to pursue a long career and to start a famous family of American actors. Junius Booth spent most of his time touring and was the first major actor to visit California; he gave America a taste for tragic acting. Charlotte Cushman started her career in opera but then became America's first dramatic actress to earn international fame. After appearing with the British actor Charles Macready in 1843, she adopted his style of acting and at mid-century became known as the world's finest tragic actress. Joseph Jefferson, as mentioned earlier in this chapter, became well-known for his outstanding portrayal of Rip Van Winkle.

Edwin Forrest rose above all other American actors of his time to earn

**Edwin Forrest as
Spartacus**

lasting fame. He began his career at age fourteen in 1820, and he gained experience in frontier theatres. After his first appearance in New York City in 1826, he soon became America's leading star, and his success continued until 1849. At that time he was connected with the Astor Place riot in New York and a sensational divorce case. The riot, which occurred on May 10, 1826, when British actor Charles Macready played Macbeth, happened because of Forrest's feud with Macready. Supporters of Forrest initiated the riot, and in putting it down the militia fired into the mob, killing 31 people and wounding more than 150 others. After that Forrest's popularity steadily diminished, and in 1872 he retired from the stage. Blessed with a powerful physique and a booming voice, Forrest introduced an American acting style of athleticism and declamation. Such heroic plays as R. M. Bird's *The Gladiator* and John Augustus Stone's *Metamora*, the story of an Indian chief, were for a time favorites of Forrest's. A staunchly nationalistic artist, Edwin Forrest established the precedent of encouraging American writers and producing American plays.

AMERICAN STAGES—CIVIL WAR TO WORLD WAR I

The course of the Civil War, lasting from 1861 to 1865, did not stimulate or impede the continuing life of American theatre, but new trends appeared soon after. In the fifty years separating the Civil War from World War I, American theatre and drama did not change so completely as did the European, but some significant alterations occurred. For example, during the nineteenth century only Bronson Howard made a living as a dramatist in the United States. After the turn of the century, however, playwriting became a profession in which a writer could make a living, dramatic criticism developed, and the drama came to be considered a respectable literary form. Although melodramas still remained popular, social issues began to show up in plays more often. The most important change during this fifty year period was the increasing emphasis on realism. Dramatists tended to follow the lead of such realistic novelists as Mark Twain, William Dean Howells, and Henry James. Theatre critics near the end of the century hailed a new era of seriousness. The American drama of the first fifteen years of the twentieth century showed some European influences, but in general it remained more true to the spirit of the nineteenth century.

During the late nineteenth century, William Dean Howells and James A. Herne were leaders in bringing realism to the American theatre. William Dean Howells has often been called the father of American realism. A novelist, critic, and playwright, Howells argued that realism in literature was simply a matter of writing truthfully about life. He utilized realistic details to an unusual degree and filled his plays with references to contemporary events and persons. He stressed "local color," which means including many details about a particular locale. James A. Herne wrote several realistic plays; his *Margaret Fleming* (1890) was among the best American realistic plays of the period. With simplicity and honesty, it tells the story of Margaret, a young woman who has recently had a child and discovers that a servant girl has died while having an illegitimate child fathered by Margaret's own husband. Margaret takes the illegitimate child as her own and indicates she will probably forgive her contrite husband. The play had a significant impact on intellectuals and writers, but it found little success with mass audiences who still preferred romantic melodramas.

Many other American writers—such as Frank Murdock, Steele MacKaye, and William Gillette—contributed to the emergence of realism in American theatre. Although realism reflected the scientific method applied to art, many different sorts of realistic plays appeared. Realism is best understood in a given period through the examination of the works of particular authors. For example, many realistic plays about the West appeared in the late nineteenth century. *Davy Crockett* (1872) by Frank Murdock was one of the most successful. Steele MacKaye worked as an all-round man of the theatre. He acted, managed, and wrote; also he was an inventor. He developed many devices that improved theatrical production. For instance, he introduced the elevator stage to American theatres. MacKaye's best-known play was the highly successful *Hazel Kirk* (1880), a rather melodramatic love story but dramatized with naturalness and humor. Another famous play of the period is *Secret Service* (1895), a complicated though realistic story of the Civil War. The author, William Gillette, participated in the original production as its starring actor. Gillette also wrote and starred in the first famous play called *Sherlock Holmes* (1898).

Melodrama was the dominant form in American drama from the Civil War until after World War I. With the rise of realism, some playwrights turned to the new style out of a desire to be truthful, but most simply combined realistic details and subjects with the established form of melodrama. Designed to thrill audiences more than to comment on life, the melodramas of the period feature strong hero-villain conflicts and as

Augustin Daly reads a new play to his New York company in the 1880s

many physical thrills as possible. In the 1980s such American films as those about Indiana Jones or Rocky Balboa are direct descendants of the form. From the 1860s to the end of the nineteenth century, Augustin Daly typified the commercially successful writers who took advantage of the new realism but stuck to the melodramatic formulas he knew so well. One of Daly's most successful melodramas is *Under the Gaslight* (1867). In it, Daly included a famous scene in which a character is tied to a railroad track and saved in the nick of time; it was the first such railroad scene, but not the last. The play was often imitated, and it is still occasionally produced. During his active years, Daly wrote many other successful plays.

As a writer and director David Belasco became the master of American melodrama, and as a producer he grew into one of the most influential men of early twentieth-century American theatre. He carried out many experiments with spotlights, dimmers, and other electrical devices for stage lighting, and more than any other producer, he was responsible for bringing full realism to the American theatre. For a play about North Carolina he insisted on having genuine North Carolina dirt onstage. When producing a play about tenement life, Belasco purchased an entire tenement, had it taken apart bit by bit, and rebuilt on stage exactly as it had been. Such incidents illustrate his enthusiasm for strict fidelity of stage detail. He adapted 23 foreign plays or books for the American stage, and he collaborated with 12 different writers on 19 plays. He wrote at least 18 plays on his own. Two of his most famous works are *Madame Butterfly* (1900), written with John Luther Long, and *The Girl of the Golden West* (1905).

At the end of the century several American dramatists wrote skillful social comedies. They offered satiric views of the follies and foibles of fashionable life that were sometimes realistic but often farcical. Augustin Daly, William Dean Howells, and Bronson Howard were writers who significantly combined the realistic style with the comic attitude. Daly's plays *Divorce* (1871) and *Pique* (1875) could be called melodramatic comedies. In an even more realistic style, Howells wrote a series of comic plays about a particular group of characters, the Robertses and the Campbells; *The Sleeping Car* (1883) was the first in the series. Bronson Howard wrote several satiric plays about American business, and he also helped establish the profession of playwright in American theatre. His Civil War play entitled *Shenandoah* (1888) was one of his most successful, and other writers have often written imitations of it. Even twentieth-century film makers have used the story.

Clyde Fitch and Langdon Mitchell brought social comedy to a peak in the early twentieth century. From 1890 through 1909 Clyde Fitch, a talented realistic writer and man of the theatre, wrote 33 original plays and 22 adaptations. Most of them achieved great popularity. Fitch devised plays with unusual details and clever stories. Some of his best-known dramas are *Beau Brummel* (1890), *The Climbers* (1901), *The Girl with the Green Eyes* (1902), and *The City* (1909). The enduring fame of Langdon Mitchell, who wrote far fewer works, rests on one play, *The New York Idea*, a good enough comedy that some companies occasionally produce it today. The play satirizes the attitudes of sophisticated people toward courtship, divorce, and marriage.

Although poetic drama appealed to audiences before the Civil War, the fad of realism made it less popular during the last quarter of the nineteenth century. But when the twentieth century began, a number of new dramatists started writing serious plays, some of them poetic. William Vaughn Moody, a University of Chicago professor, wrote three poetic plays, one of which was *The Masque of Judgment* (1900). He remains, however, best-known for his serious prose plays *The Great Divide* (1906) and *The Faith Healer* (1909). Moody was one of America's first intellectual, rather than commercial, playwrights. Rachael Crothers, the first woman to become a major American playwright, composed a work that was professionally produced nearly every year for the first quarter of the century. In such plays as *A Man's World* (1909) and *He and She* (1911), Crothers dramatized the position of women in the American society of her day. Charles Rann Kennedy, an Englishman who became an American citizen in 1917, dramatized Christian principles in a series of plays. His works, such as *The Servant in the House* (1907), stand as some of the best American religious plays of the century.

Political plays have long been a tradition in American drama. Throughout the history of the country, various authors have written plays about economic, political, or governmental issues. The Revolutionary War stim-

Left: Nat Goodwin

Center, above: Richard Mansfield

Center, below: Minnie Maddern Fisk

Right: George M. Cohan

ulated America's first plays of protest and propaganda. The 1890s saw the strongest surge of interest in economic issues in plays by such American writers as Augustin Daly, Eugene Walter, and George M. Cohan. Some of the best political plays of the period were *The County Chairman* (1903) by George Ade, *The Lion and the Mouse* (1905) by Charles Klein, and *The Man of the Hour* (1907) by George Broadhurst. The writer who could be called the father of American political drama was Edward Sheldon. A graduate of George Pierce Baker's 47 Workshop at Harvard, Sheldon became one of the first successful American playwrights trained in a university. Professor Baker was the first significant teacher of playwriting in America. Edward Sheldon also brought a vital realistic approach to the investigation of the American scene. Although Sheldon's plays display features of romantic melodrama typical of the period, they also attack serious social themes. Among his best plays are *Salvation Nell* (1908), *The Nigger* (1910), and *The Boss* (1911). In these works Sheldon depicted American life realistically and established the precedent of writing serious political plays for later writers.

In the last years of the nineteenth century and in the early twentieth century, American theatre produced many exciting actors. Some of the best were writer William Gillette, leading man Lawrence Barrett, comedian Nat Goodwin, and song-and-dance star George M. Cohan. The Booth family produced perhaps the best actors of the entire nineteenth-century

American theatre. Two actors stood out above the rest at the turn of the century—Richard Mansfield and Minnie Maddern Fiske. Mansfield was a British actor who emigrated to New York where he became a star and theatre manager. Responsible for introducing the dramas of George Bernard Shaw to American theatre, Mansfield commissioned plays from Americans such as Clyde Fitch. Mansfield also became one of the leading matinee idols of his time. Minnie Maddern Fiske grew to be the leading serious actress in American theatre when she appeared as the title character in *Salvation Nell*. Born into the theatre, Mrs. Fiske first appeared onstage at age 3, became a star in light comedy at 20, and soon developed into America's premier realistic actress. She was particularly well-known for her portrayals of Ibsen's characters.

Two families—the Booths and Barrymores—provided several stars for the American theatre. Junius Brutus Booth (1796–1852), a well-educated English actor known for serious portrayals of Shakespearean characters, deserted his legal wife in 1821 for flower seller Mary Ann Holmes and moved to America. There he established a reputation and started the famous family of actors. He and Mary Ann had 10 children before they married in 1851, the year his first wife divorced him. Junius Brutus junior (1821–1883) was only a fair actor but an excellent manager, and his son Sydney Barton also became an actor. But the elder Junius Brutus had an even more famous son—Edwin Booth (1833–1893). Edwin became America's leading actor and won a superlative European reputation. His mel-

Left: Juniús Brutus Booth as Richard III

Right: Edwin Booth as Hamlet

Above: John Wilkes Booth

ancholic personality led him to fine portrayals in the great tragedies. He began acting professionally in his father's company at age 16, and played Richard III at age 18. He came to manage the Winter Garden Theatre in New York, where in 1864 his Hamlet set a record of a hundred consecutive performances, one that remained unbroken until John Barrymore performed the role in 1923. The most infamous of the Booths turned out to be John Wilkes (1839–1865), also an actor son of the elder Junius Brutus. John Wilkes Booth was the eccentric political radical who shot

Left: Maurice Barrymore

Right: Georgiana Drew Barrymore

President Abraham Lincoln.

The Barrymores were the most famous American theatre family of the twentieth century. When Herbert Blythe (1847–1905), an Englishman born in India and educated at Cambridge, decided to enter the acting profession, he took the name Maurice Barrymore. He played his first role in 1875, the same year in which he traveled to New York to appear in *Under the Gaslight*. Subsequently he achieved noteworthy success as an actor on both sides of the Atlantic. In 1876 Maurice Barrymore married Georgiana Drew (1856–1893), daughter of another famous family of actors, and she herself had a short but fine acting career. Maurice and Georgiana's three children all earned stardom. Lionel Barrymore (1878–1954), the eldest, made his stage debut in 1893 at the age of 15 and soon became a major New York actor. Lionel, however, left the theatre for Hollywood, where he achieved success in films. Ethel Barrymore (1879–1959), the second child, made her stage debut in 1894 and rose to become one of America's most enduring stars of both stage and screen. John Barrymore (1882–1942), the youngest, followed his family's lead and began an acting career in 1903, and because of his handsome features he was sometimes called "the great profile." He soon became one of the finest actors of the English-speaking stage. His portrayal of Hamlet in the 1920s is still unsurpassed in American theatre. The Barrymores epitomized the zesty energetic talent of American actors.

Above left: Lionel (left) and John Barrymore

Above right: Ethel Barrymore

The spirit of the nineteenth century enlivened the theatres of the world. Not only did it make possible the blossoming of romanticism, but also it stimulated the development of realism and the beginning of modern theatre. The nineteenth-century influences of romanticism, melodrama, and the well-made play have proved to be considerable in the twentieth century. In the 1970s and 1980s, American drama has favored a pessimistic romanticism, and melodrama has dominated American film. Although literary critics often dismiss the American drama of the nineteenth century as inferior by comparison with European drama, the American theatre of the period was certainly varied and energetic. Such American writers as William Dean Howells, Clyde Fitch, and Rachel Crothers helped prepare the way for the serious American drama of today. Such men as Edwin Forrest, Edwin Booth, David Belasco, and George M. Cohan introduced American dynamics into the theatre.

15 The Modern Theatre

During the period from the 1870s to the 1920s, the modern theatre came into being. Amidst the excitement of new ideas, new artists, and shocking theatrical experiments, two major currents of modern drama emerged: the realistic and the nonrealistic. In the work of such writers as Henrik Ibsen and Anton Chekhov and such directors as André Antoine and Constantin Stanislavsky came the perfection of realism as a theatre style. From dramatists such as August Strindberg, Maurice Maeterlinck, and Alfred Jarry and from directors such as Leopold Jessner and Aurélien-Marie Lugné-Poë came the development of such antirealistic styles as symbolism, expressionism, and surrealism. Although the two currents sometimes separated and sometimes converged, they aroused energy and conflict among theatre artists.

Most authorities identify the decade of the 1870s as the beginning of the modern era in theatre. During that decade, Henrik Ibsen in Norway began writing realistic prose plays, and Emile Zola in France introduced the theatre to the literary movement called naturalism. About the same time, the function of the stage director was changing, and the work of the Duke of Saxe-Meiningen and Richard Wagner in Germany proved to be powerful new influences upon the directors in Europe whose theatre companies produced the new plays of realistic and naturalistic writers.

Several thinkers established the foundation of thought that led to the artistic revolution of the late nineteenth century. The philosophy of René Descartes in the seventeenth century emphasized doubt and disciplined objectivity in thought, and eventually he influenced such French writers as Honoré de Balzac and Gustave Flaubert. In the eighteenth century, critic Denis Diderot influenced authors, too, with his idea that writers should depict everyday occurrences and common social types. Auguste Comte's philosophy of positivism, published from 1822 to 1854, stressed the scientific method and even more directly stimulated the growth of realism. He caused writers to concentrate on the concrete appearance of things and upon current events.

Charles Darwin went even further. In *The Origin of Species* he argued that all forms of life gradually developed from a common ancestry and stressed the survival of the fittest. He argued that heredity and environment are the chief determinants of a person's very being, and so an ancestor or society itself is often more responsible for an individual's actions than the person himself. Darwin's ideas introduced doubts about the traditional conception of God. Suddenly God became more of an impersonal force, not a being who dealt with people directly or met them at the gates of heaven. With the denial of life after death, a new religion

The Hot Bath by V.
Mayakovsky, directed
by V. Meyerhold

of science arose, and it seemed to promise perfection of life on earth. Thus, the scientific thought of the nineteenth century looked upon human begins as natural objects, not divine at all, simply another animal species like any other. Doubt and the methodology of scientific observation invaded the world of art.

REALISM AND NATURALISM

Realism in art first appeared as a distinct style in France. From the moment of its earliest stirrings, realism depended upon four principles:

(1) the materials should come from the details of contemporary life; (2) the form should follow the chronology of the real world; (3) the style called for the artist to observe life and then present the observed details; and (4) the overall goal was to present the truth about realms of life never before explored.

Because realism arose as a revolutionary movement in art, it naturally aroused opposition. Some opponents believed realism to be immoral and held to old-fashioned romanticism, and others thought art should look for its truths in the realms of symbolic beauty. Critics argued that the realists limited themselves to ugly and trivial subject matter, to unformed slices of life, to uninspired style, and to immoral visions of life. The champions of realism replied that art ought to reflect life without making it prettier, more moral, or even more exciting than it really is. Answering the charge of immorality, the realists argued that truth is more moral than idealizations. Throughout the twentieth century and even today, most schools of art move either toward or away from realism. Later sections of this chapter treat nonrealistic theatre at length.

An important precursor of realism was Alexandre Dumas *fils* (1824–1895). Although his plays today seem romantic in emotional attitude, his "realistic" play entitled *Camille* (performed 1852), about a kept woman, was considered outrageous. He dared to place his story in contemporary Paris, and the dialogue was everyday speech. Thus the play outraged moralists of the day. He also wrote even more realistically about sex in

John Garfield (left) and Morris Carnovsky in *Awake and Sing* by Clifford Odets

his next play *The Demi-monde* (1855), in which the characters were even less sympathetic. Dumas wished to present truth about contemporary life and to encourage people to consider social problems. Thus critics labeled his works "thesis plays."

During the last quarter of the nineteenth century, realism began to multiply. Because the spirit of truth in realism was so pervasive, even the producers who favored romanticism began to change. These romantic realists began presenting authentic portraits of idealized materials in stories with upbeat endings. From the mid-nineteenth century on, many of the melodramas presented in Paris and London demonstrated that producers wanted realistic stage effects. The plays of Dion Boucicault, for example, offered such sensational sights as storms bursting, houses burning, and steamboats exploding. Instead, the genuine realists presented contemporary subject matter in settings that showed the influence of environment on character and action. From 1870 to 1890, authors like Ibsen and Zola wrote plays so shocking in subject and style that government censors prevented their works from reaching the stage until the 1890s. Only with the rise of the independent theatre movement—to be discussed later—did realism achieve its full stage potential.

Just as realistic dramatists tried to capture everyday life, so theatre people began giving more lifelike performances. Until realism became supreme in the late nineteenth century, most acting was an egoistic display. In romantic plays and in most melodramas, actor-managers took center stage, delivered the most lines, and received the most applause. Other actors got along as best they could. But with the rise of realism came the rise of the director. Because all the details of the setting, the acting ensemble, and the play itself needed to be carefully coordinated for a lifelike effect, directors began to exert the overall judgment needed for realistic plays. Thus, in many theatre companies, directors took over from the actor-managers the positions of artistic and economic power.

Duke George II of Saxe-Meiningen (1826–1914) became the first modern stage director, and he introduced many significant new production concepts. The Duke ruled a small German duchy, and his troupe played in court theatres throughout Europe in the years 1874–1890. The Meiningen Players presented 2591 guest performances in 38 cities throughout Europe. Perhaps the first woman significant in the history of directing—Ellen Franz—assisted the Duke with his productions. At first an actress in the company, she became the company expert in matters of dramaturgy and texts. Although the Duke's company presented such standard plays as those of Schiller and Shakespeare, he went beyond most previous directors in stressing historical accuracy and ensemble acting. Using a troupe of unknown actors, he asked them to play various roles, some small and some large. To make sure the settings, costumes, and properties were accurate, he designed many of them himself. Most important, he held long, detailed rehearsals. Whenever the play called for a crowd scene, he enlisted the help of Ludwig Crongk to set the movements of the minor actors as well as the major ones. The Duke influenced two especially important directors, Constantin Stanislavsky in Moscow and André Antoine in Paris. Many principles of staging that the Duke and his associates worked out have persisted in the twentieth century.

Emile Zola (1840–1902) was a significant writer who helped bring modernism to the theatre. He called himself a naturalist, and his *Thérèse Raquin* (1873) was the first major naturalistic play. But Zola's influence came more through his essays and novels than through his playwriting. In an essay, "Naturalism in the Theatre" (1881), he called the established theatre a "palace of lies," and he argued against phony romantic productions of melodramas and well-made plays. He especially argued that traditional plots were not lifelike, and he maintained that old-fashioned writers failed to present credible and consistent psychological portraits. Further, he recommended that plays show human beings struggling with their fate, fighting against forces of environment and heredity. Zola thought a play should be a fragment of existence, not a grand adventure. Along with his associates, Zola fostered the search for truth and reality. They brought about an examination of common people, of low life, and of the dark corners of society. Naturalistic writers and directors turned their attention "down" the social scale to workers, peasants, clerks, prostitutes, thieves, and derelicts. Perhaps because of the terrible reality of the lives they found, the naturalist writers tended to produce pessimistic works.

A distinction needs to be made between realism and naturalism. From the perspective of the late twentieth century, modern drama begins with the broad movement of realism. *Naturalism*, however, is a narrower term referring to one current within the realistic mainstream. *Realism* in drama means the representation of real life on stage. The characters speak naturally in everyday words, and their attitudes are contemporary. The author presents stories about ordinary people in an everyday manner. The simple goal of the realist is to present human life truthfully and without idealization. Naturalism, a narrower style, best identifies the work of a small number of European playwrights. The ideal naturalistic play is a slice of life, beginning at a randomly selected point in time and ending in an uncontrived manner. The naturalist probes like a scientist into the problem areas of society in order to expose problems.

A number of theatre directors introduced realism to the stages of Europe, and they also initiated the independent theatre movement. Among them were André Antoine in France, Otto Brahm in Germany, Constantin Stanislavsky in Russia, and J. T. Grein in England. Many of the new theatre organizations were private and depended on subscriptions for financial support. These new theatre groups had a director at their head; their actors were willing to submit to the new principles of ensemble; and their realistic, innovative stage techniques utilized three-dimensional scenery and controllable electric lighting.

In 1887, in Paris, Antoine (1858–1943) founded the first independent company, the Théâtre Libre. Influenced by Zola and the Duke of Saxe-Meiningen, Antoine formed a group of amateurs into one of Europe's most influential companies. Utilizing detailed settings and meticulous rehearsals, he created the first naturalistic productions. During his directorship the Théâtre Libre presented productions of 111 plays by 51 authors, including French premieres of such plays as Ibsen's *Ghosts*, Strindberg's *Miss Julie*, and Hauptmann's *The Weavers*. The Théâtre Libre accomplished four significant innovations: it introduced the new realism as a production style, humanized the acting of plays, introduced many new playwrights, and set a pattern for independent operation that other theatres around the world could follow.

In Germany a well-known critic, Otto Brahm (1856–1912) became the head of a new theatre in Berlin, the Freie Bühne. Beginning with a production of Ibsen's *Ghosts*, Brahm introduced the new authors of realism and naturalism to the Germanic world, and he presented the first play of Germany's most important modern playwright, Gerhart Hauptmann (1862–1946). To circumvent police censorship and the mediocre taste of most German playgoers of the time, he gave only private performances for a subscription audience. Brahm turned out to be an excellent director, and the effect of the Freie Bühne was to stimulate a rise in the level of commercial theatre in Germany. Hauptman became the first major German playwright of the modern period, and in his native country he remains one of the most frequently produced of all writers for the theatre. Many critics still consider his most famous play, *The Weavers* (1892), to be the best of all naturalistic dramas.

In London J. T. Grein (1862–1935), a Dutch drama critic, founded the Independent Theatre Society. He was associated with William Archer, translator of Ibsen, and with George Moore, the novelist. Grein's first production was, naturally enough, Ibsen's *Ghosts*. The production aroused a blizzard of outraged reviews and letters of protest. His theatre also introduced the playwright who was to become the leading genius of the modern English stage. In 1892 Grein presented *Widowers' Houses* by George Bernard Shaw (1856–1950).

Early in the twentieth century, England produced several outstanding modern directors. Two early ones established ways of working that still persist in British theatre. In London, in 1894, William Poel founded the Elizabethan Stage Society and staged many Elizabethan plays in a replica of Shakespearean theatre. He showed that numerous realistic settings were not necessary for such plays. Harley Granville Barker, a director and playwright, established a significant tradition for production in England that has lasted throughout the twentieth century. He took over the Royal Court Theatre in 1904 and brought the plays of George Bernard Shaw to prominence. For Shakespeare, Granville Barker instructed actors to make every gesture and facial expression a natural extension of the characters' thoughts and feelings, and by asking them to speak clearly but rapidly, he changed the dominant style in British acting from bombastic to realistic. Furthermore, he staged Shakespeare's plays in a stylized setting, making scene changes unnecessary, and permitted no pauses between scenes or acts, except for necessary intermissions to rest the audience. His productions often caused controversy because of their break with tradition, but they made a significant impact on later directorial practices.

In Germany the great modernist director was Max Reinhardt (1873–1943). He began his career as an actor in his native Austria and then worked for Otto Brahm in Berlin, becoming an important member of that company. While still with Brahm he began to direct songs, parodies, and

The Miracle directed by Max Reinhardt

finally cabaret theatre. By 1902, in association with Brahm's organization, he operated the Kleines Theater. In 1903 he became independent and opened the Neues Theater, and his work was so successful that he grew to be one of the world's leading directors. He produced many different types of plays in the major theatres of many different countries. Reinhardt thought of each drama as a special problem with its own unique solutions, so he experimented with numerous technical devices. He composed a master prompt book, in which he wrote all the details for each of his productions, noting everything for actors, designers, and technicians. Perhaps Reinhardt's two most important ideas were that the performance space should be modified to fit the play, and that the director is the supreme creative power in the theatre.

In the United States, realism took the stage much later than in Europe. David Belasco, an American director, became a pioneer of realism. Just after the turn of the century he employed illusionistic lighting and made the box set popular on Broadway. For *The Easiest Way* in 1909 he found a dilapidated tenement and literally transferred it bit by bit—wallpaper, doors, floor, furniture, everything—to the stage of his theatre. A few years later he faithfully copied a corner of a Child's restaurant for *The Governor's Lady* (1912). But because he pushed his actors into an exaggerated acting style, his productions only had the look of realism, not its genuine feel.

Two Russians established the most persistent modern theatre company and one of the best. In 1897, Constantin Stanislavsky (1863–1938) and Vladimir Nemirovich-Danchenko (1858–1943) met at an artists' cafe and during 15 hours of talk created the Moscow Art Theatre. Danchenko became literary manager and Stanislavsky artistic director, but both men directed productions. Also, Danchenko handled business, and Stanislavsky became a leading actor. Under the supervision of its leaders, the company became a successful ensemble theatre. The company's first production in 1898 was Alexey Tolstoy's historical play *Tsar Fyodor*. Because the Duke of Saxe-Meiningen had so thoroughly influenced Stanislavsky, the production contained a wealth of detail. The group next produced Sophocles' *Antigone* and Shakespeare's *The Merchant of Venice*. The Moscow Art Theatre then presented the dramas of playwright Anton Chekhov, who helped them become a permanent artistic force in the modern theatre, as they helped the writer to achieve international renown. The theatre's fourth production was *The Sea Gull* by Anton Chekhov. The association with Chekhov meant so much to the company that it adopted the sea gull as its logo and came to be called the House of Chekhov. The Moscow Art Theatre still persists as a major company.

Stanislavsky was always interested in acting and the problems of actors. He thought carefully about acting, and he talked to many actors throughout Europe, collecting ideas about the nature of the actor's work. He then applied his discoveries to the acting company of the Moscow Art Theatre in productions and in studio work. Developing his ideas in book form, he published a series of volumes expounding his theories and practices. The system of training and role development he perfected came to be known as the Stanislavsky Method, and his books and disciples have spread it throughout the world. American directors and actors of the Group Theatre and Actor's Studio—especially Lee Strasberg, Stella Adler, and Elia Kazan—made "the Method" the most important twentieth-century influence on acting in this country. The four most important books by Stanislavsky are *My Life in Art* (1924), *An Actor Prepares* (1926), *Building a Character* (1950) and *Creating a Role* (1961).

The following principles are among those at the heart of Stanislavsky's books. The objective of the entire system is an organic, truthful presentation of lived experience. He divided actors' work into four realms: work

Above: Vladimir Nemirovich-Danchenko (left) and Constantin Stanislavsky

Below right: The Moscow Art Theatre, 1899, with Stanislavsky (second row, fifth from left)

on self, work on a role, external work on voice and body, and internal work on feeling and imagination. Stanislavsky believed that actors' work on self is a lifelong process demanding discipline on the inner and outer self. To work on a role, actors must analyze the play, identify its action, its given circumstances, its beats, and the interrelationships of the characters. Also, actors must concentrate on the internal intentions of a given character as if they themselves had the same motivations within the circumstances of the play. Everything characters are called on to say or do can be executed with credible behavior by actors, first convincing themselves and then convincing an audience. Stanislavsky's system helps actors develop a conscious acting process for generating feeling and communicating it convincingly. He managed to evolve a method for training and rehearsing actors that has become nearly universal in modern theatre. Stanislavsky led the way among actors and directors in making realism a dominant production style for the twentieth century.

Henrik Ibsen

Other theatre artists, of course, made contributions to the rising wave of realism. But theatre people, especially directors, tend to be eclectic in their tastes, searching for the best, the most effective, or the most contemporary methods of staging. Indeed, naturalism was too limited a theatrical mode to last long. Realism was more adaptable, and it led producers of plays at the beginning of the twentieth century to approach all productions more in the spirit of verisimilitude, or lifelikeness. From the beginning of this century onward, most directors began to try to discover for each play the most unique, convincing, and appropriate manner of staging. This attitude was contrary to the traditions of the nineteenth century. In the premodern theatre, all plays would be given generally the same traditional kind of acting style, the same settings, and the same visual conventions. The adaptability of realism became apparent as twentieth-century directors stopped trying to copy life in detail; instead they began trying to create a stage setting and atmosphere to fit each play. Thus many different production styles came into being. Eclecticism and verisimilitude became the virtues of modern directors.

GREAT REALIST PLAYWRIGHTS

Henrik Ibsen (1828–1906) was the first master of the modern drama. Authorities mark the 1870s as the beginning of modern theatre, in part because during that decade Ibsen took up the mode of realism. His first realistic play was *The Pillars of Society* (1877), and then came one of his masterpieces, *A Doll's House* (1879). Soon afterward, he wrote *Ghosts* (1881) and *An Enemy of the People* (1882). Those four plays established Ibsen as both playwright and thinker, and through them he became the leader of realism. In Ibsen's dramas many of the most significant lines of development of nineteenth-century European drama came together.

In 1850, when young Ibsen started to write plays, no significant Norwegian drama existed. Coming from a poor family, Ibsen had not received much formal schooling. He quit school at 15, and apparently he never became much of a reader. Inside the theatre itself he learned about plays and about writing for audiences. In 1851 he became manager of a theatre in Bergen, Norway. During his six years there, the theatre presented 145 plays, including more than 120 by French and German romantic writers, and 21 by Eugène Scribe, master of the well-made play.

Ibsen became a great playwright because of three significant factors. First, he learned about the theatre through practical experience, and his plays come to life better on stage than on the printed page. Second, he learned storytelling from the romantics, structure from the craftsmen of the well-made play, and suggestivity from the symbolists. Third, he made an unflinching search for moral truth in modern society by exploring taboo subjects. His plays became models of dramaturgy, and his artistic audacity brought important problems to the attention of the populace. His plays often deal with an individual's quest for the absolute, and with problems of balancing personal interest with public responsibility. His deepest concern, perhaps, was with the doctrine of "free personality." Outmoded traditions of society should not, he argued, bear down on any individual and cripple their natural development of spirit, talent, or conscience.

The plays of Ibsen can conveniently be studied in three groups: (1) historical and romantic plays, from *Catiline* (1850) to *Emperor and Galilean* (1873); (2) realistic plays, from *The Pillars of Society* (1877) to *Hedda Gabler* (1890); and (3) symbolist plays, from *The Lady from the Sea* (1888) to *When We Dead Awaken* (1899). Many of his plays are well-known and often played throughout the world in the twentieth-century repertory. *Peer Gynt* (1867), a play of his romantic period, is a blend of comedy and pathos, fantasy and folklore. It tells a story of modern man searching for the key to life throughout the world and finding it in simple life, close to home. But his realistic plays, such as *A Doll's House* and *Ghosts*, established him as the leading dramatist of the modern theatre. *A Doll's House* deals with the subject of woman's subservient status in society; at the end its heroine, Nora, renounces tradition and leaves her husband and children to seek self-realization alone in the world. *The Wild Duck* (1884), an outstanding example of his symbolist period, has a clear story line; Gregers Werle, a young man who believes in truth, tries to get people to dismiss their illusions, but he only succeeds in destroying their lives.

Ibsen's plays became models for modern realistic theatre. He brought contemporary problems and logical discussion to the stage. He taught dramatists to avoid asides and soliloquies, to motivate exposition, to relate scenes causally, to establish an action that leads to a logical climax, to describe setting and physical action in stage directions, and to develop characters credibly according to environment and heredity. Ibsen's work displayed his moral indignation with the modern world—the Godless world of empty tradition, social exploitation, and industrial expansion. From a Christian existentialist named Sören Kierkegaard (1813–1855), Ibsen took the question, How can a person become a true Christian? And he transformed it into the question that suffuses all his plays: How can a person become a true human being?

Anton Chekhov

Although the Moscow Art Theatre brought the work of Anton Chekhov (1860–1904) to the attention of the world, his plays deserve their fame because of their intrinsic merit. Chekhov wrote many short stories and one-act plays, but his genius is recognized because of his four dramatic masterpieces: *The Sea Gull, Uncle Vanya, The Three Sisters*, and *The Cherry Orchard*. His plays show the influence of naturalism, but they are perhaps the best examples of realism in the modern theatre.

Chekhov's grandfather was a serf, his father a merchant, and he studied to become a physician. In 1880, at the age of 20, he began writing to support himself in medical school; about the same time he also contracted tuberculosis. After briefly practicing medicine among the peasants, he decided it was more lucrative to write. His first stories won the coveted Pushkin Prize, and about the same time he began writing short plays. In 1887 he wrote a long play, *Ivanov*, but it achieved little success. He spent a year writing *The Wood Demon*, which in a later form became *Uncle Vanya*. In 1896 *The Sea Gull* was performed at the Alexandrinsky Theatre in St. Petersburg, but it failed, chiefly because of the terrible acting. He swore never again to write plays or permit his work to be done onstage. Fortunately, Danchenko and Stanislavsky were able to convince him to let them produce *The Sea Gull*. Their version was successful, and so was their production of *Uncle Vanya* in 1899. After that, Chekhov and the Moscow Art Theatre worked together in a personal and artistic bond.

He wrote two more masterpieces for the company. It produced *The Three Sisters* in 1901, and during the same year Chekhov married one of the leading actresses, Olga Knipper. In 1904, he died at the age of 44, six months after the production of his last play, *The Cherry Orchard*.

More than any other dramatist before him, Chekhov broke many of the major traditions of dramatic structure established by the Greeks and practiced by most playwrights through the age of romanticism. He demonstrated for generations of twentieth-century playwrights a new way to write plays. Before Chekhov the best plays traditionally concentrated on "overt action," telling stories about strong-willed protagonists who set out to reach a goal, suffer emotionally because of difficulties, and then fight an opponent to a climax, thus causing a reversal in fortune. The classical plays were clearly tragedies or comedies, but in the nineteenth century the craftsmen of the well-made plays turned tradition into melodrama, a crowd-pleasing form that featured spectacular theatrical effects. Chekhov did not see the world as a melodrama, nor did he consider it to be altogether tragic or comic. Thus he came to write plays about reality as he knew it in rural Russia, plays for which no one has devised a satisfactory label. Some critics call his plays serious comedies, some think of them as tragicomedies, and still others call them ironic comedies.

Chekhov wrote plays of "covert action." Not at all static, his dramas have many striking incidents such as shootings, love scenes, fights, and deaths. But these works are so well unified, the characters so well motivated, and the scenes so tightly woven, that many observers fail to see their progressive structure. They depend on a system of covert action, a subtle pattern of human change to hold them together. Several key features can be found in all of the plays. The characters are entrapped in a situation they can neither understand nor do anything about. The scenes are arranged to explore the situation, the relationships between the people, and the threads of desire. Often a greedy person tries to overtake a victim. In *The Sea Gull* Trigorin seduces Nina; in *Uncle Vanya* Serebryakov takes away Sonia's inheritance; in *The Three Sisters* Natasha puts the Prozorov family out of its house; and in *The Cherry Orchard* Lopahin takes over the estate, displacing Madame Ranevsky and her family. In each play the central act of dispossession represents an action of ravishment, theft, or destruction. A clear structure of action is present in each of Chekhov's works, but the structures are extraordinarily well concealed. He invented what might be called the "buried plot."

Another feature of Chekhov's work is perhaps most responsible for the subtlety of his structures. He stops the play before it reaches a traditional conclusion, or he puts the major climax offstage. Thus he avoids overemotional confrontations and events; instead, he presents their results. Before a melodramatic reversal can occur, such as the triumph of virtue over vice, he ends the play. Usually the endings show his deposed and defeated characters shuffling away from their old lives, tentatively looking forward to what the future may hold. There are no villains and no heroes. Most of the characters are by turns—intense, then foolish, and angry, then pathetic. He even avoids overemotional endings because the characters somehow bring their fates on themselves. The characters express piecemeal perceptions about their lives, but the audience is permitted deeper insights. Chekhov contrives to provide an ironic view of all that happens. Through lifelike detail and avoidance of traditional structures, Chekhov tried to present a truthful version of reality in the theatre.

Sweden produced an additional master of the early modern theatre, August Strindberg (1849–1912). Born in poverty in Stockholm, Strindberg grew into an oversensitive and rebellious youth. As he tried to put himself through the University of Stockholm studying literature and science, he nearly starved. Upon winning a grant for writing a short play at age 23, he began a literary career. He supported himself as an assistant librarian from 1874 to 1882, and during the same period he married Siri von Essen. Although they had three children together, their tempestuous quarrels furnished him with material for controversial stories and plays. Between 1887 and 1901 he wrote a series of important realistic plays: *The Father, Comrades, Miss Julie, The Link,* and *The Dance of Death*. After publicizing the "battle of the sexes" in his own household, he and his first wife were divorced in 1891. He married twice more, and during the final years of his life he devoted himself to nonrealistic plays. Finally, Strindberg's frenetic psychological life came to a crisis, and he entered a private sanitarium. He recovered his mental balance but retained a tendency toward psychic fantasy. Known as one of the great innovators of the modern drama, he died of cancer in 1912.

Strindberg, like other dramatists of the period, began by writing his-

August Strindberg

torical plays of a vaguely romantic nature. But his mature work falls in two periods. The first, 1884–1892, culminates in his great plays in the naturalistic mode, especially *The Father, Miss Julie, Comrades,* and *Dance of Death*. These plays focus on the battle between men and women. But Strindberg believed naturalism should not be a mere slice of life; rather, it should light up the great battles in life and bring to light the struggles between natural forces. Strindberg's version of naturalism favored a male character in conflict with one or more females, and he was willing to forsake naturalistic detail for the sake of focusing attention on the sex war. *The Father* (1887) well illustrates his version of naturalism and of the sex war; it also demonstrates the strength of his dramaturgy.

In England the most significant realist playwright of the modern era was George Bernard Shaw (1856–1950). A gifted writer of comedy, Shaw concentrated on plays of social comment, and his works are often as didactic as they are realistic. When criticized for putting social problems on the stage, he answered that he would stop doing so when there were no more social problems. Although Shaw admitted the influence of Ibsen, Shaw never copied him, and he virtually created the modern comedy of ideas.

Shaw was born in Ireland and survived his first 20 years in Dublin as the son of an alcoholic father and a hardworking, musically inclined mother. In 1876 he went to London and educated himself, concentrating on literature, history, and the social sciences. He joined the Fabian Society

George Bernard Shaw

of socialists and tried unsuccessfully to run for political office. Shaw became a music and theatre critic. His books *The Perfect Wagnerite* (1898) and *The Quintessence of Ibsenism* (1891) were noteworthy not only for their intelligence and wit but particularly because they helped bring significant ideas about the new theatre to England. He showed his own good sense by explaining that in his thirties he became a teetotaler and a vegetarian. Perhaps he demonstrated further good sense when in his late thirties he married an extremely wealthy wife.

The range and number of Shaw's plays are astonishing. He began his playwriting career with *Widowers' House* in 1892 and continued writing plays until he was 83, when in 1939 he composed *In Good King Charles's Golden Days*. Among his more than fifty plays, some of the best are: *Arms and the Man* (1894), attacking the "romance" of war and love; *Candida* (1895), contrasting the maturity of women with the childishness of men; *The Devil's Disciple* (1897), depicting the American Revolutionary war; *Caesar and Cleopatra* (1899), dealing with political intrigue in Egypt; *Man and Superman* (1903), demonstrating the struggle between men and women; *Major Barbara* (1905), arguing that man's mind must be saved before his soul; *Pygmalion* (1913), illustrating that class distinctions stem more from environment than from heredity; and *Saint Joan* (1923), exploring the significance of sainthood.

Although Shaw took up realism, he brought many other concepts to the English-speaking stage, especially those of the philosophers Friedrich Nietzsche and Henri Bergson. Shaw took over the formulas of the well-made play and exploited them for his own comic purposes. His comedies express his ironic social opinions. Some of his pet peeves were a dislike of brutality in sports, contempt for the competitive spirit, and hatred for the killing of animals. His works show his compassion for people, and his characters are always unique. He knew that the value of an argument in a play was more in its process than its results. In his plays the arguments are as much fun as flirtations or fistfights. Shaw demonstrated how intelligence could be brought to bear in the theatre. Ultimately he was a great optimist who believed in the progressive realization of the good and in the "Life Force" as the ultimate control of all things. Furthermore, he twisted dramatic conventions in order to destroy all villains, and he showed that villains are often as good as heroes. Shaw's plays are so unique and his personality was so strong that he seems somehow to transcend the theatre itself. Few writers have shown the direct influence of Shaw; perhaps he perfected and exhausted his own special genre of philosophic comedy.

In Ireland, a group of fine writers developed the "Irish Renaissance," a literary movement stressing high quality and nationalistic fervor. Miss A. E. F. Horniman founded the Abbey Theatre in 1904, and it featured the plays of W. B. Yeats, Lady Gregory, and John Millington Synge. From 1905 on, those three writers also worked as managing directors for the Abbey; Lady Gregory continued to do so into the 1930s. During the first era of this century, John Millington Synge wrote the most enduring plays for the Irish stage. He blended folk speech, naturalistic characters, and stories about repression and fate into dramas of fascinating moods and lasting images. Two of his famous mood pieces are *In the Shadow of the Glen* (1903) and *Riders to the Sea* (1904). Often his plays are comic, yet retain poetic prose. Synge's comic drama *Playboy of the Western World* (1907) is a modern classic rendered in his unusual style. But the play so enraged some Irish people that riots occurred outside the theatre. The Abbey, however, survived and came to represent to the rest of the world the spirit of independence in theatre. Later, many of the Abbey Theatre's great actors—such as Dudley Digges, Barry Fitzgerald, and Sara Allgood—became famous in American movies.

A few key concepts summarize the revolution of realism. Hippolyte Taine, a French literary critic who influenced Zola, argued that three factors determine the character of a work of art—race, milieu, and moment. Zola saw three factors as the environmental conception of human nature. Those three elements in a person—fixed by heredity, cultural environment, and social circumstances—deeply influenced the nature of the person and the quality of his life. Thus environment became a central idea in the rise of realism. A second factor is what American critic Gilbert Durand calls the "nocturnal regime." The early realists looked down the social scale for materials, into the dark corners of life; they looked at the "night people." Karl Marx supported this view by focusing public attention on the alienation of the lower classes. Thus social problems and the seamy side of life became significant sources for the new theatre. Finally, realism stimulated eclecticism in the theatre, as writers and directors searched for ways to produce plays with truth, credibility, and lifelikeness.

Richard Wagner

THE ANTIREALIST REVOLT

Not all playwrights, directors, and designers joined the naturalist and realist movements. From the beginning some artists thought realism depended too much on superficial appearances, and they saw naturalism as a glorification of the ugly; so they led a series of revolts against realism, and such responses continue even today. The antirealistic movement in art and theatre, like realism, began on the European continent. The artists drew upon the ideas of three influential thinkers—Richard Wagner, Friedrich Nietzsche, and Sigmund Freud—as their most profound influences.

Richard Wagner (1813–1883) wrote, composed, and produced operas in Germany in the mid-nineteenth century. Among his best-known works are *The Flying Dutchman* (1841), *Lohengrin* (1848), *Tristan and Isolde* (1865), and *The Valkyrie* (1870). His ideas that most affected the modern theatre have to do with production. Although he considered music to be dominant, he conceived the idea of the *Gesamtkunstwerk* (unified work of art), meaning that all elements of production—script, music, acting, design—are brought together organically in a unified whole. Wagner further argued that only one mind, that of a master artist, should be in control of all the elements. He demanded and received the sole power to write, compose, direct, and design his productions. He disliked realism in drama because he thought of the dramatist as a mythmaker rather than a popularizer of everyday life. He wanted to represent an ideal universe rather than the ordinary world. Despite his idealist theories, he nevertheless wished to create illusion in the theatre and convince the audience that they were seeing "reality." Wagner especially believed that successful theatrical works should captivate the emotions of spectators, and he is one of those most responsible for establishing emotional effect as one of the measures of success in modern theatre.

Friedrich Nietzsche (1844–1900) was a revolutionary German philosopher of the nineteenth century. His first book *The Birth of Tragedy* (1872) pointed to emotional, ritualistic, and mythic aspects of tragedy. Nietzsche argued that creativity in humans requires two conflicting energies—the desire for order and beauty versus the impulse toward disorder and frenzy, both of which are necessary for art. He pointed out that art offers insights about existence that science cannot know. He argued that art says yes to life, whereas Christianity says no. Perhaps his most important idea for the world of art is the concept of "the will to power." Nietzsche believed each person has the capacity to use personal will to become a better, more useful, more beautiful human being; thus everyone can be more perfect and become a creator. When the will to power is perverted, a person tries to exercise power over others—a tendency that Nietzsche despised in human beings. But when the genuine will to power succeeds, a person creates himself and becomes a living work of art. Nietzsche taught the world that life is best justified as a work of art.

The ideas of Sigmund Freud (1856–1939) revolutionized the attitudes of physicians and society at large about the workings of the human mind. He also made a profound impact on the world of art, especially on novelists and playwrights. As a physician Freud first specialized in the treatment of hysteria and the diseases of the nervous system, but after studying with Jean Charcot in Paris and collaborating with Josef Breuer in Vienna, he began in 1895 to publish articles and books about the internal life of people's minds; indeed, he founded the modern practice of psychoanalysis. At first, he learned to use hypnosis in treating emotionally disturbed patients, but soon he helped develop a method that utilized free association. This manner of handling distraught personalities allowed him to study resistance on the part of the patient to the processes of uncovering repressed experiences. He also discovered transference, a circumstance that occurs when the patient becomes emotionally tied to the analyst. These two factors, resistance and transference, have remained central to modern techniques of psychoanalysis.

In 1897 Freud began to study his own subconscious mental process. All his work led to progress in the understanding of neurosis, psychosis, and perversion in comparison with the normal mind. Some of his key ideas concerned: (1) the effect of the subconscious mental process on the conscious mind; (2) the importance of mental conflict in repression and sublimation; (3) the personality structure of ego, id, libido, and superego; (4) the motivational power of instinctual drives, especially sexuality and aggression; and (5) the importance of infantile sexuality. Freud also explored human dreams as possible sources of hints about repressions. He believed that in sleep the ego and superego are at rest and repressed memories and emotions tend to surface in dreams. Freud's

Friedrich Nietzsche

work concentrated on the exploration of unconscious motivations and repressed memories and on bringing those to the conscious mind of the patient in order to alleviate disorders of personality.

Freud used four key terms to analyze the structure of personalities. *Ego* means the self, that part of the psyche which experiences the external world through the senses, organizes the thought processes rationally, and governs action. The ego mediates between the impulses of the id, the demands of the environment, and the standards of the superego. *Id* refers to instinct, or that part of the psyche regarded as the reservoir of inner drives and the source of psychic energy, dominated by the pleasure principal and irrational wishing. The impulses of the id are controlled through the development of the ego and the superego. *Libido* is the sexual urge. The libido generally produces psychic energy as well as the positive loving instincts that occur at different stages of personality development. *Superego* refers to self-control, that part of the psyche which is critical of the self or of the ego. The superego enforces moral standards; it's another version of conscience. At a subconscious level the superego blocks the unacceptable impulses of the id.

The experiments, discoveries, and theories of Freud were enormous influences on the imaginations of twentieth-century literary artists. Whereas in earlier times dogmatic authorities claimed that the supernatural or demonic forces of evil compelled mankind to perform hateful and tragic acts, Freud pointed the way for those who wish to realize the personal reasons for human behavior. He taught playwrights and novelists to probe the psyches of both themselves and their characters. Furthermore, he stimulated writers to realize the multiple motivations that people have for their actions—motivations not easily understood or expressed. He also brought to the attention of society the importance of sexual drives and helped make previously forbidden erotic subject matter the stuff of many modern stories.

Freud's emphasis on dreams, dream imagery, and dream fragmentation brought authors to understand the possibilities of organizing plays and stories as though they were more dreamlike than ordinary. Finally, Freud taught the cultural world that sometimes people wear masks in order to conceal their true identities or to shield unsuspected sides of their personalities. All these concepts became profound influences on many of the dramatists of the modern theatre, especially those who wished to work in the nonrealistic mode.

So during the final quarter of the nineteenth century, the nonrealistic, or presentational, mode of drama came into being. It contrasted sharply with the realistic, or representational, type. The antirealistic movement in theatre at first appeared as symbolism, neoromanticism, and impressionism. All three styles featured similar visions in their suggestive search for the truths behind appearances and their reflection of more symbolic details onstage. The writers of the nonrealistic persuasion took their inspiration from Wagner, Nietzsche, Freud, and certain poets, such as Edgar Allen Poe, Charles-Pierre Baudelaire, and Stephane Mallarmé.

After learning symbolism from the French poet Mallarmé, Maurice Maeterlinck (1862–1949) became the first major symbolist playwright.

***Miss Julie* by August Strindberg, Florida Southern College**

As the early leader of the symbolists, Mallarmé called for drama as a sacred ritual with symbols about the meaning of existence. Theatre was to be a revelation of life, a secular religious experience. The images should be ambiguous so that reality remains mysterious. A Belgian, Maurice Maeterlinck arrived in Paris in 1886 and began writing as a symbolist. At 28 he became the most talked-about new playwright in Europe, especially because of two short plays, *The Intruder* (1890) and *The Blind* (1890). His other best-known plays are *The Death of Tintagiles* (1894), *The Blue Bird* (1908), and *Pelleas and Melisande* (1892). Maeterlinck wanted his plays to show the transcendent reality of the soul rather than the mere everyday appearance of ordinary physical life, and he thought states of feeling could take the place of action. Maeterlinck taught the modern theatre the importance of signification, of quiet suggestivity, and of intuitive values.

Three other symbolist playwrights wrote dramas of enduring value. In France, Paul Claudel utilized symbolism and stressed the moral values of Catholicism. Preoccupied with love, death, and the beatific vision of religion, Claudel also wished to uncover the truth so often masked by human pretense. His best-remembered works are *The Tidings Brought to Mary* (1892) and *The Satin Slipper* (1924). In Russia, Leonid Andreyev wrote several fascinating symbolist plays. His most respected pieces are *The Life of Man* (1907), *Black Masks* (1908), and *He Who Gets Slapped*

(1915). His works tended to be morality plays containing a mixture of styles but always full of symbols. Irish poet William Butler Yeats also wrote perhaps the most vivid short symbolist plays in the English language. *On Baile's Strand* (1904) and *The Shadowy Waters* (1904) are two of his best works.

Among the theatre artists who opposed the strict basic tenets of realism, Adolphe Appia (1862–1928) provided the modern theatre with new ideas about scenery and lighting. In Switzerland, Appia became familiar with the operas of Richard Wagner, but when he attended Wagner's own productions in Bayreuth, he disliked them. So Appia wrote three important books: *The Staging of Wagnerian Music Drama* (1895), *Music and the Art of the Theatre* (1899), and *The Work of Living Art* (1921). He discussed the essential nature of artistic unity of elements in theatre and argued that three-dimensional scenery formed the only appropriate environment for the human actor. He wanted a "plastic" use of space through the use of "living light." He said light should come from various sources, angles, and directions, and it should change with action, time, and mood. Designers could even paint with light. Appia's ideas and designs had much in common with the poetic sensibility of the symbolists, but for him the human aura was the chief reality of theatre.

Gordon Craig (1872–1966), more flamboyant and controversial than Appia, was no less influential in projecting similar ideas. He, too, favored unified, three-dimensional scenery and lighting. The illegitimate son of Ellen Terry, a famous British actress, and Edward Godwin, a noted designer, young Gordon Craig acquired his last name because his mother liked the strength it symbolized. At age 17 he began nine years' work as a professional actor, first joining the Irving company and eventually playing Hamlet in 1897. He gradually became more interested in visual arts and scenic design. By 1903 he had designed seven stage productions, but he designed only five during the rest of his life. Still he learned enough from practical work to write innovative articles and books for more than twenty years. His chief works are *The Art of the Theatre* (1905), *On the Art of the Theatre* (1911), *Towards a New Theatre* (1913), and *The Theatre Advancing* (1919). From 1908 to 1929 he published a magazine entitled *The Mask*. His published works contain many graphics and designs that illustrate his ideas.

Craig wanted theatre to be respected as a unique art, not as a mixture of other arts. He believed it should be pure, not used for didacticism or commerce. For him the essentials of theatre art were action and acting, scenic line and color, with rhythm as the uniting factor. He believed in the shared creativity of all theatre workers, but that a master artist should coordinate everything. He initiated the idea of mobile settings and utilized neutrally painted screens that could change in color under differing light. His ideas inspired others to perfect the notion of the *unit set*, a construction of scenery on which various locales could be represented by means of minor transformations. Because he knew acting and actors so well, he sometimes argued that acting was too imprecise an art, and he suggested the use of masks, the adoption of Oriental styles, and even the employment of supermarionettes. In truth, he was more interested in making theatre people aware of the need for acting precision than he was in banishing actors from the theatre. Craig was a visionary whose ideals often infuriated workaday theatre people.

Owing to the influence of Appia and Craig, and because of innovations in mechanical and electrical technology, a new stagecraft arose. Modern theatre began to take on a new look. Whereas the nineteenth-century melodramas had painted two-dimensional scenery with footlights and overhead strip lights, the new twentieth-century plays utilized three-

A design by Edward Gordon Craig: *King Lear, the Storm* (woodcut, 1920)

dimensional structures and spotlights. A German named Karl Lautenschläger first used a revolving stage, and Fritz Brandt developed the idea of wagon stages. Steele MacKaye, an American, introduced elevator stages and other mechanical devices. For lighting, high-intensity tungsten instruments came into use, and dimmers were developed to control them. Lights began to be placed on ceiling beams in theatre auditoriums about 1910 and on balcony fronts in 1912. Scene designers borrowed from modern painters the techniques of making textured surfaces. Max Reinhardt devised many new ideas for the imaginative use of theatre space, and in his travels he introduced the new techniques to many countries. Among the Americans involved in devising the new stagecraft were Robert Edmond Jones, Lee Simonson, and Norman Bel Geddes.

EXPRESSIONISM, SURREALISM, AND THE AVANT-GARDE

Expressionism, another artistic movement, offered writers and directors a further alternative to realism, one less ethereal than symbolism. The expressionists attacked contemporary social problems more directly than the symbolists, and they wrote a more human-centered type of drama. By 1910 the expressionist movement was well underway in Germany. It soon spread throughout the world and remained strong until the mid-1920s. Expressionism requires each artist to employ personal feelings about life. Distortions in art express the individual artist's vision. Expressionism focuses on the importance of the individual human being. Most early expressionists believed that fundamental truth resides within each person rather than in the universe at large. Furthermore, they wished to express the spirit of social revolution so typical of their time. Almost any radical departure from realism is nowadays considered expressionistic. This major movement encompassed a great variety of artists and styles.

Expressionism in the theatre is understood as a term referring to a particular style of playwriting and theatre production. Two playwrights— August Strindberg and Frank Wedekind—were especially influential in its origination. Although Strindberg wrote in many styles, his nonrealistic plays such as *The Dream Play* (1902) and *The Ghost Sonata* (1907) proved most influential on succeeding generations of playwrights. In his plays Strindberg organized dramatic actions in the disconnected, freely associated patterns of dreams, and from them his imagination called up a variety of experiences, memories, and images. Wedekind combined the frankness of realism with a subjective attitude and wrote plays that shocked his contemporaries. His dramas often begin as realistic portraits and end as fantastic nightmares. His best-known plays are *Spring's Awakening* (1891), *Earth Spirit* (1895), *The Marquis of Keith* (1900), and *Pandora's Box* (1904). The genius he displayed in his 21 plays, his mixture of styles, and especially his direct treatment of sexual themes made him a significant influence on the German expressionists of the first quarter of the twentieth century.

The leader among German expressionists, Georg Kaiser, deserves to be ranked with Hauptmann and Brecht as one of the three best German dramatists of this century. Kaiser wrote more than sixty plays, most of them expressionistic. His plays usually show an individual making decisions about life, suffering because of them, and finally realizing that each human being must struggle against the dehumanized modern world. His dramas are perhaps the first great plays dealing with a solitary person facing an alien world. His best-known play is *From Morn to Midnight* (1912). Carl Sternheim, Ernst Toller, and Franz Werfel were other major German expressionist playwrights. Several Americans also

Dudley Digges in *The Adding Machine* by Elmer Rice

wrote outstanding expressionist plays. The best of them were *The Adding Machine* (1923) by Elmer Rice, *The Hairy Ape* (1922) by Eugene O'Neill, *Processional* (1925) by John Howard Lawson, and *Beggar on Horseback* (1924) by George S. Kaufman and Marc Connelly. The expressionists demonstrated to the modern theatre how to utilize distortion, caricature, and irrationality in order to attack the smug materialism and hypocrisy of the industrial world and its bourgeois society.

The desire to go beyond realism that stimulated the rise of expressionism in Germany caused corresponding artistic movements in other countries. In Italy, futurism emerged under the guidance of poet Filippo Marinetti. He published manifestos in 1913 and 1915 setting out the tenets of futurism. Rejecting the past, he pointed to potentials of the future, especially the "beauties" of speed, war, and technology. The futurists favored aggressiveness, anarchism, and contempt for women. They believed all artists over age 40 should be discarded like "useless manuscripts." Although futurist works in Italy, France, England, and Germany elicited controversial responses—sometimes boos, sometimes showers of fruit, and sometimes riots—the futurists' ideas influenced many of the artistic movements of this century. Their innovations included concrete poetry, kinetic sculpture, collage, dynamic sound (which later became electronic music), and assault on the audience. Futurist theatre featured abstraction in sets, costumes, and properties; mechanistic acting; and most important, continual attack on the audience's sensibilities. The experiments of the futurists were significant stimulants to the rise of the theatrical avant-garde during the remainder of this century.

Dadaism and surrealism together comprised the artistic movement in France that parallel expressionism in Germany and futurism in Italy. All these movements represent an attempt to extend aesthetic experience beyond the realistic, or representational. Dadaism arose in Zurich in 1916 at the Cabaret Voltaire. Tristan Tzara, a Romanian poet, became the most famous member of the group because he wrote their manifestos and edited the periodical called *Dada*. From among the dadaists, Tzara became a surrealist in Paris, Oskar Kokoschka an expressionist in Germany, and Marinetti a futurist in Italy. Dadaism clearly provided an initial stimulus to many of the avant-garde movements of the period and was a forerunner of the "happenings" of the 1950s and 1960s. The dadaists considered the world insane because it had produced a global war; so these young artists purposefully set out to avoid all "normal" logic in their art. They substituted discord, chaos, and simultaneity. After World War I ended, dadaism continued to thrive in Paris and offered an initiating force in the birth of surrealism.

Although expressionism and futurism antedated surrealism and no doubt provided ideas to its artists, a French playwright and two French directors were significant forerunners of the surrealists. The directors were Paul Fort and Aurélien-Marie Lugné-Poë (1869–1940). They gave as much stimulus to the nonrealistic theatre as André Antoine had to the realistic theatre. Fort gave theatre a new attitude, and his motto was that the word creates the decor. Fort's "word" was novel, ambitious, and

Louis Wolheim (left) in
***The Hairy Ape* by**
Eugene O'Neill

somewhat slipshod, but most of his performances caused riotous conflict in the audience. According to one critic, his theatre always brimmed with mad adventures. His friend Lugné-Poë, a better and more influential director, took from Fort the idea of theatre devoted to the word. His operation of the Théâtre de l'Oeuvre from 1893 to 1899 was dedicated to the presentation of important foreign dramas and of the new symbolist works. Lugné-Poë brought Ibsen to prominence in Paris, and he introduced such authors as Maeterlinck, Oscar Wilde, and Alfred Jarry. These two directors made a radical break with past theatre practice, and they pointed the way for later innovative directors of the modern theatre.

The playwright most influential as a forerunner of surrealism and other avant-garde movements of the twentieth century, even absurdism in the 1950s, was Alfred Jarry. His impact on modern theatre stems chiefly from Lugné-Poë's 1896 production of *Ubu Roi* (*King Ubu*). On December 10, 1896, a cultured and influential audience gathered to see this new work. First came a short lecture by the author, and then an actor named Firmin Gémier dressed as a fat, ugly king came forward, scowled at the audience, and snarled the play's first word, *Merde!* In English the word is best translated as "shit." Never before on a French stage had such an obscenity been uttered, and most of the scandalized audience booed and stopped the performance temporarily. Some people left, but many remained to enjoy the novel work. Though raucous, the play had a manic energy. Lugné-Poë set it on an almost empty stage and handled it in a frankly theatrical manner. He and Jarry wanted to confront the audience, attack it and challenge the sensibilities of all the spectators. Some critics have labeled it theatricalism, a type of drama corresponding to abstract painting. *Ubu Roi* established for the nonrealistic theatre of the twentieth century a tradition of directness and anti-illusion. Thus Jarry and Lugné-Poë set the stage for many later artistic movements, especially surrealism.

The word *surrealism* apparently originated with French poet Guillaume Apollinaire when he subtitled his play *The Breasts of Tiresias* (1917) a *drame surréaliste*. The artistic movement grew out of dadaism during the early 1920s. André Breton became the leader of the surrealists when he published crucial manifestos in 1924 and 1929. Influenced by Freud, Breton stressed the importance of the subconscious mind in creativity. He claimed that artists should write or paint automatically, with psychic abandon, and not worry about control, reason, or aesthetic principles. In practice, the best surrealist writers and painters were well-trained in their crafts, but they specialized in imaginative and surprising combinations of elements. The most popular surrealist of the theatre was Jean Cocteau (1892–1963). Although never an official member of the inner circle of surrealists, he utilized their techniques, mixing ordinary elements from everyday life with more mystical and mythical elements. Some of his best-known plays are *Antigone* (1922), *Orpheus* (1926), and *The Infernal Machine* (1932). Even though surrealism as a movement produced few major plays, it stimulated many theatre artists to consider fresh, nontraditional approaches to production. One surrealist in particular, Antonin Artaud, became a major influence on the later theatre of the absurd.

In the period from 1870 to 1920 the modern theatre came into being. Perhaps no one can yet judge it thoroughly or establish a perfect hierarchy among its artists. But during the period two major currents of drama became dominant—the realistic and the nonrealistic. Since then, few theatre artists or companies have avoided the influence of both. From the beginning of modernism, theorists spoke of ideals, while artists themselves worked eclectically, choosing first one style and then another. The leading movements of the period were naturalism, realism, symbolism, expressionism, and surrealism. The thinkers who most affected theatre artists were Darwin, Wagner, Zola, Nietzsche, Freud, Craig, and Breton. The most influential directors were Antoine, Brahm, Grein, Stanislavsky, Lugné-Poë, and Reinhardt. The playwrights who rose to international fame and whose dramas still appear on the stages of the world were Ibsen, Strindberg, Chekhov, Shaw, and Hauptmann. As always, the rise of the modern theatre saw great innovators, followed by geniuses who perfected the forms and whose work others popularized. The typically spirit of the period led most playwrights and theatre artists to struggle for personal freedom and the open expression of truth.

CHAPTER 16 Twentieth-Century Originality

The artists who worked in the theatres of the world during the 1920s and 1930s brought rebellion, social consciousness, and high artistry to twentieth-century theatre. The period between World War I and World War II (1918–1940) saw major social changes. It was a time of blossoming in the American theatre and new leaders in European drama.

Before turning to the details of theatrical art, a brief consideration of events, issues, and ideas provides a valuable intellectual perspective. The two world wars and the countless military skirmishes of the twentieth century have affected people profoundly. Wars have stimulated national economies and encouraged the growth of technology, but wars have progressively become more lethal and less decisive. Consequently, the view of war as heroic or beneficial has slowly disappeared. But also idealism has declined, and optimism has all but disappeared. Cynicism has taken over the daily attitudes of many ordinary people, and there is spreading fear. Because nuclear weaponry poses such an overwhelming threat, and because the world discovered the potentials of atomic devastation at Hiroshima, everyone somehow feels the constant pressure of imminent disaster. The fear of annihilation makes all other concerns seem small. The capitalistic prosperity of industrial countries is seriously marred by the pervasive poverty of less developed regions. Although war has produced beneficial technology, it has also engendered disillusionment and fear as constant factors in the everyday lives of people. All these factors and others have affected the nature and quality of contemporary art.

As always, great thinkers affect art and everyday life, and Karl Marx (1818–1883), one of the most significant, has touched the twentieth

Aurelie's Waltz by Arthur Schnitzler, Wabash College

century at its core. The economic theories of Marx led to the rise of socialism and encouraged new political art in Europe and the United States. The plays of Bertolt Brecht are an example. Marx, a German philosopher, developed social and economic theories known as dialectical materialism. He taught the world that economics determines people's lives and that the classes of society struggle continually. In his philosophy, known as Marxism, he argued that capitalism is unjust to workers and should be replaced by socialism in general and communism in particular.

Long Day's Journey into Night by Eugene O'Neill, with Florence Eldridge and Fredric March

His most famous publications are *Das Kapital* (three volumes, 1867–1894) and the *Communist Manifesto* (1871), to which his friend and financial supporter Friedrich Engels contributed. Marx worked in the labor movement and lived a life of poverty in England as a political refugee. Lenin and other leaders of the Soviet Union employed many of his theories in establishing that country's government. The ideas of Marx affected workers' movements throughout the world. As Marxian governments came into being in Russia, China, and Cuba, his ideas reached into the theatres of those nations.

The theories of Albert Einstein (1879–1955) produced many scientific and technological innovations, and they have made a dynamic impact on the world of art. His theory of relativity suggested to writers and painters that perception should be multiple and constantly changing rather than fixed or static. Time has become a field, not merely a series of clock ticks, and space is seen to be curved, an expanse in which a person can observe an object from several points of view simultaneously. The well-known cubist paintings of Pablo Picasso, for instance, exhibit such multiple viewpoints.

Carl Jung, a Swiss psychologist (1875–1961), extended Freud's psychoanalytic theories with ideas which have also influenced artists and playwrights. Jung added a fourth major element to Freud's three components of the mind. He argued that in addition to the ego, id, and superego, every human brain contains a "racial unconscious," a structural component of the brain because of the environmental adaptations that preceding generations have endured. The racial unconscious consists of the psychic results of countless experiences of the same sort; furthermore, it cannot be brought to consciousness, but neither can it be repressed or forgotten. When an artist draws upon his personal unconscious, he creates art with a strictly personal vision; whereas when he uses his racial unconscious, he is more apt to compose art that captures broadly meaningful archetypes, myths, and symbols. Jung stressed that the art, the social structures, and the mythology of primitive peoples can reveal the racial unconscious most directly. Thus, interest has grown in primative art, and western nations have begun to become aware of the imaginative power of art from Third World nations. Marx, Einstein, and Jung have not been the only seminal thinkers of the century, but they have been among the most telling.

Luigi Pirandello

EUROPEAN CREATORS

Early in this period the Italian theatre gave the world a dramatist of major stature, Luigi Pirandello (1867–1936). Of the dramas written in the twentieth century, those he composed between 1917 and 1936 are among the most original and challenging. He used the stage not only as a place of entertainment but also as a symbol of consciousness itself. For him the theatre offered an image of the human situation. His plays are mostly tragicomedies that illustrate the relative nature of reality and morality. He showed that people cannot be sure of anything, least of all sure of other people. He ridiculed the bourgeois tendency to thrust individuals into categories, and he revealed that in order to survive people often put on masks.

Pirandello was born into a well-to-do family in Sicily, studied in Rome, and took a doctorate in philosophy in Germany. His family arranged a marriage and provided a generous allowance for him, and he settled in Rome to become a writer. But his life brought him numerous disappointments. He lost faith in government because of its corruption. His family's fortune disappeared because its mines flooded, and the difficult delivery of his third child disturbed the mind of his wife. She became insanely jealous and easily angered. Pirandello came to realize that everyone conceives reality differently, that emotions often overturn logic, and that for people with strong feelings objectivity is impossible. At first he wrote short stories and novels as a realist, but he found the theatre more challenging. He also organized the Art Theatre of Rome; his company lasted from 1924 to 1928 and made major tours in Europe and South America. From then until his death in 1936, Pirandello concerned himself only with writing. In 1934 he won the Nobel prize for literature.

Among Pirandello's numerous plays, three are masterpieces in the world repertory. *Right You are, If You Think You Are* (1917) discusses the relativity of appearances—how people see truth differently. *Henry IV* (1922) tells the story of a rich man who after an accident has lived for years madly impersonating a Holy Roman emperor. The play illustrates how people need dreams in order to survive. His most famous play is *Six Characters in Search of an Author* (1921). Six characters interrupt a group of theatre people in rehearsal, hoping to find an author who will give "reality" to their lives by setting their story on stage. This play has become characteristic of contemporary theatre in general because of its irony, theatricalism, and perceptiveness. In his dramas Pirandello demonstrated that consciousness can be a prison that prevents people from understanding the world around them. Although his vision is pessimistic, Pirandello wrote his characters with compassion. He gave great stimulus to later developments in drama, especially the work of the absurdists. One of his best messages was that people should not pass judgment on one another and that above all they should be merciful.

In French theatre, Jacques Copeau (1879–1949) was a most influential director during the first third of the twentieth century. In 1913 he established one of France's most famous theatres, the Théâtre du Vieux Colombier. It was as important to its time as was the earlier Théâtre Libre. At first a critic, then a playwright, Copeau was most influential as a director. Dissatisfied with realism, he used simplified settings and placed actors on a bare stage to emphasize the "living presence" of the playwright. He believed a director should analyze a script carefully and translate the play into "poetry of the theatre." The first group of actors he assembled include Charles Dullin and Louis Jouvet. His theatre closed during World War I, but he reopened it with renewed vigor in 1919. Eventually Copeau became dedicated to training actors. His most important ideas had to do with the importance of studying the text and rendering all its nuances in carefully detailed acting. Copeau trained and influenced many of the next generation of leaders in French theatre.

A coalition of four men called the "Cartel des Quatre" provided artistic leadership to the entire French theatre from 1926 until 1940. These four—all friends, associates, or students of Copeau—agreed to give one another artistic help. First, Louis Jouvet began as an actor with Copeau; then he became a leading actor and director with his own company. Jouvet introduced the plays of Jean Giraudoux, the leading French playwright of the period. Jouvet believed in the primacy of the play. Second, Charles Dullin established in 1922 a theatre named the Atelier. Opposed to naturalism, he tried to combine music, movement, and dance with conventional

Jacques Copeau

acting. Dullin also helped the early careers of Jean-Louis Barrault and Jean Vilar, who later became luminaries of French theatre. Third, Gaston Baty worked from 1930 to 1947 as the leading director in the Théâtre Montparnasse. He wished to convey the text of a play and also explore the play's "zone of mystery." Baty stressed the visual elements of a production. Fourth, Georges Pitoëff, a Russian whose family emigrated to Paris, brought many foreign works to the French stage. He particularly stressed the importance of finding elements in classical plays that would communicate with contemporary audiences.

Jean Giraudoux (1882–1944) was probably the best and certainly the most well-known French playwright of the period. Well-educated, he began working as a teacher, entered the foreign service, wrote successful novels, and finally in his forties became a playwright. All of the plays of Giraudoux demonstrate his preoccupation with language, the element of drama he most respected as man's best tool of sensibility and reason. His literary style utilized irony, metaphor, and penetrating wit. The characters of his plays are seldom mean or violent but, rather, display virtues of humor and insight. Many of his plays pose a decision for a central character between two contradictory positions—for example, war and peace, life and death, or reality and fantasy. Some of his best-known plays are *Amphitryon 38* (1929), *Ondine* (1939), and *The Madwoman of*

Chaillot (1945). In all his works, Giraudoux favored humanism over materialism, the natural over the manufactured, and individual values over institutional ones.

Another French writer of this period, who became internationally renowned after World War II, was a visionary named Antonin Artaud (1896–1948). At age 24, Artaud began his career as an actor in Paris, playing roles for Lugné-Poë, Dullin, and others. He also acted in over twenty films. In the mid-1920s he was closely associated with André Breton in the surrealist movement. Then, in 1926, with Roger Vitrac and Robert Aron, he established the Théâtre Alfred Jarry, but it lasted only three years. Early in the 1930s he studied a troupe of Balinese dancers performing in Paris and began to realize the potentials of ritualistic performances in the theatre. From 1931 to 1936 he wrote a series of manifestos about the theatre, collected and published in 1938 as *The Theatre and Its Double*. In 1936 he traveled to Mexico to study primitive ritual and the cultic use of drugs. He himself was a user of drugs since his early days in Paris. Upon his return to France in 1937 he spent the next nine years in asylums for the insane. Released in 1946, he continued to write while living in a rest home. His collected works amount to nine volumes.

Although Artaud wrote no significant plays and had no success as a director, his ideas have been an inspiration to many theatre artists, especially such directors as Roger Blin of France, Peter Brook of England, and Jerzy Grotowski of Poland. Artaud verbalized the antirealist spirit of creativity, and he became a romantic symbol for those who wished to strike a rebellious attitude. He stressed the value of concrete objects over intellectual abstractions, of the body over words. According to him, the theatre doesn't require plays, only directors and actors to develop a poetry of space and movement. Furthermore, he believed in a theatre of "cruelty"—a term he borrowed from Nietzsche—not a theatre of violence but of ritualistic acts. He envisioned a theatre of alienation and absurdity, rich with symbol, hallucination, and gesture. His productions contained a series of unconnected, unrealistic, and antisocial acts. He also recommended that theatre move out of traditional buildings into barns, hangars, and abandoned factories where performances could better assault audiences. Artaud's ideas appeared in the work of some absurdists of the 1950s and still activate the work of some directors. Artaud particularly stressed that theatre is its own reality and can show the imprisoned human consciousness. He became the prophet for antitraditional theatre.

In Germany, Max Reinhardt and Carl Zuchmayer were leading theatre artists of the 1920s and 1930s. Max Reinhardt, the great eclectic director, dominated the German theatre until the rise of Hitler in the 1930s; then, because he was a Jew, Reinhardt was forced to give up his theatres and leave his country to work in the United States. But from 1905 to 1933 Reinhardt produced throughout the world 452 plays for 23,374 performances. Both in quantity and in quality he was one of the world's leading directors. Although expressionism dominated the German art theatres during the 1920s, neorealism began as a movement in the same decade. Whereas expressionism tended to be optimistic about the human condition, neorealism was pessimistic. Carl Zuchmayer was the most noteworthy neorealist playwright. His well-known play *The Captain of Kopen-*

ick (1931) satirized militarism and bureaucracy, and it became a comic classic. To escape Nazi oppression, Zuchmayer also had to flee to the United States.

In 1919 architect Walter Gropius headed a group of artists who established a school in Weimar, Germany, called the Bauhaus. The ideas which they developed were influential in all the arts throughout the world. They thought that the arts should be available and understandable to the common man, and that the environment of common people deserved to be as well designed and artistic as that of the elite. The Bauhaus taught the world that aesthetic considerations were also important in the manufacture and construction of everything. From 1923 to 1929 Lothar Schreyer and Oskar Schlemmer ran a theatre workshop. Schlemmer explored the nonrealistic use of moving bodies in stage space, also with light and color. Laszlo Moholy-Nagy experimented with light and kinetic sculpture, photography, and film. In 1925 he developed the concept of "total theatre," combining film, recordings, and light shows with live actors. The architects of the Bauhaus, especially Walter Gropius and Mies van der Rohe, became internationally influential, and their ideas about the functionality of theatre buildings continue to affect theatre design. The Nazis destroyed the Bauhaus, and the artists themselves scattered to other countries. Many came to America, and the influence of Bauhaus continues here today.

Another movement of major significance began in Germany between the wars—epic theatre. Among the many people who contributed to its development, director Erwin Piscator (1893–1966) was central. Influenced by dadaism, expressionism, and communism, he believed in subordinating drama to revolutionary goals, doctoring scripts to clarify social messages, utilizing new theatre technology, emphasizing the collective work of the entire company, and playing to working-class audiences. He started an influential company, and in the 1927–1928 season he presented the three plays that made him famous: *Hurrah, We Live!; Rasputin;* and *The Good Soldier Schweik*. In these productions he utilized many features of epic theatre—an episodic script, a bare stage with shifting cartoon projections, and nonrealistic acting. Piscator, like so many others, had to flee Germany with the rise of the Nazi political machine. He settled in the United States from 1939 to 1951 and became influential in New York theatre.

Although Piscator initiated epic theatre, Bertolt Brecht (1898–1956) brought it to high fruition. As a playwright and theorist, Brecht is now considered a leading theatre genius of the twentieth century. He wished to increase the empathic distance between a production and its audience so that the spectators would feel less and think more. Therefore, Brecht increased the narrative content of plays, "historified" his subjects (set them in other times), simplified the pictorial representation, and revealed the mechanisms of the theatre to audience view. Whereas Piscator's was a director's theatre, the theatre of Brecht was a playwright's.

Born in Augsburg, Brecht at age 19 moved to Munich to study medicine. During World War I he served as a medical orderly and became disillusioned with society and the condition of common men. He began writing in the early 1920s and joined the rebellious avant-garde in Berlin.

A Man's a Man by
Bertolt Brecht,
Hanover College

There Brecht became associated with Piscator, and from 1927 to 1933 he
wrote a number of plays. He composed his first masterpiece, *The Threepenny Opera* (1928), which brought him world fame. As a refugee from
Hitler's Germany from 1933 to 1947, Brecht wrote his greatest plays:
Mother Courage (1938), *Galileo* (1938–1939), *The Good Woman of Setzuan*
(1938–1939), and *The Caucasian Chalk Circle* (1944–1945). He also composed a body of dramatic theory that now stands as a major theatre
document of the century. He returned to East Germany in 1947, and with
his wife, actress Helene Weigel, he formed the Berliner Ensemble in East
Berlin in 1949. The company grew to be recognized as one of the major
theatres of the world, and he won the Stalin Prize in 1955. When he died
in 1956, his influence as a theorist, writer, and producer was at its zenith
the world over.

Brecht's key ideas rise from a didactic attitude. He wanted the theatre
to raise people's social consciousness, entertain them and also instruct
them. He mixed lyric, epic, and dramatic poetry in plays with open,
diffuse structures that started early in the narrative and proceeded
through many scenes. He avoided tight, climactic plays, like those of
Ibsen, and often ignored the "laws" of unity and causality. He drew
techniques from naturalism and expressionism and developed a style
that he called "narrative realism." He liked the truthfulness of naturalism
and the episodic structure and distortion of expressionism. His theatre

was anti-illusory and presentational. From Piscator he took at least two chief ideas. First, not the private stories and feelings of individuals but, rather, the relationships between individuals and society at large should be the focus of theatre. Second, the destiny of the masses should be the new heroic factor in drama.

In theatre production, Brecht developed a straightforward style. He cleared the stage and auditorium of magical elements, permitting lights to show and utilizing signs, maps, and cartoons as scenery. He told the actors to play directly to the audience, avoiding the pretense of real life. Brecht also advocated that the best dramas should contain an "alienation effect," one or more elements that would remind spectators they are watching a play. In his productions he introduced certain devices—such as interruptive songs, direct audience address, and the revelation of stage mechanics—to break the audience away from oversympathetic emotions and to get them to consider the intellectual issues more clearly. Brecht's genius as both writer and director often outstripped his objective theories. He employed theatre for serious social messages while entertaining audiences with skill and genius. Above all, Brecht wanted to make a theatre for the common people. Brecht understood the alienation around him, and his works address the spiritual and social difficulties of twentieth-century people. He does not, however, depict man caught inside a prison of consciousness; rather, he tells stories about people caught in the midst of societal changes. Also, his plays emphasize the needs and cures of social and political conditions.

In many countries and regions, the period between World War I and World War II was not a time of innovation in the theatre, nor did geniuses of Brecht's stature appear everywhere. When the Soviets came to power in Russia, playwrights and directors evidently no longer had the liberty to follow their own talents, and their creativity was smothered. An even more extreme form of restriction occurred in Germany with the rise of Nazi power under Adolf Hitler. Most of the genuinely creative artists of Germany were silenced or executed, or else they fled to other countries. Few theatre artists of worldwide influence appeared in other central European countries.

In Spain, despite the shifting winds of political change, including dictatorial rule, the theatre remained highly creative throughout the twentieth century. The early modernists among Spanish playwrights were José Echegaray, Jacinto Benavente, Ramón Maria del Valle-Inclán, and the brothers Quintero. Echegaray wrote realistic plays, some in the vein of Ibsen, and he was granted a Nobel prize for literature. Benavente, one of the most prolific of all modern dramatists, wrote more than 300 plays, and in 1922 he, too, won the Nobel prize. Whereas Benavente was a popular conventional dramatist, Valle-Inclán was essentially a surrealist even before surrealism actually came into being in Paris. With his concept of *esperpento* in literature, he is also a forerunner of the antitraditional theatre movement of the 1950s; the word *esperpento*, in fact, means absurd. Two of his most well-known works are *Divine Words* (1913) and *The Horns of Don Friolera* (1925). Valle-Inclán is also important because he was the father of avant-garde drama in Spain, especially of the tra-

dition followed by Federico García Lorca and the independent theatre movement of the late 1960s and early 1970s.

In the 1930s one Spanish writer became a world-renowned dramatist—Federico García Lorca (1899–1936). Born in Andalucia, Lorca began his career as a lyric poet. In the 1920s he joined the Madrid *vanguardia*, a young group of artists, including painter Salvador Dali and filmmaker Luis Buñuel. Influenced by the dadaists and surrealists, Lorca wrote highly accomplished surrealistic poems. Then, in the early 1930s, Lorca associated with a traveling theatre troupe called La Barraca, for which he wrote his masterpieces—such farces as *The Love of Don Perlimplin and Belisa in the Garden*, and such tragedies as *Blood Wedding* (1933) and *The House of Bernarda Alba* (1935). Especially in his serious plays he was able to write inherently poetic drama rather than merely impose verse on the material. Although other poets, such as T. S. Eliot and Archibald MacLeish, wrote good poetic plays during the twentieth century, the poetic dramas of Lorca have far surpassed all others in frequency of production in the world repertory, and they continue to be produced. Unfortunately, during the Spanish Civil War, a group of Fascists murdered Lorca at age 37, but despite his short career, he remains the leading modern dramatist of the Spanish-speaking world.

BRITISH AND IRISH THEATRE AND DRAMA

In England, theatre flourished between the wars more in the work of directors and actors than of playwrights. After World War I, actor-managers seemed to lose their hold, and a few artistic directors gained prominence. During the 1925–1926 season Theodore Komissarzhevsky, a Russian, staged a group of plays by Chekhov and other Russian authors. Not only did this series of productions introduce Chekhov to England, but also it brought professional attention to several outstanding actors—John Gielgud, Claude Rains, and Charles Laughton. About the same time, the Old Vic Theatre came to prominence; it reached artistic maturity in the 1930s under director Tyrone Guthrie (1900–1971). He adopted many of the rapid-paced, realistic production methods of Harley Granville Barker. Guthrie attracted to the Old Vic the best British actors and installed a true repertory system, in which the company presented a number of different plays on alternating nights.

Tyrone Guthrie brought the power of artistic directors to a climax. Devoted to Shakespeare and the classics, he developed new interpretations, utilized inventive stage movement, and elicited complex characterizations from actors. Some of the outstanding actors who worked with Guthrie were: John Gielgud, Charles Laughton, Flora Robson, Edith Evans, Peggy Ashcroft, Maurice Evans, Michael Redgrave, Alec Guinness, Ralph Richardson, and Anthony Quayle. After his great successes in England, Tyrone Guthrie became a major influence in spreading the gospel of classical theatre in North America. In 1953 he helped form an outstanding acting company for the Shakespeare Festival in Stratford, Ontario, and became its first artistic director. By 1957 the festival built an innovative "thrust-stage" theatre of his design. He also provided the artistic ingre-

dient for the formation of a major classical theatre in Minneapolis and worked as its artistic director for three years (1962–1965). That institution, the Minnesota Theatre Company, gave impetus in the years that followed to the rise of the professional regional theatre movement throughout the United States.

Laurence Olivier (b. 1907) typifies the high accomplishment of British acting in the twentieth century. He belongs to a generation of British actors (mentioned in the previous paragraph) that established a level of performance quality for British theatre probably unequaled in the world. Olivier spent his theatre apprenticeship in the 1920s at the Birmingham Repertory Theatre with Barry Jackson. During the 1930s he worked alongside such actors as Noel Coward and John Gielgud, and he joined the Old Vic company in 1937. He has divided his career between film acting and stage portrayals of great Shakespearean characters. Onstage he enacted, for example, the title roles in *King Lear* (1946), *Hamlet* (1948), *Richard III* (1956), and *Othello* (1964). Olivier claims the key to his success was not ability but hard work. He had the good fortune to develop his craft by performing constantly under some of the best directors of the century. Olivier came to the great roles at a time when sensible line readings were in vogue and when exciting staging was appropriate. He joined others as a leader in the formation of England's National Theatre Company.

During the era from the 1920s until the end of World War II, many skilled writers provided plays for the professional stage in London, but none originated new styles or methodologies. George Bernard Shaw wrote *Saint Joan* in 1923, but his subsequent works until 1939 were of lesser stature. Novelist John Galsworthy wrote seminaturalistic plays, the best of which was *Escape* (1926). Two writers of comedy of manners—Somerset Maugham and Noel Coward—also brought entertaining plays to the British stage. Maugham's most well-known play is *The Circle* (1921). Noel Coward wrote a special sort of mildly cynical comedy, such as *Private Lives* (1930) and *Blithe Spirit* (1941).

Some of the British drama of the period was purposefully poetic. T. S. Eliot, a lyric poet who emigrated from the United States to England in the 1920s, applied his lyric gift to writing *Murder in the Cathedral* for the Canterbury Festival (1935). After the critical success of that piece, he later wrote other verse plays, including *The Family Reunion* (1939) and *The Cocktail Party* (1949), that helped create mid-century interest in poetic drama. Christopher Fry wrote later verse plays of note, especially *The Lady's Not for Burning* (1949).

In Ireland, Sean O'Casey (1884–1964), a playwright of the first rank, appeared during the 1920s. O'Casey spent the early portion of his life as a laborer struggling to escape poverty, and he educated himself. At the age of 40 he furnished the Abbey Theatre with his first play, *The Shadow of a Gunman* (1923), and became an overnight success. In his early years he was a political radical, and later he became an artistic one. He cared less about Irish nationalism than about his country's social and political problems. His second and third plays were his realistic triumphs—*Juno and the Paycock* (1924) and *The Plough and the Stars* (1926). Because of

the satire in the latter play, it caused outraged Irish people to riot. In later plays O'Casey abandoned realism, but they never reached the quality of his two early masterpieces. The spirit of proletarian art and socialist theory affected his works profoundly, but also the music, poetry, and humor of what he wrote assumed equal importance. Few of his contemporaries wrote with the originality of O'Casey, and he probably wrote the best workers' plays of the century.

AMERICAN DRAMA COMES OF AGE

The United States used its economic and military resources to confirm itself in World War I as a world power. Somehow during that conflict the country also made a giant leap forward in the realm of art. Many authorities cite the early 1920s as the time when American theatre came of age with the plays of such authors as Eugene O'Neill and such organizations as the Theatre Guild. Undoubtedly, the innovations of European theatre artists and the plays of the modern giants—Ibsen, Strindberg, Chekhov, Shaw, and Pirandello—made a telling impact on the minds of young Americans. By the time the war began, the "new stagecraft" had already found its way to this continent. In 1917 Sheldon Cheney founded *Theatre Arts Magazine*, in which he and others wrote about the new theatre of Europe. Many influential theatre companies from Europe toured America, such as those of Copeau from France in 1917 and 1919, and Stanislavsky from the Soviet Union in 1923–1924. Max Reinhardt came here, too, in order to direct major productions and brought many European directorial practices to this country.

The major change in the United States first occurred in the "little theatre movement." It fostered new writers, directors, and actors, and it opposed standard commercial practices of the Theatre Syndicate. During the early part of the century, the Syndicate tried to gain control over key theatres in the country, and it choked off most art in American theatre. Many groups contributed to the little theatre movement. The Provincetown Players, perhaps the most influential of the new American groups of the time, was begun in the summer of 1915 on a Cape Cod wharf. After the summer season of 1916 with George Cram Cook as president, the 29 members of the company moved it from Provincetown, Massachusetts, to Greenwich Village in New York City. What made the Provincetown Players outstanding was the quality of mind of the membership and their devotion to new American playwrights. Between 1916 and 1925 they presented 93 new plays by 47 different playwrights, the most important of whom probably was Eugene O'Neill. The Provincetown Players' production of O'Neill's *The Emperor Jones* in 1920 became a commercial hit, and they moved it to Broadway. The company survived in one form or another until 1929. Some of the other groups in the movement were the Neighborhood Playhouse and the Washington Square Players in New York and Chicago's Little Theatre.

Out of the Washington Square Players evolved one of the strongest artistic theatre organizations of the 1920s—the Theatre Guild. Its board of managers included such people as Lawrence Langner, Lee Simonson,

and Theresa Helburn. Inspired by the artistic theatres of Europe, the organization devoted itself to new plays of artistic merit that commercial managers would not produce. At first it presented plays by such writers as Shaw, Kaiser, Pirandello, Ibsen, and Strindberg. Its first noteworthy American work was *The Adding Machine* (1923) by Elmer Rice. During the season beginning in 1927, the Guild began to produce the plays of Eugene O'Neill, beginning with *Marco Millions* and *Strange Interlude*. Throughout the 1930s, however, the quality of leadership in the Guild declined. Many distinguished American actors worked in Guild productions—for example, Alfred Lunt, Lynne Fontanne, and Edward G. Robinson. Another artistic theatre of its time was the Civic Repertory Theatre founded in 1926 by Eva Le Gallienne. On Broadway itself producer Arthur Hopkins put together many artistic productions and helped raise the international reputations of John Barrymore and his brother Lionel. The Barrymore brothers and their sister Ethel were among the most compelling actors of their era.

Eugene O'Neill (1888–1953), America's most renowned playwright, came to prominence in the late 1910s and early 1920s. The son of traveling actor James O'Neill, Eugene was born in a Broadway hotel and educated at various Catholic schools, plus a year at Princeton. He took to the sea as a laborer and lived such a strenuous life that he contracted tuberculosis. During convalescence, O'Neill began to read, think out, and write plays. In 1914, at age 26, he took a course at Harvard from the first

The Great God Brown by Eugene O'Neill, with Leona Hogarth and William Harrigan

Elmer Rice

university teacher of playwriting, George Pierce Baker. In the summer of 1916, the Provincetown Players gave him his first production, when they presented *Bound East for Cardiff*, a moody short play written about his experiences at sea. O'Neill's first full-length play, *Beyond the Horizon*, won a Pulitzer prize in 1920. O'Neill never suffered as a neglected artist because the Provincetown Players and then the Theatre Guild placed on the stage nearly everything he wrote. After 1934 he lived in seclusion with his third wife on Sea Island, Georgia, and in California's Valley of the Moon, and in 1936 he received the Nobel prize for literature. From that time until his death he wrote many more plays, often withholding them from production for several years.

The prolific O'Neill led the American theatre into the modern age with his intense and experimental dramas. Claiming only the influence of Strindberg, he obviously knew the work of Ibsen and many other European dramatists, especially the expressionists. Philosophy and psychology also fascinated him, and the influences of Nietzsche and Freud are obvious in his work. Although he wrote some landmark dramas, not all his plays were outstanding, and generally his use of language lagged behind his sense of action and his vision of life. Six of his best plays are generally realistic: *Beyond the Horizon* (1920), *Anna Christie* (1920), *Desire Under the Elms* (1924), *Ah, Wilderness!* (1932), *The Iceman Cometh* (1946), and *Long Day's Journey into Night* (1956). Five are expressionistic or stylized: *The Emperor Jones* (1920), *The Hairy Ape* (1922), *The Great God Brown* (1926), *Strange Interlude* (1927), and *Mourning Becomes Electra* (1931). The element most responsible for the greatness of O'Neill's work is a vision of man's quest for a new God, a new set of values to replace those destroyed with the creation of the modern world. He dramatized the idea that if human beings search hard enough, they can find an underlying order in the universe. Although only his realistic works are persistently produced today, Eugene O'Neill remains America's leading dramatist.

Four other particularly outstanding writers of serious plays were Elmer Rice, Sidney Howard, Maxwell Anderson, and Robert Sherwood. Elmer Rice, a native New Yorker, got his first play, *On Trial* (1914), produced on Broadway at the age of 22. From that time until his death in the 1960s, he was an active dramatist who wrote in many styles and forms. *The Adding Machine* (1923), the first significant American drama produced by the Theatre Guild, remains Rice's most frequently produced play. This expressionistic work alternates between serious and comic scenes and follows the career of Mr. Zero, a modern everyman who is victimized by work on earth but who after murdering his boss does no better in the hereafter. His other significant drama from the 1920s is *Street Scene* (1929), an intensely naturalistic play about life in a tenement. Other important works by Elmer Rice are the didactic plays *We, the People* and *Judgment Day* (1934) and the imaginative *Dream Girl* (1945).

Maxwell Anderson (1888–1959) wrote many fine plays, some in verse. His first major success came in collaboration with Laurence Stallings; they wrote *What Price Glory?* (1924), a landmark piece because of its ironic depiction of war and plentiful use of profanity. Anderson wrote historical verse plays such as *Elizabeth the Queen* (1930), *Mary of Scotland* (1933), *Valley Forge* (1934), and *Anne of the Thousand Days* (1948). Perhaps his best play was *Winterset* (1935), in which he attempted to put poetic dialogue into the mouths of everyday people. The play drew inspiration from the famous Sacco-Vanzetti murder case, and it follows the story of a young man bent on avenging the unjust execution of his father. During the 1930s and 1940s many authorities considered Anderson the leading American playwright, but his plays have not often been produced in the last quarter of the century.

Robert E. Sherwood (1896–1955) began his career with an antiwar comedy, *The Road to Rome* (1927), but in the 1930s he turned to more serious work that mixed comic and melodramatic elements with significant themes. *The Petrified Forest* (1935) established a special type of play in American theatre. Set in a crossroads cafe, it presents a varied group of ordinary people held hostage for a time by gangsters. Many subsequent plays by other authors have used a similar situation. The play served as a vehicle for actor Humphrey Bogart's rise to stardom on the stage and later in motion pictures. Others among Sherwood's best plays are *Idiot's Delight* (1936), *Abe Lincoln in Illinois* (1938), and *There Shall Be No Night* (1940).

Not all of the playwrights who came to prominence in the 1920s turned out serious pieces; some wrote comedies. Philip Barry wrote such plays

Robert E. Sherwood

as *You and I* (1923), *Hotel Universe* (1930), and *The Philadelphia Story* (1939). The latter is frequently produced even today. From the 1920s to the 1950s, George S. Kaufman was perhaps America's best writer of farce. As the names of his coauthors indicate, Kaufman was a good collaborator: *Beggar on Horseback* (1924, with Marc Connolly), *The Green Pastures* (1930, with Marc Connolly), *Stage Door* (1936, with Moss Hart). *You Can't Take It with You* (1936), by Kaufman and Hart, has turned out to be one of the most frequently produced of all American plays—a classic American comedy. S. N. Behrman had his first success with *The Second Man* (1927) and later wrote other outstanding comedies such as *Biography* (1932) and *No Time for Comedy* (1939). These dramatists and others set a high standard for later writers, and they established comedy as a mainstay of American theatre.

AMERICAN THEATRE IN THE 1930s

During the 1920s, American theatre hit a peak of economic success, but after the stock market crash of 1929, theatre like all other businesses suffered financial difficulties. About 190 plays reached the Broadway stage in the 1930–1931 season, but by the 1939–1940 season only 80 were presented. Nevertheless, new groups appeared, and theatre artists found inspiration in the social issues of the time. A number of visionary theatre groups came into being, and many new writers, directors, and actors stepped into the lights of Broadway.

The most influential production company of the 1930s was called the Group Theatre. In 1931, Cheryl Crawford, Harold Clurman, and Lee Strasberg—all Theatre Guild employees—formed the organization. The Group Theatre became not only the leading professional theatre organization of the decade but also the one with the most long-range influence, especially in the realm of acting. The Group Theatre's impact is still apparent in American acting and rehearsal techniques. The three founders, wishing to establish a permanent acting company with a unified approach to acting, adopted the Stanislavsky Method. They also wanted to bring forth the work of new playwrights, especially those concerned with immediate social and political problems. Some of the important playwrights that the

Left: Harold Clurman

Right: Cheryl Crawford

Lee Strasberg

Group produced were Robert Ardrey, Paul Green, Sidney Kingsley, John Howard Lawson, William Saroyan, Thornton Wilder, Irwin Shaw, and Clifford Odets.

During the ten years of its life the Group Theatre presented 23 plays, 13 of them focusing on social problems. Although the Group Theatre always stressed artistic collaboration and economic community, during the first three or four years of production Lee Strasberg was the dominant stage director. He developed his own version of the Stanislavsky Method, particularly stressing "emotion memory." In later years Harold Clurman became the more dominant director, and he emphasized Stanislavsky's concepts of "given circumstances" and the "magic if." The actors in the organization were even more talented than the directors. The performers themselves turned out to be one of the best collections of actors in the history of American theatre. The acting company included stage stars Luther Adler, Stella Adler, Morris Carnovsky, and Sanford Meisner, as well as those who became film stars—Lee J. Cobb, John Garfield, and Franchot Tone. Actors Elia Kazan and Robert Lewis later became significant New York directors. Kazan, who eventually became a major film director, was probably the best stage director to emerge from the Group Theatre. After the company's demise, Clurman, too, continued to direct and also to write theatre criticism. In the last third of his life, Lee Strasberg became a major force in American acting in the 1940s and 1950s as founder of and major teacher at the Actors' Studio.

Clifford Odets

The major playwriting discovery of the Group Theatre was undoubtedly Clifford Odets (1906–1963). He first joined the Group as an actor, but soon, with Clurman's encouragement, he began to write plays. His first major effort was a long one-act play, *Waiting for Lefty* (1935), which he wrote in a hotel room in three days. The play contained a group of short scenes about a cab drivers' strike, and it was so successful in a small, experimental production with Group actors that it moved to Broadway. So emotionally exciting was the play that each night at the end of the production most spectators rushed out of the theatre to demonstrate in the streets. Few other plays by Odets generated the same sort of audience enthusiasm, but several were highly praised, especially *Awake and Sing!* (1934), *Paradise Lost* (1936), and *Golden Boy* (1937). All of his plays of the 1930s were didactic—built upon a system of ideas with the story and characters subsumed to the social message. His best works embodied the ideas rather than preaching them. For this reason the plays of Clifford Odets turned out to be among the best didactic pieces from any American writer. In the late 1930s and after, his career led him to Hollywood, but he also wrote two other plays for Broadway *The Country Girl* (1950) and *The Flowering Peach* (1954).

Several major scenic designers were associated with the Group Theatre, especially Boris Aronson, Mordecai Gorelik, and Donald Oenslager. Like the actors and directors, the designers were among the artistic leaders of the American theatre between the wars. Indeed, the Group was a dominant artistic force in American theatre during that period.

Another theatre organization of the 1930s also deserves special mention—The Federal Theatre Project. It was the largest organization in the history of American theatre, and the financial support for it came from the Federal government. Because so many Americans were out of work during the 1930s—theatre people included—the government formed the Works Progress Administration (WPA) and established projects that provided jobs in various fields. The Federal Theatre Project was one such arm of the WPA. Hallie Flanagan, one of the most dynamic women in the history of American theatre, became the head of the Project. She gained her experience by studying with George Pierce Baker and developed her theatrical touch by directing experimental productions at Vassar College. She envisioned this governmental program with its immense (for its time) financial subsidy—$46 million for four years—as an opportunity to create a national theatre. She divided the nation into five regions, assigned directors in each, and encouraged them to foster regional playwrights, actors, designers, and directors. The results were amazing in both amateur and professional theatre presentations—over 1200 productions of 830 works, 105 of which were new scripts. The Federal Theatre Project lasted from 1935 to 1939.

Among the Project's most unusual innovations were the "living newspapers." These informative, didactic productions were startlingly original. Elmer Rice helped originate the concept, and Arthur Arent acted as chairman of the writing committees that created them. Three of the living newspapers were especially outstanding. *Triple-A Plowed Under* (1936) presented facts about farm production and offered commentary about the government's farm policy under the Agricultural Adjustment Administration (AAA). *Power* (1937) explored the system of Tennessee Valley Authority (TVA) installations for electricity. *One-Third of a Nation* (1938) dealt with the housing shortage and nationwide rental malpractices. The scripts always focused on the difficulties of a "little man," a common citizen with curiosity and a problem. The dialogue and the set speeches often came directly from news sources, such as interviews, public speeches, and statistics. The settings were in the tradition of Erwin Piscator's epic theatre. The designers used projections, constructivist scenery, and complicated lighting.

Although the living newspapers were among the most original creations of the Federal Theatre Project, they also were the most controversial in politics and thus contributed to its downfall. In 1939 Congress chose not to renew the funding for the Federal Theatre because the living newspapers had supposedly espoused too many radical views, although the attitudes expressed were never more radical than those of the Roosevelt administration. Perhaps the most important lesson the nation can learn from the Federal Theatre Project is the impact that the government of the United States could have in benefiting the arts if such a program were followed as normal policy. Some problems and many arguments would no doubt result, but also the increase in artistic opportunity would be great.

The Federal Theatre helped create theatre companies in New York and throughout the nation. The best of them was the Mercury Theatre, which

The Mercury Theatre production of Shakespeare's *Julius Caesar* directed by Orson Welles

313

Orson Welles and John Houseman formed in 1937. Young Welles furnished artistic genius as actor and director, while Houseman managed the business. They produced an all-black rendition of *Macbeth* (1935) and a modern-dress version of *Doctor Faustus* (1937) starring Welles. When they produced the satirical leftist musical *The Cradle Will Rock* (1937), the WPA ordered the show not to open. Welles and the cast trudged to another theatre; author-composer Marc Blitzstein played the music on a lone piano; and they opened the show anyway. So, the Mercury Theatre declared its independence from the government. Welles directed such innovative productions for the Mercury as *The Shoemaker's Holiday, Heartbreak House,* and *Danton's Death.* The Mercury was also the nucleus of many creative radio productions during the late 1930s—for example, *War of the Worlds.* In the early 1940s Welles took the group to Hollywood to create such landmark films as *Citizen Kane* and *The Magnificient Ambersons.* Welles, Houseman, and many of the Mercury's actors—for example, Joseph Cotten—have had long, influential careers in American theatre and film.

During the 1930s, three other writers wrote significant plays for the American stage—Lillian Hellman, John Howard Lawson, and Thornton Wilder. Lillian Hellman (1905–1984) became well-known with *The Children's Hour* (1934), a story about how a girl attempts to destroy a woman who is her teacher through a series of lies which society accepts as truth. Hellman clearly wished to write seriously about subjects of moral concern. She put together carefully structured stories for her plays, but the ideas the stories illustrated were even more important. Like Clifford Odets, she was a master of the didactic play. Probably her most lasting play is *The Little Foxes* (1938), a descriptive picture of rapacious capitalism at the turn of the century in the South. Other well-known plays of Hellman's are *Another Part of the Forest* (1946), an adaptation of Jean Anouilh's *The Lark* (1955), and *Toys in the Attic* (1960). Although she disliked the label "well-made," which some critics gave to her plays, her works are indeed well-crafted and thoughtful. Late in life she wrote a series of fine autobiographical volumes.

John Howard Lawson (1895–1977) became known as a playwright in the 1920s with two expressionistic plays, *Roger Bloomer* (1923) and *Processional* (1925). But his reputation as a theorist and radical playwright grew even more important in the 1930s. For many years a confirmed Communist, he became "the dean" of leftist writers. Three of his plays were important productions of the 1930s—*Success Story* (1932), *Gentlewoman* (1934), and *Marching Song* (1937). The latter play serves as the best American example of socialist realism. Even more important than his plays were his book *Theory and Technique of Playwriting* (1936) and the influence he exerted on writing theory when he left New York and became a leading screenwriter in Hollywood. Lawson brought the "conflict" theory of drama to this country and promoted its widespread acceptance, especially among Broadway professionals and screenwriters. Like several European theorists before him—especially Brunetière—Lawson believed drama is best structured around a character with conscious will who struggles toward a goal and endures conflict with opponents.

To the basic theory, Lawson added the Marxian idea that human conflicts reflect the class war. His ideas about playwriting and screenwriting remain so pervasive and influential today that many of those influenced by him are unaware of it.

Thornton Wilder (1897–1975) is one of America's most respected and produced playwrights. Wilder succeeded both as playwright and novelist. Born in Madison, Wisconsin, he grew up in China and attended Yale. He taught in high school and at the University of Chicago, and he served in the Army in World War I and with Air Force Intelligence in World War II. Because he was a linguist, producers often asked him to adapt foreign plays. His fame came first as a novelist, and his most distinguished book, *The Bridge of San Luis Rey* (1927), won a Pulitzer prize. He began writing short plays at Yale, and Richard Boleslavsky's Laboratory Theatre first produced a play of his in 1926. In 1932 he adapted a French play by André Obey, *The Rape of Lucrece*, for actress Katharine Cornell. Max Reinhardt successfully produced his play *The Merchant of Yonkers* (1938). Wilder later rewrote it for Tyrone Guthrie to direct as *The Matchmaker* (1954), and he rewrote it again for the musical *Hello, Dolly!* (1964). In 1938 came the first production of Wilder's best play, *Our Town*. As an outstanding American example of theatricalism, *Our Town* shows the universal experiences of life, love, and death among simple, ordinary people.

During the 1930s Paul Green (1894–1981) also achieved success as a playwright in New York and subsequently lifted the outdoor pageant to the heights of genuine art. Green wrote plays about the South, such as *In Abraham's Bosom* (1926) and *Hymn to the Rising Sun* (1936). The Group Theatre presented his *House of Connelly* (1931) as their first major production. Green wrote *The Lost Colony* (1937) to be performed in an outdoor auditorium on Roanoke Island in honor of the 350th anniversary of Raleigh's colony. A combination of regular theatre, scenes of spectacle, and segments of dance, the play met with such success that it has played every summer season since then. Green wrote similar productions such as *Texas*, for other outdoor sites. Among all types of live theatrical presentation, outdoor drama appeals most to ordinary Americans, and thus it comes perhaps the closest to being the genuine theatre of the people.

In the 1930s, theatre also reached colleges and universities. George Pierce Baker began teaching a class in playwriting at Radcliffe College as early as 1903, but theatre courses were not then common in college curricula. Baker's course became available to Harvard students, and he added a producing group as well, the 47 Workshop. Such playwrights as Edward Sheldon, Eugene O'Neill, Sidney Howard, and Philip Barry studied with him. In 1914, at the Carnegie Institute of Technology (now Carnegie-Mellon University), Thomas Wood Stevens started the first college degree program in theatre. Baker followed in 1925 with a program at Yale. During the 1930s theatre became a widely practiced discipline. Among the leaders in the spread of theatre to campuses were Frederick Koch at the University of North Carolina, A. M. Drummond at Cornell, and E. C. Mabie at Iowa. In the 1940s Hubert C. Heffner brought Stanford to the top rank of theatre schools. Even today, Yale, Iowa, and Stanford retain reputations in theatre that began before mid-century. University theatres provide instruction and experience for students, and they offer productions to many communities throughout the nation. Most theatre artists today get their start and early seasoning in campus theatres.

The American musical also came of age during the 1920s and 1930s. Although music and dance found their way into theatre in nearly every age of cultural history, twentieth-century America has brought it to a state of sophisticated art. Musicals grew ever more important in American consciousness during the 1920s, but when *Of Thee I Sing* won the Pulitzer prize for drama in 1931, the musical stepped into the realm of art. George S. Kaufman and Morris Ryskind wrote the book for *Of Thee I Sing*, while Ira Gershwin wrote the lyrics and George Gershwin the music. From that time forward, musicals have become the most popular form of American theatre. But mere popularity does not explain the rise in quality that occurred in musicals during the 1930s and early 1940s. *Porgy and Bess* (1935) brought black performers to the musical theatre. *On Your Toes* (1936) utilized ballet. *Knickerbocker Holiday* (1938) balanced poetry and music. Another climax occurred when in 1943 Oscar Hammerstein II and Richard Rodgers transformed a play by Lynn Riggs into *Oklahoma!*, and director Rouben Mamoulian balanced all production elements harmoniously in what historians call the first "integrated musical." Throughout the last fifty years the musical has evolved into a unique genre of art with principles, forms, and craftsmanship all its own.

HISTORY

Harvey by Mary Chase at Brown County Playhouse

**John Garfield and Lee J.
Cobb in *Golden Boy* by
Clifford Odets**

In the 1920s and 1930s many artistic movements blossomed. Stimulated by the great modernists of the late nineteenth and early twentieth centuries, theatre reached artistic heights. As always, the schools and movements arose chiefly in Europe—futurism in Italy, surrealism in France, and expressionism in Germany. England established a tradition of great actors and directors, while America produced writers, theatre companies, and a theatre genre of international significance. The major figures of the period were playwrights Pirandello, Brecht, Giraudoux, Lorca, O'Casey, and O'Neill. The leading directors were Reinhardt, Copeau, Guthrie, Jouvet, and Piscator. So many actors achieved greatness that they are too numerous to list, but Laurence Olivier best symbolizes the artistry to which they all aspired. Among the best designers of the time were Americans Normal Bel Geddes, Robert Edmond Jones, Jo Mielziner, and Lee Simonson. In the 1920s theatre experimentation became intense, and in the 1930s theatre artists themselves became intensely concerned about social issues. But the 1940s brought another world upheaval—World War II. The theatre faced change once again.

CHAPTER 17 *Contemporary Innovations*

World War II occupied the last years of the 1930s and the early 1940s, but contemporary theatre rose like a phoenix out of the ashes of the conflict. During the war itself, the men and women of the theatre naturally entered the conflict as active soldiers or home-front workers. Serious drama nearly disappeared because audiences apparently preferred diversion or propaganda. Nearly every major playwright in America, as well as other countries, lost creative vitality during the war years, as their attention turned elsewhere. The social disruption of the war destroyed many cultural traditions, and the new theatre of the 1950s through the 1970s reflected the disillusionment of the times. Often the new spirit was more cynical and self-centered than original or humane; nevertheless, new talent, energy, and styles revitalized the theatre.

This chapter concentrates on the significant artists who created new drama during the period from World War II until the present, the late 1940s to the mid-1980s. This contemporary period has been one of disillusionment, rebellion, and change, and it has been a time of rising social concern about the survival of humanity. Fortunately or not, the economic winds of change affect the contemporary theatre profoundly. For the sake of clarity the chapter proceeds country by country, since most theatre in the last forty years has been rather narrowly national. Only a few geniuses in art, such as Samuel Beckett, or a few commercial hits, such as *My Fair Lady*, have been able to leap international borders. Contemporary innovations in the theatre are here discussed by country in the following order: France, England, Ireland, Germany, Italy, Spain, central Europe, and the United States.

***Waiting for Godot* by Samuel Beckett, The Acting Company**

THE ABSURD ARISES IN FRANCE

The most pervasive intellectual vision after World War II, and still a prevalent one, is existentialism. It identifies problems of the individual adrift in a threatening world, facing walls of loneliness, and trying to find something to believe in. The term *existentialism* signifies many things, but it is important here in three regards. First, existentialism is a philosophic movement that utilizes the methods of phenomenology, or the descriptive analysis of subjective processes. Jean-Paul Sartre and others turned existentialism into a literary and psychological movement. Second, existentialism became popularized in France during the 1950s, stimulating the work of artists and writers and leading the young rebels in Paris to act out the alienation of the times. They began the antiestablishment behavior so characteristic of the contemporary youth of all nations. The third application of existentialism is to describe a commonly held vision of humanity in today's universe. No matter what religion or philosophy a person believes, everyone is likely to feel alienated by the growing population, the world's increasing technological complexity, and the shrinking importance of the individual. Existentialism in all three senses has become a key to understanding the culture and the art of the contemporary world.

Most perceptive people, especially artists, sense the tendency of the

world to become more and more dehumanized. The individual's feeling of helplessness arouses what Albert Camus called the "sentiment of the absurd." At one time or another, most people feel that life is hopeless, that political leaders no longer have perfect answers, that a lone person is helpless, and that even science has betrayed mankind with atomic technology and industrial pollution. Most people feel to some degree alienated, lonely, or vulnerable. Existential thinkers analyzed these human states, and existential writers reflected such human situations onstage. Sometimes the works were serious, sometimes distorted, and sometimes comic. Both Sartre and Camus pointed out that a person should not surrender to feelings of absurdity but should respond to life's challenges by making a commitment to some greater cause than self. Contemporary theatre is strongly colored by existential thought.

Jean-Paul Sartre (1905–1980), a French playwright and political activist, became a leading philosopher of the times. His fame arose during the war when he published a philosophic book *Being and Nothingness* in 1943, the same year he also wrote and saw the production of his first play, *The Flies*, which was soon followed by his most influential play, *No Exit* (1944). In the French resistance movement, he had seen men who faced life-and-death situations and made choices that defined their very being. Such situations became the heart of his plays, and the process of such choices became the heart of his philosophy. Sartre saw each human standing free but alone in the world. Living in a meaningless universe at first gives a person a false sense of freedom, but later a sense of anguish, or nausea, when facing walls of nothingness. To escape anguish each person must "create" himself by making a commitment to some cause, and Sartre naturally recommended socially beneficial ones. He stressed that each person has only himself to blame for what happens and must take personal responsibility for all of his decisions. More than any other twentieth-century thinker, he induced in the people of the modern world a heightened sense of consciousness and responsibility.

Far left: The Bread and Puppet Theatre production of *The Stations of the Cross* by Peter Schumann

The best of Sartre's works embody his ideas instead of preaching them, but all his plays have didactic structures. *No Exit*, for example, is a situational play in which a man and two women find themselves in a room in hell. As they explore their situation and the possible relationships it holds, they realize that as people look back on their lives with the eyes of outside observers, hell is the realization of missed opportunities or mistaken decisions. People can change themselves for the better any time they really want to. Some of Sartre's other major plays are *The Respectful Prostitute* (1946), *Dirty Hands* (1948), and *The Devil and the Good Lord* (1951). Ultimately, Sartre demonstrates in his plays that modern man cannot afford to permit the absurd condition to sap his energy or trap him into lethargy. Although Sartre's drama is often philosophical and sometimes difficult to understand, some of his dramas were pacesetters for the present era, and his ideas are universally pervasive.

Albert Camus (1913–1960), born to a poor French-Algerian family, studied philosophy, went to Paris, and became a celebrated writer and a friend of Sartre. His thought took a similar current, and he, too, helped spread ideas about the absurd. He published novels, plays, and philo-

Albert Camus

sophical works on existential questions. Like Sartre, Camus wrote plays about moral decisions. Two of his best plays are *Caligula* (1945) and *The Just Assassins* (1949). A chief idea that appears in his work is the "dynamic imperative." Nearly every modern person at some time or another, Camus says, feels that life is pointless, ridiculous, or absurd. But the problem for the modern person is how to get around that feeling. In everyone there is a "dynamic imperative" that makes them go on trying, continuing life even when life is bleak. A person does indeed stand alone, he says, facing an alien universe, and the best attack on feelings of the absurd is to take action—live, love, and create in order to give life meaning.

Another French writer, less a thinker than Sartre and Camus but perhaps a better dramatist, is Jean Anouilh (b. 1910). While young he committed himself to the theatre by working as secretary to Louis Jouvet, a leading actor-director in France. Anouilh married an actress and used stage furniture to set up their first apartment. His first play was produced in 1932, but not till five years later did he become successful with *Traveler without Baggage*. From that season onward, Anouilh brought out a new play nearly every theatre season. With his *Antigone* (1943), produced during the war, he became one of France's leading dramatists. He wrote comedies like *Thieves' Carnival* (1932) and *Waltz of the Toreadors* (1952), and serious plays like *Becket* (1959), *Eurydice* (1941), and *The Lark* (1952). His plays contain a fascination with the conflict between innocence and cynicism, truth and betrayal, and hope and despair. He claims that the plays of Pirandello, especially *Six Characters in Search of an Author*, most influenced his work, and he also admits the influence of Jean Giraudoux. Perhaps the greatest strength of his plays lies in their focus on a strong central line of action and careful storytelling. Several of his plays, including *Ring Round the Moon* and *Antigone*, remain in the active repertory of world theatre.

Jean-Louis Barrault (b. 1910), a leading French actor and director, began as an actor with Charles Dullin. He also worked with mimist Etienne Decroux and the visionary Antonin Artaud. Barrault married a leading French actress, Madeleine Renaud, and they performed many plays together. During the war, Barrault directed several productions at the Comédie Française, one of the two leading state-supported theatres in France. Because of his multiple background, Barrault became an eclectic director, combining a love of fine plays with a magical touch in stage movement. He staged his productions with a "total theatre" concept, utilizing many of the tools of the stage to create new effects and new conventions for each play. Never satisfied with mere psychological realism, he argued that the live actor was central in theatre. Barrault often revived difficult classics, such as *The Suppliants* by Aeschylus, and staged works of many controversial playwrights. For instance, his production of André Gide's adaptation of Franz Kafka's novel *The Trial* during the early 1950s was one of the earliest absurdist theatre pieces. He also produced original works by such writers as Albert Camus, Samuel Beckett, and Eugène Ionesco.

Jean Vilar, Roger Blin, and Roger Planchon are directors of major importance in contemporary French theatre. Jean Vilar, of the same generation as Barrault, directed his first major production during the war, then formed his own troupe, and in 1951 became the head of the Théâtre National Populaire (TNP), the other major state-supported theatre in France. Roger Blin, at first a film critic, worked with Artaud and then acted for other major directors. He began directing late in his career, and in 1953 he became famous with the first production of *Waiting for Godot* by Samuel Beckett. During the 1960s he became the leading French director of absurdist plays. Roger Planchon started his directorial career as an innovator with avant-garde plays during the 1950s in the French city of Lyon. He remains there and operates one of the world's best working-class theatres. His productions are innovative, in the theatrical manner of Piscator and Brecht, but they are always entertaining.

Absurdist drama developed from the existential vision of contemporary life and depicted man as alone and lost. Three dramatists writing in French brought absurdism into vogue—Samuel Beckett, Eugène Ionesco, and Jean Genêt. Absurdist dramatists denounced traditional theatre conventions. Most of their plays avoid cause-effect stories to explore a situation. Their characters are usually stylized, puppetlike figures. Most absurdist plays appear more abstract than real because their authors use ambiguity to stress the unknown. In most dramas dialogue approximates how people communicate, but in absurdist plays language becomes an obstacle. Likewise, absurdist plays tend to be more theatrical than dramatic. Movements, gestures, and scenery gain symbolic significance because they take the place of words. By investigating the depths of human alienation, anguish, and despair, absurdist drama offers a pessimistic view of life. The absurdists of the 1950s and 1960s narrowly followed the long Parisian antirealist tradition, and the movement generally harmonizes with Artaud's attitudes. The theatrical ambiguity and cynicism of the absurdist writers pervaded a portion of contemporary theatre from the 1950s until the 1980s.

Samuel Beckett (b. 1906), who wrote *Waiting for Godot* (1953), brought absurdist drama to international acclaim. Born in Ireland, Beckett became a language teacher, but in the late 1920s he went to Paris to be a poet. Influenced by James Joyce, Beckett began writing other types of works. *Waiting for Godot* was his first published play, and in Roger Blin's production in Paris it succeeded artistically and financially. By the end of the 1950s, *Godot* was one of the world's most frequently produced plays. A situational drama without a story, *Godot* depicts Beckett's existential vision of life, pessimistic but basically religious. Mankind is shown to be longing for some meaning beyond everyday triviality, and since God never shows up, each person is left alone, suffering daily anguish in an alien universe. Beckett's other plays are variations on similar themes. Among them are *Endgame* (1957), *Krapp's Last Tape* (1958), *Happy Days* (1961), *Play* (1963), and *Come and Go* (1966).

Eugène Ionesco (b. 1912) was another genius among the absurdists. A native Rumanian, he, too, found fame by writing in French and living in Paris. His first play, *The Bald Soprano* (1950), came from a series of nonsense exercises he had to memorize when he learned English. He continued to write mostly short plays—*The Lesson* (1951), *The Chairs*

(1952), and *The Killer* (1958)—until Jean-Louis Barrault produced *Rhinoceros* (1960). His international reputation soared, and his influence grew throughout the 1960s and 1970s. Ionesco concentrated more on social man and woman, and most of his work is satirical. He poked fun at middle-class habits, traditions, and worries. Over the years his plays have become more humanistic, and story values have grown more important to him. He has also written prolifically about dramatic theory and the function of art in the human community.

Left: Boris Vian

Right: Jean Genêt

Jean Genêt (1910–1985) wrote some of the most unusual absurdist plays, and certainly the most cruel in the manner of Artaud. Filled with hallucination, degradation, and depression, his plays are fascinating and poetic. They are natural extensions of his life. An illegitimate son of a mother who abandoned him, he grew up as an orphan, delinquent, and outcast. He spent his first thirty years as a professional thief, except for a short term in the French Foreign Legion and several long terms in prison. In 1940 he began writing poetry, fiction, and plays. His play *Deathwatch* appeared in 1949, and his other dramas followed in the 1950s and 1960s. Louis Jouvet produced his short play *The Maids* (1957); avant-garde critics praised it while traditional critics considered it scandalous. Genêt also wrote *The Balcony* (1957), *The Blacks* (1959), and *The Screens* (1961). He celebrated evil and referred to his theatre as a "hall of mirrors" that show man caught in a series of distorted reflections. As projections of subjective fantasies transformed, his works are primitive in structure and illogical in characterization, but they make an emotional impact on most spectators because of their sexual and deathly overtones. The plays of Genêt are examples of absurdist fantasy, myths of the outcast.

Several other French writers added to the absurdist movement. Arthur Adamov was born in Russia but educated in Europe. He, too, moved to Paris and came under the influence of surrealists, especially Artaud. He attracted world attention in the 1950s and is generally associated with absurdism. *Ping Pong* (1955) is perhaps his best-known work. Jean Tardieu first wrote as a poet previous to World War II; then he began to compose nightmarish short plays that attracted attention in the 1950s—for example, *The Information Window* (1956). Boris Vian, a Parisian jazz musician, wrote several surrealistic plays, the best of which is *The Empire Builders* (1959). This play is often performed throughout the world because it so well symbolizes the plight of a family in the atomic age. Robert Pinget, a New Wave novelist in France, wrote some absurdist plays during the sixties. A close friend of Samuel Beckett, his plays exhibit certain similarities to *Waiting for Godot*. From France, absurdism soon spread to the rest of the world. But the vision of human alienation began to appear in guises other than in the tradition of surrealism or expressionism.

In the late 1970s another French director came to world attention—Ariane Mnouchkine (b. 1940). In the mid-1980s she is one of the most influential directors in Europe. Other contemporary French directors of note are Patrice Chereau, Antoine Vitez, and Daniel Mesguisch. Mnouchkine, a Parisian born to a Russian family, began directing while a student at the Sorbonne, attracting attention with her production of *Blood Wedding* by Federico García Lorca. Soon afterward, she joined a theatre commune numbering about 40 members and became one of its leaders. The group was called the Théâtre du Soleil. They performed their plays on the outskirts of Paris, first in the Cirque d'Hiver, a warehouse in which the audience space was redesigned for each production. The first two presentations of the Théâtre du Soleil, beginning with *The Kitchen* by Arnold Wesker and then Shakespeare's *A Midsummer Night's Dream*, were masterpieces of environmental theatre. When the company temporarily lost its theatre in France, it worked in Milan as guest of the Piccolo Teatro, a major Italian theatre company. There, the commune, with Mnouchkine at its heart, created one of their most famous productions, entitled *1789—The revolution must stop only at the perfection of happiness—Saint-Just*. The Théâtre du Soleil is one of the most highly regarded artistic companies in Europe.

Of course, a number of other Parisian playwrights continue to create contemporary plays. One of the significant contemporaries writing in French is Fernando Arrabal (b. 1932). Although he was born in Spain and grew up there, and even though many of his plays utilize his Spanish memories and sentiments, Arrabal is in a broad sense a French writer. His plays mix scenes of absurdist comedy, agonizing introspection, and intense social protest against governmental tyranny. Among his best early plays was *Fando and Lis* (1958), and among his later plays are *The Architect and the Emperor of Assyria* (1967), *And They Handcuffed the Flowers* (1970), and *Young Barbarians Today* (1975). Other contemporary French playwrights of note are Françoise Sagan, Marguerite Duras, René de Obaldia, and Jean-Claude Grumberg.

To summarize contemporary French theatre, the temptation is to mention only absurdist authors and influential directors, but many fine artists work in all three major categories of theatre in Paris. First, the boulevard, or commercial, theatre consists of a thriving number of groups playing new and old plays of the conventional sort. Second, a number of directors run experimental theatres, ranging in magnitude from the theatres headed by Jean-Louis Barrault and Ariane Mnouchkine to shoestring operations by young people in the process of learning their craft. Third, the French government contributes to three theatre organizations and many provincial companies. The Comédie Française, a traditional theatre, produces mainly classics. The Odéon, with a more contemporary slant, plays a repertory tuned to the taste of its current manager. The Théâtre Nationale Populaire (TNP), founded by Jean Vilar, presents a mixed repertory aimed at the popular audience. The government also subsidizes more than 20 provincial theatres. Contemporary drama thrives in France.

ANGER AND STYLE IN ENGLAND

After World War II theatre in England began not so much with absurdism as with anger. Great Britain faced many social problems during the 1950s, and a new group of playwrights led by John Osborne (b. 1929) dramatized them. Osborne's play *Look Back in Anger* took stage in 1956 at the Royal Court Theatre under the aegis of the English Stage Company and its leader George Devine. *Look Back in Anger* brought them financial and artistic success. John Osborne spent the early years of his professional life as an actor, and his plays captured the spirit of the late 1950s and 1960s in socially rebellious speeches. Osborne has written several other plays of value, especially *The Entertainer* (1957), *Luther* (1961), and *Inadmissable Evidence* (1965).

Harold Pinter (b. 1930), another British dramatist first produced in the 1950s, writes in the absurdist vein and has risen to international acclaim. He, too, began his professional career as an actor. From the beginning his plays have been simple and direct, but they also contain a strange aura of ambiguity. Naturalistic in detail, they are absurdist in impact. Through vulnerable, directionless characters, the plays often display everyday trivia. Indeed, the people appear comic up to a point in the action, and then they become terrified, haunted, or violent. Pinter utilizes menace as a significant element of interest. Often the characters have anxieties about some unexplained force outside the play, and sometimes that force destroys them, as in *The Birthday Party* (1958). Pinter's plays are naturalistic but mysterious, comic but violent. Most important of all, his work suggests the precariousness of human life on earth and the uncertainty of any truths. Some of his other well-known plays are *The Caretaker* (1960), *The Homecoming* (1965), *Old Times* (1971), and *Betrayal* (1981).

Other fine playwrights have contributed serious plays to the contemporary theatre in England. John Arden, whose best play is probably *Sergeant Musgrave's Dance* (1959), deals with contemporary problems, usually social or political ones. Arnold Wesker, the most politically oriented of the "angry generation," achieved world fame with *The Kitchen*, a play produced during the 1960s in most of the world's major theatres. Edward Bond wrote truthful grotesques and aroused controversy with such violent plays as *Saved* (1965), *Lear*, and *Stone*. Peter Shaffer, perhaps the best craftsman of all, has written such hits as *Five Finger Exercise* (1958), *The Royal Hunt of the Sun* (1964), *Black Comedy* (1965), *Equus* (1973), and *Amadeus* (1979). Other serious British dramatists of note are Peter Nichols, David Storey, Robert Bolt, and David Hare.

Throughout the history of drama, England always seems to produce good comic dramatists, and many have appeared in contemporary theatres. Joe Orton wrote three absurdist comedies—*Entertaining Mr. Sloane* (1964), *Loot* (1966), and *What the Butler Saw* (1969). Tom Stoppard, whose plays feature verbal gymnastics, found world fame with his play *Rosencrantz and Guildenstern Are Dead* (1967). Other plays by him are *Jumpers* (1972), *Travesties* (1974), and *The Real Thing* (1983). Simon Gray has written a number of brittle absurdist comedies, such as *Butley* (1971) and *Otherwise Engaged* (1975). Alan Ayckbourn, perhaps the funniest of them all, writes such entertaining farces as *How the Other Half Loves* (1971), *Absurd Person Singular* (1972), and *Bedroom Farce* (1975).

Although the contemporary theatre in England has produced a number of writers, the era there is even more blessed as an age of directors. Joan Littlewood (b. 1914) is an outstanding example. In the 1930s she formed the Theatre of Action in Manchester, and in 1945 she founded the Theatre Workshop in London. The company toured working-class districts and settled in London's east working-class district. Using her own version of ideas from Brecht and Stanislavsky, and adding improvisations and political discussions, Littlewood developed superb acting ensembles. She

Sisterly Feelings by Alan Ayckbourn, Indiana University

also favored new scripts by unknown, working-class writers. Some of her most widely known productions were *The Quare Fellow* (1956) and *The Hostage* (1958), both by Brendan Behan; *A Taste of Honey* (1958), by Shelagh Delaney; and *Oh, What a Lovely War!* (1963), an ensemble piece. Especially during the 1950s and 1960s, no more dynamic director worked in England than Joan Littlewood.

One of the two largest theatre organizations in England is the Royal Shakespeare Company. Beginning about 1957, Peter Hall developed it out of the Stratford Memorial summer theatre festival. Next he leased the Aldwych Theatre in London and put actors under year-long contracts. He increased the productivity of the company from 5 to more than 25 productions a year. In 1962 he expanded the management and direction of the company to involve Michel Saint-Denis and Peter Brook. The repertory of the theatre ranged from ancient classics and Shakespeare to modern classics and highly experimental works, such as *Marat/Sade* (1964), written by Peter Weiss and directed by Peter Brook. In 1969 Trevor Nunn became the artistic director, and in 1982 the company moved into its new home in the Barbican Arts Center in London. The Royal Shakespeare Company continues to receive a large subsidy from the British government. Since developing a reputation as both a classical and an avant-garde company, it has achieved world renown.

Peter Brook (b. 1925) is certainly one of England's leading directors of the century. A chief exponent of "concept directing," he stamps each of his productions with the power of his personal imagination. Two of his most well-recognized productions achieved world renown: *A Midsummer Night's Dream* and *Marat/Sade*. In more recent years he has experimented with theatre, especially trying to examine the anthropological roots of theatre's appeal. His book *The Empty Space* is one of the best for understanding the role of directors in the contemporary theatre.

An idea for the National Theatre, the other major theatre company in England, occurred as early as 1848, but almost a hundred years passed before Parliament approved it. Even then it took until 1962 to work out the details; in 1963 the Old Vic Theatre was purchased as a temporary home, and a production of *Hamlet* was mounted. Laurence Olivier became artistic director and critic Kenneth Tynan became literary consultant. Olivier led the company into an eclectic approach dedicated to fine acting in a broad range of styles under the guidance of numerous guest directors. Under Olivier the National's best productions tended to be classics. In 1973 Peter Hall became artistic director, and in 1976 he opened a lavish new theatre, again with *Hamlet*. Other significant directors in England are Terry Hands, Frank Dunlop, John Dexter, John Barton, and Barry Kyle. Some of the leading actors and actresses of the period are Maggie Smith, Ian McKellen, John Neville, Albert Finney, Alan Bates, Nicol Williamson, Alan Howard, Richard Burton, Glenda Jackson, Joan Plowright, Antony Quayle, Donald Pleasance, Diana Rigg, and Paul Scofield.

In contemporary Ireland, playwrights continue to appear. The most noteworthy contemporary Irish playwright is, of course, Samuel Beckett, who grew up in Ireland but settled in France. Next, chronologically, came

Brendan Behan whose play *The Hostage* was performed all over the world. Two other dramatists of importance are Brian Friel and Hugh Leonard. Friel's two most well-known plays in the United States are *Philadelphia, Here I Come* (1964) and *Lovers* (1967). Hugh Leonard, too, has met with success in this country, especially with his plays *Da* (1978) and *A Life* (1980). The Abbey Theatre continues as the major production entity supported by the government. It moved into a new playhouse in 1966. Some of the best contemporary directors are Frank Dermody, Hugh Hunt, Tomas MacAnna, Rita Mooney, and Alan Simpson. Ireland also continues to turn out excellent actors, some known internationally: Cyril Cusack, John Hurt, Michael MacLiammoir, Jack McGowran, Siobhan McKenna, Peter O'Toole, and Susannah York. Ireland produces an unusual number of writers who have gifts of verbal fluency and freshness.

GERMANY AND THE REST OF EUROPE

The contemporary theatre in Germany began immediately after World War II with renewed energy. Since bombs destroyed many theatres during the war, the state and private investors built many new theatres. As a result, more new theatres came into being in the 1950s and 1960s in Germany than any other country. With the German penchant for advanced technology, the new theatres are filled with the latest in stage equipment and lighting instrumentation. Also, Bertolt Brecht returned to Germany in 1948, bringing with him a number of untried plays and a lot of newly expanded theories that he had developed as an exile during the war years. By the mid-1950s, Brecht had not only established himself as Germany's leading dramatist but had also created the country's leading theatrical company—the Berliner Ensemble. Brecht acted as managing director of the company until his death in 1956, and he proved the value of his theories in productions of his own plays as well as those of others. The Berliner Ensemble, located in East Berlin, remains a vital company in the 1980s. Many other fine companies are at work, especially in Berlin and Munich.

Swiss playwrights Max Frisch and Friedrich Duerrenmatt became the

Lynn Fontanne and Alfred Lunt (front right) in *The Visit* by Friedrich Duerrenmatt

329

first postwar dramatists produced by German theatre who were worthy of international acclaim. Max Frisch was born in Zurich and educated to be an architect, but under the influence of Brecht he turned to playwriting. Three of his most frequently produced plays are *The Chinese Wall* (1946), *Biedermann and the Firebugs* (1953), and *Andorra* (1961). All are theatrical in style, didactic in structure, and poetic in diction. Friedrich Duerrenmatt, also a resident of Zurich, first studied theology and philosophy before turning to drama. He, too, saw his early plays staged in the late 1940s and early 1950s, but he came to world attention with his two best plays, *The Visit* (1956) and *The Physicists* (1962). His dramas employ strong stories, well-developed characterizations, and a great deal of intelligent conversation. Duerrenmatt, too, writes under the influence of Brecht, and he claims the influences of Thornton Wilder and Luigi Pirandello.

Documentary theatre, one of the major new types of contemporary drama, arose in Germany during the 1950s. Like Brecht, Erwin Piscator also returned to his native Germany after the war, in 1951. He staged a number of productions and probably coined the term "documentary drama" or "theatre of fact." In the early 1960s Piscator became managing director of the Volksbühne in West Berlin, and there he developed his theories while directing productions of new dramatists who were able to write with enough intelligence and social consciousness to suit him. Three authors in particular have written documentary dramas—Rolf Hochhuth, Peter Weiss, and Heinar Kipphardt. Documentary drama as Piscator developed it is similar to his earlier epic theatre and to the living newspapers of the American Federal Theatre Project of the 1930s. The first of the documentary dramas, *The Deputy* by Rolf Hochhuth, took the stage under Piscator's hand in 1963; that play aroused social and religious controversy by criticizing the pope. Another of Hochhuth's documentary dramas was *The Soldiers* (1967). The best-known play by Heinar Kipphardt is *In the Case of J. Robert Oppenheimer*, which Piscator produced in 1964.

Peter Weiss (1916–1982), the most widely acclaimed documentary dramatist, moved his family out of Germany in 1934, and he has since lived in a series of countries. He began writing plays in the 1960s and achieved fame in 1964, when at the Schiller Theater in West Berlin, Konrad Swinarski and Weiss himself directed *The Persecution and Assassination of Jean-Paul Marat as Performed by the Inmates of the Asylum of Charenton Under the Direction of the Marquis de Sade*. Peter Brook directed the piece later in 1964 for the Royal Shakespeare Company in London, and his production traveled to New York. The two productions were enough to establish Weiss as a playwright of genius and to spread Brook's fame as well. Weiss's next play, *The Investigation* (1965), presented an arranged series of documents taken from the hearings about the Auschwitz war crimes in Germany. In 1968 Weiss published an article that outlined "Fourteen Propositions for a Documentary Theatre." Among the most noteworthy points, he wrote that documentary theatre reports facts and shuns invention, that it concentrates on social and political themes, and that it opposes the absurdist view of life. Other major works

Marat/Sade by Peter Weiss, Indiana University

by Peter Weiss are _The Song of the Lusitanian Bogey_ (1967), _Vietnam Discourse_ (1968), and _Trotsky in Exile_ (1970).

Although today's German theatre seems to be a director's theatre, in recent years it has produced several other writers of note. Günter Grass, one of Germany's noted postwar novelists, has written several plays, among them _The Wicked Cooks_ (1962) and _The Plebeians Rehearse the Uprising_ (1966). Austrian playwright and novelist Peter Handke has written a number of stage pieces utilizing linguistic alienation in order to startle and irritate the audience. Some of his works are _Offending the Audience_ (1966), _Kaspar_ (1969), and _The Ride Across Lake Constance_ (1971). Tankerd Dorst, Heinrich Henkel, and Ulrich Plenzdorf are other playwrights of note. Among contemporary directors in East Germany, Anselm Perthen, Manfred Wekwerth and Heinz-Uwe Haus have staged major productions. In West Germany, notable recent directors are Peter Stein, Claus Peymann, and Peter Zadek.

Since 1950 the contemporary Italian theatre has produced several artists who have risen to international prominence, and in the 1980s they are helping generate a new artistic energy. Two outstanding Italian theatre artists are director Giorgio Strehler and playwright Dario Fo. Because the star system and commercial theatre have so long dominated Italian theatre, the country has no long tradition of theatrical training. Another barrier to the rise of a national theatre tradition is the multiplicity of regional dialects and cultures throughout the country, so productions might be successful in one region and fail badly in another. Giorgio Strehler is, however, one distinguished director who has created unusual theatre in Italy, and through his influence, governmental support of theatre companies is more common than ever before. From 1947 to 1968 Strehler started and masterminded the Piccolo Teatro in Milan, and because of his work there, he has achieved international renown. Since 1968 he has been in great demand in other countries—for example, he managed the Odéon in Paris in the 1970s. Luca Ronconi, another director of note, has also had an impact on Italian theatre. Ronconi developed large-scale outdoor productions, such as *Orlando Furioso*, in which scenes are performed simultaneously around a piazza and the audience moves around to witness the scenes. Film directors Luchino Visconti and Franco Zeffirelli have also staged challenging theatre productions.

The theatrical genius of Italy in the 1970s and 1980s is perhaps Dario Fo (b. 1926). As playwright, actor, and director, Fo is a master of comedy and political satire. He has taken the long popular tradition of Italian improvisational theatre and transformed it into a farcical theatre of protest that appeals to the working class of the country. Fo entered the theatre as a designer, became an actor at the Piccolo Teatro, and then with his wife, Franca Rame, created an enormously popular comic television series. But they renounced commercialism and middle-of-the-road politics and created Il Colletivo Teatrale La Commune, a leftist theatre troupe to play mainly for workers. Dario Fo and his company improvise

We Won't Pay! We Won't Pay! **by Dario Fo, Indiana University**

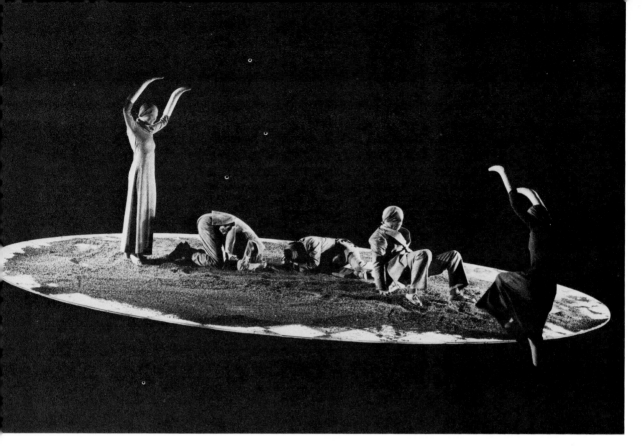

Els Joglars performs
Laetius

early versions of his plays, accept suggestions from workers, and then perfect the scripts in performance after performance. His farces are some of the most outrageously funny and politically stinging of the century. His best plays of the 1970s and 1980s are *Mistero Buffo, Accidental Death of an Anarchist,* and *We Won't Pay! We won't Pay!* By the middle of the 1980s Dario Fo had become one of the most influential avant-garde theatre artists in Europe.

The Spanish theatre was hidden from the world for nearly thirty-five years at mid-century. While dictator Francisco Franco ruled Spain from 1939 to 1975, the rest of the world guessed that genuine art there was unlikely. To the contrary, the Spanish theatre did not die. Indeed, the best Spanish theatre created in the second half of the twentieth century came from artists protesting political oppression. Antonio Buero Vallejo started the renewal of Spanish theatre with his play *The Story of a Stairway* (1949). He wrote plays of social significance that audiences would understand but censors could not. His dramas—for example, *The Concert at Saint Ovide* (1962) and *The Sleep of Reason* (1970)—have established him as Spain's leading dramatist. Alfonso Sastre disliked Buero's moderation, and he has sought a dramatic form that best demonstrates humanity's need for social change in such plays as *The Condemned Squad* (1953), *Blood and Ashes* (1965), and *Roman Chronicles* (1968). Sastre is also a fine dramatic theorist. His books of essays—

Drama and Society (1956) and *Anatomy of Realism* (1965)—stand as humanist manifestos for the theatre. Among the best Spanish directors are the inventive Adolfo Marsillach, Albert Boadella, and Lluis Pasqual; Spain's leading actress is Nuria Espert. Probably the most creative theatre in Spain has come from the *vanguardia*, especially such groups as Els Joglars, La Claca, and Tábano.

Since mid-century a number of outstanding creative theatre artists have surfaced in eastern Europe. Josef Svoboda (b. 1920) of Czechoslovakia is one of them. Through his experiments with multimedia and the use of modern technology in scenic and lighting design, he established the concept of "scenographer" for the modern theatre. A scenographer is a visual artist of the theatre who controls all the design elements for a production. Svoboda has been particularly skilled in using nontraditional scenic materials, a completely flexible stage, and projections on diverse surfaces. An extremely eclectic designer, he has worked in most conceivable styles, and he is not committed to any particular artistic methodology. He does, however, adhere to principles of flexibility and functionality. Among his most significant designs are settings for *The Insect Comedy* and *Romeo and Juliet* at the Prague National Theatre.

Poland has given contemporary theatre one of its most original directors in Jerzy Grotowski (b. 1933). Also an eclectic artist who draws techniques and inspiration from all possible sources, Grotowski has experimented perhaps more widely than any other modern director. He believes that theatre productions should occur in the intimacy of small theatres and that theatre companies ought to be cohesive, well-trained, and have a singularity of purpose. To him theatre is ritualistic in rehearsal and in performance. Grotowski has reestablished artistic ethics in modern theatre, and he has argued that actor training is a matter of removing barriers. Thus he tries to help each actor purge anything physical or psychological that gets in the way of artistic creativity. Actors cannot hide things, he says, and they should not try. Any actor who uses tricks of any sort to hide himself, makes creativity in himself impossible. The creative process consists in revealing the self and in structuring the revelation. Grotowski also stressed the taking of risks, because in order to create a person must try for something so new, so extreme that the risk of failure is great. Artists cannot repeat old or familiar routes. The final principle of Grotowski's work is that artists should concentrate on process more than on results. Among his most distinguished productions are adaptations of Marlowe's *Doctor Faustus* and Wyspianski's *Akropolis*.

Among the other theatre artists of eastern Europe, several writers are worth noting. In Czechoslovakia, Vaclav Havel wrote such plays as *The Garden Party* (1963) and *The Conspirators* (1974), and other satires about bureaucracy and restricted behavior. During the contemporary period the works of Polish dramatist Stanislaw Ignacy Witkiewicz came to world attention. In the 1920s he wrote nonrealistic, pessimistic plays that concentrated on violence, sexuality, and drug-inspired fantasy. Some commentators considered his dramas forerunners of the absurdist plays of the 1950s. Two of his best plays are *The Water Hen* (1921) and *The Madman and the Nun* (1923). Tadeusz Rosewicz and Slawomir Mrozek are contemporary Polish writers of note. About the only internationally prominent Russian playwright of recent years is Aleksey Arbuzov with two plays written in the 1960s—*The Prodigal Son* (1961) and *The Promise* (1965). Yuri Ljubimov is a Russian director of international repute who now lives and works in London. A great deal of fine theatre also occurs in Rumania and Yugoslavia, but those countries have not produced writers who have made an international impact.

ECLECTICISM IN THE UNITED STATES

Shortly after the end of World War II, American theatre came to life again, and the survivors of the Group Theatre were among the most influential reigning artists. Elia Kazan became the preeminent director of the period, especially because he directed the first productions of *A Streetcar Named Desire* (1947) by Tennessee Williams and *Death of a Salesman* (1949) by Arthur Miller. Most of the actors Kazan used were trained in the Stanislavsky Method. Some of them had worked in Group Theatre productions—for example, Lee J. Cobb, who starred in *Salesman*—and some were new, specially trained young actors—for instance, Marlon Brando in *Streetcar*. Kazan's method included careful analysis of the play's action, clarification of character intentions, and meticulous emotional work with the actors. Every element of his productions contributed to an overall poetic realism especially appropriate for the plays of Tennessee Williams. Kazan and two former members of the Group Theatre—Cheryl Crawford and Robert Lewis—also founded the Actors Studio in order to provide a place for young actors to develop internal acting skills. Lee Strasberg became the principal teacher, and some of the early students who later became stars of the American stage and cinema were Marlon Brando, Paul Newman, and Geraldine Page.

The plays of Tennessee Williams (1911–1983) rank with those of Eugene O'Neill and Thornton Wilder as some of the best American dramas of the century. He reached prominence during the 1940s and continued to write into the 1980s. Influenced by such European writers as Strindberg and D. H. Lawrence, Williams wrote mostly realistic plays about social outcasts who are too sensitive for the conventional world. Although Williams often focused on the decadence of alcohol, drugs, and sex, he nevertheless was able to infuse his works with haunting poetry. A native southerner, he wrote rich, atmospheric tragedies of destruction that take place when the conventional, the hypocritical, or the violent bullies of society enforce their wills upon sensitive, fugitive, and lonely individualists. Not only did Williams achieve monetary success with genuinely artistic works, but he also became and has remained a pervading influence on succeeding generations of writers. His most enduring plays are *The Glass Menagerie* (1945), *A Streetcar Named Desire* (1947), and *Cat on a Hot Tin Roof* (1954).

Another contemporary American playwright of international significance, Arthur Miller (b. 1916), also came into prominence in the late 1940s. Miller wrote less poetically than Williams but with more social impact. His first successful play, *All My Sons* (1947), carries an overt message, and most of his works attack the evils of materialism and the false dreams of capitalism. But with the skills of a master dramatist, Miller surpassed mere didacticism and wrote two of the best tragedies of the contemporary age—*Death of a Salesman* (1949) and *The Crucible* (1953). Some call his work realistic, but in truth he wrote with a wide eclectic range of styles, utilizing surrealism in *Salesman* and epic theatre in *The Creation of the World and Other Business* (1973). Ultimately his work reaches beyond sectarian social concerns and concentrates on the moral struggles of mankind. Other American playwrights—such as William Inge, Robert Anderson, and Paddy Chayefsky—also captured the American spirit in plays written during the 1950s.

During the 1960s, while numerous experiments were going on in American theatre, three important playwrights began their careers—Edward Albee, Neil Simon, and Arthur Kopit. Albee became the leading American writer of absurdist plays. He composed ironic, menacing works that projected a deeply pessimistic view of existence. His best plays of the decade were *Who's Afraid of Virginia Woolf?* (1962) and *A Delicate Balance* (1966). Neil Simon began writing a series of comic plays in the early 1960s that have turned out to be among the best comedies by an American in the entire century. He began with *Come Blow Your Horn* in 1961, continued with such plays as *Barefoot in the Park* (1963) and *The Odd Couple* (1965), and was still going on in the mid-1980s with *Brighton Beach Memoirs* and *Biloxi Blues*. Financially Simon is the most successful

Rose Hume in *Ma Rainey's Black Bottom* by August Wilson, directed by Lloyd Richards

playwright in the history of American drama, and perhaps in the history of the world. Arthur Kopit reached the professional stage in 1960 with the production of his absurdist farce *Oh, Dad, Poor Dad, Mama's Hung You in the Closet and I'm Feeling so Sad* (1960). Since then Kopit has written several lively works filled with insight and paradox, especially *Indians* (1968), *Wings* (1980), and *End of the World* (1984).

One of the most energetic and artistically promising currents in contemporary American theatre is the black theatre movement. Although many fine black actors and directors have worked in American theatre in nearly every generation, the 1960s saw them rise to new creative heights because of their devotion to the black experience and their commitment to black audiences. No longer do black theatre productions or companies have to depend on white audiences for success. Some of the outstanding black writers of recent times are James Baldwin, Lorraine Hansberry, Imamu Amiri Baraka, Douglas Turner Ward, Ed Bullins, and Lonnie Elder. Among the best black actors have been James Earl Jones, Ruby Dee, Diana Sands, Robert Hooks, and Ossie Davis. The number of outstanding black theatre artists is growing each year.

The Off Broadway movement became important in the 1950s, gained energy during the 1960s, and became the heart of American theatre in the 1970s. Throughout the history of New York theatre, small companies with limited budgets have offered an alternative to the commercial theatres of Broadway. Such groups as the Washington Square Players, Jean Dalrymple's City Center, and the Civic Repertory Company of Eva Le Gallienne gave fine productions during the first half of the century. But when a company called Circle in the Square produced *Summer and Smoke* by Tennessee Williams in 1952, the Off Broadway movement came of age as a genuine force in American theatre. This group, formed in 1951 by José Quintero and Theodore Mann, has presented many outstanding productions—including O'Neill's *The Iceman Cometh* (1956)—and it has helped many actors come to prominence—for example, George C. Scott, Jason Robards, Jr., and Colleen Dewhurst. The Phoenix Theatre was another outstanding Off Broadway company of the 1950s. A final artistic innovation of the 1950s was the development of "happenings." Named by painter Allan Kaprow, the best happenings were artistic occasions in which an aesthetic concept simultaneously involved artist, environment, event, and audience.

During the 1960s, the Off Broadway movement gained considerable momentum and exploded into Off Off Broadway. The explosion occurred because the most energetic young artists not accepted in the established theatre invariably begin noncommercial theatres of their own. But since the Off Broadway theatres had themselves become established and ever more commercial, the new theatre people of the 1960s were again excluded; so the Off Off Broadway movement began. Among the many initiators, Ellen Stewart became the most influential noncommercial producer of the period by establishing the La MaMa Experimental Theatre Club. She provided a place for many new playwrights to see their works on stage. Cafe Cino, the Judson Poet's Theatre, and Theatre Genesis were other daring theatres of the 1960s and 1970s.

***The Hot l Baltimore* by Lanford Wilson— Indiana University**

337

The Ontological-Hysterical Theatre's production of *Sophia= (Wisdom) Part 3: The Cliffs* directed by Richard Foreman

Many productions of the American avant-garde also occur Off Off Broadway, and several companies have led the way during the contemporary period, especially the Living Theatre and the Open Theatre. Julian Beck and his wife, Judith Malina, began the Living Theatre in the early 1950s, and by 1963 it blossomed into a leading avant-garde company. In the mid-1960s the Becks gave the company a more activist political stance, and they took it on the first of several trips abroad. Their style of life, politics, and artistic excellence made an impact on young theatre people in Europe and South America. Two of their best-known productions were *Frankenstein* and *Paradise Now.* Joseph Chaikin and others started the Open Theatre in 1963 as a workshop to explore improvisation. Attempting to find means to acting outside the Stanislavsky method, the Open Theatre performers and writers developed "transformations," in which the actors move freely from one role to another during the course of one performance. Several playwrights became involved—for example, Jean-Claude Van Itallie with *The Serpent* (1969) and Susan Yankowitz with *Terminal* (1970). The Open Theatre also brought current social problems to the stage.

Other manifestations of the American avant-garde in theatre have taken place in New York and elsewhere. Under the tutelage of Richard Schechner, the Performance Group, which lasted from the late 1960s to the late 1970s, brought concepts of environmental theatre to audiences. Its most renowned production was *Dionysus 69*, and Schechner has come to be known as a leading American theorist of contemporary drama. Peter Schumann, a German, came to New York and founded the Bread and Puppet Theatre in 1961. Devoted to self-sufficient ritual, the company uses giant puppets, live actors, and sometimes spectators themselves. One of its best productions was *The Cry of the People for Meat*. Since 1959 the San Francisco Mime Troupe has given countless performances of scripted and improvised plays for workers, demonstrators, and ordinary people. Their theatre is most often an open space in a field, factory, or street. The company has combined commedia dell'arte techniques with social messages to make a brand of theatre all its own.

Three other wildly fascinating avant-garde artists in the United States are Richard Foreman, Charles Ludlam, and Robert Wilson. All are involved in the creation of unusual and nontraditional theatre experiences. Foreman, primary creator in the Ontological-Hysterical Theatre, emphasizes interior and subjective aspects of theatrical experiencing. Ludlam founded the Ridiculous Theatrical Company, and his avowed objective is to be outrageous; thus some of his productions present unconventional attitudes toward sexuality and purposefully inept acting. Wilson concentrates more on images than stories in his striking productions, such as *Einstein on the Beach*, and he has already become a major theatre influence among avant-gardists throughout the world.

Perhaps the most important non-Broadway theatre organization in the

***Henry IV, Part I* by William Shakespeare, Indiana Repertory Theatre**

United States is the Public Theatre, headed by Joseph Papp. In the 1950s Papp began producing the New York Shakespeare Festival, offering free performances in Central Park, for which an outdoor amphitheatre was built there in 1962. Then, in the late 1960s, he established the Public Theatre with its several performing spaces Off Broadway in the old Astor Library building. The first production was the landmark musical *Hair* (1967), which eventually moved to Broadway for a long run. Subsequently, the Public has presented a startling variety of plays and musicals, including *A Chorus Line*, and it has introduced many fine new playwrights, one of the best of whom is David Rabe.

The repertory theatre movement that blossomed in the 1960s has made fine productions available in most American cities. Since the beginning of American society, excellent professional theatres have existed outside New York City, but in the 1960s a new wave of theatres blossomed throughout the country. Among the most important early leaders and their theatres were Nina Vance at the Alley Theatre in Houston, Tyrone Guthrie at the Guthrie Theatre in Minneapolis, Zelda Fichandler at the Arena Stage in Washington, D.C., and William Ball at the American Conservatory Theatre in San Francisco. For the most part, these theatres utilize professional companies to present mixed seasons of classical and modern plays. Some of the producers—such as John Jory at Actors Theatre of Louisville, Gordon Davidson at Mark Taper Forum in Los Angeles, and Arvin Brown at Long Wharf Theatre in New Haven—present a surprising number of new plays. Indeed, the repertory theatres of the country are responsible for discovering and producing a significant number of new works. During the 1970s, for the first time in history, theatres outside New York hired more professional actors than those in the city. Because these theatres have lesser economic pressures than those in New York, more original and daring productions now first occur in other cities.

In fact, most of the new American playwrights now develop their works Off Off Broadway and in regional theatres. Among the best new dramatists are Lanford Wilson, Marsha Norman, Beth Henley, David Mamet, and Sam Shepard. Wilson received a first production of his short play *The Madness of Lady Bright* at the Off Off Broadway Cafe Cino in 1964,

The Road to Mecca by Athol Fugard (left), Yale Repertory Theatre

and with director Marshall Mason he helped found the Circle Repertory Company in New York in the early 1970s. His play *The Hot l Baltimore* was performed there in 1973. Other well-known plays by Lanford Wilson are *The Rimers of Eldritch* (1967) and *The 5th of July* (1978). Actors Theatre of Louisville first produced Marsha Norman's play called *Getting Out*, and she has also written *'Night, Mother* (1983). Beth Henley, whose most well-regarded play is *Crimes of the Heart* (1981), also began her career with productions in repertory theatres. David Mamet, who won a 1984 Pulitzer prize with his play *Glengarry Glen Ross* (1983), regularly sees first productions of his plays in Chicago's Goodman Theatre. All of Sam Shepard's plays have first appeared in regional theatres or Off Off Broadway. Some outstanding dramas by Shepard are *Curse of the Starving Class* (1977), *Buried Child* (1978), and *Fool for Love* (1983). At present the theatres of America probably produce more new plays each year than ever before in the history of theatre.

In the mid-1980s theatre observers note a renewal of social consciousness and a new concern with morality. Strangely, a major problem for artists in the contemporary age has been the "problem of freedom." It arose because World War II stimulated a spirit of disillusionment and because people began to rebel against traditional values. Artists the world over suddenly found they could write about any subject at all and put any act onstage. They had total freedom. So, in the 1960s and 1970s productions often presented pessimistic views of human decadence and violence—anything that might be shocking. But the genuine artists have come to realize that when total freedom is possible, the artist faces more pressure than ever to choose what's truly important in human existence. After the depths of pessimism have been explored, and after *everything* has been tried on stage—from religious ritual to sexual promiscuity—then suddenly artists have the responsibility once again to identify and dramatize experiences of more lasting value.

Perhaps, as some cultural commentators have observed, theatre is embarking on a period of post-modernism. In the 1920s Spanish critic Ortega y Gassett wrote a landmark essay entitled "The Dehumanization of Art," in which he explained the vision of existence that gave rise to the abstract art of the first half of this century. Perhaps now, in the final quarter of the century, it is time for someone to write an essay called "The Humanization of Art" to herald the beginning of a new artistic era. Maybe theatre could use a period in which artistic quality became more important than news appeal, originality more significant than quirkiness, and moral vision more appealing than personal noteriety. In the face of economic pressures, theatre is too often judged according to financial success. While most writers, actors, directors, and designers live frugal lives, investors are expected to benefit most from theatre's earnings. Still, theatre artists in all societies persevere and continue to produce works that reflect and affect the age in which they live. In any case, theatre is sure, somehow, to go on trying to affirm the human.

Henry Fonda and
Katherine Hepburn in
the film version of *On
Golden Pond* by Ernest
Thompson

Part Four

C O N N E C T I O N S

18 *Theatre Environments*

Environment affects theatre performers and audiences profoundly. One theatre space may stimulate a certain drama, while another may stifle it. Some plays, like *Talley's Folly* by Lanford Wilson, fit best in an intimate theatre, but others, like the musical *La Cage aux Folles* by Jerry Herman and Harvey Fierstein, belong in a large theatre. If 80 people crowd themselves into a tiny theatre, they are more likely to enjoy a performance than if they see it in a large auditorium with empty seats. Part of theatre's magic depends on the right kind of place. Every theatre company tunes its productions to the available theatre space.

This chapter explores theatre environments and investigates how buildings function as houses of creativity. First comes a discussion of the aesthetics of theatre architecture, to see what buildings and audience contexts really do for performances. There follows an explanation of spatial functions in the theatre and a description of the basic theatre configurations. Finally, there is an exploration of the current state of theatre environments in the United States.

Performance at Café La MaMa

THE AESTHETICS AND REALITY OF PERFORMANCE SPACES

In nearly every civilized era, theatre has appeared in numerous locations. Each special environment has affected both the performance and its reception. The physical setting and the social milieu for performances have helped make each drama what it turned out to be as a human experience. For example, the first production of Jarry's *Ubu Roi* occurred in a small theatre, and its audience became intimately aware of the "outrageous" behavior of the performers. Actors have created theatre in streets, courtyards, and churches; on wooden planks, polished marble, and raw dirt; in union halls, gymnasiums, and ballrooms; beside rivers, on hillsides, and in skyscrapers. Sometimes a lot of people have crowded in to watch, and sometimes the actors have outnumbered the spectators. Often the audience liked the play; occasionally they worshiped it; and at times they rioted against it. The history of theatre can be told by tracing types of performance spaces and exploring social circumstances.

Everyone likes comfort while watching a play. So no matter how humbly a theatre company may begin, nearly every group tries to acquire better and better facilities for its productions plus more and more comfortable accommodations for its audiences. Each place, every different building affects the aura of the performances given there, both in sensory detail and in audience unification. The actors feel differently about the performance if they can hear voices reverberate back to them. Audiences

The Canadian Shakespeare Festival Theatre, Stratford, Ontario

respond more positively to performances when the air is neither too hot nor too cold in the theatre building. Whenever a few people can't see or can't hear a production, they can disrupt the rest of the audience. Even the smallest physical circumstances can make a difference because, after all, everyone in a theatre is human, and human beings respond physically to their surroundings.

Although buildings are important as physical surroundings, people actually create theatre space. For every production, a group of people agree to stage a drama in a certain location. Sometimes they use "found space," simply setting their minimal scenery in the street or inside a nontheatrical building. Perhaps they own or rent a theatre. No matter where they stage their dramatic work, they must make the significant decision about the physical nature of their performance by saying where it will be presented. Furthermore, they must consider how they want the audience disposed in relation to the performance space. If they use an existing theatre, they must accept an arrangement of seats, or if they use an open space, they must devise an arrangement. Each space is so different in its physical detail and in its mental effect on performers and audience members alike that the selection of theatre space amounts to one of the most critical theatrical decisions. Sometimes those in charge are right and sometimes not.

The effect of place on people, though difficult to measure, is profound.

The details of a performance space affect each spectator physically and emotionally. If a theatre is small, its surfaces varied, its colors warm, and its atmosphere intimate, how different an audience member will feel than in a huge auditorium full of cool light, overwhelming space, and an institutional atmosphere. Often a new theatre company, or a poor one, begins producing plays successfully in humble surroundings, perhaps in found space. Audiences discover the company, and people come. They get packed in, sit in uncomfortable seats, breathe hot air, and love the show. With the encouragement of popularity and a bit of money jingling in the box office, the company moves to a bigger space, a better auditorium, or maybe even a new theatre; and often their art goes to pieces. Suddenly, the small, unified company faces yawning space that changes its vision, disappoints its audiences, and dilutes the quality of its work. But theatrical production is so unpredictable that the opposite can happen, too. A drama or a troupe that is mediocre in one space may be marvelous in another. In every case the effect of place on people establishes certain potentials for feeling.

Certainly audiences appreciate certain comforts, and in this country they take some of them for granted. For most productions, people prefer to sit on comfortable seats. It is difficult to concentrate on a play when one's backside aches. But maybe the seats shouldn't be too comfortable, because when that happens, so the theory goes, too many audience members go to sleep. Also, people like to see, and so sightlines are important. Whatever the arrangement of audience and stage space, everyone who comes to a performance deserves to see all that happens, and they like to hear. Acoustics in normal-sized theatre spaces ought to be adjusted with panels and drapes so that everyone hears well. Today in outdoor amphitheatres and huge auditoriums sound amplification is employed. Audiences have also come to expect temperature control so they don't become too hot or too cold. Sometimes even odors are a concern, especially in small spaces with musty draperies or old paint. Also, audiences like to be seen before and after a show and at intermission, but it makes them self-conscious to be lighted during a performance. Simply speaking, theatre producers try to control any physical stimuli that might prevent spectators from concentrating on the production and enjoying it.

Some plays work in intimate theatres but not in big auditoriums, and vice versa. Likewise some actors perform dynamically in small theatres but cannot fill the space in big ones. Some directors stage plays adroitly on proscenium stages but fail on thrust stages. Certainly, different audiences like different sorts of theatre places. Some people like opulent theatres that present lavish musicals. Others want modern spaces with odd new plays, while others look for traditional playhouses presenting classics. Still others prefer scrufty theatres that house shocking avant-garde pieces. Most intelligent theatregoers, however, desire a variety of experiences and are willing to go to many different kinds of theatres.

Many new theatres are adapted or built each year. Although real estate owners in New York have had relatively few theatres constructed during the last twenty-five years or so, outside Manhattan many organizations move into new theatres every year. New high school, community, university, and repertory theatres are mushrooming across the country. Not all the so-called new theatres have new architectural surroundings; often a theatre group transforms a space into a theatre. Any spectator can encounter many different kinds of theatre buildings. Most people frequently have a chance to go to a new theatre. A special excitement usually accompanies the opening production and the first season of a company in a new space.

Economic conditions today require that many alternative theatre groups adapt strange architectural spaces and transform them into theatres. For example, the Phoenix Theatre, a dynamic theatre organization in Indianapolis, opened a new theatre in the fall of 1983. Brian Fonseca, the artistic director, found an affordable place, a connected group of offices in a downtown apartment building. The group pitched in and dismantled the old walls, built new ones, and hired electricians and plumbers to complete the job. Now the Phoenix has a warm, intimate theatre seating about 90 people. So the story goes with many groups around the country. Sometimes warehouses, churches, or barns are transformed. In each case the theatre people ingeniously devise the necessary facilities for performances—taking care of scenery, lighting, dressing rooms and the like—and also look after audience comfort as well as they can.

Sometimes, of course, a theatre production company gets to build a new theatre. When the time comes to dream up an entire building, a great deal of careful analysis and planning must go into all the decisions. Few groups are as inventive as theatre companies about the use of space. Theatre producers are skilled at seeing needs, establishing priorities, and planning finances. Three sorts of people, however, ought to be involved in planning every new theatre: the client, the architect, and the consultant. The clients for theatre buildings—both owners and users—suggest the basic requirements of function and govern the overall economics. An architect arranges the building's spaces, selects the materials, and establishes a working budget. A theatre consultant provides specialized information, mostly about theatre technology, mechanics, and engineering.

Architects naturally control the design of theatre buildings. When commissioned, an architect must fit the building to its use as well as to its site. Since a physical milieu always affects the work of the people who use it, theatre architects attune themselves to the human processes that happen in a theatre's working spaces. They must know about traditional principles of theatre architecture and yet have enough artistry to be original. Not only should architects design attractive exteriors and interiors, but also they need to solve the many mechanical problems associated with theatre design. Theatre architects are nearly always wise enough to engage theatre consultants to advise them. Specifically, an architect furnishes plans and specifications for the construction of the theatre. When construction takes place, the architect remains in contact with the contractor. The architect's artistry should provide economical, imaginative, and attractive solutions to the physical and spatial needs of the theatre company, but an amazing number of people contribute ideas and work to the process of planning and constructing a theatre. The process is always the effort of a human community—a group devoted to the cultural expansion of society.

THE FUNCTIONS OF THEATRE SPACE

Theatres normally contain eight basic kinds of spaces. Each fulfills an important function or houses significant activities. An architect must consider each sort of space when designing a theatre. The basic spaces are exterior, public, business, auditorium, stage, backstage, production, and mechanical. The following discussion defines each of the spaces as an architect might consider them when planning a theatre.

The exterior space of a theatre includes the location, the site, and the external shape of the building. An architect seldom selects the location, simply because ownership boundaries restrict most properties. But the architect does identify the proper site within a given external space. Sometimes the exact site depends on testing the composition of the earth beneath the surface to determine its support capabilities. Among the next most important considerations are the automobile traffic patterns and the pedestrian channels. The parking problem, too, arises early. As the architect contemplates the exterior shape of the building, he or she also begins to conceive the landscaping and the external wall design and treatments. Some sort of outdoor advertising may also be a factor in the

John F. Kennedy Center for the Performing Arts, Washington, D.C.

exterior plan. Usually the architect alone is responsible for the exterior design of theatre buildings.

The public space within a theatre consists of numerous segments and facilities. In a new building, an architect takes into consideration all the potential uses of foyers, lobbies, lounges, rest rooms, and other public areas. If those spaces are pleasant and commodious, then an audience is more likely to enjoy the entire theatregoing experience. Public spaces are not only functional but also social—and significantly so. People want

The Kennedy Center lobby

to see and be seen. The lobby space needs to be the proper size and shape for the numbers expected in the auditorium and for the type of circulation that may occur inside the building. Sometimes lobbies are used for receptions, lectures, and exhibitions. Of course, adequate and pleasant spaces for portions of the audience to occupy during intermissions are also important in theatre design. Other public facilities are lavatories, cloakrooms, lounges or powder rooms, and refreshment areas; and certainly people must have adequate space in halls and passages to move through the building.

The business space consists of areas for the box office, managerial personnel, and theatre administration. Box offices vary in size and shape, but they are always readily available to the public. In large theatres more than one sort of ticket window may be necessary—one for advanced reservations and one for current tickets. The managerial offices house such people as the business manager, the promotion and publicity staff, the literary staff, secretaries, and the house manager. The custodial crew and their equipment also need space. In addition, the artistic director and all the artistic staff normally have offices in the theatre building. For the numerous meetings necessary in the operation of a theatre, at least one conference room may be useful. The overall management space can be as small or as large as the magnitude of the theatre's business dictates.

The auditorium of any theatre is its most definitive space. The size of the stage and its arrangement in relation to the seating area defines the physical theatre more than any other feature of the building. The size, shape, height, width, and depth of each stage ought to be unique. But an even more significant factor about stage design is its proximity to the audience. Figure 18.1 illustrates the six spatial arrangements most often used today in new theatres—proscenium, thrust, arena, amphitheatre, corner, and combination.

Each of the types of stage-auditorium arrangements diagramed in

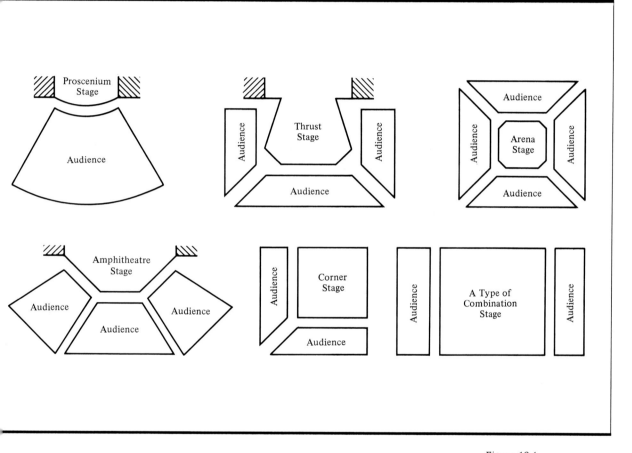

Figure 18.1

Diagrams of six common spatial arrangements in new theatres

Figure 18.1 has its advantages and disadvantages. The next segment of this chapter explains them in more detail and shows ground plans of typical theatres in existence. The important factors to note here are that each theatre arrangement emphasizes space differently and each establishes varying distances between performers and audience members. The proximity between stage and auditorium can also be studied in another way—in a cross-sectional diagram. Whether the stage is above or below the viewers makes a difference. Figure 18.2 shows the three most common solutions.

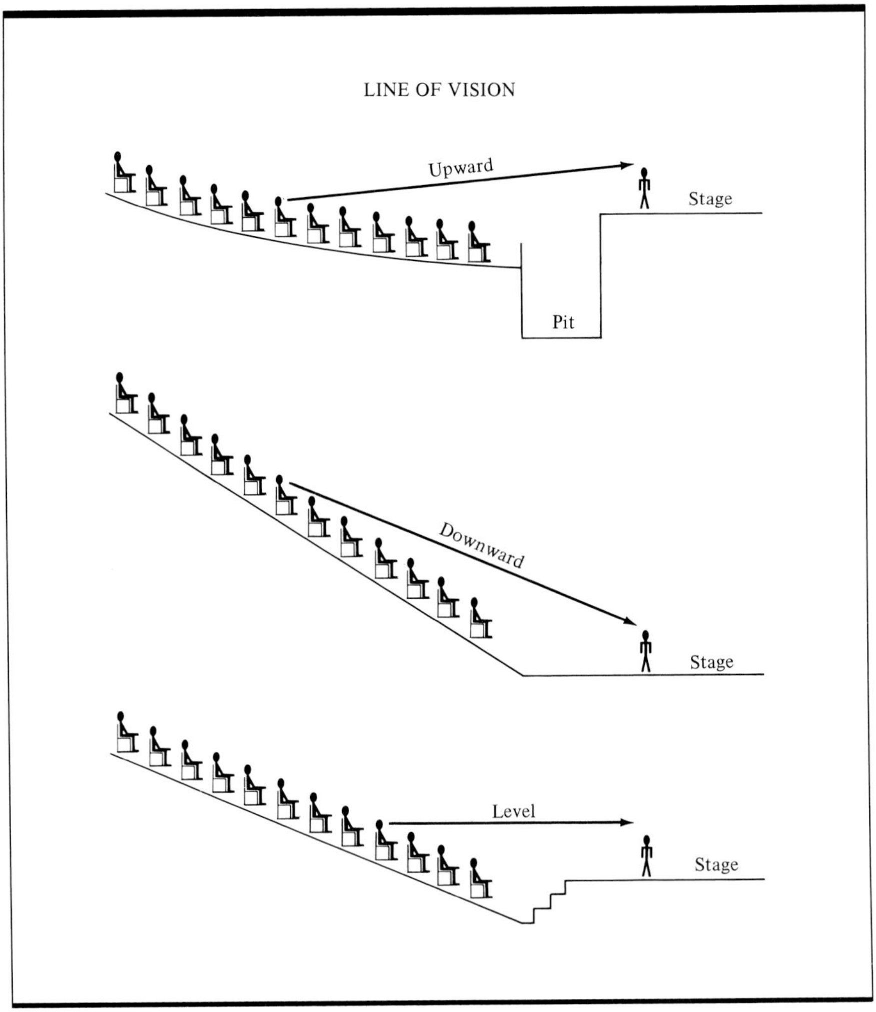

LINE OF VISION

Figure 18.2

**Diagrams of audience
proximity to stage**

Considerations about the stage space itself are numerous and complex. Each dimension of the playing space—its width, depth, and height—dictates in part what sort of scenic presentation can be made on that stage. Every production should somehow employ the potentials of a theatre's available playing space. A theatre can have too little or too much space for the sort of productions that will happen in it. In addition, the spaces above and at the sides of the stage make a difference in how the scenery can be shifted during a production. The fly gallery is a part of the stage space (Figure 18.3).

Every theatre also needs backstage space. The unseen spaces at the sides of the visible acting area are called wing spaces. Some theatres have a trap room beneath the stage. All such auxiliary spaces are necessary for scenery, lighting, properties, and the traffic flow of actors on and off the stage. Figure 18.4 indicates a few of the backstage spaces for a typical proscenium stage.

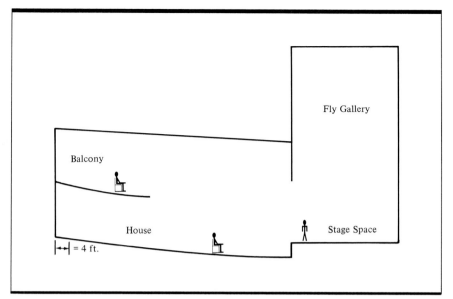

Figure 18.3

Cross section of auditorium, stage, and fly gallery in a proscenium theater

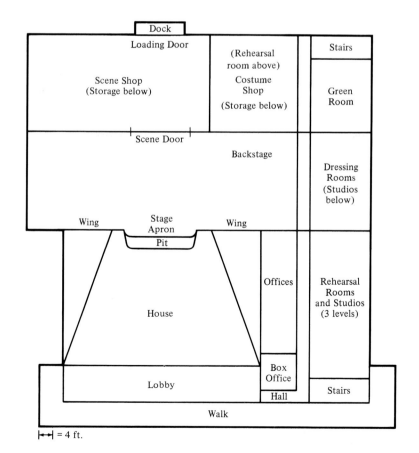

Figure 18.4

Diagram of typical backstage spaces in a well-designed theatre

Production areas are all those working spaces where work is done in preparation for a production. Some are rehearsal rooms; others are shops where construction work of one sort or another is accomplished. The production areas include rooms for actors, musicians, designers, technicians, and crews. The performers, of course, need dressing rooms with adequate space and facilities. They also may need quick-change rooms near the stage. Most theatres contain a greenroom, which is an offstage lounge for the working personnel. A warm-up area for musicians near the orchestra pit is desirable in big theatres. Theatres typically have at least four shops for scenery, lighting, properties, and costumes. Near the shops, designers often have a studio with drawing equipment. A show's crews need such spaces as a lighting booth, a sound booth, and a stage manager's station. In addition, theatres need storage spaces, especially for lighting, costumes, and properties. Any production company will use all the space available and want more.

Mechanical spaces are necessary for all the equipment that any public building needs. These spaces house equipment for ventilation, heating, cooling, electricity, water, and sewer. Other services that somehow must be provided in theatre buildings are security against theft, fire protection, audience lighting, noise control, loading access, vending machines, and first aid, plus internal and external communication systems.

Planning a theatre is a fascinating experience for a theatre company,

A proscenium stage, the Dorothy Chandler Pavilion, Los Angeles

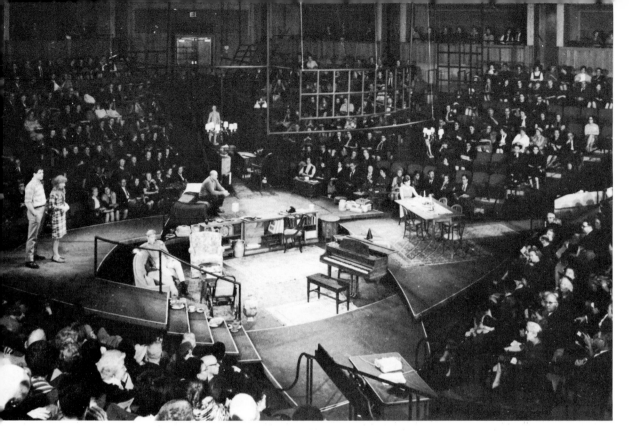

for its administrators, and certainly for the architect. The spatial and mechanical problems unique to theatre are nearly overwhelming, and many good minds must check and recheck every detail of planning, design, and construction. Because so many theatres have burned, numerous fire regulations are imposed on builders. Furthermore, because so many people use theatre buildings, safety features are crucial in theatre planning. Despite all the difficulties, however, the conception and opening of a new theatre building or a fresh theatre space are stimulating human experiences. With the considerations mentioned in this chapter, everyone should better be able to evaluate and enjoy theatre buildings, whether old or new.

THEATRE SHAPES

The possible configurations of performance spaces in theatres are nearly infinite. But most theatres in use today set performers and spectators in certain proximities. Each type of theatre utilizes a performance space with a particular shape. Theatres naturally vary in size and capacity, but still the basic patterns remain the same. Each type of theatre arrangement has a long developmental background in history; some of the earlier versions of the basic stages are treated in Chapters 10–17. The text and illustrations in this section identify the basic shapes for theatre and explain the conditions for flexible theatre types.

Theatres with a *proscenium stage* are the most common type in use today. Developed mostly in the nineteenth century to house illusionistic scenery, proscenium theatres best suit realistic melodramas and comedies with interior settings. In a proscenium theatre the audience generally sits in one-half of the space and the stage takes up the other half. The seats are arranged in rows, all facing the stage at about the same angle. The word *proscenium* refers to the "picture frame" through which the

A thrust stage, the Guthrie Theatre

audience views the play. Theatre productions occur in proscenium theatres of all sizes, ranging from huge houses seating more than a thousand to tiny theatres with about fifty to a hundred seats. The proscenium arrangement provides ample opportunity for elaborate scenery. In most proscenium theatres the seats are fixed permanently, and the performers occupy space that is visually separate from the spectators.

An *arena stage* features a performance space in the middle of the audience. Spectators sit on all four sides of the stage. Some theatres are permanently constructed with this configuration, but more often arena arrangements are set up within flexible theatre spaces. The great advantage of arena staging is that more people can be close to the performers, thus making the life in a drama more vivid for more people. The disadvantages are the lack of scenery space and the difficulty of making entrances and exits.

Theatres with a *thrust stage* have people seated on three sides of the action. Thus, more audience members sit close to the action. The most modern of the three basic types of audience arrangement, thrust stages also make audiences more aware of three-dimensional space. The term *thrust* refers to the fact that the performance area, or stage, juts into the audience area. In most theatres of this sort, the audience is arranged on three sides of the performing space, and the fourth side is used for scenery. Since the Globe Theatre for which Shakespeare wrote his plays had a thrust-stage configuration, his plays are particularly effective in this type of arrangement. Other plays with episodic structures and frankly theatrical styles also work well on thrust stages.

A *flexible theatre* refers to a building in which the performance and audience spaces can be rearranged for each production. In such theatres, directors can choose between different audience-stage configurations for each play. Still, the basic arrangements possible are usually proscenium, arena, or thrust. Many theatres have some flexibility in the use of the apron, the area between a proscenium stage and the audience, but a genuinely flexible theatre is one that is fully convertible.

Some theatres are simply a *black box*, a large empty room painted black in which chairs, rugs, risers, or bleachers can be set up in any desired configuration. More different arrangements are possible in black-box theatres than in any other sort of architectural space. Spectators can be set in literally any proximity to performers. Besides proscenium, arena, and thrust arrangements, some of the possibilities are corner, center, reversing ends, and "L" stages. Universities often have this type as a second theatre, available for student-directed productions. In such theatres students can beneficially experiment with the various arrangements. Most of these theatres house or seat small audiences, thereby permitting a run of several performances for each production without requiring large numbers of people to fill the designated audience space.

Environmental theatre refers to performances that occur in spaces not arranged like other conventional theatres. Sometimes the performance occurs in a large open room, similar to a black box, but instead of seating audience members in a usual proximity to performers, audience areas and performance areas are unpredictably intermixed. The audience environment and the performance environment interpenetrate so that a single atmosphere pervades all the human beings present—spectators and actors alike. Sometimes environmental theatre utilizes a building with many rooms, and the performance occurs in multiple places at once. In such cases, some spectators witness one scene while others witness another; often the spectators then move on to another room for another bit of action; or one group of viewers follows one group of actors

Gloria Foster in Bertolt Brecht's *Mother Courage*, New York Shakespeare Festival

from room to room. Sometimes environmental theatre occurs in art museums as one type of "performance art."

Some productions simply employ *found space*. Theatre troupes that travel a lot or ones that present street theatre must find their spaces or take any area made available to them. They use streets, factory yards, ballrooms, dining halls, city squares—anywhere they can find an audience. Sometimes their viewers sit, and sometimes they stand. The actors in such productions are free to improvise movement, adjusting what they have rehearsed to fit the space. This type of theatre is perhaps the oldest, the most primitive, the most flexible, and perhaps the most permanent of all.

CONTEMPORARY SPACES

One of the fascinating factors in theatregoing is the variety of theatre spaces now in use. Attending one theatre regularly is of course pleasant, but going to different theatres provides strange and new experiences. Each theatre building has its own personality and indelibly marks the productions that occur there. This section explores a number of theatres to provide examples of different types of production. The theatres illustrated earlier in this chapter show a variety of spaces in size and arrangements.

In most Broadway theatres the space and facilities are severely limited;

Guys and Dolls, the Alliance Theatre Company, Atlanta

nevertheless, most of them communicate the special flavor of professional theatre at its best. Since many of the theatres were built early in this century, and since the owners wish to seat as many people as possible in the spaces available, spectators must endure cramped seating and abbreviated lobby spaces. The sight lines are not good over the entire auditorium, but the acoustics are usually adequate. The stages are often small and by contemporary standards not well-equipped; they handle single-set shows best. Actors have little space and few comforts. Still many fine productions come into being in these rather old-fashioned

I never Sang for My Father **by Robert Anderson, Repertory Theatre at Christian Theological Seminary, Indianapolis**

theatre spaces. Most theatre owners have modified their theatres as best they can to meet contemporary needs. Two good examples of Broadway houses are the Palace Theatre, where musicals often play, and the smaller Golden Theatre, a space more appropriate for straight plays.

Off Broadway and Off Off Broadway theatres abound throughout the city of New York. Few of them have ideal space or facilities, but they vary greatly. Most of the theatres are transformed spaces that formerly served some other function. Many of the theatres, however, provide intimate and stimulating environments for good productions. The Manhattan Theatre Club has long survived in this kind of theatre. Though the space is unusually small, the WPA theatre turns out fine productions. Producer Joseph Papp is master of the Off Broadway theatre scene in New York. His Public Theatre complex is exemplary and contains more than one theatre performance space.

America's repertory theatre companies present many fine productions throughout the country. Although few of them have brand new buildings, most of the theatres are modern in design and conception. Many of the companies have several fully equipped stages. Some have proscenium theatres, some have thrust stages, and some are arenas. When a company has more than a single theatre, usually one is full-sized for the major productions, and the second is smaller and houses more daring, experimental works. The Mark Taper Forum in Los Angeles is not only

Kip Niven in *The Tempest*, University of Evansville

one of the best companies artistically but also has a functional theatre complex. The Guthrie Theatre in Minneapolis features a well-designed thrust stage. Actors Theatre of Louisville, Kentucky, contains two good performance spaces.

Arts centers contain excellent theatres in many major cities. The John F. Kennedy Center in Washington, D.C., houses several different theatres. Its production management often books shows of different types and sometimes initiates productions for the Kennedy Center alone. Other arts centers sometimes house community theatre groups or semiprofessional theatre companies. An unusual theatre of this sort is the Oklahoma Theatre Center in Oklahoma City.

Festival theatres present many excellent summer productions across the country, and some of the companies have unique contemporary buildings in which to work. Shakespearean festivals are particularly popular. Three of the most well known take place in Ohio, Oregon, and Colorado. The Ashland Shakespeare Festival Theatre in Oregon more closely approximates the plan of an Elizabethan theatre.

College and university drama departments and theatre groups furnish more drama of quality than any other sort of theatre organization, one of the reasons being that educational institutions are blessed with fine theatre buildings. On campuses all types of theatres exist—some with proscenium stages and others with flexible and thrust stages. Some large universities, such as the University of Illinois, in Urbana, have entire theatre complexes. Some flexible theatres are simply open rooms, but others are carefully designed theatres. The Ace Morgan Theatre at Denison University in Granville, Ohio, is capable of a number of variations in staging patterns. The seats are folding chairs, which can be arranged in any of the basic areas for proscenium, side-stage, or arena production. The Shanklin Theatre at the University of Evansville in Indiana is one of the best small thrust-stage theatres. Summer theatre productions occur in many types of theatres throughout the United States. Professional, semiprofessional, and amateur companies work in conditions that range from remodeled barns to new open stages, from restaurants to amphitheatres. Most of America's professional summer theatres are located in the upper segment of the East Coast. The Cape Playhouse in Dennis, Massachusetts, is one of the most famous, and it has a typical new summer stock company. A semiprofessional company occupies the thrust stage of the Brown County Playhouse in Nashville, Indiana.

About two dozen outdoor dramas are presented each summer in spacious amphitheatres throughout the South and Southwest. The plays celebrate historical personages and events. Together these plays make up a unique type of drama. More than any other playwright, Paul Green is responsible for developing the genre. The theatre built for *The Lost Colony* on the coast of North Carolina was the first of its kind. One of the most recent outdoor dramas is *The Battle of Tippecanoe* near Lafayette, Indiana.

Dinner theatres abound throughout the country. Sometimes plays are presented on tiny bandstands in cramped restaurant conditions, and sometimes buildings have been constructed especially for dinner-theatre operation.

Community theatres operate in many different kinds of theatre spaces. Year after year people in cities and towns throughout the nation band together to produce plays. They put on their works in ballrooms, gymnasiums, and regular theatres. Sometimes they rent or lease the spaces, and sometimes they are successful enough or rich enough to erect fine buildings. The energetic civic theatres of the country not only offer a place for nonprofessional theatre people to create but also help keep drama genuinely alive. A representative of a large organization of this type is the Indianapolis Civic Theatre.

High school productions far surpass any other kind of theatre production in sheer number. These groups, like many other amateurs, work in a variety of circumstances. Most often, however, high school groups are asked to produce their plays in giant all-purpose auditoriums. Such structures are perhaps necessary for convocations, band concerts, and graduation ceremonies, but they make good theatre difficult because of their size. Still, such giant auditoriums tend to be better production spaces than those which feature a stage at one end of a gymnasium. Some high school drama teachers have more freedom than others and are able to devise intimate theatres for special productions. Since most high school productions use large numbers of students, large theatres are often useful. The drama group at Bloomington South High School in Indiana produces many plays in a typical auditorium.

The number of hours that the artists spend in theatre buildings is simply amazing. Actors and directors, designers and crews, and producers and business personnel occupy theatre spaces most of the hours of the day and of the night. Seldom does a theatre building stand empty, and even then during the few quiet hours the custodial staff is likely to be hurriedly cleaning in preparation for the next working day. A theatre is always full of life. A theatre's total environment touches actors deeply because they spend so much of their lives there. They absorb the very atmosphere. A theatre is a building where the human creative process goes on and on, days without end.

For audiences, too, where theatre happens makes a difference. Most people go to the theatre to enjoy themselves, or to have special experiences. To fulfill its function, a theatre building must somehow be special. The physical surroundings affect audiences in sensory and emotional ways. When people walk into a theatre, the division of space and the very atmosphere stimulate them to expect a ritual of social communion or at least a couple of hours of entertainment. They walk in with anticipation, with a sense of occasion, and with high hopes of having a memorable experience. A good theatre space promises life intensified. Insofar as space, shelter, light, temperature, color, and comfort affect human beings, so theatres affect audiences deeply. A well-designed theatre increases the artistic potentials of the productions it houses. A good theatre building stimulates the art of drama.

19 *Cinema*

Narrative motion pictures are one of the most important types of dramatic art. Without doubt, more people go to see movies in their local cinemas than ever go to see live theatre. But, of course, people watch feature-length films nowadays on home television even more often than on screens in movie theatres. Although a narrative motion picture is not the same as a live play on a stage, movies are closely enough related to theatre that they can appropriately be discussed here. Indeed, the first course in many college theatre departments includes films as a means of illustrating theatre techniques. Knowing details about the theory and craft of motion pictures promotes an understanding of dramatic art in general, just as knowledge of certain ideas and techniques regarding theatre can provide better understanding of narrative motion pictures.

This chapter explores cinema as art in order to define it and to show the similarities and the differences between it and theatre. The discussion deals only with feature-length, narrative films. Such film genres as documentaries, cartoons, and short subjects are not treated. Covering four areas of information, the chapter first delves into film aesthetics, especially examining the psychic involvement of viewers and the principles of montage and closure. Second, it then defines basic elements, forms, and styles of film. Third, it describes some of the essential procedures in movie production. Finally, the discussion turns to finances and the economic determinants of cinema.

BASIC CINEMA AESTHETICS

Although cinema and theatre are different arts, they share many common techniques and have many corresponding elements. The materials of plays and screenplays are, broadly speaking, the same. The men, women, and children of the real world or of fantasy worlds, along with their thoughts, words, and deeds furnish both the screenwriter and the playwright with the details of their art. The essential form of both plays and screenplays depends on the essential principle of a pattern of action. In both media, a writer establishes one or more situations and then aligns a series of events in a particular sequence. When such a sequence of events follows one or more lines of action, then the story takes on a comprehensible form. The manner of presentation differs greatly between film and theatre; thus the style of communication in the two is vastly different.

The essential difference between theatre and film is that plays use words as key materials whereas films use photographs. In the material sense, drama is verbal, and film is visual. For theatre a writer emphasizes the verbalization of experience. Drama depends on deeds, too, but in the theatre sensitive and imaginative speeches most fully reveal the deep perceptions or the comic twists of human experience. For cinema, however, a writer concentrates first on single visual images and then on a stream of such images in sequence. A movie also features deeds, but the externalization of most feelings and thoughts is best presented in one or more pictures. In order to contrast the styles of these two arts,

one might think of cinema as the art of external human action and of theatre as the art of internal human action.

The overall aesthetic function of a film is also essentially different from a play. A film usually establishes a close empathic bond between the viewer and the series of images—the life he observes. Indeed, the aesthetic distance is so close that the emotions of a movie ideally occur inside the spectator. The bond is not so close in the theatre; rather, theatre permits a group of spectators to sit as a communal witness to the living

Far left: Orson Welles in *Citizen Kane*

Left: Ben Cross in *Chariots of Fire*

experience of real people. In cinema the viewer participates, whereas in theatre the spectator witnesses. Plays and screenplays are alike in material and form, but their eventual presentation to an audience differs in style and function.

The most telling difference between cinema and drama concerns *psychic participation*, or self-projection. This phenomenon occurs when a person *watches* a projected movie, in contrast with when a person *witnesses* a live play. A movie stimulates a viewer's imagination differently. An analogy with novels and poems clarifies the experiential contrast. When people read a novel, they look at word symbols printed on paper. Literally, there are no people in a novel, only words. The people and places occur imaginatively inside the reader's head. A novel is a set of symbols that trigger mental images and feelings in a person's mind. But a lyric poem is quite different. Also made up of verbal symbols, the words of a poem are the expression of a poet. A poem's words are what the poet, or his or her mouthpiece, says directly to the reader. Poets do not try to create a fictive world so much as they attempt to reveal how some experience made them feel or how some thought occurred to them. Novels are *expansive* and stimulate a person's mind to fantasize an imagined world. Poems are *intensive* and communicate a view of human experience. Similarly, for psychic participation, movies are expansive, and plays are intensive.

365

Maureen O'Hara, Victor McLaglen, John Wayne, and Barry Fitzgerald in *The Quiet Man*

Cinema is rightly associated with the novel and theatre with the lyric poem. A motion picture no more contains people and places than does a novel. It represents people by presenting photographic images—of light, shadow, and color—on a screen. A viewer takes these symbols to be people, and an imagined stream of images registers inside the head of the person watching. As the moviegoer observes the patterns of light and color, registering images of people's activities in given places, then the viewer begins to feel emotion. It all happens inside the viewer's head. The viewing of a movie, like the reading of a novel, is essentially a solitary experience. Even as a person sits before a film with someone else, he must make a psychological break away from the film in order to communicate with the other person.

While watching a live play in a theatre, a significantly different psychological experience is likely to occur. A play, like a lyric poem, is a more aesthetically distanced event. It does not unfold so much within the viewer's imagination. A piece of live theatre really occurs in front of the audience, and it stimulates associations but doesn't enfold the play. Living people onstage permit a social group—an audience—to witness intimate life experiences. The fact that the people onstage are live makes all the difference. The fact that the audience witnesses as a group also makes a difference. Seeing a play alone is not at all the same as seeing it with a friend or a crowd; the full effect is not possible when one sees a play alone. A movie can perhaps be more fully enjoyed alone. Listening to a produced play is akin to hearing a lyric poet read his or her work. Just as poets express their feelings, so do actors, as the characters, talk with immediacy of their emotions. A film, like a novel, occurs chiefly within a viewer; a play, like a poem, occurs chiefly outside the spectators. Of course, plays and movies have certain features in common—for example, story, character, and dialogue. Naturally, both films and plays stimulate the imaginations of audience members, but between film and theatre the manner of the imaginative perception is quite different.

One other general principle is essential for an understanding of cinema theory—the principle of *montage*. It is associated with the psychological tendency in human beings to make *closure*. Early in the twentieth century, a Russian filmmaker named Sergei Eisenstein developed the idea of montage, which refers to a series of cinematic shots shown one after another in a sequence. For example, the first shot of a movie depicts a small sailboat on the ocean; the second shot shows a freighter steaming along; in the third shot a beautiful woman lies beside a pool; and in the fourth shot a fat man walks up beside the pool. Although the four shots display four different things, a viewer seeing them in sequence "closes" them together, making a connection between them. Seeing the sequence, a viewer might realize that the fat man is approaching the woman like a freighter approaching a sailboat. Whatever the images in a sequence, audience members will imaginatively put them together. This principle

Henry Fonda (third from right) in *The Grapes of Wrath*

of montage is as essential to movie construction as is the principle of psychic participation.

THE ELEMENTS OF FILM

CONNECTIONS

To consider the essential elements of narrative films, the causal approach is useful. What are the basic materials of film? What are the principles of form that it exhibits? What is the nature of filmic style? And what is the aesthetic function of a full-length, narrative film?

First come the materials. The smallest, yet the most essential, material unit of cinematic art is an *image*, or the single photographic frame. The individual image is closely tied to moment and shot. Individual visual images are the principal components of a film. Above all else, what a film director does is to select and arrange details for one photograph after another as a series of visual images. Thereby he controls exactly what individual audience members see, and what the viewers see has an intense impact on their feelings as well as their senses. By means of the images presented, a film controls the quality and direction of an audience member's sense perceptions. The principle of montage works on each person's sense of closure. Audiences respond to the cumulative effect of seeing a flow of images projected on a screen—a flow that fools the human eye into seeing movement instead of a mere series of stills. All the planning that goes into a film concentrates on the solitary image.

Charlie Chaplin in *The Gold Rush*

The director contrives the strategy of employing script, actors, camera, and technical elements in order to capture a narrative in photographs. The basic material of cinema is a series of pictorial images captured one after another on a strip of film.

Each visual image on film captures a *moment* of reality, at best a moment of significance in the life of a person. To comprehend the essence of narrative motion pictures, this concept is among the most important. One strategy of motion picture technique rests on the idea

**Jill Clayburgh in *An
Unmarried Woman***

that if a filmmaker can capture one significant moment after another in a person's life, then observers will follow the stream of photographs with sympathetic emotion. But one moment in a person's life is not like another. Life varies. Some moments are more important than others, and often a series of relatively unimportant moments lead up to one of high significance. To photograph a significant moment in a person's life is to capture externally the essence of that life.

An example of a significant moment happens in the film *An Unmarried Woman*. A husband and wife are sitting in a restaurant one day. The husband suddenly tells his wife that he no longer loves her and is having an affair with another woman. In that moment the wife discovers the truth about her husband, and her social and economic world collapses. A stunning change instantly occurs in her life. Words are not necessary. When that moment happens, all the director needs to do is photograph her face, and a viewer empathically knows how she feels. Such realization and the associated feelings occur as much in the imaginations of the spectators as in the mind of the woman. The best filmmakers are able to photograph a series of such big moments as strong visual images. A movie is composed of a series of interesting moments in the lives of a group of characters. In the best films the moments show changes in a character's life.

Another important term associated with filmmaking is *shot*. In order

369

**Ingrid Bergman and
Gary Cooper in _For
Whom the Bell Tolls_**

for an image to be recorded, a camera must operate for a given length of time. The mechanical process of capturing an image, or a significant moment, is best understood as a shot. Technically, a shot demands one setup of the camera and involves the time from when the camera begins running to when it stops. Even if the composition of the image changes during that period—the camera might pan, dolly, or approach—the shot remains singular. Film directors cannot think merely of one shot at a time; they must know how each shot will join with those that go before or come after it. Thus filmmakers often point out that no shot can be conceived statically for its own sake; every shot must be conceived as merely one unit in a constantly changing flow. Nevertheless, a shot of a moment makes a single image that is the basic ingredient of a movie.

Frame is another term that has to do with how an image is captured on film. Every shot consists of a visual image somehow framed by the limits of the camera lens and by the edges of the film stock. Framing has to do with how much of a particular scene is to be included in the shot. Another consideration about framing is that of the angle from which the shot is to be made. Such particular descriptions as "long shot," "medium shot," or "close-up" refer as much to framing as to the camera's distance from the subject. The way the camera frames a particular scene controls its visual impact on viewers.

A _scene_ is a unified series of shots occurring at a single time and in a single place. It may consist of one extended shot or a series of shots spliced together. For example, the following series of shots illustrates a scene:

Long shot: Six runners are sprinting down the lanes of a track toward the camera.

Medium shot: Two of the runners stride side by side and pull away from the others.

Close-up: The face of one of the two leaders shows great pain.

Close-up: The other runner's face looks relaxed.

Medium shot: The relaxed runner begins to inch ahead.

Long shot: The runners are nearing the finish line.

Medium shot: In a view from across the track, the relaxed runner wins.

Long shot: All the runners are now across the finish line and slowing down when suddenly the pained runner falls.

A film *sequence* is a group of scenes that make up a major unit of the action. For instance, in the film *Tender Mercies* with Robert Duvall, the opening sequence shows a number of scenes in a small, country motel. In the first scene, a boy and his mother, who owns the motel, watch shadows of two drunken men arguing in a distant window. Then, inside the motel room, Duvall passes out on the floor. The mother and boy go back inside their house. The next scene shows Duvall waking up in the morning. He goes outside, and the young woman tells him he's been asleep two days and his partner has taken the car and left without paying. Duvall goes back into the motel room, finds his bottle, and takes a drink. In a climactic scene, he hunts up the young woman, admits he's broke, and asks to work off his debt. Those scenes taken together make up a sequence. All feature-length narrative movies contain similar sequences of scenes, varying in length and complexity. As with shot and scene, no standard rules exist about how long a sequence should be. The duration of a sequence varies within a film, and each filmmaker uses it differently as a rhythmic, story-telling unit.

Environment is also an important factor in moviemaking. All the physical surroundings of a particular place make up an environment. When a film begins, the camera reveals the specific details of a place; the first shots in any film establish some specific environment. The camera eye records and the human eye recognizes the specific details of a place and then its aspect as a whole. The more details presented, the more specific is the place depicted. A shot of the open ocean, for example, reveals a generalized sort of environment, but unusual details of wind and wave could make the shot more specific as an environment. As directors and cinematographers make a film, their attention must focus upon the suggestive and credible details of particular places. Indeed, part of the appeal of films is that they take an audience to either exotic places or familiar ones. Visual environments establish the visual and emotional

371

grounds for a story, and the establishment of detailed environments is crucial in any film.

The concept of *situation* is also important. The establishment of a situation is crucial to the beginning of a film, and the progressive changes in situation must be shown as the story progresses. A situation amounts to a set of relationships between people, or between people and a place. A situation occurs when characters are somehow caught in a web of difficulties. For example, in one film situation the sea might be a prison, confining a shipwrecked family to an island, but in another situation the sea might represent an opportunity for escape—say, from Devil's Island. Most situations in films depend as much on the visual details of environment as on the interactions of people. For example, a young couple, recently married are happily eating breakfast together—a situation. They sit in a modern kitchen with sunlight streaming in a window—an environment. Everything is ready for something to happen. When a clear, challenging situation appears at the beginning of a film, the story starts more surely, and as the various situations clearly appear throughout the film, then interesting events are more likely to occur.

Surprising, unusual *events* are also significant matters for the composition of a film. An event is something that happens. In the previous example, when something or someone disturbs the young couple at breakfast, then an event takes place, and the situation changes. Maybe the young husband accidentally discovers a strange love letter addressed to his wife, or maybe an escaped convict bursts through the door. Either occurrence would be an event, because suddenly all the relationships are forced to change. The quality of every film depends in part on the inventiveness of its writers and directors as they devise unique and startling events within the given environment of the film.

The final and perhaps most telling sort of material for any film is human character itself. Every person living, dead, or even imaginable is potentially material for a film. So when a screenwriter makes a selection of characters, the choice is a material one. To tell a story about people in a Swiss village attempting to save a party of mountain climbers obviously needs different characters as materials than a story about two Spanish gypsies living in a cave and stealing food, horses, and babies

Harrison Ford in *Raiders of the Lost Ark*

**Marlon Brando in
*One-Eyed Jacks***

from nearby villages. All the details of each character are important, because these too are materials. The author, director, actors, and designers of a film want to know the physical, social, psychological, and ethical nature of each person in the story. In fact, the process of dreaming up and selecting character details occupies a lot of the generative time of the creative team. Together they choose and assemble the characters, and the quality of the film depends to a degree on perceptiveness of those who select and depict them.

The major materials of a film, then, are images, moments, shots, frames, environments, situations, events, and characters. With such details as these, a writer and director put together a work of cinematic art.

MAKING A FILM

The technology of film is complicated enough to appear mysterious to the ordinary moviegoer, and it certainly involves the expert work of many skilled technicians. This section examines the particular functions and work of some of these specialists—such as producers, writers, directors, cinematographers, designers, and actors. From the beginning, anyone interested in movie production must realize that in one sense technology controls cinematic art. The master filmmakers understand and control a vast technological complex. Not only must a script and actors be chosen, but also there are choices to be made regarding cameras, film stock, color, lenses, lighting, film developing, editing, opticals, titles, sound mixing, and printing. All those details and many others require the work of expert technicians in order for a film to reach the screen. If a person is interested in film production, each of those areas deserves careful study. Here the discussion is not so concerned with technology as with the most important functions of the people who create cinematic art.

At the head of every film production organization stands a producer, who manages everything. Often the producer conceives the project in the first place by finding a worthy script, raising money, and hiring the necessary talent to shoot the film. He or she oversees every detail as the movie is shot. Next, the producer masterminds the promotion of the finished product and then places it with a distribution company, selling foreign and television rights as well. Eventually, the producer pays off everyone, including the investors, and if he or she is lucky and the film is successful, pockets a nice portion of the profits for himself. Most films nowadays have more than one producer because there is so much complex work involved. Good producers are a combination of businessperson and artist. Although they have little time for the meticulous creativity of writers, directors, and actors, they must be creative in the realms of planning, administration, and management. Because a producer controls everything, sometimes other cinematic artists, such as actors or directors become producers themselves, in order to retain control over an entire film. Good producers are well-organized, hard-working, and respectful of others. The best producers have thoughtful visions of the social function of films. A poor producer is often a money grubber with little vision but great greed. All producers have savvy, and some are intelligent.

A writer provides the creative heart of a motion picture. For producers, directors, and actors, the search for good scripts is unending. They stay in touch with the best screenwriters, and they scrutinize most published novels. Movie studios and producers have arrangements with major publishing companies to look at new novels even before they are published. Without a good script, no movie can proceed. Movies are as much a writer's art as they are a director's. Even scripts put together by a famous director—Ingmar Bergman, perhaps, or Federico Fellini—must be *written*. When a director composes a script, he's a writer. Although many directors write films, all who write must know the requisites of a good screenplay. Most of the principles of dramatic writing are operative in screenwriting, too. Principles of story and character, for example, work well for both media. The essential difference between screenwriting and playwriting can be summarized in two questions: A writer for the stage asks, What is going on? A writer for the cinema asks, What is going on that can be photographed? Screenwriting is a solitary and difficult art, and among expert filmmakers, the writer is regarded as one of the central creators.

The master of the process of making a film is the director. He or she plans and oversees the work of all the artists and technicians who are involved. At first alone and eventually with a cinematographer, the director studies a screenplay and develops it into a shooting script. Then, during the filming the director actually works with the actors and technicians to see that his or her conceptions are carried out. Although some of the director's work is improvisational during the shooting, most of the camera setups and shots are meticulously planned. Sometimes directors have little control over the editing, but those who have strong enough artistic reputations or large enough financial stakes often oversee the editing of their films as well. The best directors create films that execute their inner conceptions of particular stories and that carry out their broad visions of cinema as art.

A cinematographer provides all the technological expertise about cameras, film, and photography needed for a production. Writing a screenplay is literary, and preparing a production is administrative; only when a camera starts rolling does filmmaking become a reality. The physical quality of a movie depends on the quality of the component photographs which a cinematographer makes. The three most important elements a cinematographer has to control are film stock, the composition of elements in each frame, and the lighting of those elements. Some segments of movies are shot outdoors on "location," where weather and light are difficult to control, and other segments are shot indoors on location or in a studio, where conditions are easier to manipulate. Cinematographers also have to deal with two kinds of movement problems. Moving a camera from place to place in order to photograph different scenes means mul-

Yul Brynner presents an Academy Award to director François Truffaut

Malcolm McDowell in *A Clockwork Orange*

tiple setups. For each setup all the equipment must be carefully readjusted. In addition, the movement of actors as they are photographed sometimes occurs within a frame, and sometimes their activities require a moving camera. All types of movement present special problems to the cinematographer. With regard to lighting, such qualities as intensity, color, and quality are crucial. The cinematographer is also one of film's central creators.

Designers of many kinds provide the visual essentials of location, setting, costume, and properties. Working closely with a film's director, the production designer helps select the appropriate outdoor locations where a film will be shot. He or she designs and oversees the construction of any necessary scenery. Scenery construction is often as essential for location shooting as it is in studios. For example, many of the old-fashioned buildings and stagecoaches used in westerns have to be built. Costume and properties designers do their work for movies much as they do for the theatre. In film work the lighting designer is often considered the most important. He works closely with the cinematographer to create studio light or to supplement natural outdoor light. If the subjects to be photographed are lighted well, then the actors look good, the director is seen to be skillful, and even the cinematographer's work seems better. Viewers seldom notice the designers' activities because in most films the sets, costumes, lights, and properties all appear natural.

Making all these items integral and credible is the chief job of the designers.

Actors bring the characters to life. Although most moviegoers have become sensitized to the work of actors, many do not understand the work or the business of acting. Some of an actor's creative process for a film is identical with that necessary for theatre. Psychological transformation is the most difficult aspect, and the one least understood even by some actors themselves. It would seem that because actors walk and talk like everyone else that anyone can act, but not everyone can. Acting demands self-transformation for the sake of a character, and it requires the externalization of all thoughts and feelings. Most people cannot transform themselves sufficiently, and few people externalize their feelings very well in front of others. Film acting differs from stage acting in scale of externalization and in subtlety of expression. The business of acting in the movie world is complicated. Most professional actors never become stars and never get to be well known. Actors go to audition after audition, and more often than not they do not get cast. Directors want actors who look and sound right, and because there are so many actor's nowadays, casting agents are necessary to find and select actors for a director's final approval. Actors are the central objects photographed in a movie.

The film editor is more of a second director than audiences realize, because he or she literally constructs a film. Pudovkin, a famous early Russian director, once said about editing that "a film is not shot, but built." With the film a cinematographer has shot and technicians developed, an editor analyzes the frames of film that make up each shot. The editor next cuts away excess frames and often separates the film of some shots into smaller pieces. Then considering hundreds and sometimes thousands of pieces of film, the editor literally constructs the movie by joining the ribbons of film together. More than anyone else, an editor controls the rhythm and flow of a film, thus determining the clarity of the final assemblage. Most major directors participate in the editing of their films, not usually by doing the mechanical work but by making most of the decisions. For some films the editing is "invisible," meaning unobtrusive, not calling attention to itself. But in other films the editing is "emphatic," meaning purposefully attracting attention. Many dramatic films use both. For example, in portions of *High Noon* with Gary Cooper, the editing is invisible, but at the end when the scene jumps from place to place with each tick of the clock, the editing becomes emphatic.

Some of the mechanics of film editing are worth noting. Editing is sometimes "chronological," with one scene coming after another in logical or causal sequence. Editing can also be "relational," stressing intellectual or emotional connections between images. "Interconnecting" refers to making connections between contrasting or disparate visual images. "Linking" means connecting similar, noncontrasting images. "Cutting" is a quick shift from one image to another. For example, a shot might show a man walking along the street of a Greek town and suddenly cut to a woman looking out of a nearby window. A "jump cut" is an especially abrupt change. In the example above, a jump cut might be from the man in Greece to a shot of his son in a school playground in Paris. A less abrupt way to make a transition in film is with a "dissolve," in which the old image fades out slowly while a new image fades into view. A "fade in" refers to the beginning of a shot appearing out of visual oblivion, and "fade out" means an image disappears. Of course, there are other editing techniques, but these are enough to indicate the work of a film editor.

Many people contribute to a movie sound track. Composers, musicians, effects people, sound mixers, and many electronic technicians help with each narrative film. Even sophisticated moviegoers sometimes fail to recognize the importance of sound in films, because cinematic sound is not usually intended to draw attention to itself. It supports other elements. The sound of actors' voices supports the actors by matching the movements of their lips. Atmospheric sounds—such as traffic passing or waves hitting the shore—must credibly connect with visual images. Music supports the emotions of the characters. All these sounds exert a subtle psychological effect on audiences, providing information, mood, or symbols. Since an editor cuts apart and reassembles film footage, a sound designer must synchronize sound with every frame, making sure that the sounds occur when they should. He must establish a volume level for each sound, and whenever two or more occur at once, he must balance them. Sound also helps make transitions with cuts or dissolves. Composers often create original music for films, and arrangers orchestrate melodies appropriately. Musical passages frequently become emotional motifs in films, and the repetition of a melody becomes identified with a mood, a character, or an action. Sound is one of the most sophisticated and complex aspects of film production.

THE BUSINESS OF CINEMA

The expense of motion pictures makes them different from all the other fine arts. The seven traditional fine arts—music, poetry, dance, architecture, painting, sculpture, and theatre—have been practiced for centuries by cultures everywhere. Although they all now take advantage of modern technology, none of the other fine arts must have such complex equipment. A shepherd can sing a tune, an Amazon Indian can draw a picture in the sand, and a group of students can put on "poor" theatre; but so far the making of a dramatic film requires a lot of money. In order to justify the amount of money it takes to rent equipment, to buy film, and to pay technicians' salaries, films are mostly made as products for sale. Since they must be money-making commodities, the decisions that control their creation are often made more for economic than artistic reasons. The artists who can deal with economic complexities and still create a movie that achieves a high artistic level are rare indeed. Nevertheless, most movies, even the most crassly commercial, are to some degree artistic. For the most part, creativity motivates the cinematic artists, but the profit motive certainly is the energy behind the movie business.

One necessary step for any prospective producer is raising money. Motion picture financing is a complicated affair, normally involving large companies. Most movies are made by six or seven major production companies. But independent companies also make some of today's films. In any case, the money for a production comes principally from banks, corporations, and individuals who are willing to make loans to a production company. These investors speculate that they can get their money back from the investment along with a profit. Investors are more likely to take a chance with their money if the project has a marketable "team"—producer, director, writer, and stars who have "track records" of recent success. Newcomers have a difficult time breaking in, except as assistants or minor figures in a successful production company. Occasionally, a new production group succeeds in raising enough money, from $4 million to $7 million, for a modest film and thus breaks into the business.

Business procedures control the destiny of every film. Whether or not money can be raised and how much is raised determine whether a movie goes into production and its prospect for coming to fruition. Thousands of movies are written every year, but only a few hundred are optioned for prospective production. Of those optioned, quite a few are planned, but many more never get filmed; of the ones shot, a number are never released. In the United States, fewer than a hundred films made each year get released in theatres. Most are destined for television. After producers raise the money for a film and production begins, financial control becomes crucial. Simply put, whatever organization or executive controls the finances of a project has true control of everything. Promises, agreements, and contracts are often broken for the sake of control. The final word, even about such matters as who gets cast or how many horses are used, comes from the top. Budgets, accounting, and purchasing in their way make as much difference to the outcome of a film as the artistic vision of a director or the talent of a leading actor or actress.

Distribution is also a matter of great importance to filmmakers. Once a movie is completed, or often while it is still in production, the producer and fellow executives must arrange for the film to be shown in movie theatres throughout this country and overseas. This process is called distribution. They must also sell rights for television use of the film. Nowadays they also arrange for videocassette sales. Naturally everyone wants to make a profit from the movie, and everyone gets a cut, a fee or a percentage of the profits. Most major movie companies—for example, Columbia or Universal—arrange for the release, or distribution, of their own films and of some films from independent producers. Because certain companies own many theatres or can influence theatre owners, distribution problems for independent or foreign producers can be great indeed.

The financial paradox of contemporary cinema is that money can hire the greatest talents of the world, but it cannot insure great art. Movies attract the finest directors, writers, and actors the world over. Outstanding stage directors, such as Ingmar Bergman and Elia Kazan, have handled both theatre and film production. American writers as great as F. Scott Fitzgerald, Clifford Odets, and William Faulkner have written movies. Such fine stage actors as Laurence Olivier, George C. Scott, and Kevin Kline also work in films. But no amount of talent can guarantee the success of a film artistically or financially. To make a profit, a film must be released in so many places in North America and all over the world that movie executives want to make their product as universally appealing as possible. Often the very process of working so hard for universality tends to water down all the artistic "spice" of a film and make it bland. Sometimes in the attempt to be original and entertaining, a film turns out to be an unclear jumble of scenes. There's nothing wrong, of course, with attempts to be universal, entertaining, or even commercial. Some films, like Steven Spielberg's *E.T.*, accomplish all that quite well and do so with artistry. But nobody in the movie business can guarantee success, let alone genuine art.

In the mid-1980s the health of the film industry seems assured. Movies such as *Star Wars, Raiders of the Lost Ark*, and *Terms of Endearment* have helped revive the popularity of going out to the movies. Television networks compete for the right to broadcast major films, and they use as many made-for-TV movies as they can find. TV stations everywhere continue to show old movies over and over. Colleges and universities now teach the history of cinema, and some offer courses in filmmaking. Many young people see the film industry as a world of opportunity for careers, if not for fame and fortune.

The wave of the future for moviemakers is, however, the videocassette revolution. More and more people are buying video recorders capable of showing movies on home television. Most movies, old and new alike, are

Jack Haley, Ray Bolger, Judy Garland, and Bert Lahr in *The Wizard of Oz*

now available on videocassettes. As retail outlets for videocassettes increase, small production companies are likely to start producing films primarily for videocassette sale. When that occurs, one of the movie industry's traditional controls may fall; no longer will major film companies act as barriers to the distribution of the films of independent producers. Also with the rapid technological advances in cameras and film stock, and with their continual reduction in price, more and more new filmmakers will be able to afford to make movies. Finally, as film schools improve, more young people are acquiring cinematic expertise, so that the talent pool is growing rapidly. These factors are likely to affect the future of the film world.

For an audience member the practical and aesthetic differences between film and theatre are many. First, going to a theatre to see a live play is necessarily more of a social event. A theatre evening requires more time and usually costs more money, whereas people now can simply stay at home to see most movies. Second, theatre is best enjoyed with other people. In fact, an audience made up of a group of people is essential to theatre. Not so for movies. Although it can be fun to see a film with a crowd, movies can be enjoyed just as well alone as with a group. Aesthetically, a film engages a person's imagination in a special way; a play involves the viewer differently. Film provides perhaps more empathy and theatre more immediacy. Certainly they are different arts, and when well produced, both are worthy of attention.

Cinema as an art has great power for mythmaking. Throughout its history, movies have created many heroes—many figures whom people have attempted to emulate. Indeed, people today in many economically disadvantaged countries come to know and perhaps to envy life in more well-developed nations through the medium of movies. The patterns of life and modes of behavior that movies display affect almost everyone in conscious and subconscious ways. From fashions to emotional attitudes, movies have undeniable power to affect the peoples of the world.

CHAPTER 20

The Business of Theatre

In the United States, theatre takes place within the economic context of capitalism. The means of production and distribution are privately owned and operated for the sake of personal profit. The market is open, presumably, and free competition prevails. Everyone has an equal chance, and the best or the cheapest products succeed—they make money. Productivity is the key to success, and money is the object of all effort. Of course, in the capitalist system, wealth and power tend to accumulate in the hands of those who have it in the first place. Today the most powerful and wealthy "individuals" in society are the enormous, financially diverse corporations. To protect individual workers, unions exist. Governments at the local, state, and national levels regulate everything and everybody. The government also enforces a system of economic adjustments, so that the poor and disadvantaged receive financial aid. Theatre companies and theatre workers in this country have to survive amidst these prevailing economic conditions; they have to make money.

Everyone in theatre faces continual financial problems. Actors, writers, and all the other theatre people have to earn a living. Theatres must somehow make enough money to meet ever-increasing expenses. Although Broadway companies try to turn a profit, most theatre groups struggle just to break even. When a hit show comes in at the highest economic level of theatre, the financial rewards are stunning. Producers, investors, stars, and everyone else make incredible amounts of money. But hits are rare, and during any year few theatre workers make it to Broadway. Most theatre workers don't make much money, and the companies that do survive face economic difficulties every day. In such an

A theatre box office

**Van Heflin and Charles
Bickford in *Casey Jones*
by Robert Ardrey**

atmosphere of penury and pressure, theatre people have to pay attention to business.

COSTS, BUDGETS, AND FUNDING

What does the drive for money do to theatre as art? Financial concerns in the theatre often come to control both the process and the product. In fact, with many companies the product to be sold becomes more important than the process of creation. As the foregoing chapters have explained, the co-creative process of theatre is the chief reason for its existence. The process of preparing and playing a drama or a musical is more experiential than productive. Theatre at its best is not primarily an object to be bought and sold; it's a system of experience both for the artists and their audiences. Art isn't art for the sake of consumption. When the money motive invades the realm of creativity, art tends to disappear.

In every country and in every age haven't theatres needed money to survive? Of course they have. Yet, the problem nowadays is that show business tends to overwhelm dramatic art. Although every play is meant somehow to be entertaining, people come to think that entertainment is all-important. Too many people believe theatre is supposed to provide a pleasant diversion instead of an intense life experience, whether serious or comic. Of course, most art theatres today are nonprofit organizations and thus escape the normal rate of corporate taxes. But every play that reaches the stage costs something, and every person who works in the theatre has to eat. Money—and lots of it—is a necessity.

Although every theatre production anywhere is expensive, professional theatre on Broadway costs the most. Broadway productions are the most expensive in the world—both to generate and to attend. On January 15, 1984, the *New York Times* stated that the cost of producing *Kean*, a show with only one actor, in London was $30,000, whereas in New York it cost $150,000. According to the same *New York Times* article, the elaborate musical *Cats* cost $1.1 million in London, but $5.3 million in New York.

A production number in *Evita*

Most Broadway productions range in cost from a quarter of a million to $3 million. In 1985 single ticket prices ran as high as $45 for musicals and $37.50 for straight plays, and in 1986 they were going higher.

CONNECTIONS

Why does it cost so much? Most experts answer "labor costs," but the cost of money (interest on loans) and excessive profit-taking are also factors. Perhaps the most elusive condition of all is how many different pockets the Broadway dollar must fill. The following budget items for the production of *Kean* reveal some of the problems.

Partial Weekly Expenses for *Kean**

Theatre rental	$10,000
Star's salary	12,500
Business manager	1,250
Stage manager	1,000
Press agent	914
Box office manager	670
Stage carpenter	658
Curtain man	549
Wig keeper	500

**New York Times,* January 15, 1984, sec. 2, pp. 1 and 25.

Not all stars demand so much money for appearing on Broadway, and some even work for minimum in order to help a production survive. For example, Al Pacino acted in *American Buffalo* for actors' union minimum salary of $610 per week.

Some producers say production costs are high because of Broadway expectations. New York audiences, so the argument goes, expect the best from a Broadway show. The result is more elaborate scenery and technical support for all presentations. For instance, no straight play is presented on Broadway with less than several hundred lighting instruments, and musicals have three times that many. Every production that takes the stage in one of the 30 or so Broadway theatres is very costly, and the chances of a profitable return are slight indeed. The income for a Broadway show is strictly cash receipts from ticket sales; the production companies are not diversified corporations with multiple revenue structures. Most shows do not earn back their investments, let alone make money. Thus, Broadway theatre is a major financial gamble for extremely high stakes. In such a situation it's amazing that art takes place at all. Broadway shows and their touring companies are the largest theatre-for-profit organizations in the country.

Some people blame unions for the high costs and high prices of Broadway, but others blame ticket sellers, investors, producers, or theatre owners. Unions undoubtedly serve their members in useful ways, or they would not continue to exist. No doubt the economic interests of unions have helped push production costs upward, but unions alone are not responsible for the upward spiral of costs. A number of unions provide services to the artists and technicians who work in professional theatre and film. Appendix I describes the seven most dominant unions in the worlds of theatre, film, television, and radio. All professional theatre unions have entry requirements, initiation fees, and annual dues, and all of them periodically negotiate higher salaries or improved benefits for their members. Most unions have useful publications that are available to associate members or outsiders for a fee. Normally, if asked, each union will provide useful informative materials about its operation.

Other profit-making ventures in the theatre world are some summer theatres and most dinner theatre operations. Nearly all production budgets for single shows in these theatres are below $50,000, and many shows get staged for a lot less. The lion's share of the costs in these theatres goes to salaries. Although there are theatres in which people make livings, not many producers get rich running those companies. Such theatres make money to operate from the box office and also from sales of food and refreshments.

Professional repertory theatres are for the most part nonprofit companies. Compared with the million dollar budgets of Broadway shows, the cost of individual productions in repertory theatres is small indeed, Still, the annual budgets for the many fine theatres across the country are usually sizable. Their nonprofit status simply gives them some tax relief and indicates that no one is making more than a salary from their operation. Professional repertory theatres must pay union salaries for all services and labor. Often these theatres depend on gifts from corporate and private donors in order to survive financially. Most repertory theatres have budgets ranging from $1 million to $10 million. For most, about half of their operating budget comes from sources other than box office.

Most alternative theatres, some repertory theatres, and many summer stock theatres are semiprofessional. That normally means that the theatres do not use many, if any, union actors or workers. Although in major cities, such as New York, Chicago, and Los Angeles, Actors Equity Association (the actors' union) permits waiver appearances. In such cases, actors appear in plays for less than the normal minimum wages so that they can help their careers by being seen. Most of the people who work in semiprofessional theatres are paid a minimal amount. Such theatres usually have some volunteer or apprentice labor. Some of these theatres

Balm in Gilead by Lanford Wilson, Phoenix Theatre, Indianapolis

are associated with a university. For example, the Asolo Theatre in Sarasota is administratively connected with Florida State University. The budgets for each production in theatres such as these vary greatly and range from about $10,000 a production to more than $50,000. These theatres get their operating money from the box office and perhaps from associated institutions. Most alternative theatre organizations in the major cities last only a short time, normally two to five years. Most outdoor theatres are also semiprofessional. They pay good salaries for theatre people who wish to work for a summer season.

Many universities and colleges offer elaborate theatre productions to their communities, and their production budgets are surprisingly large. Most college theatres don't have to pay salaries from box office receipts. The parent institution pays the requisite salaries of faculty directors, designers, and shop supervisors. Students make up most of the labor force, working voluntarily or for course credit. Small college production budgets for a season of plays range from $10,000 to $50,000. Medium-sized institutions have seasonal production budgets in the range of $50,000 to $100,000, and large universities almost always have season-long budgets far above the latter figure. Funding in universities varies, too. Occasionally, they provide their theatre departments with some production funds, but more often the departments must generate their own income for productions through ticket sales, grants, or gifts. In some schools, a portion of the student activity fee is given to the theatre department in exchange for free student admission. In most cases, however, universities and colleges have a good deal of money to spend on the technical aspects of production.

Many other organizations operate amateur theatres, but they, too, must worry about finances. Civic and community theatres vary in size and economic strength. Some civic theatres have large budgets of several hundred thousand dollars, and these groups usually hire a professional staff. Volunteers, however, run most community theatres, and their production budgets run from a few hundred to several thousand dollars. Most high schools sponsor theatre productions as well. Sometimes they spend surprising amounts of money, and in some cases they make it back at the box office. Most high school productions, though, receive financial support from the system's operating budget, and they do not make back their expenses.

In other countries, theatre financing occurs in a variety of ways. Many national governments subsidize theatres. In fact, most European countries point with pride to the national funding of major theatre troupes. England, for example, subsidizes a number of theatre organizations, including the National Theatre and the Royal Shakespeare companies. In Germany, even local municipalities sometimes sponsor their own professional theatres. Most European countries also have independent companies that depend upon ticket sales and gifts for their financial liveli-

And a Nightingale Sang
by C. P. Taylor, Indiana University-Purdue University at Indianapolis

389

hood. The same countries have fewer semiprofessional and amateur theatres per capita than the United States, and entrance into theatre professions overseas is much less open. In socialist countries, most theatres are state supported, but these countries have relatively few theatres.

CONNECTIONS

THE BUSINESS STAFF

The business process is as important to a production as the artistic process, and for the continuing life of a theatre company it assumes even more importance. Before any work can happen in the theatre, money has to be raised. In early planning, finances affect many of the artistic decisions. As a staff chooses a show or maps out a season, they have to pay attention to numerous business matters. They must be sure the selected plays can be designed and built within the budgetary limitations. If the working staff would not be able to handle the construction tasks, then more labor must be hired. Performance scheduling makes a difference, too. The staff must find an appropriate play for a particular time of year, and it must set openings on advantageous dates. Soon after a play is selected for presentation, budgets must be established before planning and purchasing begin. All supplies, salaries, and services together must not exceed the established financial limits. Uneconomical spending can wreck a theatre. Finally, someone must promote, publicize, and sell tickets to the production. That activity, too, helps determine a play's success. So the whole process of funding, budgeting, purchasing, and selling a play are crucial to its life.

A theatre staff is made up of several groups. The managerial group consists of a producer and his immediate associates, including the business manager; sometimes this group amounts to an artistic director and a managing director. The artistic staff consists of one or more directors, designers, and technical supervisors. On the office staff are secretaries, accountants, and clerical personnel. The house staff has a house manager, box office agents, and ushers. Finally, the maintenance group includes engineers and custodians necessary for the upkeep of the building. Also a theatre may have an advisory staff of lawyers and public-

Above: Producer David Merrick

Right: Producers Bernie Jacobs (left), Nelle Nugent, and Gerald Schoenfeld (right) of the Shubert Organization, with author David Elgar (second from right) accept Tony Awards for _Nicholas Nickleby_

relations experts.

In the world of theatre, a producer is in charge of everything. In fact, a producer usually conceives it all in the first place. Initially, the producer must find a property, a play he or she can believe in. Producers want one that is original but won't stretch audiences too far, a quality piece that is also commercial, and one not hard to cast or mount but easy to promote. Sometimes Broadway producers find a play in a repertory theatre, Off Off Broadway, overseas, or even in manuscript. Then they must raise the money, no easy task in today's tight-fisted society. Next they have to assemble a good business staff and a skilled creative group—especially an experienced director and a talented cast. They must mastermind the entire constructive process, oversee everyone's work, and remain in charge for the run of the show. In the non-Broadway theatre, someone must assume the same duties, although in many groups the responsibilities are divided. For example, in professional repertory theatres an artistic director and a managing director often share the producer's function. But usually in the American theatre system, the intelligence and personality of one person—the producer—holds an entire theatre company together.

A managing director, or business manager, and the rest of the "front office" staff look after the budget, accounting, purchasing, payments, personnel records, and ticket sales. Although these matters have more connection with regular business practices than with artistic creativity, they are nonetheless essential factors in theatre operation. Many intelligent and hard-working people in these positions make theatre possible. All people in the artistic realms of theatre depend mightily on the industry, honesty, and wisdom of the business people. Some of a theatre's most important budgetary items are:

CONNECTIONS

Producer Joseph Papp

Salaries	Programs
Scenery	Tickets
Lighting	Taxes
Properties	Utilities
Costumes	Maintenance
Music and musicians	Theatre rental or
Scripts	mortgage payments
Royalties	Reserve fund
Advertising and publicity	Miscellaneous
Box office operation	(petty cash, etc.)

Many theatres operate under the general control of a board of directors. Boards are supposedly composed of men and women experienced in business, the arts, or both. Such groups fulfill many useful functions. Their expertise comes into play at the very origin of a theatre company. They help with organization, fund raising, and staff selection. A board of directors operates thereafter as an advisory group, to which the working management is responsible. A board usually gathers four times a year, and its executive committee meets more often. In regular meetings they review reports from the operating staff, help solve current problems, and consider future plans. The best theatre boards depend on the artistic director to establish the creative vision of the organization, but they offer business advice and long-term continuity to any theatre company.

SELLING THEATRE

To sell a series of productions in any community, a theatre company needs to have two things—good productions and effective organization. Well-staged plays alone won't fill the seats. In modern society, too many other people are after the public's entertainment dollars. Therefore, theatres have to develop careful organizations to promote their productions and sell their tickets. Experts in the business world have long realized the need of facts for successful marketing, and sophisticated theatre organizations now carry out audience-research projects, using polls and questionnaires to investigate the nature of their audiences. They also seek marketing advice from experts. For example, the Theatre Communications Group in New York helps repertory theatres plan audience research and promotional campaigns. Every theatre has a public image, and its promotional staff can keep it positive and well known. Also, good organization is responsible for keeping regular spectators, attracting new ones, and importing large groups. Finally, most theatre people now recognize that some sort of subscription campaign is essential for establishing an audience, and some type of gift campaign is necessary for balancing the annual budget.

Without volunteers and auxiliary organizations many American theatres would not long survive. Most professional repertory companies, many summer theatres, and all university and civic groups utilize volunteers. Every community contains many people willing and eager to help with phoning, mailing, and running the box office. Except for Broadway, ushers usually work voluntarily for free admission to see the show. Auxiliary organizations are made up of interested people who wish to help theatre groups over a long period of time, and they certainly contribute in many ways. Most important, they help circulate news about the productions and make theatre attendance socially attractive. Fre-

Lloyd Richards, Artistic Director of the Yale Repertory Theatre and of the National Playwrights Conference at the O'Neill Center

quently they assist with season ticket campaigns and fund-raising drives. These useful organizations provide a pool of volunteers for all sorts of jobs, such as meeting stars at airports, hosting receptions, and hunting up unusual stage properties. Volunteers of all ages love to work in the theatre, and most theatres could ill afford to get along without them.

For a theatre to have a continuing existence, it depends on good promotion and public relations. Promotion means working for a theatre's long-term reputation and involves attracting the attention of groups of people who might attend together or as individuals. Public relations means gaining the attention of society at large. Often theatres hire a specialist to handle promotion and public relations. Promotional activities include the development of season brochures, the presentation of luncheon or evening programs to other organizations, and the sale of ticket blocks. Public-relations activities are devoted to getting the name of the theatre and its artists before the public. For example, public-relations experts are able to get actors and playwrights on television talk shows, and they manage to develop news stories that don't seem to be advertisements.

Only through publicity does a theatre's audience come to know about its productions. Somehow business managers and their staffs must let potential audience members know the what, when, and where of each production. They can communicate the information in various ways. Most theatres pay for advertisements in newspapers, on television, and on radio. Many groups also utilize posters, although posters are not highly regarded as publicity devices. Sometimes cafe cards are placed in restaurants. Perhaps the most effective means of publicity is direct mail to regular or prospective audience members. Every theatre tries to develop a good mailing list and keep it up to date. Ultimately, the best publicity about any particular production is by word of mouth, which can happen before and during the run of a show. Word-of-mouth publicity prior to the opening of a show comes best from theatre auxiliary groups, but once a show opens, it takes care of itself. For fine productions audiences always tend to grow larger over the course of a run because positive word of mouth is the best possible publicity.

Another way theatres have always attracted attention is through the use of stars or other celebrities. Well-known actors always fascinate people, and for attracting audiences to the theatre the more well known the better. Professional theatre utilizes stars for two reasons. Their very names attract audiences. And most of them are particularly good at their art, or else they wouldn't be stars. On Broadway, producers want one or more stars in a production because their names help attract investors and later bring audiences to the box office. Other large professional organizations and many summer theatres also depend on the drawing power of stars. Of course, not all well-known actors are genuine stars. Some so-called stars, especially those from other media, can't act very well on the stage in a live situation. Theatres also utilize other celebrities for publicity purposes. For example, a well-known playwright, director, or designer can help attract attention to a production. Even on the local level, talented people come to be known in a community, and their

**George C. Scott and
Maureen Stapleton in
Plaza Suite by Neil
Simon**

presence in a show helps attract that particular audience. The careful
use of celebrity is a major tool for promoting theatre.

ECONOMIC ISSUES

Contemporary theatre artists face many financial difficulties, and the
economic issues behind their problems are worth some thought. Society
is becoming more and more specialized, technology more and more
expensive, and so theatres have to face increasing budgets. No company
in any business survives easily in today's competitive marketplace, and
because so much of theatre's labor is done by hand, it is less competitive
than most. Building maintenance, utilities, and custodial labor alone have
put some theatres out of business. The materials for sets and costumes
cost more than ever, not to mention the price of the latest dimmer boards,
lighting instruments, and sound equipment. Theatre workers must have
salary increases, too, and union demands drive them up annually. The
key economic question is clear. In the face of current financial pressures,
how is artistic theatre going to survive?

There are some answers about theatre's survival. One solution is to
present a greater number of commercially appealing shows. Many of
American producers are apparently trying this solution, and their efforts

appear among the shows that were running on and off Broadway in April 1985 and February 1986.

| | Broadway | | Off Broadway | |
	1985	1986	1985	1986
Musicals	15	13	12	10
Comedies	7	11	11	12
Dramas	4	6	8	8
Total	26	30	31	30

Just because musicals have commercial appeal doesn't mean they are artless, but neither are they automatically successful. Still, the dominance of musical productions and the relative lack of serious plays indicates the difficulty of maintaining an artistic theatre in American society.

Many observers have suggested that the United States should follow the example of European nations and establish subsidies for the arts. In fact, American government at all levels already supports the arts in general and theatre in particular. The federal government provides some money through the National Endowment for the Arts. The amount, however, is tiny by comparison with appropriations for other agencies, and as pressure rises for tax cuts and the balancing of the federal budget, the amount that the federal government designates for the arts appears to be diminishing. At present the federal government allows nonprofit theatres a tax-exempt status, which helps a lot. It also makes annual financial appropriations to state arts commissions, but again the amounts are so small and the artists so many that hardly anyone benefits enough to really make a difference. All the states provide money for the arts. Those with the foresight to realize that theatres raise cultural standards give money to repertory theatres and outdoor theatres, hoping to attract tourists and new industry. State aid to the arts is also channeled through universities; thus, state funds help support many college and university theatres plus their associated semiprofessional companies. A few municipal governments help assist local theatres, but the number doing so changes with each election. Yes, American government supports the arts—but not nearly enough.

Subsidies from the corporate and private sectors of society are another source of support for theatre. Fortunately, one result of capitalism has been the creation of philanthropic foundations, such as the Ford and the Guggenheim. They often help fund theatre companies and make grants available to individual artists. Some foundations, such as the Pulitzer, give annual prizes. In addition to the famous foundations, many smaller ones exist, and each year throughout the nation they give a great deal of money to the arts. Individual citizens also help with donations ranging from a few dollars to many thousands of dollars. Without this sort of private support, most theatres would have great difficulty surviving at all. Unfortunately, the amount of foundation support remains about the same over a period of years, while theater budgets keep increasing. Most

CONNECTIONS

Producer Craig Anderson

economists and cultural observers think that in the future more of the nation's successful corporations will need to help the arts financially. Without a future increase in aid, theatres are likely to become economically weaker and weaker.

Most people fail to realize that the theatre programs in colleges and universities amount to America's most elaborate subsidized theatre system. Six hundred or more of these theatres provide a repertory of classical and modern plays to communities throughout the nation. They provide a place for many theatre professionals to practice their art. Not all talented theatre artists work in New York or even in professional repertory theatres; many good directors, designers, actors, and writers make a living doing their creative work alongside students. American universities are the Medici of the age in the sense that they provide the means for so many artists to practice their art. Naturally the range of talent and expertise in theatre faculties varies greatly; some college theatre teachers are excellent at their job and others far less so. Nevertheless, the institutions of higher education must be recognized for what they are—strong supporters of theatre. University theatre departments are not, of course, simply havens for creative artists; they also provide communities and generations of students with opportunities to see the world's greatest plays, and many fine scholars in such departments diligently work to uncover and preserve treasures of information about the past. The cul-

The Federal Theatre production of *One-Third of a Nation,* a living newspaper.

tural impact of university theatre departments in this country is truly remarkable.

A final economic issue that may interest many readers of this book is the question of theatre as a career. What are the prospects, for example, of a college student who considers making a career in the theatre? Do college and university theatre departments justify their existence by turning out young professionals ready to go to work? All such questions tend to oversimplify the problems, and answers to them are necessarily general. Many college students do choose the theatre as a profession, and they begin serious study during their undergraduate years. After graduation, a few talented students enter the professional theatre immediately. But a majority of the hopefuls discover they need more training and experience before they can compete in the professional world. A great many decide they don't want to live in New York or another metropolitan center, and so they help create energetic semiprofessional or amateur theatre elsewhere. Furthermore, a theatre major is as good as any other major in a university for providing a young person with a liberal education. Not all theatre majors can or should go into theatre as a profession. But no one with genuine talent needs to be frightened by the prospect. The theatre provides many places to work in various cities. Those students who have genuine talent and the grit to follow through with it can and will make a place for themselves.

If the economic prospects for theatre are so grim, what is the hope for the future? Will theatre die? No way! It will survive. In every age, theatre people have always lived on the edge of disaster. It is no profession for the timid. It will survive, but it could use some help. Theatre always casts a marvelous spell on a community. Sometimes it scares people or offends them, but sometimes, too, it makes them laugh or cry. Above all, drama makes everyone see further into human existence, and it exercises a strange power over people. It intensifies their experience. This special magic that theatre arouses is worth more than any community can pay, and so theatre people have faith that support will always come from . . . somewhere.

CONNECTIONS

Children learning about theatre through participation

21 *Theatre in Society*

People do not live by bread alone. Besides food, human beings need warmth, light, water, sex, and sleep. Even those physical requirements aren't all a person needs. People also need ideas. In order to live, everyone must know the necessities of survival and how to satisfy them. Without ideas to live by, life would be perilous and empty. And what about feelings? What kind of monsters do people become without them? Ideas and feelings help people penetrate their physical experiences and make meaning in life. The theatre is a place where people can come together and share intense feelings, ideas, and experiences. The foolishness of Shakespeare's clowns in *Twelfth Night*, the decision of Ibsen's Nora in *A Doll's House*, or the groping energy of Sam Shepard's lovers in *Fool for Love*—to witness such things is to see more deeply into life.

Art is a necessity in human society, not a frill. It is more than decoration or entertainment. Even if some government made rules against the fine arts, people would still create. They would whistle, hum, and sing. Without oil paints, they might use berry stains to make pictures on cave walls. If sculpture and architecture were forbidden, children would still make castles in the sand, and their parents would try to create the best shelter possible. Then when people would gather in groups, somebody would naturally start to dance, and others would happily join in. Off to the side, some oldster would probably start telling tales, maybe even in rhyme. Eventually somebody would start to act the stories out, and everybody would turn to watch. People cannot do without the arts, and this concluding chapter offers a few reminders about the necessities of art and the basics of theatre.

VISION

Vision in art refers to the life perceptions of artists as reflected in their work. Vision means how a person sees, both physically and intellectually—how a person looks at the external world and comprehends it. An artist's vision includes the entire complex of personal attitudes and beliefs about existence. A playwright reveals vision in a drama in the actions and the speeches of the characters. For example, the Greek tragedian Aeschylus saw the world as a place where divine justice works itself out. Writers' vision gives them ideas to express and words to speak. In order to make art of high quality, a playwright needs to have something to say and attitudes about how to say it. The same is true of directors, designers, and actors.

Artistic vision is both conceptual and aesthetic. That means every artist

***Buried Child* by Sam
Shepard, Magic Theatre**

has philosophic thoughts about the world and artistic ideas about how
to make a work of art. A playwright, for example, thinks about such
matters as the nature of human existence, the influence of economics
on politics, or the violence often performed in the name of love. He might
make a play to illustrate or communicate his thoughts. Also, individual
artists' aesthetic attitudes affect their work. Aesthetic attitudes are the
ideas artists have about making an art object. As artists work, their prior
experience comes in to play. With every project, artists must decide what
to create and how to create it; thus, every work reveals by its very nature
the artist's aesthetic vision.

Vision in a theatrical performance is more complicated than in a poem or a painting. The complexity arises because theatre is a social art. In a live drama a number of people join their visions. A dramatist makes a play of a certain kind, exhibiting a particular view of life and revealing his vision. As in any literary work, the vision of a play can be discerned in a printed version, but a play is only partially realized until it is brought to life by actors, designers, technicians, and a director. The visions of all these people are in some measure combined with that of the playwright, and their vision makes a great difference in the nature of any drama.

CONNECTIONS

Each spectator also has a vision of life, and a given drama may clash or harmonize with it, but in every case true art expands that individual's vision. If a performance doesn't much affect a spectator's vision, then boredom sets in. Of course, a viewer can disagree with details of the philosophic or artistic vision of the performance, but in our time mental confrontation is an apparent necessity for art. Genuine art almost always expands the vision of any spectator. When art operates at full power, somehow artists and spectators meet and join visions; indeed, artists are often called visionaries.

Craftsmanship alone does not make art. Artists definitely need to be skilled at their craft, but when pieces are merely crafted, when items project no vision at all, they fail to affect anyone's inner spirit. True artists—writers, designers, directors, actors—have specially developed ways to express their vision. The quality of an artist's vision profoundly

***The Tempest* by William Shakespeare, The Guthrie Theatre**

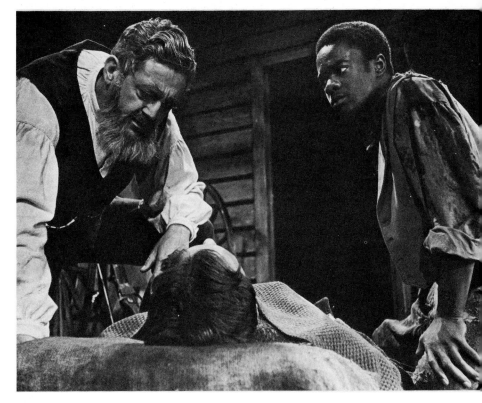

Right: *Harpers Ferry* **by Barrie Stavis, The Guthrie Theatre**

Below: *Picnic* **by William Inge, Brown County Playhouse**

affects the value of the art objects or performances he or she creates. Genius in the world of art begins with vision and extends to craftsmanship. The degree to which an artist becomes a visionary, one who sees into life in a special way, controls the quality of the work produced. Innovators, originators, and geniuses are not the only artists of value, but they are the ones with special powers of vision that make their artworks more dynamic and thus more stimulating. Vision begins as an experience of an artist, who extends it into an artwork and ultimately projects it in such a way that it affects the experience of a viewer.

ACTION

The major circumstance of all theatre is human experience, and the key principle of all drama is human action. By dramatizing human experiences, playwrights draw the attention of a community to certain characters, revealing their fears and dreams, their mistakes and successes, and their joys and deaths. To see what one person experiences helps others to understand what they might experience. Any character is

C O N N E C T I O N S

The Road by Wole Soyinka, The Goodman Theatre

worthy of interest for a while, but for a play to hold the interest of intelligent men and women for very long something must happen. A drama that lasts for more than half an hour needs to show something going on. That's where action comes in. Action is a pattern of human experience, a series of experiences wound together, and it usually shows people changing. Without action there is not much drama in a play, and life is exactly the same.

The clearest sort of action occurs whenever somebody tries to do something. Inaction involves nothing but sitting around. Passive characters do not care, do not try, and do not do anything. Such characters might be worth a look, but they are not worth an hour or two. Hamlet takes action when he attempts to find out if the Ghost told the truth, when he tries to catch the King, and when he struggles to get revenge. Action takes over Romeo and Juliet when they fall in love and try to get together. The miser Harpagon in Molière's play strives as hard as he can to keep his money. Willy Loman in *Death of a Salesman* tries to discover what went wrong and what he can do to help his sons succeed. Action lies at the heart of every great play.

Drama at its best explores the potentials of human action. Some plays demonstrate the obsessions of certain characters as they struggle against overwhelming forces—for example, *Oedipus the King*, *Macbeth*, and *The Cherry Orchard*. Other dramas depict people wrestling with evil—as in

Medea, Othello, and *The Wild Duck*. Still other plays show people doing ridiculous things—for example, *A Midsummer Night's Dream, The Miser*, or *Arms and the Man*. The action of many plays is clear, as in *Hamlet*, but in other plays, as in *Uncle Vanya*, the action is hidden. Drama demonstrates action or hints at it, but in plays that hold an audience it is always there. Action in dramas makes them compelling for a length of time; without it people get up and leave. Ultimately, action in the theatre helps people understand the values of action in life.

PAST, PRESENT, FUTURE

In all art—the theatre is no exception—value adheres to both the old and the new. In common language, the best of the old has stood the test of time and has become classic, and the best of the new is original, pertinent, up to date, and popular. For every artist who has a high degree of awareness, one of the serious problems of creativity is the balancing of the old and the new. Each artist must utilize some of the principles of the past. Every director, for example, marshals visual, auditory, and internal stimuli in time-proven ways, although some directors use the best of the universal principles more consciously or perhaps more skillfully than others. But for art of high order, each artist must also introduce some factors of originality. In one sense, genius in art is judged as the ability to devise new principles and new techniques. No innovative genius

Ethel Barrymore (right) in *Captain Jinks of the Horse Marines* by Clyde Fitch

can be fully original until he or she knows what has gone before; so the best artists are likely to be well informed and have good insight into the art of the past.

Theatre of the past is difficult to study, not because there are no good theatre historians to collect and present facts, but because theatre is such a temporal art. It exists fully only during performances, and thereafter it persists only as images in the memories of witnesses. Thus, the theatre of times gone by must be studied through written facts and opinions, and even the best historians can only report informed hints about what some artist or performance was like. Still, without the work of theatre scholars today's theatre would not be so well wrought, so inventive, or so fresh.

The creative accomplishments of all theatre artists are difficult to comprehend. Actors of the past are hard to evaluate because the work of all stage actors is so temporal; it does not last. Of course, some actors appear in films, but the nature of stage performance is very different in style. Film acting usually demands relatively less inner transformation and not much projection from an actor. Therefore, the first-hand reports of viewers and the personal thoughts of actors themselves are the main sources of information about actors of bygone days. Photographs and graphic renderings, however, provide a clear and faithful record of the work of scenic designers and costumers of other times. The play script preserves the work of the playwright most thoroughly, but no one can fully understand or appreciate a play in its totality until it comes to life on a stage. The work of a theatre director is perhaps the most ephemeral of all. How a director envisioned a performance, evoked particular portrayals from various artists, and put all the pieces together—all this work is not particularly apparent to spectators. Therefore, the study of directors of the past is perhaps the most difficult of all.

Although theatre is best studied alive, many fine books relate the facts and the spirit of history. A selected list of such volumes appears in this book's bibliography. The theatre performances of the past are irretrievable as living events, but to read about the world's great performers and to study the plays that have survived helps one to recreate the best of the old. Also many old plays survive today and are staged again and again, so that the creativity of other times comes to life once more in contemporary productions.

In order to know and understand the theatre of the present, one can start with the perspective of the past, but nothing can substitute for direct experience. The more live plays one sees, the deeper is one's awareness, and the more different kinds of theatres one attends, the wider one's understanding. "The Theatre" is not singular; it is unpredictably plural. American theatre, for example, does not exist on Broadway alone, or just in New York, or in professional theatres only. Live theatre is available nearly everywhere in the United States, and all the productions of all theatres from Broadway shows to local high school productions, from professional repertory performances to summer stock presentations, together make up today's theatre. Some traditions persist, and new ones constantly arise. But it is possible to tell the difference. An observer must

Hemingway **by Sam Smiley, Indiana University**

look for what is truly original in the subject matter, the unity, and the style of a given production. What sort of performance is it meant to be, and in what ways does it live up to expectations or change them? A study of materials, organization, and style always reveals the true nature of an artwork, the degree to which it is derivative or original.

Audiences, however, take joy in the familiar as well as in the original. People take genuine pleasure in hearing a song that is an old favorite, and so do they respond in theatre. There is pleasure in seeing the work of a familiar playwright as he attacks new subject matter, or in the performance of a favorite actor in a new play, or in the innovative staging by a familiar director of an old play. The new may also produce a thoroughly different experience. Theatre often probes new psychological states or emotional experiences. One may even be shocked by the vibrant strangeness of an artist's materials, vision, or craft. The kinds of theatre available today are nearly as diverse as the experiences of human life. Attending many theatre productions, one need not admire them all, endure them all, or even remember them all. But every production has the potential for providing insight into life, for stimulating pleasure, and for producing a peak experience. The magic of life is always there somewhere in every theatre, just waiting to be discovered.

No one can accurately predict exactly what forms the theatre may take in the future or what styles it may exhibit. Humans naturally seem to enjoy contemplating what the future holds. Artists frequently tend to pay the most attention to their present work, but they labor toward the future, especially in self-development and in planning new works. For each artist, as for everyone else, the future is problematic. Some playwrights, for example, wish to write only about their own time, and they are willing to examine the sort of problems, handle the type of people, and use the kind of language that have little chance of enduring. Other writers carefully compose their plays to insure as much as possible the endurance of their work. But most playwrights, like most other artists, produce the best work they can, hoping it may have an impact on people in their own time as well as in the future. Every artist, then, somehow faces the problem of the future.

CONNECTIONS

THE NECESSITY OF THEATRE

Occasionally people question the very future of theatre itself, wondering about or even predicting its slow demise. They usually point to statistics on how many more people buy movie tickets than theatre seats; or they speculate about how many hours the average person watches television, arguing that television has replaced the theatre as an entertainment necessity. Broadway is shrinking, they say; movies are more popular; and television is on for about seven hours a day in most people's homes. None of those facts has much relevance to the existence or

Playwright Athol Fugard (left) directs his play *Master Harold . . . and the Boys*, Yale Repertory Theatre

persistence of theatre. Even to argue about the financial difficulties of Broadway, the cinematic entertainment industry, or the companionship factor of television is to miss the point of theatre completely.

Theatre—like other fine arts such as music, dance, and painting—has existed in some guise in most human societies, and the more well developed the society, the more well developed their theatre has become. Fine art persists because people want to make fine art; artists want to occupy themselves with it. Whatever fascinating, well-crafted, startling

***Peer Gynt* by Henrik Ibsen, The Guthrie Theatre**

worlds that theatre people produce, others want to see. Some people realize how much richer life can be because of multiple contacts with art, and others never find out.

Theatre persists first because certain people want to write, act, design, and direct. The most significant need art fulfills is not to generate products for a market but rather to occupy the human potential for creativity. Theatre of a high level of artistry exists today throughout the country and the world; indeed, play-leasing companies report that more performances of more plays are now being given than ever before. Insofar as the future is concerned, theatre of a high level of artistry will no doubt persist as long as there are people capable of creating art at a high level. Financial profits, quantity of production, or widespread popularity matter far less than the creative experience itself.

The most imaginative people in any society will continue in the future as they have in the past to produce fine art, and the most sensitive people in every society will pay attention to that art. Just as music, poetry, and painting will flourish in the future, so will theatre.

Theatre and the other fine arts grow ever more necessary in human society, ever more crucial to human survival. In some respects people do not need art, not biologically or politically, but in other respects people cannot do without it. Because in every segment of human society so many people are involved in the process of creativity, people evidently need the activity of art and the beauty of it. The world would be difficult to imagine without songs, celebrations, stories, decorations, or performances. Creativity is a significant humanizing process. By testing deeds, thoughts, and ideas in a crucible of action, drama examines human behavior and provides insights about human values. Drama is not an animal necessity, but it is a human one. The amount of artistic endeavor in most societies is indicative of the long history and unceasing persistence of the arts. Theatre has earned its place in the world's cultural life, a place as permanent or as precarious as the survival of humankind itself.

Drama as a fine art persists year after year on the strength of the people devoted to creating it, enjoying it, or studying it. Theatre happens in a startling variety of places, in widely differing modes, and for countless reasons. People produce more drama today than ever before in the history of the world—from the National Theatre in London to a university theatre in Iowa City, with a play by Shakespeare or one by a new young playwright, featuring a great actor or a student. Drama lives on in regular theatres and also thrives in high school gyms, outdoor amphitheatres, grand auditoriums, noisy restaurants, barns, and even the streets. Theatre art endures in the very lives of human beings.

Bibliography,
Appendix,
Photo Credits

Books About Creating or Responding to Theatre

Appia, Adolphe. *The Work of Living Art and Man Is the Measure of All Things.* Coral Gables, Fla.: Miami University Press, 1960.

Aristotle's Poetics. Trans. S. H. Butcher. New York: Hill & Wang, 1961.

Artaud, Antonin. *The Theatre and Its Double.* Trans. Mary C. Richards. New York: Grove Press, 1958.

Bay, Howard. *Stage Design.* New York: Drama Book Specialists, 1974.

Bellman, Willard F. *Lighting the Stage: Art and Practice.* 2d ed. San Francisco: Chandler Publishing Co., 1974.

————. *Scene Design, Stage Lighting, Sound, Costume & Makeup: A Scenographic Approach.* New York, Harper & Row, 1983.

Benedetti, Robert L. *The Actor at Work.* Englewood Cliffs, N.J.: Prentice-Hall, 1976.

Bentley, Eric. *The Life of the Drama.* New York: Atheneum, 1964.

Blunt, Jerry. *The Composite Art of Acting.* New York: Macmillan, 1966.

Bobker, Lee R. *Elements of Film.* 2d ed. New York: Harcourt Brace Jovanovich, 1974.

Brecht, Bertolt. *Brecht on Theatre.* Trans. John Willett. New York: Hill & Wang, 1965.

Brook, Peter. *The Empty Space.* New York: Atheneum, 1968.

Brustein, Robert. *Revolution as Theatre: Notes on the New Radical Style.* New York: Liveright, 1971.

Burdick, Elizabeth B., et al., eds., *Contemporary Stage Design.* Middletown, Conn.: Wesleyan University Press, 1975.

Burian, Jarka, *The Scenography of Josef Svoboda.* Middletown, Conn.: Wesleyan University Press, 1971.

Burris-Meyer, Harold, and Edward C. Cole. *Scenery for the Theatre.* 2d rev. ed. Boston: Little, Brown, 1972.

————. *Theatres and Auditoriums.* 2d ed. New York: Van Nostrand Reinhold, 1964.

Camus, Albert. *The Rebel: An Essay on Man in Revolt.* Trans. Anthony Bower. New York: Knopf, 1956.

Casty, Alan. *The Dramatic Art of the Film.* New York: Harper & Row, 1971.

Chaikin, Joseph. *The Presence of the Actor.* New York: Atheneum, 1974.

Champlin, Charles. *The Movies Grow Up 1940–1980.* Athens, Ohio: Ohio University Press, 1981.

Chekhov, Michael. *To the Actor: On the Technique of Acting.* New York: Harper & Row, 1953.

Clark, Barrett H., ed. *European Theories of the Drama.* Rev. ed. New York: Crown Publishers, 1947.

Clurman, Harold. *On Directing.* New York: Macmillan, 1972.

Cohen, Robert, and John Harrop. *Creative Play Direction.* Englewood Cliffs, N.J.: Prentice-Hall, 1974.

Cole, Toby, ed. *Playwrights on Playwriting.* New York: Hill & Wang, 1961.

————, and Helen K. Chinoy, eds. *Actors on Acting: The Theories, Techniques, and Practices of the Great Actors of All Times as Told in Their Own Words.* New York: Crown Publishers, 1954.

————. *Directors on Directing.* Rev. ed. New York: Macmillan, 1963.

Corson, Richard. *Stage Make-up.* 5th ed. Englewood Cliffs, N.J.: Prentice-Hall, 1975.

Craig, Edward Gordon. *On the Art of the Theatre.* 2d ed. Boston: Small, Maynard, 1924.

Croce, Benedetto. *Guide to Aesthetics.* Trans. Patrick Romanell. New York: Macmillan, 1965.

Dean, Alexander. *Fundamentals of Play Directing.* 3d ed., rev. by Lawrence Carra. New York: Holt, Rinehart and Winston, 1974.

Goldman, Michael. *The Actor's Freedom: Toward a Theory of Drama.* New York: Viking, 1975.

Grotowski, Jerzy. *Towards a Poor Theatre.* New York: Simon & Schuster, 1968.

Guthrie, Tyrone. *A New Theatre.* New York: McGraw-Hill, 1964.

Hagen, Uta. *Respect for Acting.* New York: Macmillan, 1973.

Hainaux, Rene, ed. *Scene Design Throughout the World, 1960–1970.* New York: Theatre Arts Books, 1972.

————. *Stage Design Throughout the World since 1935.* New York: Theatre Arts Books, 1956.

————. *Stage Design Throughout the World since 1950.* New York: Theatre Arts Books, 1964.

Heffner, Hubert C., Samuel Selden, and Hunton D. Sellman. *Modern Theatre Practice: A Handbook of Play Production.* 4th ed. New York: Appleton-Century-Crofts, 1959.

Henry, Mari Lyn, and Lynne Rogers. ***How to Be a Working Actor.*** New York: M. Evans & Company, 1986.

Hodge, Francis. ***Play Directing: Analysis Communication and Style.*** Englewood Cliffs, N.J.: Prentice-Hall, 1971.

Ionesco, Eugène. ***Notes and Counter Notes: Writings on the Theatre.*** Trans. Donald Watson. New York: Grove Press, 1964.

Izenour, George. ***Theatre Design.*** New York: McGraw-Hill, 1977.

Johnstone, Keith. ***Impro: Improvisation and the Theatre***. New York: Theatre Arts Books, 1980.

Jones, Robert E. ***The Dramatic Imagination.*** New York: Meredith Publishing Co., 1941.

Kerr, Walter. ***Tragedy and Comedy***. New York: Simon & Schuster, 1967.

Koestler, Arthur. ***The Act of Creation.*** New York: Dell, 1964.

Langer, Susanne K. ***Feeling and Form.*** New York: Scribner's, 1953.

Lawson, John Howard. ***Theory and Technique of Playwriting.*** New York: Hill & Wang, 1960.

Lessac, Arthur. ***The Use and Training of the Human Voice.*** New York: Drama Book Specialists, 1967.

McCandless, Stanley R. ***A Method of Lighting the Stage.*** 4th ed. New York: Theatre Arts Books, 1958.

McGraw, Charles J. ***Acting Is Believing.*** 2d ed. New York: Holt, Rinehart and Winston, 1966.

Mast, Gerald. ***A Short History of the Movies.*** 2d ed. New York: Macmillan, 1980.

Mielziner, Jo. ***Designing for the Theatre.*** New York: Atheneum, 1965.

———. ***Shapes of Our Theatres***. New York: Potter, 1970.

Moore, Thomas Gale. ***The Economics of the American Theatre.*** Durham: Duke University Press, 1968.

Morison, Bradley G., and Kay Fliehr. ***In Search of an Audience: How an Audience Was Found for the Tyrone Guthrie Theatre.*** New York: Pitman, 1968.

Oenslager, Donald. ***Scenery Then and Now.*** New York: Norton, 1936.

Olson, Elder. ***Tragedy and the Theory of Drama.*** Detroit: Wayne State University Press, 1961.

Parker, W. Oren, and Harvey K. Smith. ***Scene Design and Stage Lighting.*** New York: Holt, Rinehart and Winston, 1974.

Plummer, Gail. ***The Business of Show Business***. New York: Harper & Row, 1961.

Rubin, Joel E., and Leland Watson. ***Theatrical Lighting Practice.*** New York: Theatre Arts Books, 1954.

Russell, Douglas. ***Stage Costume Design: Theory, Technique and Style.*** New York: Appleton-Century-Crofts, 1973.

Saint-Denis, Michel. ***Theatre, the Rediscovery of Style.*** New York: Theatre Arts Books, 1960.

Sartre, Jean-Paul. ***Sartre on Theater.*** Trans. Frank Jellinek. New York: Random House, 1976.

Schechner, Richard. ***Environmental Theater.*** New York: Dutton (Hawthorn Books), 1973.

———. ***Public Domain: Essays on the Theater.*** New York: Macmillan, 1969.

Smiley, Sam. ***Playwriting: The Structure of Action.*** Englewood Cliffs, N.J.: Prentice-Hall, 1971.

Sellman, Hunton D. ***Essentials of Stage Lighting.*** New York: Appleton-Century-Crofts, 1972.

Spolin, Viola. ***Improvisation for the Theatre.*** Evanston, Ill.: Northwestern University Press, 1963.

Stanislavski, Constantin. ***An Actor Prepares***. Trans. Elizabeth Reynolds Hapgood. New York: Theatre Arts Books, 1946.

———. ***Building a Character.*** Trans. Elizabeth Reynolds Hapgood. New York: Theatre Arts Books, 1949.

———. ***Creating a Role.*** Trans. Elizabeth Reynolds Hapgood. New York: Theatre Arts Books, 1961.

Staub, August. ***Creating Theatre: The Art of Theatrical Directing.*** New York: Harper & Row, 1973.

BIBLIOGRAPHY

Adams, John C. *The Globe Playhouse: Its Design and Equipment*. 2d ed. New York: Barnes & Noble, 1961.

Amico, Silvio D'. *Storia del Teatro Drammatico*. Vol. 2 of *Dal Rinascimento al Romanticismo*. Milan, Italy: Garzanti, 1950.

————. *Storia del Teatro Drammatico*. Vol. 3 of *Parte Quarta: L'Ottocento*. Milan, Italy: Rizzoli, 1940.

Arnott, Peter. *The Ancient Greek and Roman Theatre.* New York: Random House, 1971.

Barton, Lucy. *Historic Costume for the Stage*. Boston: Baker's Plays, 1935.

Bentley, Eric. *The Playwright as Thinker: A Study of Drama in Modern Times.* New York: Morrow (Reynal), 1946.

Berthold, Margot. *A History of World Theatre.* New York: Ungar, 1972.

Bieber, Margarete. *The History of the Greek and Roman Theater.* 2d ed. Princeton, N.J.: Princeton University Press, 1961.

Brockett, Oscar G. *History of the Theatre*. 3d ed. Boston: Allyn and Bacon, 1977.

————, and Robert R. Findlay. *Century of Innovation: A History of European and American Theatre and Drama Since 1870.* Englewood Cliffs, N.J.: Prentice-Hall, 1973.

Brustein, Robert. *The Theatre of Revolt: An Approach to Modern Drama.* Boston: Little, Brown, 1946.

Carlson, Marvin. *The French Stage in the Nineteenth Century*. Metuchen, N.J.: Scarecrow Press, 1972.

————. *The German Stage in the Nineteenth Century*. Metuchen, N.J.: Scarecrow Press, 1972.

Chambers, E. K. *The Mediaeval Stage.* 2 vols. Oxford: Clarendon Press, 1903.

Cheney, Sheldon. *The Theatre: Three Thousand Years of Drama, Acting and Stagecraft.* Rev. ed. New York: MacKay, 1972.

Clurman, Harold. *The Fervent Years: The Story of the Group Theatre and the Thirties.* New York: Knopf, 1950.

Couty, Daniel, and Alain Rey, eds. *Le Théâtre.* Bordas, 1980.

Craig, Hardin. *English Religious Drama of the Middle Ages*. Oxford: Clarendon Press, 1955.

Croyden, Margaret. *Lunatics, Lovers and Poets: The Contemporary Experimental Theatre.* New York: McGraw-Hill, 1974.

Duchartre, Pierre L. *The Italian Comedy: The Improvisation, Scenarios, Lives, Attributes, Portraits and Masks of the Illustrious Characters of the Commedia dell' Arte.* Trans. R. T. Weaver. New York: Dover, 1966.

Esslin, Martin. *The Theatre of the Absurd.* Rev. ed. Garden City, N.Y.: Doubleday, 1969.

Fergusson, Francis. *The Idea of a Theatre*. Princeton, N.J.: Princeton University Press, 1949.

Freedley, George, and John A. Reeves. *A History of the Theatre.* 3d rev. ed. New York: Crown, 1968.

Gassner, John. *Masters of the Drama*. 3d ed. New York: Dover, 1954.

Gorelik, Mordecai. *New Theatres for Old*. New York: Samuel French, 1949.

Guicharnaud, Jacques. *Modern French Theatre from Giraudoux to Beckett*. New Haven, Conn.: Yale University Press, 1961.

Heffner, Hubert. *The Nature of Drama*. Boston: Houghton Mifflin, 1959.

Herrick, Marvin. *Italian Comedy in the Renaissance*. Urbana: University of Illinois Press, 1965.

————. *Italian Tragedy in the Renaissance.* Urbana: University of Illinois Press, 1965.

Hodges, C. Walter. *The Globe Restored: A Study of the Elizabethan Theatre*. 2d ed. London: Oxford University Press, 1968.

Kirby, Michael, ed. *The New Theatre: Performance Documentation.* New York: New York University Press, 1974.

Kitto, H. D. F. *Greek Tragedy: A Literary Study*. Garden City, N.Y.: Doubleday, 1955.

Krutch, Joseph W. *Comedy and Conscience After the Restoration*. New York: Columbia University Press, 1949.

Meserve, Walter. *An Emerging Entertainment: The Drama of the American People to 1828.* Bloomington: Indiana University Press, 1977.

————. *Heralds of Promise: The Drama of the American People During the Age of Jackson, 1829–1849.* Westport, Conn.: Greenwood Press, 1986.

Molinari, Cesare. **Teatro**. Milan, Italy: Arnoldo Mondadori, 1972.

Nagler, Alois M. **A Source in Theatrical History**. New York: Dover, 1952.

Nicoll, Allardyce. **The Development of the Theatre: A Study of Theatrical Art from the Beginnings to the Present Day**. 5th ed., rev. London: Harrap, 1966.

————. **History of English Drama, 1660–1900**. 6 vols. London: Cambridge University Press, 1955–1959.

————. **Masks, Mimes and Miracles**. New York: Harcourt Brace Jovanovich, 1931.

————. **Stuart Masques and the Renaissance Stage**. London: Harrap, 1937.

Nietzsche, Friedrich. **The Birth of Tragedy**. Trans. Walter Kaufman. New York: Random House, 1967.

Oxford Companion to the Theatre. 3d ed. London: Oxford University Press, 1967.

Payne, Blanche. **History of Costume from the Ancient Egyptians to the Twentieth Century.** New York: Harper & Row, 1965.

Pickard-Cambridge, A. W. **The Dramatic Festivals of Athens.** 2d ed., rev. by John Gould and D. M. Lewis. Oxford: Clarendon Press, 1968.

Quinn, Arthur H. **A History of the American Drama from the Beginning to the Civil War**. 2d ed. New York: Appleton-Century-Crofts, 1943.

————. **A History of the American Drama from the Civil War to the Present Day.** 2d ed. New York: Appleton-Century-Crofts, 1949.

Roberts, Vera Mowry. **On Stage: A History of Theatre**. 2d ed. New York: Harper & Row, 1974.

Smiley, Sam. **The Drama of Attack: Didactic Plays of the American Depression**. Columbia: Missouri University Press, 1972.

Tolstoy, Leo. **What Is Art?** Trans. Aylmer Maude. London: Oxford University Press, 1930.

Turnell, Martin. **The Classical Moment: Studies in Corneille, Molière, and Racine**. New York: New Directions, 1948.

Wickham, Glynne. **The Medieval Theatre**. London: Weidenfeld and Nicholson, 1974.

Willett, John. **Expressionism**. New York: McGraw-Hill, 1970.

William Shakespeare and Stratford-upon-Avon. London: Pitkin, 1975.

Wilson, Edwin, and Alvin Goldfarb. **Living Theater: An Introduction to Theatre History.** New York: McGraw-Hill, 1983.

Woods, Leigh. **Garrick Claims the Stage: Acting as Social Emblem in Eighteenth-Century England.** Westport, Conn.: Greenwood Press, 1984.

A P P E N D I X

Actors' Equity Association (AEA)

Alan Eisenberg, Executive Secretary
165 W. 46th St.
New York, NY 10036
(212) 869–8530

Founded: 1913. Members: 35,000.
This union serves professional stage actors and stage managers. It limits membership and maintains basic entry requirements and fees. AEA also maintains Actors' Equity Foundation, which makes awards and grants to organizations or charities that are in the best interests of theatre and the union's members. It also publishes a monthly newspaper.

American Federation of Television and Radio Artists (AFTRA)

Sanford I. Wolff, Executive Secretary
1350 Avenue of the Americas
New York, NY 10019
(212) 265–7700

Founded: 1933. Members: 10,000.
The membership of AFTRA is composed of professionals in television and radio. An initiation fee and dues are charged its members. It publishes news bimonthly and a magazine quarterly.

Directors Guild of America (DGA)

Michael H. Franklin, Executive Director
7950 Sunset Blvd.
Hollywood, CA 90046
(213) 656–1220

Founded: 1959. Members: 7,300.
This union principally serves professional film, television, and radio directors, assistant directors, and managers. It negotiates agreements for members, bestows awards, and publishes an annual membership directory. It has certain membership requirements, fees, and annual dues.

Dramatists Guild (DG)

David E. LeVine, Executive Director
234 W. 44th St.
New York, NY 10036
(212) 398–9336

Founded: 1920. Members: 7,600.
This union is the major professional organization for playwrights, lyricists, and composers. It is a corporate member of the Authors League of America. The Dramatists Guild conducts symposia and weekend workshops. It also bestows the annual Hull-Warriner Award and maintains a library of theatre reference texts.

It advises members on business problems and publishes a useful newsletter and a quarterly magazine.

Screen Actors Guild (SAG)

Ken Orsatti, Executive Secretary
7750 Sunset Blvd.
Hollywood, CA 90045
(213) 876–3030

Founded: 1933. Members: 55,000.
SAG is the major union for professional film and video actors. There are certain professional requirements for membership, and an initiation fee and annual dues are charged. It issues a number of useful publications, including "Screen Actor News," "Screen Actor News Hollywood," and *Screen Actor Magazine.*

Society of Stage Directors and Choreographers

A. Harrison Cromer, Executive Secretary
1501 Broadway
New York, NY 10036
(212) 391–1070

Founded: 1959. Members: 950.
This independent national labor union represents directors and choreographers who work in the professional theatre. Its membership is restricted, and an initiation fee plus dues are required of its constituents.

United Scenic Artists (USA)

John Van Eyck, Business Representative
575 Eighth Ave.
New York, NY 10018
(212) 736–4498.

Founded: 1918. Members: 1,600.
USA is the union of professional designers, and its membership also includes scenic artists, costume designers, lighting designers, diorama and display workers, mural artists, and television artists. The union has jurisdiction in legitimate theatre, motion pictures, and television. Prospective members of the union must pass a thorough examination, consisting of practical and written parts. It publishes an annual directory.

Photo Credits

The numbers of the pages on which the illustrations appear are printed in **bold.**

Purchase, Carl Otto von Kienbusch, Jr., Memorial Collection. **171** Granger Collection. **173** © 1986, courtesy Museum of Fine Arts, Boston: Bequest of Charles H. Parker. **177** Culver. **179** Sam Smiley. **180** Photo Bibliothèque Nationale, Paris. **182** Metropolitan Museum of Art, Rogers Fund. *Chapter 11:* **186** Culver. **187** Wabash College. **189** Culver. **190** Bettmann. **192** Harvard Theatre Collection. **195** Granger Collection. **199** Harvard Theatre Collection. **202** Granger Collection. **204** Harvard Theatre Collection. *Chapter 12:* **207** Lucas, University of Evansville. **208** Culver. **209** *(left)* Bettmann Archive; *(right)* Culver. **211** *(above)* Culver; *(left)* Indiana University Photo Service. **213** *(above)* The Hampden-Booth Theatre Library at The Players; *(left)* Anderson/The University of Evansville Theatre. **215** Granger Collection. **216** Devonshire Collection, Chatsworth Library. *Chapter 13:* **221** Harvard Theatre Collection. **222** Nationale Forschungs-und Gedenkstätten der Klassischen deutschen Literatur in Weimar. **223** Culver. **225, 226** *(both)* Harvard Theatre Collection. **228, 231** *(both)* Henry E. Huntington Library and Art Gallery. **232** Granger Collection. **235** The Hampden-Booth Theatre Library at The Players. **237** Bibliothèque Nationale, Giraudon, Art Resource. **238** Victoria and Albert Museum. **241** Nationale Forschungs-und Gedenkstätten der Klassischen deutschen Literatur in Weimar. **242** Granger Collection. **244** Nationale Forschungs-und Gedenkstätten der Klassischen deutschen Literatur in Weimar. *Chapter 14:* **247** Culver. **248** The Hampden-Booth Theatre Library at The Players. **250, 251, 252** *(all)* Culver. **255** Harvard Theatre Collection. **259** Culver. **260, 262** The Hampden-Booth Theatre Library at The Players. **264** *(all)* Culver. **265** *(far left)* The Hampden-Booth Theatre Library at The Players; *(left and above)* Culver. **266** *(left and right)* Culver. **267** *(above left)* Culver; *(above right)* Dartmouth College Library. *Chapter 15:* **270** Novosti, Sovfoto. **271** Theatre Collection, The New York Public Library. **275** Culver. **276** *(both)* Sovfoto. **277** Granger Collection. **279** Culver. **281** Granger Collection. **282, 284** Culver. **285** Granger Collection. **287** Florida Southern College. **289** *On the Art of the Theatre* by Edward Gordon Craig, 1920. **290** Theatre Collection, The New York Public Library. **291** Culver. **292** Indiana University Photo Service. *Chapter 16:* **295** Wabash College. **296** Culver. **297** Granger Collection. **299** Culver. **302** Hanover College. **307, 308, 309** Culver. **310** *(left)* Bettmann Newsphotos; *(right)* Wide World. **311** Regan, Camera 5. **312, 313** Culver. **316** Indiana University Photo Service. **317** Culver. *Chapter 17:* **319** © Martha Swope. **320** © 1972, Peter Moore. **322** Wide World. **324** *(left)* Wide World; *(right)* Photo Trends. **327** Indiana University Photo Service. **329** Theatre Collection, The New York Public Library. **331, 332** Indiana University Photo Service. **333** Ros Ribas. **336** Wide World. **337** Indiana University Photo Service. **338** © 1973, Peter Moore. **339** Courtesy Leon Brauner. **340** Carter, Yale University Repertory Theatre.

Part Four opener **344** Wide World. *Chapter 18:* **345** © Jerry Vezzuso. **346** The Stratford Shakespearean Festival Foundation of Canada. **349** Buxbaum, J. F. Kennedy Center. **350** John F. Kennedy Center. **354** Courtesy Welton Becket and Associates, Architects. **355** Courtesy Arena Stage. **356** The Guthrie Theatre. **357** © 1983, Martha Swope. **358** Rafshoon, Alliance Theatre Company. **359** Blake, Repertory Theatre at Christian Theological Seminary. **360** University of Evansville. *Chapter 19:* **364** Culver. **365** Photo Trends. **366, 367, 368** Culver. **369** Photo Trends. **370** Culver. **372** Wide World. **375, 376** Wide World. **380** Culver. *Chapter 20:* **383** © T. Charles Ericksen. **384** Culver. **385** © Martha Swope. **387** Heitz, Phoenix Theatre. **388** Hanover College. **389** Indiana University—Purdue University at Indianapolis. **390** *(above)* © 1983, Martha Swope; *(right)* Wide World. **391** Susan Cook, Martha Swope Associates. **392** Wide World. **394, 395** © 1985, Martha Swope. **396** Culver. **397** © Holland, Stock, Boston. *Chapter 21:* **400** Blanchette, Magic Theatre. **401** Goldstein, The Guthrie Theatre. **402** *(right)* The Guthrie Theatre, Minneapolis; *(below)* Brown County Playhouse. **403** Lascher, The Goodman Theatre. **404** Culver. **406** Indiana University Photo Service. **407** © T. Charles Ericksen. **408** Giannetti, The Guthrie Theatre.

Index